Courage and Tools:
The Florence Howe Award for Feminist Scholarship
1974–1989

Edited by

JOANNE GLASGOW

and

ANGELA INGRAM

The Modern Language Association of America

~ New York 1990 ~

Library of Congress Cataloging-in-Publication Data

Courage and tools : the Florence Howe Award for Feminist Scholarship, 1974–1989 / edited by Joanne Glasgow and Angela Ingram.
p. cm.
Includes bibliographical references and index.
ISBN 0-87352-344-X (cloth) ISBN 0-87352-345-8 (paper)
1. American literature—History and criticism—Theory, etc.
2. American literature—Women authors—History and criticism.
3. English literature—History and criticism—Theory, etc.
4. English literature—Women authors—History and criticism.
5. Feminist literary criticism—Awards. 6. Feminism and literature.
7. Women and literature. I. Glasgow, Joanne. 1943–
II. Ingram, Angela J. C.
PS25.C6 1990
810.9′9287—dc20 90-44932

Published by The Modern Language Association of America
10 Astor Place, New York, New York, 10003-6981

~ CONTENTS ~

~ ACKNOWLEDGMENTS ~

EDITING THIS VOLUME has been a most unusual—and amazing—book project for both of us. Because the records of the Women's Caucus for the Modern Languages are incomplete, scattered all over the country, archived nowhere—in short, a mess (there's another project for someone!)—we had to begin at the beginning, even though initially we did not even know when that was. We tracked down all the winning essays—word of mouth and the wonderful network of Women's Caucus members helped immensely here. Then we had to contact the authors—the task was easy enough when it came to current MLA members, but the search for those who had left the academy was rather formidable. Thank goodness for alumnae offices, the memories of our friends and colleagues, and the wonders of telephone-answering machines. All this in less than two months!

For introducing the project to the MLA Publications Committee, we want to thank especially Ellen Cronan Rose and Carol Martin and, for supporting their proposal, the MLA Commission on the Status of Women in the Profession. For enthusiastically welcoming the proposal, for providing material assistance in numerous large and small ways, and for moving with blazing speed, we thank the entire MLA publications staff—but notably Adrienne Ward, who gave more of her time and assistance than we ever dared to expect. To the authors of the essays collected here, we express our thanks for their generosity and especially their promptness in meeting our impossible deadlines, as well as for the leads and investigative searches several of them provided as we did our detective work. Our most heartfelt thanks go to the many WCML friends and colleagues who made all this possible. Three women in particular spent countless hours on the telephone with us and even more time researching documents: Judith Johnston, Ellen Cronan Rose, and Susan Koppelman. We also wish to thank (in alphabetical order) Florence Boos, Dorothy H. Brown, Lee R. Edwards, Hannah W. Hopp, Frances Kavenik, Kathleen Gregory Klein, Melissa Sue Kort, Susan Pace, Peggy Prenshaw, Emily Toth, and Jacqueline Van Baelen. We are grateful for the opportunity this project provided to make or to renew acquaintance with so many superb MLA women. And finally we thank each other for being exemplary "work partners."

Permissions Acknowledgments

Phyllis Franklin, "Traditional Literary Study—in the Subjunctive Mood," *Female Studies* 6 (1972): 38–56. Copyright © 1972 by the Feminist Press. Reprinted by permission of the Feminist Press.

Ellen Elizabeth Morgan, "Isabel Archer: Resistance to the Patriarchal Order," *University of Michigan Papers in Women's Studies* 1.4 (1975): 95–106. Copyright © 1975 by University of Michigan. Reprinted by permission of *Michigan Feminist Studies*.

Joanna Russ, "What Can a Heroine Do? Or, Why Women Can't Write," *Images of Women in Fiction: Feminist Perspectives*, ed. Susan Koppelman Cornillon (Bowling Green: Bowling Green U Popular P, 1972) 3–20. Copyright © 1972 by Bowling Green University Popular Press. Reprinted by permission of Bowling Green University Popular Press.

Susan Stanford Friedman, "Psyche Reborn: Tradition, Re-vision, and the Goddess as Mother Symbol in H. D.'s Epic Poetry," *Women's Studies* 6 (1979): 147–60. Copyright © 1979 by Gordon and Breach Science Publishers. Reprinted by permission of the author.

Annette Kolodny, "Dancing through the Minefield: Some Observations on the Theory, Practice, and Politics of a Feminist Literary Criticism," *Feminist Studies* 6.1 (1980): 1–24. Copyright © 1979 by Annette Kolodny. Reprinted by permission of the author.

Ellen Pollak, "Pope and Sexual Difference: Woman as Part and Counterpart in the 'Epistle to a Lady,' " *Studies in English Literature* 24 (1984): 461–81. Copyright © 1984 by *Studies in English Literature*. Reprinted by permission of *Studies in English Literature*.

Patrocinio P. Schweickart, "Reading Ourselves: Toward a Feminist Theory of Reading," *Gender and Reading: Essays on Readers, Texts and Contexts*, ed. Elizabeth A. Flynn and Patrocinio P. Schweickart (Baltimore: Johns Hopkins UP, 1986). Copyright © 1986 by Johns Hopkins University Press. Reprinted by permission of Johns Hopkins University Press.

Beth Kowaleski-Wallace, "Milton's Daughters: The Education of Eighteenth-Century Women Writers," *Feminist Studies* 12.2 (1986): 275–94. Copyright © 1986 by *Feminist Studies*, Inc. Reprinted by permission of *Feminist Studies*.

Celeste M. Schenck's "Feminism and Deconstruction: Reconstructing the Elegy" appeared in a different version in *Tulsa Studies in Women's Literature* 5.1 (1986): 13–28. Copyright © 1986 by *Tulsa Studies in Women's Literature*. Reprinted by permission of *Tulsa Studies in Women's Literature*.

Deborah Byrd, "Combating an Alien Tyranny: Elizabeth Barrett Browning's Evolution as a Feminist Poet," *Browning Institute Studies* 15 (1987): 23–42. Copyright © 1987 by *Browning Institute Studies*. Reprinted by permission of *Browning Institute Studies*.

Linda Kauffman, "Special Delivery: Twenty-First-Century Epistolarity in *The Handmaid's Tale*," *Writing the Female Voice: Essays in Epistolary Literature*, ed. Elizabeth Goldsmith (Boston: Northeastern UP, 1989) 221–44. Copyright © 1989 by Northeastern University Press. Reprinted by permission of the author.

~ PREFACE ~

What Was It Like Then?

FLORENCE HOWE

TWENTY-ONE YEARS AGO, a whole generation. I was forty, and I was the "old lady" even then. What was it like then? Well, for one thing, it was very clear. There were no blurred moments, no ambiguous responses, no liberals. There were only the "radicals" and the "conservatives." There were only "us" and "them." And there were very few of "us" and very many of "them." Also, there were some men among "us" and some women among "them." That was not confusing, however, for, again, the numbers and the expectations made everything clear. There was no time for infighting, and nothing at all to fight about: the enemy was clear, visible, armed, and dangerous. All the power was theirs, all the money, all the institutions, even all the mailing lists.

What did we have on our side? The special power that came from the urgency of our fresh consciousness, our analysis of "patriarchy," a new word and a concept that transformed us from token women to radical activists. It is hard to describe how it felt then without seeming to color the events romantically, for we live in a time that has, at best, grown a layer of lassitude over that green consciousness; at worst, a deep cynicism denies all. But in those days we were high on consciousness, on the vision that allowed us to see with what Joan Kelly has called "double vision." Even the grief with which we encountered the "oppression of women"—a new expression—even that grief was spiced with the high of anger, new feelings for many of us.

What did we do? Perhaps the most radical thing we did does not seem radical at all today: we gathered information about matters hitherto perceived as nobody's business, as inevitable circumstances, or as accidental occurrences. We gathered statistics and labeled them discrimination and cried injustice. Where there were victims, there had to be oppressors. And those nice gentlemen both inside and outside the MLA did not care to be oppressors. Indeed, some of them were eager to prove that they were truly our friends, even that they could do a better job with statistics than we could.

The Women's Caucus for the Modern Languages held its initial informal meeting following the first official session of the MLA Commission on the Status of Women at the 1969 MLA annual meeting in Denver. At this session, one nice gentleman cited statistics on women that he expected would be pleasing information. Indeed, even more than Kate Millett's reading from the second chapter of her still unpublished *Sexual Politics*, his was information incendiary enough to lead to the founding of WCML.

The commission had come out of the 1968 MLA annual business meeting, one of those truly revolutionary moments of the sixties. At the close of this lengthy meeting, a resolution passed unanimously calling for the Executive Council to set up a commission that would "establish equity for women in the profession." The resolution might have come to nothing, except that, earlier at this meeting, Louis Kampf had been elected second vice president in an unprecedented vote, the outcome of which was most surprising both to him and to his supporters. One of his first acts as second vice president was to remind the council of this resolution and to name me as chair. At the same time that I was named chair of the commission, another woman with clearly conservative politics was appointed as member. Between us, we were to staff the rest of the commission, as well as to plan and execute its program. While I did not consider myself formally a feminist at the time, I was rapidly turned into one by the tone and actions of meetings with the Executive Council and other individuals within and without the MLA. My conservative colleague proceeded to do her job, and we managed to work together amicably. It seemed important in those days to have men on this commission, and since I was alert to the ineffectuality of tokens (having been one for decades), I insisted on naming two men, and thus we petitioned to enlarge the commission from the original five to seven. We each appointed one woman and one man to the commission, and we agreed on another woman.

For our first public meeting, in December 1969, we each named one speaker. I named Kate Millett, who would read from chapter 2 of *Sexual Politics*, on the ideology of patriarchy; and my colleague named a professor of French at Yale, who, she said, would talk about women at Yale. And he did just that, citing statistics proudly to prove that, for most of the century, women had earned one-third of Yale's doctorates in several MLA-connected departments. He was, to the amazement of the group, bragging about Yale's record with regard to women. I didn't have long to wonder what might follow. As chair of the session, I began to fear for the professor's safety, for there were several feminist Yale doctorates in the room who demanded to know how many of the women the professor bragged about had been hired into Yale's faculty. There was no soothing response possible, since of course Yale had hired its male doctorates in substantial numbers. I took it as my responsibility to see the professor out, and he left, not really understanding the lack of graciousness on the part of the audience he had been addressing.

But many among the audience stayed behind to organize the Women's Caucus for the Modern Languages. Earlier that evening, as chairwoman of the commission's panel, I had talked about the politics of organizing women within the Modern Language Association and other professional groups. If the "official" commission were to be effective, I theorized, it needed to be motivated by a base of energy, even a level of discontent. The commission, a feminist arm within the MLA, needed a political mass that would support its efforts and press it to work harder and more effectively. Thus, independent of the MLA, the

Women's Caucus for the Modern Languages was formed that evening in December 1969; it met for the first time at the convention in 1970.

With the advent of the commission and the caucus, we gained two special powers: the power to organize sessions and to speak out at meetings focused on the status of women and the power to encourage scholarship on women and to help distribute, and eventually publish, such scholarship and other materials that would stimulate the transformation of our academic discipline.

Perhaps it is hard to imagine a time when, at an MLA convention, there were no sessions on feminist literary criticism, much less on theory, none on women writers, not even on Virginia Woolf. If you came to consciousness in the mid-seventies or the early eighties, it would be only natural to assume that the several hundred sessions devoted to women writers and, in general, the visibility of women at the MLA annual convention constituted the natural order of things.

We also had what now seems most precious of all to me: that generosity of spirit called sharing. Perhaps it is difficult to imagine a world in which course syllabi were published and distributed at MLA annual meetings, when one could see the books that others were using and even their lecture topics and the research questions assigned to students. We would not have had the rapid growth of women's studies in the United States were it not for the brilliance of Sheila Tobias, who thought of printing up course syllabi in the first place, and for the willingness of our colleagues to share their teaching with others. This sharing was not for a moment only: between 1970 and 1975, Know, Inc., a small press in Pittsburgh, and the Feminist Press published course syllabi in ten volumes called *Female Studies*, a few of which can still be found in my office, though officially they are out of print. Six of these volumes were edited by members of the Commission on the Status of Women and sold chiefly at MLA annual meetings each year, the ones published by the Feminist Press earning royalties for the commission. In 1982, the Feminist Press published a volume edited by three commission members, Barbara Smith, Gloria Hull, and Patricia Bell Scott, *All the Women Are White, All the Men Are Black, but Some of Us Are Brave: Black Women's Studies*, a volume that included course syllabi, bibliographies, and essays, a large proportion of them literary.

As I look back through these two decades of the MLA, the commission, and the caucus, I am aware that work inside these institutions was, in part, responsible for the growth and development of the Feminist Press and of my own and the press's contribution to women's studies, especially in literature. The early success of the Feminist Press depended on our presence at MLA annual meetings each year and on caucus and commission members who were using and thus helping to distribute our published books and who were also advising us about what else needed publishing. I am aware also that, without the caucus, I might not have won that write-in election in 1971 that made me president of the MLA in 1973.

I was not, as many thought, the first woman president but the third, since there had been two women presidents before me. But the half century that had elapsed, as well as the characteristic disappearance of the history of women, made it seem as though I was the first. The three years in office as second vice president, first vice president, and president of the MLA were not pleasure-filled for me. I had had to resign from the commission and thus give up the useful and collegially congenial work I had begun, or take it with me to the Feminist Press and *Women's Studies Quarterly*. As "token" on MLA's Executive Council, I was politically powerless, except as symbol for those outside. And it was impossible to explain any of this in the early seventies without seeming to be either an ungrateful wretch or a crybaby. What I missed was perfectly obvious: colleagues with whom I could do useful work. Today, feminists inside MLA's Executive Council enjoy such pleasures.

Perhaps it is thus understandable why, at first, I was horrified when, following my presidential address at the MLA annual meeting in Chicago in 1973, the Women's Caucus for the Modern Languages announced the Florence Howe Award for feminist scholarship. What I heard that evening was the word *memorial*. I heard the "Florence Howe Memorial Award." The word rang clearly enough in my head so that I remember also the thought "but I am not dead yet." No, and today, a full generation further on in the work of building feminist institutions, we are more alive than we were then, more alert to the reality of classrooms and consciousness transformed by the many literatures of the world written and to come. In 1990, I am grateful to the caucus and others inside the MLA for making it possible for me to appreciate the honor of this award once again, to enjoy this volume, and to look forward to the volumes to come.

~ WINNERS OF THE ~ FLORENCE HOWE AWARD

~ 1974 ~

Phyllis Franklin, "Traditional Literary Study—in the Subjunctive Mood"
Joanna Russ, "What Can a Heroine Do? Or, Why Women Can't Write"
Ellen Morgan, "Isabel Archer: Resistance to the Patriarchal Order"

HONORABLE MENTION

Coppélia Kahn, "The Rape in Shakespeare's *Lucrece*"
Harriet R. Allentuck, "The Will to Refuse in *The Princess of Cleves*"
Judith Fetterley, "*A Farewell to Arms*: Ernest Hemingway's 'Resentful Cryptogram' "
Madelyn Gutwirth, "Madame de Staël, Rousseau, and the Woman Question"

~ 1975 ~

Mary Cohen, "Sylvia Plath's Children's Poems"

~ 1976 ~

No prize given

~ 1977 ~

Susan Peck MacDonald, "*Middlemarch*, *Daniel Deronda*, and Hegel's Master-Slave Relationship"

HONORABLE MENTION

Marcia Tillotson, "Mary Shelley, the Monster and Frankenstein: The Creator's Relationship to Her 'Hideous Progeny' "
Susan Sniader Lanser, "*Nightwood*: A Feminist Perspective"

~ 1978 ~

Susan Stanford Friedman, "Psyche Reborn: Tradition, Re-vision, and the Goddess as Mother Symbol in H. D.'s Epic Poetry"

HONORABLE MENTION

Elizabeth Abel, "Women and Schizophrenia: The Fiction of Jean Rhys"
Suzanne Juhasz, "Toward a Theory of Form in Feminist Autobiography: Kate Millett's *Flying* and *Sita*; Maxine Hong Kingston's *The Woman Warrior*"

~ 1979 ~

Annette Kolodny, "Dancing through the Minefield: Some Observations on the Theory, Practice and Politics of a Feminist Literary Criticism"

Honorable Mention

Dorothy Ann Brown, "Guidelines for a Critical Discussion of Aesthetics of Feminism in Virginia Woolf's Fiction"

Nancy K. Miller, "Emphasis Added: Plots and Plausibilities in Women's Fiction"

~ 1980 ~

Corinne Dale, "The Domestic Alternative: Beyond Feminist Criticism"

Honorable Mention

Mary Suzanne Schriber, "The Role of Convention in the Fiction of Edith Wharton"

~ 1981 ~

Cynthia A. Davis, "Archetype and Structure: On Feminist Myth Criticism"

Honorable Mention

Carol Cantrell, "The Unmanly Man in the Novels of Ernest Hemingway"

Charlotte Goodman, "The Lost Brother, the Twin: Twentieth-Century Women Novelists and the Male-Female Double Bildungsroman"

~ 1982 ~

Ellen Pollak, "Pope and Sexual Difference: Woman as Part and Counterpart in the 'Epistle to a Lady' "

~ 1983 ~

Faye M. Lenarcic, "The Virgin Shapeshifter: Melville's Quarrel with Maids"

~ 1984 ~

Patrocinio P. Schweickart, "Reading Ourselves: Toward a Feminist Theory of Reading"

Honorable Mention

Alice Fox, "Literary Allusion as Feminist Criticism in *A Room of One's Own*"

Betsy Erkkila, "Dickinson and Rich: Toward a Theory of Female Influence"

~ 1985 ~

Beth Kowaleski-Wallace, "Milton's Daughters: The Education of Eighteenth-Century Women Writers"

~ 1986 ~

Celeste M. Schenck, "Feminism and Deconstruction: Reconstructing the Elegy"

HONORABLE MENTION

B. K. [Bradford] Mudge, "Burning Down the House: Sara Coleridge, Virginia Woolf, and the Politics of Literary Revision"

~ 1987 ~

Deborah Byrd, "Combating an Alien Tyranny: Elizabeth Barrett Browning's Evolution as a Feminist Poet"

HONORABLE MENTION

Françoise Lionnet-McCumber, "*Metissage*, Emancipation and Female Textuality in Two Francophone Writers"

~ 1988 ~

Linda Kauffman, "Special Delivery: Twenty-First-Century Epistolarity in *The Handmaid's Tale*"

HONORABLE MENTION

Michael Danahy, "Marceline Desbordes-Valmore and the Engendered Canon"

~ 1989 ~

Rosemarie Garland Thomson, "Speaking about the Unspeakable: The Representation of Disability as Stigma in Toni Morrison's Novels"

HONORABLE MENTION

Ellen Dupree, "Jamming the Machinery: Mimesis in *The Custom of the Country*"

~ INTRODUCTION ~

Joanne Glasgow and Angela Ingram

THE ESSAYS COLLECTED in this volume are a tribute to the many successes of feminist scholarship and to the work of women scholars in the fields of language and literature study over the past twenty years. They are also, as their name attests, a tribute to one of the women most responsible for that scholarly success, Florence Howe. And they are a celebration of the Women's Caucus for the Modern Languages, an organization that Florence Howe and others began twenty years ago.

To understand the significance of this celebratory tribute, we should perhaps think back to 1970, those of us who can remember those early years, and recall the academic structures and assumptions that contributed to the marginalization of women—undergraduate and graduate students, faculty members, and the handful of women administrators. The explosive tensions of peace activism, civil rights, and campus unrest during those years, tensions romanticized by many and deplored by as many others, have often been read as the signature of 1970. But for academic *women* it was the year of beginnings, the founding of the Women's Caucus for the Modern Languages, the MLA Commission on the Status of Women,[1] and shortly thereafter the MLA division Women's Studies in Language and Literature, all of which Florence Howe helped establish. It was also the year that she cofounded the Feminist Press[2] and *Female Studies*, publishing enterprises vital to the work of women scholars. As Deborah Rosenfelt has written, ''[Howe] helped us build on such strong foundations that a younger generation of feminist scholars can *join* an association rather than having to invent it, and does not *have* to know how deeply it is in [her] debt'' (9).

The generation of the seventies did, however, know how deeply indebted we all are to Howe's work, almost from the very beginning. Since 1969, Howe had been lecturing on feminist criticism and pedagogy, developing early feminist critical texts (published in *Soundings* and, in 1972, Susan Koppelman Cornillon's *Images of Women in Fiction: Feminist Perspectives*) and presenting at regional MLAs many of the ideas that she was to publish in *No More Masks!* in 1973. Her early work provided a model for many feminists writing on issues of race and class. In recognition of her pioneering work, the Women's Caucus, acting on a suggestion of WCML president Dolores Barracano Schmidt, at its third annual meeting, established the Florence Howe Award for feminist scholarship. Writing in *Concerns*, the official newsletter of the caucus, in April 1974, the editor, Betty Richardson, reported:

> At its December, 1973, business meeting in Chicago, the Women's Caucus for the Modern Languages established the Florence Howe Award, which will include

> a first prize cash award and an unspecified number of honorable mentions. The award will be made annually for essays written by women scholars treating (1) feminist criticism in general, (2) feminist criticism of a woman author, (3) feminist pedagogy, (4) pedagogy from a feminist perspective. Manuscripts may deal with any period or field. (3–4)

Richardson went on to detail the regulations for preparation and submission of manuscripts and to solicit, as well, reader-judges for the award, which was to be administered that first year by caucus founding members Susan Koppelman Cornillon and Leonora Woodman.

Because the subsequent history of the award reflects many of the tensions and struggles within the feminist movement, it seems relevant to the presentation of this volume to record what those regulations were. In 1974, as in all following years, submissions had to be written in English, a regulation that had the effect, presumably unintentional, of reinforcing the Anglo-American literary hegemony within the MLA. Then, as now, it was stipulated that the essay must have been written within the preceding four years. This regulation would ensure the relevance of the essays to current feminist considerations and foster scholarship from promising young academics as well as from more established women. Related to the idea of "making it new" was the rule that the essay could be either published or unpublished, although it had to be submitted without reference to its publication status. Women scholars were, of course, under intense pressure to publish current research and literary studies and thus were not to be restricted by WCML or required to delay publication. This regulation, however, was to create problems in later years, as did the wording that the author need not be a member of WCML. It is interesting to note that the language of the report in *Concerns* specifies an award for a woman scholar—a stipulation that was never again mentioned in the regulations. Indeed, two of the honorable-mention winners have been men. The other rules spelled out in 1974 governed the documentation style, number of copies, deadline for submission, and procedures for ensuring author-anonymous readings. Thus the Florence Howe Award was launched.

The history of the award in the following fifteen years provides an interesting sociological and historical study paradigmatic in some ways of feminist institutions in general. Despite the wording of the initial announcement concerning a "first prize . . . and an unspecified number of honorable mentions," the Awards Committee in 1974 gave the Florence Howe Award to three women (an additional four received honorable mention): Phyllis Franklin, who was to go on to become a member of the Commission on the Status of Women, director of the Association of Departments of English, and now executive director of the MLA; Joanna Russ, who was to become celebrated as the author of *The Female Man* and other novels, as well as of the insightful critical work *How to Suppress Women's Writing*; and Ellen Morgan, who has left both the American academy and America altogether. Franklin's essay concerned feminist pedagogy, Russ's contributed to feminist critical theory, and Morgan's provided feminist analysis of a specific author—three of the four categories listed in the initial announcement of the prize.

The prize was won in 1975 by Mary Cohen, then at Temple University, for her essay "Sylvia Plath's Children's Poems." No honorable mention was reported in *Concerns*, nor has any other record surfaced in the scattered archival materials available to us. But we surmise, given the explosive controversy that followed almost immediately, that no honorable mention was given. Indeed, by 1975 there were tensions building within the caucus over the meaning of feminist achievement and feminist process, tensions that mirrored the debates within the larger feminist community.

By 1976 some of these political conflicts had emerged full-blown within the Women's Caucus. In that year the WCML Executive Committee decided not to award a prize at all, not because no submissions were found worthy but because there was a deeply felt disagreement about prizes in themselves. Under the leadership of WCML president Helen Batchelor, there was a push to award a single first prize, a decision resisted by Florence Howe Award Committee chairs Susan Koppelman Cornillon and Leonora Woodman. In the May 1976 issue of *Concerns*, extracts from position papers regarding this controversy were published.[3] From these extracts it seems evident that Batchelor was concerned about the obligation of WCML to award an unlimited number of prizes carrying cash awards. Koppelman [Cornillon] quotes Batchelor, who wrote that "a prize and an award necessarily mean that there is competition" (14). Koppelman resigned from the Awards Committee, stating that she wanted "the number of women whose work met the standards established . . . [to] be named as either first prize winners or winners of honorable mention" (14). Koppelman went on to state her philosophical opposition to the concept of competition among women, favoring instead cooperation and the establishment of standards of achievement:

> I am comfortable with a contest that encourages winners rather than one that mass-produces losers. . . . I think . . . that we are learning to build cooperatively on each other's ideas, that we are carrying on some of the most exciting critical dialogues that have ever been entered into. . . . I think the women's movement is characterized by co-edited anthologies because of these dynamics that energize feminist activity—cooperative, multi-faceted, complex. (15)

Koppelman's next statement enters the controversy more directly and personally:

> I agreed to act as co-chairwoman of this contest because I love and respect Florence Howe for what she has accomplished for all of us and I wanted to work on a project that would honor her for that work in a way that was in accordance with the spirit of that work. The kinds of sharing that have been characteristic of the women's movement, the kinds of sharing that have been characteristic of Florence's career, are not, in my opinion, most appropriately honored by the choosing of one from among the many as the best of all. I believe that we should set standards and publicly honor all those among us who achieve those standards be there one woman or one hundred. (15)

Koppelman's objection to the naming of a single prizewinner was echoed in a letter from Howe herself, in which, among other things, Howe stated: "If the Women's Caucus is interested in the prize's reflecting my life and concerns, then it should proceed to support Susan's position to select prizewinners as she has outlined. . . . I do not think that competition for its own sake is a valuable mode of behavior" (16). The caucus president for 1973, Ruth Altmann, agreed, outlining again the reasons for the establishment of the prize, particularly the encouragement of serious feminist writing: "We knew of no prize being given for such endeavors and we felt that they merited recognition" (16). According to Altmann, the pattern of competition seen as characteristic of the male-dominated academy of the time was not the aim of the caucus that established the prize.

The issue was joined on the other side by thoughtful and equally impassioned positions, expressed by Phyllis Franklin, Mildred B. Munday, Nancy Joyner, and others. In general, those favoring the "competitive prize" model criticized the assumption that competition itself is bad or destructive or unfeminist. "Is it unsisterly, too?" asked Munday. Pointing out that competition is inherent in current academic life, these women advocated a feminist arena of publication, argument, and discourse in which feminists offered their work to, and in competition with, other feminists rather than to the reigning critical establishment, most often the men with whom they would otherwise still have to compete—for jobs, tenure, promotion.

To resolve the conflict, ballots were sent to all WCML members. Less than 10% of the membership responded, but of those who did, the overwhelming majority (73%) voted for what was called "flexibility" in the granting of the award, leaving the decisions about numbers of awards up to the Awards Committee. Less than 1% voted to award only a single prize, while 18% voted to award four to six prizes annually. Clearly those who cared enough to cast ballots were not utterly convinced by the arguments of either faction, preferring instead to see what was submitted each year and to trust the judgment of the Awards Committee. But a major change was introduced by this same ballot. It was decided by a 93% to 7% vote to rotate the Awards Committee among the regional caucuses affiliated with the national WCML. This change was made primarily to reduce the work load of those who volunteered their time to read and judge a growing number of manuscripts. That regional system has been in place ever since.

It will be evident to readers of this volume that a "single prize" model was in fact what resulted from this early controversy. It is nevertheless clear, from reports submitted by various awards committees over the years, that many readers still wanted to recognize other fine submissions, and so the honorable-mention designation continued to be given. In the spirit of that recognition, we have provided, following the preface, as complete a list of the honorable-mention recipients as we were able to compile from the incomplete records of the caucus.[4]

When we examine the published record of the Florence Howe Award in the subsequent thirteen years, we see very few changes in the system of granting the prize. In 1979 there was an impressive list of thirty judges for the contest, a roster that was to become for a short-lived period the WCML Readers' Service, a group of established feminist scholars willing to devote time to reading manuscripts of younger women scholars, an early form of network mentoring that unfortunately did not sustain itself. By 1979 the Awards Committee found itself overwhelmed by the number of submissions and introduced the regulation that the award be given only to *unpublished* manuscripts. Five years later the conditions had changed again, with fewer essays being submitted. The Executive Council of the WCML decided once more to accept submissions of articles that had been accepted for publication or published within the preceding year. The reasoning was similiar to that in 1974—that the pressures of hiring, tenure, and promotion dictated that feminists seek almost immediate publication of their work. The one-year delay imposed by WCML rules discouraged many promising young scholars, as well as established feminists, from submitting their work for the award. Two other changes in administering the prize occurred in 1979: the categories for submissions were reworded as feminist pedagogy, feminist studies in language and literature, feminist theory, and the present state of feminist studies in literary history and criticism, and it was now stipulated that authors must be members of the WCML. There the rules remain. Little has changed in the history of the prize since 1984.

There is, however, another sense in which little has changed. As we began collecting the essays, we were struck by the total absence of African Americans (until 1989), Native Americans, Chicanas, Asian Americans (except for 1984), and non-English-speaking women writers either as authors of award-winning essays or as subjects of discussion. Nor does lesbian literary criticism ever once surface. Is this all-white, heterosexual image a reflection of the best feminist scholarship being written, as the prize was intended to be? It would certainly not have been Florence Howe's wish or, we suspect, the wish of any of the women involved in the Women's Caucus as we have known it. Yet the fact remains.

Perhaps it is more relevant to ask if this mostly all-white image is a reflection of the best feminist essays being *submitted* to the prize committees. According to the records available, awards committees seemed to have had few minority essays to select from. There are no archives that contain the lists of submissions, but in 1979 the committee, chaired that year by Jacqueline Van Baelen, deplored the British-American white domination of the prize. Van Baelen's report acknowledged that such monopolization could be reduced only by active and committed outreach to feminists working in underrepresented areas.

This is not the proper forum for a detailed analysis of the racial, class, ethnic, and sexual demographics of either the Modern Language Association or the Women's Caucus for the Modern Languages. Nor is it within the scope of this introduction to present the history of exclusion, marginalization, or partial inclusion that has kept many women of color from participating in these institutions. Still, it must be said that the history of the Florence Howe Award of the WCML reflects the sociohistorical matrix out of which the award comes. And that matrix has been overwhelmingly white, middle-class, heterosexual, and devoted to English-American literature. This composite profile, by and large, reflects the membership of the profession and of the Women's Caucus.

Historians of the feminist movement may recognize that by the late 1970s many white, middle-class feminists had begun, even if only imperfectly, to struggle with the challenge that African American and Third World feminists had been posing for years. For a brief period in 1979 and 1980, *Concerns* published a section devoted to what were called "minority women." Certainly by 1979 the inclusionary vision and revision of feminist scholarship had already started; indeed, it was well-established. We had powerful, insightful criticism from Barbara Smith and Audre Lorde, from Hortense Spillers and June Jordan. In texts available to English speakers, Chicanas began exploring feminist issues. Paula Gunn Allen's research and writing gave Native American literature a new voice in the academy, and the MLA Commission on American Languages and Literatures had been established. *MELUS* existed. Adrienne Rich, Monique Wittig, Catharine Stimpson, and Bonnie Zimmerman, among others, were challenging the heterosexist biases of thought and writing so ingrained in the received canon.

The WCML had itself sponsored panels at the MLA convention that included lesbians, women of color, older women, working-class authors, and academics. Caucus panels continued to address issues of pedagogy and the profession. That it took ten years for these movements to be reflected in the Florence Howe Award prompts us to ask why authors engaged in these issues seemingly chose not to submit essays for the award. We cannot, of course, provide answers—we can only raise questions that we hope will generate further debate and discussion within the caucus and the MLA.

Perhaps the first question is whether a prize that depends on voluntary submission can generate the range of critical inquiry its sponsors hope for. It is a truism, after all, that we usually think in terms of where our work will receive the most sensitive and most positive reception. Did, do black feminists find the MLA and the WCML congenial audiences? While the MLA Commission on the Status of Women has almost from the beginning included African Americans, that inclusion has been marked by struggles and controversy, as commission records indicate. The WCML has never had an African American officer. Did, do African American feminists think their work has better prospects of recognition and publication in other forums?

The same questions can be asked regarding Hispanic feminists and lesbian feminists. Did, do Hispanic women find *Feministas Unidas* and Spanish and bilingual publications more congenial? Did, do they perceive that their work will be more fully understood in other forums, among readers familiar with their concerns? Did, do lesbian feminists prefer to submit their scholarly essays to the Lesbian and Gay Caucus of the MLA? Did, do they feel more comfortable, more certain of a careful reading by peers who share their concerns? Perhaps a more basic question can also be asked: Do writers "on the margins" seek a wider impact than the WCML Florence Howe Award can give them?

We raise these questions in the spirit of feminist solidarity, not to blame or accuse anyone. Given our own long involvement with the caucus, we recognize clearly one of the realities of the feminist movement, indeed, of human institutions—that much is always asked of volunteers. We know well how many are the demands on caucus volunteers who still have to teach, write, struggle for our place in the academy.

Nevertheless, a celebration of twenty years can be a time for taking stock, for gauging how we can make progress, for renewing our dedication to the goals that seemed important when we began and that still seem important. Perhaps now is the time to commit ourselves even more strenuously to reflecting the diversity that we as feminist scholars represent.

At the same time that we recognize what is not in this collection of essays, we want to celebrate what is. And it is rich indeed. In the context of the concerns of feminist literary scholarship over the past fifteen years, these essays exemplify the healthy variety, in terms of both subject and approach, we should want always to associate with feminist criticism. While we have no way of reconstructing the collective thinking of any Florence Howe Awards Committee, we know that the selection of people asked to read essays submitted has been guided by criteria agreed on by caucus members and that, in line with those criteria, the readers have represented the widest possible range of specialization, of period, of critical or theoretical approach.

The result has been that the prizewinning essays provide us with examples of many of the approaches feminist scholars have chosen, and created, since the early 1970s. It is noticeable that there are no instances of psychoanalytic criticism or of criticism largely inspired by French feminist theories of *l'écriture feminine*, though there are certainly honorable-mention essays we would probably want to place in those categories. Represented among the essays collected here, however, are numerous critical methodologies: empirical "images of women" criticism, linked often to a close reading of texts by women and by men; archetypal and myth criticism; deconstruction; reader-response criticism; readings grounded in sociological or historical contextualizing; revisionary literary history; and genre criticism. These critical modes are applied in ways that, while they focus on particular texts, often re-vise the approach. Thus these essays form a body of work that carries within it a part of the history of feminist criticism and is itself a record of the ongoing discoveries made by feminist scholars when we read and when we write—and when we teach.

In 1974 Phyllis Franklin declared, "We must not be afraid of heuristic studies." Ellen Morgan, validating Isabel Archer in Henry James's "pre-feminist" *Portrait of a Lady*, wrote that "whatever freedom she has must be a small affair indeed and of small comfort to her except in the largest sense of her being able to approve of her choice and to be responsible for it. But that approval and responsibility make all the difference between the dignity of resistance and the smallness of surrender." Joanna Russ asked (several times, as is her wont), "What can a heroine do?"

A decade and a half after the conception of the Florence Howe Award, we can look back on essays that reflect similar concerns: all of them are, at some level, necessarily heuristic; they continue to describe ways to enlarge freedom and to take responsibility for doing so; and they suggest that we are all still looking for—and creating—heroines who can *do* something. While these essays show that feminist scholarship has moved from the avowedly "subjunctive mood'' (in Phyllis Franklin's words) to something like the indicative mood, they show, too, that feminist scholars are loath to give up the ''possibleness,'' the ''contingency'' of the subjunctive—and that is something to be thankful for.

''Milton's daughters,'' says Beth Kowaleski-Wallace, ''are emblematic of all Miltonic daughters who participate in a literary tradition they do not comprehend. But,'' she goes on, ''a patriarchal literary tradition demands only compliance, not comprehension from its daughters.'' There are no willing Miltonic daughters here. The tenor of this collection is not one of compliance, however seductive that might be. These voices—as different as they are from one another, as resistant to categorization in terms of content, intent, and whatever kinds of tents the speakers inhabit—comprehend fully the patriarchal voices with which they contend. It would be disingenuous to impose on them some sort of ''theme,'' an overall ideology, or a methodology to which they all subscribe. Indeed, to do so would be to subvert, even to pervert, the intentions of the founders of the Florence Howe Award. It seems fair, though, to suggest that they share a point like the one defined here by Patrocinio Schweickart: ''Feminist criticism [and we might add pedagogy], we should remember, is a mode of praxis. The point is not merely to interpret literature in various ways; the point is to *change the world*.''

Given the revision of exclusionary canons and literary premises, which is surely one function of the MLA and certainly a mission of the Women's Caucus, it is not at all surprising that most of the essayists in this volume eschew the ''dog-eared myth of intellectual neutrality'' (Annette Kolodny), the notion of ''ideological innocence'' (Ellen Pollak), the ''objectivist illusion'' (Patrocinio Schweickart). This is not to say—to switch metaphors—that all the methodological babies are thrown out with various kinds of ideological bathwater. One strength of this collection is its focus on the conflicting claims between what, in 1972, Phyllis Franklin uneasily recognized as the need to have students do ''some good reading'' (as defined by her male colleague) and the determination of feminist scholars to resist the ''immasculation'' that seems to require us to ''render up our dead'' (Celeste Schenck) and forget our history.[5]

Neither is it surprising that there are recurrent concerns here about whether, female characters *can* be heroines; about whether, as feminist scholars, readers, writers, or students, we can find a response to the equation ''culture = male'' (white, Euro-American, heterosexual male); about whether, whatever she does, a woman does not ''stink.'' This last issue, in various forms, emerges frequently in the essays; the ''straw woman'' Phyllis Franklin derived from her students' magazine reading in 1972 figures here with remarkable resilience—as writer, critic, or character. The composite female reader, as Franklin describes her, is ''sincerely, even terribly worried. . . . She worries about her body—is it the right size and shape? Does it stink? . . . Who is she? What is she? Does she stink? What does she want to be? What is she brave enough to be?'' And even if it were possible (should we wish it) for the writer or critic to achieve the odor of sanctity, we would still face in our classrooms those women whose aim is to ''delight others, and to smell good.'' And there are no sophisticated words with which to deconstruct a smell.

Joanna Russ concludes: "Women cannot write—using the old myths. But using new ones—?" and these essays tell us that, using the "old myths," women cannot easily or honestly read, or make critiques either. Thus many of these writers suggest ways in which we might re-read/re-vise/re-place the myths we have been taught. In reminding us that those female bogeys, Eve and Pandora, were moved by a desire for knowledge and by curiosity, Phyllis Franklin invokes for us, without body odor, two traditions of women's urge to know. In a similar spirit, Susan Stanford Friedman shows us, H. D.'s mythmaking transforms the Goddess from what is for male mythmakers something like the embodiment of "otherness" and the "eternal feminine" to "a projection of the mother-daughter bond and the creative capacity of women." And, perhaps more important, H. D. deals effectively with that most influential of modern mythmakers, Sigmund Freud, by turning his "categories upside down—or right side up, if you will." Corinne Dale, though her purpose is larger than this suggests, seeks in part to "demystify the American Adam/frontier myth" and put before us the (possibly smelly) "domestic alternative" in American fiction. The then current myth that Sylvia Plath was "hurtling herself toward death" comes under scrutiny in Mary Cohen's analysis of Plath's use of the Mary and Christ-child myth in the "children's poems." Rather, Cohen suggests, the theme serves to voice Plath's increasingly urgent feminism.

At the (chronological) center of this collection, Cynthia Davis devotes an essay to "feminist myth criticism." In a different way from Joanna Russ, she points to the dangers of simply turning Jungian mythic patterns upside down according to gender, insisting that "myth criticism cannot ignore either gender or its social definition" and that simple "role reversal" just will not work. Celeste Schenck shows how the male myths of mourning, enshrined in elegy, do not speak to women, whose mourning is recuperative rather than competitive, whose myths constitute ways to hold on to the dead rather than to send them off (or up). And Linda Kauffman suggests how Margaret Atwood's Offred figures, bodily, the oppositional forces of myth ("received history," as it were) and history as an account of "real life."

In 1981 Cynthia Davis said that "the hidden patterns of feminine experience and perception must be revealed in new forms [of myth] and in versions of old ones." Perhaps the clearest analysis of how new myths can empower both characters and readers comes in Rosemarie Garland Thomson's discussion of Toni Morrison's "disabled" and "stigmatized" women. Their resilience, their immense will to survive both originate in and create an "alternative domain" that enables us, forces us, to see the "everyday" order for what it is. "Myth," she says, "allows [Morrison's] novels the potential to clear away the oppressive ubiquity of the dominant perspective and to establish a space . . . where things are run differently." For those who read these essays in sequence, it will be a joy and a reward (though *surely* not for doing things "properly") to find Joanna Russ's questions about myth "What can a heroine do?" and "But using new ones—?" answered so gracefully and so affirmatively.

Joanna Russ suggested "back then" that detective stories, supernatural fiction, science fiction, and political fiction might be genres that allowed space for fictional accounts of "the kinds of experiences we are actually having now." Though we can, perhaps, force Atwood's novel *The Handmaid's Tale* into the science fiction category, those genres are not, in general, the topics of these essays. There are, however, numerous ways in which the essayists, and their subjects, struggle with or against established genres—both literary and critical. Revision of a traditional myth obviously means revision of traditional genre: thus, rewriting the Goddess as Muse, H. D. restructures the patriarchal epic for her own purposes. For another example, numerous female elegists have constructed a mode of their own, refusing to shove the dead out of the way in order to inherit their place and thereby creating an "intertextually verifiable tradition" that calls elegy "as patriarchally codified, into question" (Schenck 199). Novelists without a myth (and therefore a generically "proper" plot) to call their own (not even a Freudian or a Jungian modernization) are immediately open to charges of "formlessness" because, as Davis observes, "in the search for patterns not 'accessible' to a 'public,' androcentric consciousness can go on even as new forms are created" (117). And when Atwood creates her own myth and thus her own genre out of the fabric of a present horribly projected into the future, she is criticized for "lack of realism" (Kauffman).

It is just as problematic to subscribe in some way to the established modes and perspectives. So, as Deborah Byrd suggests, Elizabeth Barrett Browning spent a good deal of time "competing" with or trying to emulate the men who wrote the poetry she admired. George Eliot somehow encourages a reader's sympathy for Lydgate rather than for Rosamond or even Dorothea, as Phyllis Franklin and Susan Peck MacDonald show, in different ways, in their discussions of *Middlemarch*. Such propensities will seem perfectly explicable if we consider the power of what Beth Kowaleski-Wallace calls "Locke's pedagogical paradigm," the concealed coerciveness of the "myth of the benevolent patriarch." When it is a critic rather than a nineteenth-century poet or novelist who does not feel the "awe and fear" attendant on such "education," and *most* especially when that critic comments on writers as canonized as Alexander Pope or Herman Melville, she is accused of "case-making," as MacDonald was, or of being "a shade too polemical," as Faye M. Lenarcic was. Fortunately, Schweickart offers some suggestions for a way out of this dilemma, arguing persuasively that "an interpretation . . . is not valid or invalid in itself," its validity being "contingent on the agreement of others," and that "feminist reading and writing are alike grounded in the interest of producing a community of feminist readers and writers."

Most of the concerns addressed by these essays might be categorized under feminist studies in language and literature and feminist theory. Another category is the present state of feminist studies in literary history and criticism. It was with "presentness" in mind that when we asked each award winner to contribute her essay to this volume, we asked, too, whether she would want to write a short piece to accompany the essay. We suggested that such an afterword might, for example, explain the context(s) of the essay, might develop the conclusions the writer drew "back then," might radically revise or even repudiate the arguments presented in the essay. We were aware that, as writers and scholars, none of us remains immutably in the spaces we have at various times occupied, and we did not want the essayists to feel frozen in the time and place of the essay represented here. When we invited afterwords, then, we were not imposing an obligation. We were delighted that all the award winners were able to send their essays, and grateful for the afterwords we did receive—which add a valuable contextualizing element, as well as some timely caveats. At the same time we honor the feelings of essayists who for various reasons did not wish to write an afterword. ''It was like looking at a ghost,'' one said. Another wrote that she didn't want to ''go back, rethink, reread, rewrite what I thought then.'' The strict deadlines we had to impose prevented others from writing new material. But the volume had the enthusiastic endorsement of each writer or her representative.

We hope that the afterwords, as well as the silences, help us situate feminist literary criticism in historical perspective, for we are nearly ready for another overview, ten years after Annette Kolodny's ''Dancing through the Minefield.'' In that essay she called on feminist critics to ''expose [the minefield] for what it is . . . and deactivate its components''—and that was before almost everyone started using French words and putting parentheses in odd places, or male critics started reading ''as women.'' Taken in sum, of course, these essays point to the dangers of the minefield both before and after 1979. Susan Peck MacDonald still, and with good reason, finds the standards of literary criticism ''capricious''; Ellen Pollak, having fairly analyzed the vulnerability of some ''established'' critical approaches, appreciates that she still might be the lunatic on the fringe (albeit a prizewinner); Beth Kowaleski-Wallace contends that ''we have no choice'' but to struggle against being ''daddy's girls'' who are ''condemned . . . to live under the weight of a patriarchal tradition we ourselves have helped to perpetuate''; and Annette Kolodny, in 1990, speculates that we might now face a ''minefield of our own achievements and their implications.''

We might be tempted to read these comments on the present state of feminist studies as warnings that we should avoid particular topics, texts, approaches—might see the minefield, that is, as uncrossable, its components impossible of deactivation. But that would be to misread the Florence Howe Award and the Women's Caucus (members of which have crossed various minefields of our own, as this introduction makes clear), to misread (is this possible?) Florence Howe.

In December 1973, Florence Howe delivered the MLA presidential address, which she called ''Literacy and Literature.'' It is not without significance that she had been elected, in 1971, in a write-in campaign—crossing thereby a minefield of, one imagines, vast proportions. In her address she called for ''courage and tools, [the] . . . not unreasonable goals of literary study,'' and asked: ''Dare we admit that literature . . . matters to our lives?'' (122). Like many others after 1971, she referred to Adrienne Rich's definition of ''re-vision'' as ''an act of survival,'' calling for an extension of the ''process of survival'' to those ''omitted from literary study and from the curriculum in general,'' including students whose needs had not been met, ''not only women but most of the invisible masses that have always peopled this earth'' (123). Those ''masses'' are, of course, "invisible" usually to eyes dimmed by ethnocentrism, class privilege, heterosexism, and ageism (at least), and it is regrettable that generally—though not, thank goodness, finally—the Florence Howe Award essays focus on the most privileged of all—always excepting that those in focus are women.

However, in this twentieth anniversary year of the Women's Caucus for the Modern Languages, the 1973 president of the MLA—an institution she was recently said to have helped "if not to overthrow, . . . to thoroughly subvert . . . and transform . . . into a hotbed of feminist activity" (Rosenfelt 9)—might justifiably be pleased with these essays gathered together in her name. Representing as they do many acts of courage, they are certainly the kinds of tools for which she and we well understand the need if we are both to "admit that literature . . . matters to our lives" and to "*change the world.*"

NOTES

[1] The MLA Commission on the Status of Women was officially founded in 1968 but is celebrating its twentieth anniversary in 1990 because its present configuration and mission began in 1970. For a fuller account of the commission, see Florence Howe's preface to this collection.

[2] Since 1985 the name has been the Feminist Press at the City University of New York.

[3] For a complete discussion of this debate as published in *Concerns*, see that publication, vol. 6.2 (7 May 1976): 14-22. Selected excerpts of this material are offered in the text here to reveal the contours of the debate.

[4] We have searched all the records available to us and have concluded that no honorable mention was given in 1975 or in 1985. If any reader has access to documentation of honorable-mention awards for those years, we urge her or him to contact the editors so that lacunae in the archives might be filled in.

[5] "Immasculation" was first defined by Judith Fetterley in *The Resisting Reader*; several Florence Howe Award essayists make use of the concept.

~ THE "OTHER" ~ FLORENCE HOWE AWARD

RECALLING FLORENCE HOWE'S concern for "the invisible masses that have always peopled this earth," we want here to draw attention to another way in which Howe's concerns about feminism, education, and women's lives have been addressed. At Santa Rosa Junior College, in California, members of the Women's Staff and Faculty Support Network call the WCML Florence Howe literary prize the "other Florence Howe Award."[1] In 1980, network women devised an award to honor campus colleagues doing "superior jobs, giving . . . extra effort above and beyond their job requirements." Originally the Woman of the Month Award, in spring 1983 it was named for "a woman who represented all the aspects of the women the award was honoring." The SRJC network chose Florence Howe because, besides being a scholar and a university professor, she provided (through the Feminist Press) "teaching materials on women writers and women in history to educational institutions." The 1987 award-winning grounds manager at SRJC, who found "receiving an award . . . a bit nerve-wracking," discovered in the library a Florence Howe compilation of stories and poems of working women in "nontraditional careers." That volume made her "feel more comfortable." The network's decision and the grounds manager's discovery are just two reasons for the WCML to be glad we share, nominally, an award with the SRJC network. Florence has told us she is proud of the SRJC award; we are proud to share an idea with women whose concerns, transposed into only a slightly different key, are ours.

Following are the names of the women who have been honored with the Santa Rosa Junior College Florence Howe Award:

~ 1980–81 ~

Ruth Craig, Foreign Language Instructor (deceased)
Cathy Maddux, District Accountant (retired)
Nancy Yoshioka, Administrative Secretary
Allene Hankla, Assistant Dean of Instruction (retired)
Edna Hughes, Administrative Secretary (retired)

~ 1981–82 ~

Evelyn Pollard, Assistant Dean, Counseling
Betty Goulart, Administrative Secretary (retired)

~ 1982–83 ~

Dianne Smith, Instructor, Behaviorial Sciences
Susan Baldi, Assistant Dean, Instruction
Marian Kaus, Instructor, Health Occupations (retired)

~ 1983–84 ~

Joan Ringler, Financial Aid Technician (retired)
Carol Olmstead, Instructor, Math (resigned)

~ 1984–85 ~

Laurie Beard, Administrative Assistant and Secretary, President's Office
Raquel Rodriguez-Rasor, Instructor, ESL English

~ 1985–86 ~

Joyce Welch-Griffin, Instructor, English
April Chaney, Testing Technician
Linda James, Administrative Secretary

~ 1986–87 ~

Marge Ling, Department Chair, Vocational Nursing
Nancy Moorhead, Grounds Manager

~ 1987–88 ~

Paula Coulson, Reentry Assistant, Reentry Office
Pat Miltenberger, Vice President, Academic Affairs (resigned)
Kerry Campbell-Price, Manager, Public Relations

~ 1988–89 ~

Sue Amalia, Director, Vocational Studies
Nancy Luke, Programmer Analyst, Computer Services
Maryanne Michaels, Director, EOPS
Sandy Martinez, Manager, School Outreach (resigned)

~ 1989–90 ~

Lynn Garlock, Accounting Clerk I, Telecommunications
Elizabeth Carlson, Learning Specialist, Learning Services

NOTE

[1] The information about the Santa Rosa Junior College Florence Howe Award is taken from copies of *Insider*, the college staff newsletter, and from a letter from Melissa Sue Kort, who sent us copies of the *Insider*.

~ 1974 ~

Traditional Literary Study—in the Subjunctive Mood

PHYLLIS FRANKLIN

THESE DAYS OF women's liberation may be the times that try men's souls, but these are also the times when it feels particularly good to be a woman. One looks to the future with interest; for women are beginning, if not to come into their own, at least to undertake, in a concerted way, a search for what that "own" might be. For me, this sense of exciting prospects is new. I didn't have it eight months ago when I agreed to teach an experimental course called Women in Literature for the University of Miami. And it didn't happen all at once. As the semester progressed, I thought frequently, at first with deep misgivings, and finally with amusement and self-confidence, of William Vaughn Moody's poem "I Am the Woman." The woman he describes states her challenge in this way:

> I am the Woman, ark of the law and its breaker,
> Who chastened her step and taught her knees to be meek,
> Bridled and bitted her heart and humbled her cheek,
> Parceled her will, and cried, "Take more!" to the taker,
> Shunned what they told her to shun, sought what they bade her seek,
> Locked up her mouth from scornful speaking: now it is open to speak.
> (127)

No longer chastening steps, or teaching knees to be meek, women have begun to speak. We are no longer simply holding out cupped hands to receive attributes from men. Instead, and this for me is at the heart of women's studies, we are trying to assess our heritage—scientific, economic, social, and cultural—in an attempt to discern what we were in that first shining hour in Eden; what we might have been before man came to see us, made us see ourselves, paradoxically enough, as both the ark of the law, his law, and the breaker of that law.

This project of self-discovery is not only complex (how does one go about stripping away centuries of socialization?) but, at first, frightening. As I gathered materials, prepared lectures, I felt myself threatened and depressed, and my students had a similar emotional experience. After all, hostility rarely reassures.

The subject seemed complicated, uncertain, and hopeless. In the course of the semester, however, we lost the sense of hopelessness, though we could not forget the complexities or uncertainties; for most of us concluded we were uncertain about the nature of woman, that there were mysteries to solve. And mysteries are frightening.

My particular concern in this paper deals with the question of how those of us engaged in the study of literature can contribute to the development of women's studies in both our teaching and our research. What are the possibilities? Virginia Woolf totted up in *A Room of One's Own*: "women and what they are like; or . . . women and the fiction they write; or . . . women and the fiction that is written about them; or . . . all three . . . inextricably mixed together . . ." (3). And she did not even begin to concern herself about a method, which is at least as important as subject matter.

While I was planning my course, I talked with women who had already taught such courses. They admitted many difficulties. One had used a sociological orientation, and I could see that most of the newly published texts reflected this approach. But it seemed unsatisfactory. For one thing, it wasn't literature, and so evaded the possibility of finding out truths from literature. And besides, I wasn't trained to conduct such a study, though I supposed I could bone up. Another woman told me she had concentrated on literature that presented strong women, so that she could provide her students with good role models. This sounded more attractive. Obviously there was a desperate lack of varied role models for women in our society.

But this too seemed unsatisfactory. What bothered me most was that it meant accepting as valid the literary models provided by our culture. For example, she was teaching *Antigone*. I found myself wondering whether it would be a good thing for my students to simply accept Antigone as a role model. It's true that she is a brave young woman who has the strength of her convictions, and so is admirable. But it's also true that she is admirable because she risks and suffers death to fulfill religious and familial obligations, an act of female self-sacrifice not unlike the self-effacement expected of the nineteenth-century woman. And surely we have had enough of that. Of course, there is more than self-sacrifice involved in *Antigone*. There is an abstract problem too, that of duty to one's conscience and duty to one's state, a problem of conflicting loyalties.

Well, why use a woman to exemplify such a problem? Aeschylus in the *Oresteia* had dealt with a not totally dissimilar dilemma and had used a man. But Sophocles, early in the play, makes the point fairly clear, and we can see why a woman is a clever choice. It is not the way of a woman to disobey, says Ismene, who exemplifies the well-behaved young lady. And just because it is not the way of a woman to disobey, the importance of family tradition and the importance of duty to one's conscience are intensified when *even* a woman musters up courage to die for her belief. Her daring is more significant than a man's because she is weaker; her challenge more surprising. I concluded that the fact of her sex was structurally significant and that although she wasn't a bad model, still, studying the play wouldn't particularly clarify the problems women face in our society.

It is interesting, too, that compared with ancient tragic heroes, she is rather passive. To be sure, she makes her initial decision to disregard the edict, but she simply decides to do the deed and take her punishment. Her heroism rests on her willingness to accept an early death, a timeworn literary solution for most female dilemmas. Consider Oedipus—he doesn't set out to destroy himself. Or Orestes—he doesn't just wait for his fate. Also, while we have passivity before us—look at the suicides in Sophocles's trilogy: Jocasta and Oedipus, generally speaking, share the same kind of guilt. But Jocasta kills herself, while Oedipus puts out his eyes; unpleasant, but he endures so as to suffer and live and finally to triumph. Similarly, Eurydice is so overcome with grief that she kills herself, while Creon, who has precipitated the situation, like Oedipus, chooses to suffer, and live.

No, I decided, simply using strong female characters as positive role models was not enough. I wanted to understand patterns, try to get beyond, beneath cultural and literary assumptions, and not just accept them. But my particular teaching assignment was such that I could not engage in elaborate studies in single areas. I had been asked to teach a sophomore-level course that would be open to all undergraduates. After some agonizing, I put together a reading list and determined an approach for my classroom. Looking back on it now, I see that my decisions reflected three kinds of obligations: to my discipline, to the subject itself, and to my prospective students.

I wanted whatever I did to be academically respectable. I confess to thinking—well, if the course doesn't do anything much for women or women's studies, at least it will be a solid course in literature, just topically oriented. Actually, my chairman's responses to my reading list revealed that he had the same thing in mind: "They will be doing some good reading," was what he said. I was also interested in the problem of methodology. I thought that once I was safely behind my academic barricade, I could, perhaps, try to discover whether such a course as Women in Literature should exist. Was it a legitimate subject? What kinds of things could be discovered? And more important than answers, I decided, were questions. What were the right questions to ask, so that problems could be defined and directions for research marked out?

And I wanted to fulfill as best I could my students' special needs and expectations; in this area, I felt most presumptuous, most on my own. I knew from talking to some of them before the semester began that they were enrolling because they had questions about their own identity as women and questions about the ways they might develop their lives. Because of this, I was afraid to go too far into the past for reading materials. It seemed to me that before they could answer their questions, they had to have some insight into the pressures women experience in our society. And so the books I selected ought to reflect aspects of a woman's life that were still worth worrying about; that is, they should involve questions related to life-styles. From this point of view, the problems of such figures as Antigone and Joan of Arc seemed less important.

My final reading list consisted of books about women by both men and women writers of various nations. I asked my students to read *The Romance of Tristan and Iseult*, so that we could examine one source of the love myth in Western society; *Madame Bovary*, so that we could see the effect of this myth; *Little Women*, so that we could examine the very real attractions of a warm and strong family and consider also the question of sentimentalism; *Middlemarch*, so that we could consider women characters drawn by a woman, account for their evolution, and consider why women had not seemed suitable figures for tragedy; *Anna Karenina*, so that we could consider the value of living within tradition, and the danger, from Tolstoy's point of view, of fulfilling emotional needs outside marriage; *A Doll's House*, for historical reasons and because it raises the question of male law, male and female values; *Miss Julie*, because it clearly reveals the male as sexual aristocrat and sex as degrading for women, so that sexual intercourse becomes the cause of the tragedy; *The Portrait of a Lady*, so that we could consider the concept of the lady and the danger of denying sexuality; *The Awakening*, because it is a modern statement of woman's dilemma by a woman who touches the center of the problem and then, in 1899, doesn't know what to do about it; *Mrs. Dalloway*, because it is a woman's portrait of the hostess, the mother, the virginal wife; and a new paperback anthology, *The Bold New Women*, because it is worth exploring for its defiant antiromantic attitude. The poetry we considered throughout the semester to exemplify one thing or another, we read as a group in the classroom, and I provided copies. In addition, I asked students to read either *The Second Sex* or *Sexual Politics* or *The Female Eunuch* or *Man's World: Woman's Place*, recommended in that order.

Also, in response to my students' special needs, I worried about classroom atmosphere. I knew that all of us would be personally involved with the subject and with testing our attitudes and arguments on each other, because to a great extent the subject had to be made. So personalities would matter, classroom relationships would have to be different, less formal than in my other classes, I decided, and (oh, dear) my own sense of myself as a woman would matter. Should I, I wondered, be objective or reveal myself? And on personal or literary matters? At the beginning I wasn't sure.

But I was certain that the classroom atmosphere had to be comfortable, that the students should participate. I had chosen the reading list, and though this might have the taint of autocracy, I felt justified. But I wanted them to get to know each other as quickly as possible and to work together. It was with this in mind that I arranged the first assignment, which required group work. As I made the assignment that first day of class, I reminded students of the general notion that women could not work well together, and I asked them to examine their own feelings. Actually, I regarded this as an integral part of the assignment, and later, after the class project was complete, we talked about the problem of women working together.

This assignment required that, as a group, we develop a picture of what we called our "straw woman," the modern American woman as she could be seen in the magazines she reads, magazines written to appeal to her. I explained that a jointly created description of this straw woman would provide us with something to react to as the semester progressed. I also hoped, though I did not say this, that it would help us more quickly become a group with a common goal. We discussed the various popular women's magazines, decided which types to study, and divided into six groups on the basis of expressed interest in the magazines. Each group was charged with analyzing a magazine and describing its typical reader. What was she concerned with, interested in? How bright did the editors think she was? They were to consider the cover, fiction, nonfiction, advertising, editorials, illustrations, general layout. On the basis of their reports, I put together a profile of this straw woman. This I duplicated and handed out by the end of the second week of the semester, and the class had visible proof of the group effort. The magazines we considered were *Good Housekeeping, MS., New Woman, Cosmopolitan, Glamour, Playboy*, and two confessional magazines. As I considered their comments, I was led to make the following generalization:

> Our straw woman is sincerely, even terribly worried. Heaven only knows how she lives longer than her mate! She worries about her body—is it the right size and shape? Does it stink? How should she do her hair? What about body odor? What should she wear? Whom should she vote for? What kind of furniture, car, food, appliances, or stocks should she buy? And what about body odor? How should she cook the food, take care of the furniture and clothing? What should she do about sex (marital or premarital or adulterous)? How should she feel about the family, marriage, and day-care centers? And what about body odor? Should she make love to one man or more than one man—seriatim or simultaneously? Or should she just let him make love to her? Should he chase her or should she chase him? Is guilt necessary? Desirable? Who is she? What is she? Does she stink? What does she want to be? What is she brave enough to be? Is women's lib a threat or a ray of hope—or both?
>
> One thing seems very clear. While the classical purpose of literature is generally assumed to be dual—to teach and delight—the purpose of popular journalism for American women has only a single aim: to teach them how to delight others, and to smell good.

And this was one of the first truths I learned about literature for women: in general, such literature is, however artistically admirable, designed to be monitory. It was not just the class analysis that made me aware of this but an interesting complaint lodged by a male colleague who had borrowed my copy of Doris Lessing's *The Golden Notebook*. He complained that the book was depressing because there weren't any admirable male characters he could identify with. And he was aggrieved because this was clearly a new situation for him. At first I felt apologetic because I had praised the book; and then I realized how rare it was for a woman to find an admirable female character to identify with who didn't practice self-sacrifice. There are lots of stories about more or less wicked or silly women who are more or less admirable and with whom one can sympathize, but their stories are warnings: they come to a bad end so often. On the other hand, there was Mary Poppins, I thought, frantically casting about, or Alice (maybe), or the nice old-lady detective in mystery stories; and I recalled something a cynical woman had once said to me—that the only women people could feel neutral about sexually, and perhaps therefore the only ones they could write about in a neutral way, were those who by vocation were exempt from sexual possibility—nuns and witches, she had said. I added to the list Mary Poppins, Alice (maybe), and old-lady detectives who were clever.

Aside from the first assignment, I stayed close to the traditional. This seemed important because books frequently taught and frequently written about would be likely to have influenced generations of readers and therefore would be worth studying. That is, if we're trying to find out what women are and might have been, it seems important to look at books that may have helped make us what we are. Such a book as *The Awakening* was included for its insights and for its differences from the more widely read and taught *Madame Bovary* and *Anna Karenina*, but an entire reading list of books not widely known would have defeated my immediate purpose.

My approach to these books was traditional too. It seemed natural to use my professional training. If I were willing to accept one or several methods of literary study when I wanted to learn other things, why shouldn't these methods be helpful now—if only I handled them in a more open, hopeful way—use old methods but stay in the subjunctive mood. And so I decided that we would study a book a week, that I would rather briefly review for the class traditional approaches to the book and then we would look at it from our own perspective—that of women in 1972. To give students some sense of how we might begin to see things in a new way, I discussed with them approaches to literature found in Katharine Rogers's *Troublesome Helpmate* and Mary Ellman's *Thinking about Women*.

Recalling Wayne Booth's list of the various ways one might look at fiction, I rather quickly decided that two of the approaches he reviews would be most fruitful for classroom analysis. First, we should examine the work as an art object, Booth's "autonomous," "well-wrought urn" category. It seemed important to understand what it was in the artwork we were responding to, what in the structure and imagery, what quality of language that made us feel as we did about the characters and situations. I hoped that after we had studied the book in this way, we could look at it as a "work of rhetoric," "an imposition by one man on another" ("Rhetoric" 158). And having determined the nature of the book's pattern and its effect upon us, we could then consider the implications of the book's rhetoric for women. What might aesthetically effective books that conveyed values so persuasively have meant to women in the past? What could they mean for us now?

Because of this particular emphasis, I abandoned any serious attempt to deal with biographical questions or even questions concerning the author's conscious or unconscious intentions. The fact that a book or a poem was well known, frequently taught, and, therefore, perhaps, influential was fact enough. How or why it got that way was a good question, but I chose not to try to answer it.

This approach proved useful for us, opening up a number of problems. For one thing, we gained some interesting insights into attitudes toward sex. The first book in the reading list was *The Romance of Tristan and Iseult*, which I had gone back to the Middle Ages for, although many of my colleagues and students thought it a strange choice. From the point of view of methodology, however, it was a good book to start with because Denis de Rougemont's study of the Tristan legend showed how an analysis of structure could get beyond a book's charm to a more complete understanding of its rhetoric. For charm the story does have. Even the most hardened antiromantics in the class found themselves responding to and involved with the lovers. Yet the pattern in the book is clearly not what a reasonable reader would expect: two young people very much in love who, instead of avoiding obstacles so that they may freely fulfill their love, accept obstacles, and when none exist, actually create their own. But the pattern does reveal a truth about the book—that is, that it is just as important for the lovers to be apart as it is for them to be united.

De Rougemont has explored this pattern of unhappy love, love accompanied by the "exquisite anguish" of parting, which he sees as very significant. He says that there is no literary tradition of happy love in Western society and that the very charm of the myth rests on our desire for unhappy love, which in turn he relates to an unconscious death wish (1–47). This last I am not sure of. Certainly the legend is effective on a much simpler and more obvious level. That is, it seems directly related to the rhythm of sexual desire—restraint and increased tension, climactic coming together, and separation—and all this under the influence of a love potion which excuses, explains, and justifies; so that for a time, while under the spell of the tale, along with the lovers, we willingly abandon moral considerations. And so moved, so caught up in the story, we accept the rhetoric of the legend, which is, that the fulfillment of passionate love under these conditions is rightly bigger than we are and creates its own morality. To yield oneself in a perilous situation, to give all for love, has a very real power to charm us, and we respond for a number of more or less civilized reasons. The legend does ennoble sexual love; it compels our response to the rhythm of sexual desire when rational control gives way to passion; and it reflects the intensity of sexual desire, or perhaps just the intensity of unsanctioned sexual desire.

Well, then, what is the significance of this rhetoric for us? A crucial one, I think. Men as well as women are carried away by passion, but women much more than men are defined by the terms of their sexual participation, and so passion can have a more devastating effect when women make decisions "under the influence." A consideration of the legend and its tremendous power as a myth to affect us, "usually without our knowing," de Rougemont says, can lead, at least, to an intellectual awareness of the aura that surrounds sexual fulfillment in our society. I say "at least" because I suspect that intellectualizations about passion are rarely helpful; but, still, knowledge is supposed to be power. Certainly it is helpful to know that though there are many centuries between Iseult and *True Confessions*, there is a connection.

Studying the legend in this way does not represent a plea to ignore passion. Rather, it is a plea to know with what part of our bodies we respond to the legend, to know that we may respond positively to the idea of unhappy love, and, perhaps, most important of all, to recognize that what we are dealing with is unattainable desire, so that to fulfill it easily is to destroy it. Events that take place somewhere between "Once upon a time" and "They lived happily ever after" cannot take place in everyday time and stay the same. If we do not understand this, we may be left, as was Emma Bovary, with destructive dissatisfactions. One must decide whether one wants to live always on the brink of ecstatic passion and suffer the consequences, or live with fewer intensities more generally diffused. Knowledge involves recognizing that on the one hand there is Keats's "Heard melodies are sweet, but those unheard / Are sweeter" and on the other hand there is e. e. cummings's very practical he-man, who says: "A pretty girl who naked is, / is worth a million statues." One must remember that if Tristan had married Iseult, she would be driving a car pool, and he would be taking out the garbage.

A study of August Strindberg's *Miss Julie* yielded a different insight into sexual matters. As in the Tristan legend, emotional appeal is based on increasing sexual tension between Jean and Miss Julie. This tension results finally in intercourse, and then we are privileged to observe the aftermath. Involved in the erotic tension of the play and influenced by Strindberg's rhetoric, we can hardly help but feel the woman's debasement and the man's pride. Jean, despite his dishonesty and social inferiority, is, according to Strindberg, "In the sexual sphere . . . the aristocrat" (xx). He is the natural winner; Julie, the natural loser. A sexual encounter cannot diminish him, but not even aristocratic birth can help her. Because she is a woman and because she experiences physical desire, she is doomed either to fall or repress her sexuality. As E. M. Sprinchorn notes: in this play "fate takes the form of erotic passion" and "the tragedy lies ultimately in the act of love itself" (xiii). Julie's recurrent dream reveals the kind of stress she and so many women have experienced. She dreams of falling from the top of a pillar. She fears the fall, she desires the fall, and she knows that she will have no peace until she falls. But she also knows that once fallen, she will not be able to stop herself from sinking into the dirt. So persuasive is Strindberg's rhetoric that we accept the fact that when a lovely woman stoops to folly, the only act that can cover her guilt is death.

Obviously the message here about the nature of sex is quite different from that of the Tristan and Iseult legend, and it is an important message for women to recognize and talk about. Strindberg's view of the male as sexual aristocrat and his dramatization of woman's fall in sex is illuminating. As far as my class was concerned, one had not only to watch out for the Scylla of idealization but also to beware the Charybdis of degradation.

We learned other things too. A study of implicit comparisons, for example, led us to see that a sense of women as helpless, animal-like creatures has evolved at least partly because writers either make direct comparisons between women and animals or because in more subtle ways they make us see the fate of women as being like that of animals. Flaubert's very famous scene of the agricultural show in *Madame Bovary* sets up this kind of comparison. He describes the

> long lines of girls—servants from farms, wearing blue stockings, low-heeled shoes and silver rings and smelling of the dairy when they came close. They walked holding hands, forming chains the whole length of the meadow, from the row of aspens to the banquet tent. It was time for the judging, and one after another the farmers were filing into a kind of hippodrome marked off by a long rope hung on

stakes. Here stood the livestock, noses to the rope, rumps of all shapes and sizes forming a ragged line. (154)

The cinematic possibilities of the scene are good. Few directors would miss the link between the judging of lines of animals inside the hippodrome and the judging of the female animals lined up outside. Moreover, Flaubert's emphasis in this scene on winning prizes—farmers for their animals or men winning women—not only underscores Rodolphe's campaign to win Emma; it also makes us see the relationship between men and women in a particular way—the superior male cleverly winning the less clever female. Using ironic juxtaposition, Flaubert presents Rodolphe's seductive entreaties against a background of voices announcing prizes for the best manures. And the creature who is going to be won by this "manure" is at that very moment held "like a captive dove," while outdoors the peasant women's headdresses look "like fluttering white butterfly wings." Finally, we see Rodolphe, his siege well on the way to success, lead Emma away. In this scene, she wears a green bonnet, and Flaubert also describes the other "masters" leading off the animals: "their horns decked with the green wreaths that were their trophies" (168–70). Again, few directors filming the scene would miss the intended comparison between the two kinds of green-hatted creatures, each led away by a master.

Tolstoy also makes use of animals in *Anna Karenina*. D. S. Merezhkovsky points out the similarities between Tolstoy's description of Vronsky's horse Frou-Frou and his description of Anna. By making us see Frou-Frou as like Anna, by making us see Vronsky treat the horse as he would a woman he loves, Tolstoy also makes us see the possibility of Anna's death. Frou-Frou dies because Vronsky makes an "unpardonable mistake"; and we watch him kick the fallen horse that is already in great agony (211). This we see just before Anna puts her future in Vronsky's hands.

The scene is brilliant and conveys several kinds of information. Merezhkovsky says: "In the death of the woman, as in the death of the animal, a tragedy has been accomplished—the eternal violation of the strong against the weak, the crime of a sensual eros against another, spiritual one . . ." (802–10). The male critic sees a valid moral injunction against the exploitation of the weak by the strong. The self-conscious feminist reader agrees, but also sees that such a comparison intensifies for women a sense of weakness and dependence. Surely there is a message here for us, in addition to the one intended by the author: beware of subtle persuasions hidden in juxtapositions.

Just as we learned to question the effects of implicit comparisons, so did we learn to question the implications of imagery. For example, we found William Wordsworth's poem "She Was a Phantom of Delight" a particularly interesting hodgepodge of genuine admiration for a woman, nineteenth-century ideas of women, and older antifeminine attitudes, although when first the poem gleamed upon our sight, it seemed just another nineteenth-century glorification of woman.

In each of the poem's three stanzas, Wordsworth considers different aspects of a woman he admires. He is first impressed by her appearance; later, he is impressed by her womanly qualities; and, finally, he recognizes her as a being, presumably a human being. This last view is the way many of us would like to be seen, and so it is worth starting with. What matters in this stanza is that the woman, like other beings, is "A traveller between life and death," and so, we assume, like other beings must suffer the slings and arrows of fortune and the angst beings experience who know that one day they will not be. In the face of this, she is thoughtful, reasonable, temperate. She has endurance and foresight and strength and skill. She is, he says, a perfect woman, and she has been endowed with these qualities so as to use them.

There is nothing here to offend, nothing here like the misogyny one finds in the literature of the Renaissance, which Katharine Rogers associates with ambivalent attitudes toward love. In this tradition, if women were attractive, it was common to point out that their very attractions were dangerous illusions, that painted exteriors hid weakness, or impurity, or evil. John Marston, for instance, "described women as 'Glowe wormes bright / That soile our soules, and dampe our reasons light,' " and Rogers explains that "the glowworm comparison was popular, since a glowworm, bright and pretty from a distance, is seen in the hand to be an ugly black bug" (109). The dangers and disappointments of these glowing creatures were also explored by John Donne in "Loves Alchymie," where he denies that physical love between a man and a woman can result in an ennobling transformation. A lover may glorify the woman he loves—"his pregnant pot," Donne calls her—but he is deluded. The lover gets only a "winter-seeming summer's night"—a short night that seems long and is therefore dull, and chill instead of warmth. And so Donne concludes, emphasizing the lack of substance in women and love,

> Our ease, our thrift, our honor, and our day,
> Shall we, for this vaine Bubles shadow pay?

With this in mind, it is interesting to look again at Wordsworth's poem, the first stanza this time, in which he praises the woman's appearance. Wordsworth describes her as a phantom, which may simply suggest that she is ethereal. Of course, what the word means is that she lacks substance. Moreover, she is not only a phantom, a being that seems to appear but has no physical presence, but she is also a phantom of delight, which, like Donne's winter-seeming summer's night, suggests unfulfilled promise. And she is an apparition, a "moment's ornament," one whose decorative quality is ephemeral. Here we have the gather-ye-rosebuds theme, that charming *memento mori* so frequently addressed to women. (Wasn't it *Newsweek* that described women's studies as the latest "wrinkle" in higher education?) And when we reach the last lines of the stanza, we find that this "image gay" (still not the real thing) has appeared only "To haunt, to startle, and waylay." Now this may simply describe the impression a beautiful woman can make on a man, but being haunted can be both unpleasant and pleasant; being startled is never particularly comfortable; and who wants to be waylaid? Even if it does not involve hostility, it still keeps you from doing whatever it was you set out to do.

Well, how different is Wordsworth's phantom of delight that, like the ignis fatuus, will startle and waylay, from John Donne's "vaine Bubles shadow"? A major difference lies in the fact that the negative elements in Donne's poem are obvious. Donne is disgusted because he finds the "Myne of love" empty. Wordsworth accepts a woman's lack of substance as fact, and his compliments echo with reverberations of ancient fears that attraction may not be pleasant. I suppose such ambiguous compliments are only unfortunate for women who may be led to think of themselves as haunting creatures and concentrate so on this that they do in fact become phantoms, without substance as people.

If Wordsworth's first stanza reflects ancient attitudes about the illusionary qualities of female beauty, the second stanza most clearly exemplifies nineteenth-century assumptions about woman's personality and work. She is a competent housekeeper and accepts as the extent of her mobility something described as "virgin liberty." She is sweet, and neither too bright nor too good for her everyday housekeeping chores; her responses are emotional but not deep; and her wiles are simple. That is, not being overly bright, her more or less devious ways are not dangerous, a charge that reflects an old attitude toward women. Edward de Vere had described man's pursuit of woman in this way:

> Yet for disport we fawn and flatter both,
>   To pass the time when nothing else can please;
> And train them to our lure with subtle oath,
>   Till, weary of their wiles, ourselves we ease;
> And then we say, when we their fancy try,
> To play with fools, O what a fool was I.

There may be a little confusion here as to who is manipulating whom, but at least there is disgust at the quality of the relationship, though the earl thinks man superior and woman at fault. But again, Wordsworth accepts the fact of female wiles, which are not only not to be feared or disapproved but to be encouraged, because they and she are so simple.

This poem, then, is much more than a poem of praise. From a woman's point of view, it exemplifies very nicely centuries of confusion during which men have assigned attributes to women—but we have to remember that it is their confusion and not necessarily a natural result of our nature.

By far the most dangerous and tragic phrase in the poem, however, is "transient sorrows." Surely a being capable of breathing thoughtful breath, who travels as we all do between life and death, ought to be capable of more than transient sorrow. Why couldn't Wordsworth see the contradictions inherent in a creature who was simultaneously a lovely flimsy who came trailing yards of silk chiffon, a competent housekeeper who was sweet and silly, and a monolithic Roman matron? And there is a still more important question for women to ask. Why was it that the limitation of woman's nature, as it was conceived in the nineteenth century—when she achieved a position somewhere between responsible male adult, child, and idiot—was not viewed as potentially tragic? Why did no artist see her suffering or struggling in her intermediary position in such a way that she could achieve the dignity of tragedy? Even a Caliban can get some literary sympathy, and there is a well-established literary tradition that deals with men who strive against limitations—men like Faustus or Ahab.

To be sure, there are women whose struggles involve the violation of sexual mores and who come to a bad end, but that's not what I mean. George Eliot, in the prelude to *Middlemarch*, recognizes the possibility of unexpressed tragedy in women's lives as she talks of Saint Theresa, whose "passionate, ideal nature demanded an epic life." She writes:

> Many Theresas have been born who found for themselves no epic life wherein there was a constant unfolding of far-resonant action; perhaps only a life of mistakes, the offspring of a certain spiritual grandeur ill-matched with the meanness of opportunity; perhaps a tragic failure which found no sacred poet and sank unwept into oblivion. (1)

And one expects, after such a beginning, that Eliot herself may play the part of sacred poet, that in Dorothea Brooke this tragic failure will be exemplified.

This is not the place for a lengthy discussion of why Dorothea's dilemma falls short of tragedy. But briefly, it is obvious that marrying your heroine to the man she loves and letting her live happily ever after provides at least one reason. George Eliot lets us see that Dorothea is a woman with heroic possibility who settles for domesticity, but the settling has its satisfactions and so we do not see her life as wasted. It is interesting, though, that there is a much stronger sense of loss in Eliot's description of Lydgate's failure to fulfill his potential. Lydgate, whose career has been limited by an unfortunate marriage, calls his wife "his basil plant" and explains that basil flourishes "wonderfully on a murdered man's brains." Clearly, this "murder" of his brains cannot be compared with the vague feeling we have that Dorothea might have done something "better"; and the difference in intensity reflects a sharp difference in attitude toward the quality of disaster when both a man and a woman fail to utilize their intellectual capacities. Despite her prelude, Eliot evades the tragic and accepts the traditional.

But even if she does not dramatize the potential tragedy in a woman's life, at least Eliot only partially diminishes her heroine: Dorothea is not sweet or little. It was far more frequent in the nineteenth century to diminish women so as to gain a sentimental effect, and I believe that a study of sentimentality will be important in an understanding of literary attitudes toward women. The tendency to diminish women was so widespread that Bret Harte, writing about Charles Dickens's children and women, satirized it:

> I see a child, . . . a most unnatural child, a model infant. It is prematurely old and philosophic. It dies in poverty to slow music. It dies surrounded by luxury to slow music. . . . Previous to its decease it makes a will; it repeats the Lord's Prayer, it kisses the "boofer lady." . . .
>
> I see a good woman, undersized. I see several charming women, but they are all undersized. They are more or less imbecile and idiotic, but always fascinating and undersized. They wear coquettish caps and aprons. I observe that feminine virtue is invariably below the medium height, and that it is always simple and infantine. . . . (98–99)

Harte, who was himself a clever user of formulas for developing character, certainly picked up on the technique of gaining sympathy. For the child, enhance his unchildlike qualities. For the woman, the adult, enhance her childlike qualities. It is with all the little Libbies, sweet and small and angelic, with all the Beth Marches' dying slowly with amazingly sweet acceptance that we must deal—and whom we must analyze. Diminishment is a necessary aspect of sentimentality, and the interesting thing about sentimentality is that it

> is a gross form of emotional reassurance. It tells us that everything is really all right and that suffering, although sad, is only temporary and not really serious . . . . Wherever it has appeared, . . . it has relied heavily on the creation and repetition of stock response materials (''emotional triggers'') which are centered around the emotional values of injustice to the self, manifested as self-pity, victimization, and martyrdom. (Benson 23)

And women, little, sweet women, are part of the stockpile of emotional triggers.

Because it is emotionally reassuring, sentimentality keeps us from looking beyond the situation for solutions. Consider a nonsexual example. The old poem about the poor little newsboy shivering in tattered clothing in the snow as he tries to sell his newspapers is a perfect example of a poem so satisfying within itself that we do not question its resolution. Our sympathies are aroused for the poor boy, unable to sell his papers. But at last, along comes a man, well-to-do, warmly dressed, in a comfortable fur-collared greatcoat, perhaps—there are few details:

> . . . The kind eye glistened
> As the stranger took the sheet,
> And glanced at the stiffened fingers,
> And thought of the icy feet.
>
> Then dropped in his hand the value
> Of his fifty papers sold,
> 'Ah, Poor little friend,' he faltered,
> 'Don't you shiver, and ache with cold?'
>
> The boy, with a gulp of gladness,
> Sobbed out, as he raised his eye
> To the warmth of the face above him—
> 'I did—sir—till you—passed by!'
> (Furness 99–100)

The trouble with this ending is its capacity for providing emotional satisfaction. The immediate problem is solved. There is an exchange of human warmth and gratitude, and the boy's papers are sold. But only for today. The price of the fifty papers obviously means little to the man, who, let us hypothesize, will go home to his warm fire and sumptuous dinner, while the newsboy, the next evening, will be back shivering on the corner. Nothing has really changed. But because of the easy emotional response and the easy emotional resolution, the deeper, more significant aspects of the situation are avoided. Instead of thinking, we feel. We feel good about the newsboy; we feel good about Dorothea's marrying Will; we feel good about poor Beth—we feel so good that we never look past the poem's solution to a larger solution which might involve serious questions about justice or tragedy.

Well, these are the kinds of things we learned, the kinds of questions we asked, as we examined an artwork's aesthetic appeal and its rhetoric. This procedure was useful, particularly useful in an undergraduate classroom because it required no special dogmatism, no certainty as to who the good and bad guys had to be. And it can be used with any number of different combinations of books that explore various aspects of female experience. Though I was satisfied with this approach, I also saw, as the semester progressed, that there were a number of traditional approaches to literature that offered other possibilities, particularly for research.

Questions about sentimentalism and tragedy, for instance, get one into the study of genre, which might be productive. Why, for example, do women appear more frequently and in more important roles in sentimental literature, in comedy, melodrama, and comi-tragedy? Why do they appear rarely in significant ways in epic or in tragedy? What kinds of genre have attracted women writers? Why? What kinds have they excelled in? Failed in? Why? What kind of reading attracts, is designed for, and influences women readers? Have these types changed in time? Will they continue to change? And perhaps most important of all—what have been the conditions of heroism for women?

And there are still other approaches that might be fruitful. One could go back to Hippolyte Taine, for instance, and his assumptions about literature described in the introduction to *History of English Literature*. To him, literature was a transcript of contemporary manners, a type of a certain kind of mind. It was a "monument," a "fossil shell" behind which there was a man, whose nature had been affected by his race, his surroundings, and his epoch (1–21). The object of literary study was to try to understand the man, the organism that had created the monument, the literary shell. He assumed that by studying the external aspects of life one could come to an understanding of man's inner nature. Man's products were

> but avenues converging to a centre; you enter them simply in order to reach that centre; and that centre is the genuine man, I mean that mass of faculties and feeling which are produced by the inner man. . . . This under-world is a new subject-matter, proper to the historian. If his critical education suffice, he can lay bare, under every detail of architecture, every stroke in a picture, every phrase in a writing, the special sensation whence detail, stroke, or phrase had issue; he is present at the drama which was enacted in the soul of artist or writer; the choice of a word, the brevity or length of a sentence, the nature of a metaphor, the accent of a verse, the development of an argument—everything is a symbol to him; while his eyes read the text, his soul and mind pursue the continuous development and the ever changing succession of the emotions and the conceptions out of which the text has sprung: in short, he unveils a psychology. (4)

At this point we might make use of his approach. If one can read the nature of a man as he is molded by his nature and instincts in his writings; if one can read the nature of a nation in its accumulated writings, as Taine also believed one could, perhaps one can undertake a study of the nature of woman in the same way. Could we not add sex to Taine's race, surroundings, and epoch as a formative factor that might be isolated and examined?

Certainly Taine's assumptions do not violate the beliefs of those modern psychologists and physiologists who remind us that the body makes the mind. Thus the art object, which the mind creates by externalizing aspects of itself (mind, body, and environmental influence), can legitimately be examined so as to determine sexual influences, sexual manifestations—if we develop our "critical education" sufficiently so that we can read back through the process.

Perhaps long-range studies of the works of women writers of all nations and times which attempt to do this may be helpful. Much thought would have to be given to the project, but we might gain valuable insights, perceive common factors not only in themes and attitudes but in structures, styles, rhythms. Virginia Woolf long ago talked about the difficulties women writers faced, and cited the sentence as a particular problem. She wrote:

> To begin with, there is the technical difficulty—so simple, apparently; in reality, so baffling—that the very form of the sentence does not fit her. It is a sentence made by men; it is too loose, too heavy, too pompous for a woman's use. Yet in a novel, which covers so wide a stretch of ground, an ordinary and usual type of sentence has to be found to carry the reader on easily and naturally from one end of the book to the other. And this a woman must make for herself, altering and adapting the current sentence until she writes one that takes the natural shape of her thought without crushing or distorting. ("Women" 145; 1966 ed.)

Is there, can there be such a thing as a female sentence? Are there structures, styles, rhythms that women find more comfortable, more expressive? And, if so, what do they tell us about the nature of woman? This is just one kind of question we might ask. There are many others.

And legends, and myths. Much might be done in this area to reevaluate ancient messages. Take the stories of Eve and Pandora, for instance. In both Hebraic and Greek tradition, the introduction of evil in the world is ascribed to women; and, though I imagine that fewer and fewer people take these accounts seriously, I think that we should, because certain common elements in both legends convey a very special message for women. You will recall that both women are ordered by men not to do something—Eve is not to eat the apple, Pandora is not to open the box. They both disobey, and by their disobedience bring evil upon all of humankind. Although generally we focus on the result of their disobedience with some degree of regret and frustration, it seems far more important to consider the motivation for their disobedience, which is the same in the two cases. It is the prospect of knowledge that finally tempts Eve; it is curiosity that leads Pandora to open the box.

Curiosity. Interestingly enough, in modern times, human curiosity has not been feared at all, but praised instead. George Sarton, in his monumental *History of Science*, says that curiosity is "one of the deepest of human traits, indeed far more ancient than mankind itself," and that it "was perhaps the mainspring of scientific knowledge in the past as it still is today'' (16). But curiosity was apparently not so valued in the past, at least not in women. From a man's point of view, the woman who sought knowledge was dangerous, so dangerous that female curiosity was seen as bringing down the worst of disasters. It seems important, therefore, for those of us involved in women's studies, to remember that proscriptions against female knowing are both ancient and male.

Not that keeping this in mind will simplify the problem of women's studies, which remains both complex and exciting. But it may be comforting to remind ourselves that we are not the first women eager for knowledge and that though men have feared female knowing, we need not fear it—even if the best way of finding out is not yet perfectly clear. And until we find the best way to solve our problem of methodology, I believe that any valid approach to literary study is at least capable of yielding insights, if our considerations make use of the subjunctive mood—if we remain open to the possible, the hypothetical, the contingent. We must not be afraid of heuristic studies. That, of course, is what this paper represents.

~ 1974 ~

Isabel Archer: Resistance to the Patriarchal Order

ELLEN MORGAN

THE PORTRAIT OF A LADY, like many of the portrayals of women which have traditionally been regarded as great literature, is a nonfeminist work. Typically, the author of the nonfeminist novel about a woman creates a heroine—Anna Karenina or Madame Bovary, for example—whose attractiveness and charm determine the course of her existence. Her gestures are shaped and given their significance by the reactions of others to her as a sexual being. Usually, she unprotestingly permits her charms and the responses they evoke to have sway over her identity and destiny. But nevertheless, the author does not consider her incomplete, deficient, and unrealized in personhood, or flawed in her beauty and humanity. One can only presume her creator feels that as a female she is largely a function of her sexual appeal rather than of her interior growth. Her development during the course of the story is likely to consist in the heightening which attends falling in love or the increase in poignancy which attends victimization borne gracefully.

Unlike an Edna Pontellier (in Kate Chopin's *The Awakening*) or a Martha Quest, or an Isadora Wing (in Erica Jong's *Fear of Flying*), the heroine of the nonfeminist novel does not try to break out, to free herself from the constrictions her society's value system imposes on women. She may disobey the system, but she does not take a genuinely critical stance outside it, and thus she does not transcend it. Unlike a Sasha Davis (in Alix Kates Shulman's *Memoirs of an Ex-Prom Queen*) or an Orlando, or a Beth Phail (in Marge Piercy's *Small Changes*), she does not come home to herself by acquiring the degree of self-knowledge on which to build an independent value system and a life consistent with it. Hers is the tale of an essentially subordinated personality, of a personality which does not develop the autonomy to go psychically beyond the limits of a social milieu which interferes with its growth.

But some books on the literary continuum between misogyny and the all-inclusive humanism of which feminism, like all other egalitarianisms, is a necessary component lie in the area where the nonfeminist novel begins to display a prefeminist sensibility. *The Portrait of a Lady* is an example of a work in this area. Not only does it emphatically contrast the meagerness of its heroine's real opportunities for action and free choice with her desire to choose and grow, but it depicts a woman *nearly* capable of developing a transcendent selfhood and passionately desirous of becoming a fully independent person. In this sense, Isabel Archer, with her introspective, questioning nature, is much closer to a Martha Quest than to an Anna Karenina. But still, James did not give Isabel the force of intellect and character to take a critical view of her society and detach herself from it either before or after her marriage. It is true that given the extremely restrictive set of social circumstances which follow upon Isabel's marriage, any woman would be hard put to devise an independent life. Divorce or separation would be impossible to obtain from a man like Osmond, and a comfortable separate domicile would be a financial impossibility without his cooperation. But in the final analysis, it is Isabel's inability fully to confront the institution of marriage, to question its appropriateness for her and its "sacredness," her inability or disinclination to face the frightening isolation which awaits the woman who steps outside the marital convention, and to carve out a life in the shape of her own values, which mark *The Portrait of a Lady* as a nonfeminist book.

However, *The Portrait* is a signally intriguing example of nonfeminist literature because Isabel behaves so bravely within this small sphere out of which she is not forceful enough to break that her modest victory takes on the cast of genuine triumph. Her gifts are inadequate to the task of true self-development and liberation, but her spirit is noble despite its slenderness, and to her rightfully belongs respect, if not the measure of admiration which must be reserved for a larger courage and capacity. My effort in the following pages will be to describe the combination of factors, some within Isabel and some in the society which surrounds her, which makes it impossible for her to "affront her destiny." I shall try to analyze the significance of her final act, and show what kind of book the nonfeminist novel is at its best and most sympathetic toward women.

The most salient quality about Isabel Archer is her love of "liberty." "I'm very fond of my liberty" (30), she tells Ralph early in their acquaintance. Later she tells Mme Merle that neither her house, furniture, and clothes nor the books she reads and the company she keeps express her. Although she is not sure she succeeds in expressing herself, she remarks:

> nothing else expresses me. Nothing that belongs to me is any measure of me; everything's on the contrary a limit, a barrier, and a perfectly arbitrary one. (173)

Isabel is aware of constraints upon her freedom of a most subtle nature. She seeks, by learning what can influence her away from being her real self, to discover and defend the autonomy of that self.

Early in the book, Isabel sees herself as a free agent able to determine her destiny. But as the story progresses, it becomes clear that the freedom she believes she has is illusory, and that she must eventually discover that it is illusory. What her temperament and adequate social position and Ralph's beneficence really add up to is simply that she will not have to marry for money—nothing more. She will be able to choose her husband. But as a woman of her nature, time, and milieu, she will have almost no other opportunities for autonomous action. By the laws of patriarchal society she will be forbidden to exert direct control over her money and thus to use it directly to express her ideals and will. Whether as wife or spinster, within the family she will be obliged, both legally and by force of social custom and accepted morality, to defer to the guidance of men. As the story unfolds, her individual needs for security and love will be forced into open conflict with her desire for liberty, and she will discover that fulfilling these needs means acceding to the unfavorable terms on which love and security are offered to women in her society. Thus Isabel will be faced with a dilemma: What can a human being who is largely unfree to act directly and independently, and who must therefore seek to define herself otherwise, do and become?

One way out of the dilemma which Isabel rejects, as is evident from the conversation with Mme Merle, is the substitution of possession for action, the defining of oneself by what one has rather than by what one does. Early in her marriage, Isabel tries two other ways, nearly simultaneously, and, later, a third. One way is voluntarily to submit to her husband's wishes, thus "choosing" to obey him, rendering her very imprisonment an act of will and making a virtue of the moral necessity she feels to remain imprisoned. The second is to rebel, if ever so quietly, by choosing to obey in order not to confirm her subjection but to undermine it; an example of this type of behavior is her following to the letter Osmond's directions concerning his daughter. "Perhaps," James observes, "as regards some of them, it was because her doing so appeared to reduce them to the absurd" (362). The third way is limited open defiance of her husband.

Of course, at least in the earlier part of her marriage, before she begins to defy Osmond, Isabel is in bondage: in order to act so that she may approve of her conduct and respect herself, she feels forced to meet standards of behavior in her marriage which are inimical to her own well-being and happiness. She submits to the bondage of these standards because of her belief in the sacredness of marriage and her conviction that she freely chose to marry Osmond. She never completely detaches herself from either of these notions, and so her tragedy is the delusion that the rules of the game are fair and thus that it is a point of personal honor to be guided by them. James never explicitly examines the rules, but the game is implicitly exposed as Isabel's problems and choices are described and as James situates the other female figures of importance in this book.

The first of these figures to appear is Mrs. Touchett. She is very independent, "likes to do everything for herself" (24), and has "her own way of doing all that she did" (30). She makes Isabel admire her for her truly personal point of view, her personal standard of judgment (60). She values people for their independence—their ability to get along without her as well as she gets along without them seems to her to provide "ground for a relation with her" (229).

At first glance this description sounds highly flattering. Mrs. Touchett would appear to be a "liberated woman," self-directing, possessing the kind of wholeness of selfhood and maturity which enable a person to develop and be guided by internal standards rather than merely acceding uncritically and passively to the fashions of the times. Such a person might be a fit model for the young woman who loves her liberty—except, of course, that a second glance shows how utterly inappropriate Mrs. Touchett is as a model for anyone. For her independence and individuality are maintained at the expense of warmth and love. To begin with, she has a very underdeveloped capacity to feel. Then by leaving the husband with whom she could not be happy she has forfeited intimate companionship and her child. "Isabel," James tells us, "came at last to have a kind of undemonstrable pity for her" because she "offered so limited a face to the accretions of human contact" and "nothing tender, nothing sympathetic had ever had a chance to fasten upon" her nature (188). So much for Aunt Lydia Touchett as a role model of the independent woman.

At the opposite pole is Serena Merle, the perfectly social animal. She, however, is "too flexible, too useful . . . too ripe and too final" without enough "tonic wildness" (165), too artificial, in a word, and tinged with the sinister. Having brought about Isabel's disastrous marriage in order to secure a dowry for her illegitimate child, she suffers the frustration of all her hopes and dreams, the corruption of her soul, and, along the way, Osmond's rejection of her. Finally, upon exposure, she is forced to go into exile alone. Her own daughter dislikes her (445). She has no husband and thus no economic base or social position. The life she has so carefully built up around her daughter and former lover, who still has the power to give her pain although he is indifferent to her, is destroyed in spite of her adherence to all the proprieties. So much for Mme Merle as a model of the woman who, having ambitions and talents of her own, transgresses conventional domestic morality.

The next female figure of any significance in *The Portrait* is Henrietta Stackpole. Henrietta is important to Isabel as "a proof that a woman might suffice to herself and be happy" (55). She has a career and is financially and professionally successful. One might begin to think her an encouragement to any young woman in search of a way to "affront her destiny" on her own terms, to seize control of her own life and develop a self in the image of her ideals. But Henrietta's "peculiarities," one learns, are "marked enough to give loyalty a spice of heroism" (398). She is faintly ridiculous most of the time and is, in short, the stereotype of the meddling, unsubtle, vulgar—although in this case, in an exasperating way, lovable—emancipated American female. Most important, in the end, she marries, making Isabel feel that "the dreariness of the world took on a deeper tinge" (462); her marriage invalidates her example of independence.

Pansy Osmond and Lord Warburton's almost negligible sisters can be taken for the perfectly docile and well-behaved women often idealized as images of feminine perfection by Victorian writers. They exist in the shadows of the men in their families, and, in Pansy's case, the cost of survival is total submission to male authority, even when that authority is pitted against her own interests and deepest happiness.

Thus James has provided in the women around Isabel a catalog of consequences for breaking the rules of the game: exile into an emotional and social Arctic like those of Mrs. Touchett, Serena Merle, and the Countess Gemini or, at best, assignment to the ranks of barely tolerated eccentrics like Henrietta. In addition,

James has sketched in something of the circumscribed but approved life of the woman who conforms, as do Pansy and the Misses Molyneux.

It is in the context of this catalog and of the centrality of freedom to Isabel that her reactions to her suitors should be examined. I believe it would be a great mistake to explain the fear of her various admirers which James consistently says she feels by imputing to her a terror simply of sex or of passion which cannot logically be connected with or accounted for by any feature of her personality or background. Fear certainly controls her sexual and passional life, but the fear is not specifically sexual. It is related directly to Isabel's fondness of her liberty, her *most* characteristic trait. Fear dominates Isabel's behavior with her suitors only because the expression of sexuality for a woman of her time and milieu entailed submission to a sexual and marital convention which, except in unusual circumstances, denied women the rights to their own persons and to any real independence of action.

When Isabel suspects that Lord Warburton is about to "make up" to her, she does not find the prospect totally disagreeable. There was a "pleasant part" in the idea, we are told (93), and we understand that Isabel is not insensitive to the man's evident masculine charm. But at moments, James remarks,

> the possibility of admiration by a personage represented to her an aggression almost to the degree of an affront. . . . He appeared to demand of her something that no one else, as it were, had presumed to do. What she felt was that a territorial, a political, a social magnate had conceived the design of drawing her into the system in which he rather invidiously lived and moved. A certain instinct, not imperious, but persuasive, told her to resist—murmured to her that virtually she had a system and an orbit of her own. (94)

When Warburton, sensing that perhaps Isabel objects to the idea of living in England, assures her they can live anywhere she chooses, Isabel feels keenly the attractiveness of his strength, protectiveness, and ability to accommodate her—but, as the story goes,

> though she was lost in admiration of her opportunity she managed to move back into the deepest shade of it, even as some wild, caught creature in a vast cage. The "splendid" security so offered her was *not* the greatest she could conceive. (99)

Clearly, for Isabel, security has something to do with feeling sure she will not be caged in someone else's life. She decides she cannot marry Lord Warburton because "the idea failed to support any enlightened prejudice in favour of the free exploration of life that she had hitherto entertained or was now capable of entertaining" (100–01). The proposal is essentially a "big bribe" (104), to the temptation of which she feels she must not succumb.

As for Caspar Goodwood, Isabel does encourage him in the beginning (91), thus indicating again that she is not immune to a powerful sexual presence or to the attractions of allowing someone else to look after her, to shape her life. And Goodwood seems at first relatively unlikely to snuff out Isabel's liberty. Unlike

Lord Warburton, he has "no system at all" (94). James says that Goodwood has never supposed that Isabel "hadn't wings and the need of beautiful free movements—he wasn't, with his own long arms and strides, afraid of any force in her" (140–41). When Isabel tells him she does not like him "watching" her because she likes her liberty, he feels a sense of "common ground" (140–41). "Who," he asks her, "would wish less to curtail your liberty than I? What can give me greater pleasure than to see you perfectly independent—doing whatever you like? It's to make you independent that I want to marry you" (141).

But his fine words do not fool Isabel. She replies, "that's a beautiful sophism" (141). And so it is. What is being said about liberty when it is accounted a thing to be conferred by one person upon another? Goodwood's generosity is basically of the same order as Warburton's. Each can afford to indulge Isabel because both—Warburton with his social and political position and his wealth, Goodwood with his own wealth and his ability to manage and command, and both with their status simply as men—know they will always have the option of patronizing Isabel. Each can afford to be guided by the principle of noblesse oblige. Isabel rightly perceives her own position vis-à-vis each of the men as that of a dependent whose "liberty" will be contingent upon whether the uses she makes of it are approved, upon whether she pleases her patron. Goodwood may safely "admire" (140) Isabel's love of liberty; it will give him greater scope for such patronage. In spite of the restrictions she knows will be imposed upon her as a single young woman, Isabel judges that more binding ones would attend upon marriage (141).

Sometimes Isabel fears that she will capitulate to Goodwood. But although occasionally "Caspar Goodwood had seemed to range himself on the side of her destiny, to be the stubbornest fact she knew"—a fact she "might evade . . . for a time, but that she must make terms with . . . at last" (104)—she perceives that these terms "would be certain to be favourable to himself" and, by implication, not to her. She dislikes his refusals to leave her alone when she asks and to accept her decisions about whether and whom she will marry and how she will interpret her marital responsibilities. "It was," James says, "part of the influence he had upon her that he seemed to deprive her of the sense of freedom" (104). She feels always a need to "defend herself against a certain air that he had of knowing better what was good for her than she knew herself" (135–36).

Isabel has the satisfaction of refusing these two suitors and thus exercising power, control over her own destiny. But this is about the limit of her power. Its negative and small potential becomes increasingly evident as the story progresses. Reducing further this potential is the inner factor, the natural human desire for "a clear and quiet harbour enclosed by a brave granite breakwater" (191), for love from a solicitous and dependable man and the comforts of an established order. There are pretty obviously two mutually antagonistic drives in Isabel—the one for liberty, self-determination, responsibility, selfhood, and the other for this kind of security. The drive for independence leads her to reject Warburton and Goodwood, but the need for security is what has made their solidity attractive and tempting to her. It is a need, moreover, to which Isabel is pushed to succumb by forces outside her control. For, as James shows throughout the book, in the life-styles of the other female characters and in the attitudes of Warburton, Goodwood, and Osmond, the inclination toward inertia, toward passive acceptance, toward external direction, is encouraged in women, thought proper to them, and its opposite is punished. They have few opportunities for action (at one point Isabel gives "an envious thought to the happier lot of men, who are always free to plunge into . . . action" [317]) and are expected to accept the status of wards in their families before marriage, of dependents after. This duality in Isabel between the freedom and the security impulses forms the true pivot or focus of the book, and makes *The Portrait* as significant a depiction of a woman as it is.

The first time, chronologically speaking, that James gives the reader a picture of Isabel, she is seated alone reading a book, "so occupied . . . that her solitude did not press upon her"; but James adds that there was a "want of fresh taste in her situation" which her Aunt Lydia's advent "did much to correct" (31), thereby modifying the degree of self-sufficiency implied in the picture. Next we learn that as a child, having spent a single day in the local primary school and having "protested against its laws," Isabel had been allowed to stay home, where she felt both "the elation of liberty and the pain of exclusion" (32). Thus it is stressed from the beginning of the story that Isabel is not only self-sufficient and freedom-loving but also a person who needs to belong to a social world and to be subject, at least to some degree, to externals in order to find her life interesting. Her deepest wish—which should not be interpreted as a sign of immaturity but rather of potential for autonomy and self-development—seems to be to have the amusement and security of the social and external without unduly compromising her liberty in the process. Again and again she reveals fear that her desire for security may sabotage her desire for liberty. Her early views of marriage especially bear out this idea: she believes that "if a certain light should dawn she could give herself completely" but holds that "a woman ought to be able to live to herself" and finds the idea of giving herself completely "too formidable to be attractive" (55).

At the same time, Isabel is both intrigued with and afraid of the challenge of freedom. Although she admires people for having standards of their own, she is far from fully confident in her ability to assert herself and use freedom wisely; her self-esteem seems to rest largely on what others think of her. One notes that she is capable of hiding parts of her real self, as girls are so often urged to do —her interest in books, for instance (41), even her "emancipation" (75) and her eagerness to explore life (132–33)—in order to be more attractive and acceptable. And her experience is so narrow that a want of self-confidence is not unreasonable. When she first inherits her fortune, as she tells Ralph, she is afraid because she feels it gives her the power to act and the responsibility for choosing how to act (190), and she is totally ignorant of how to meet this responsibility. It is only after a time that she makes up her mind that to be rich is a good thing because "there was a larger grace" than to be stupidly weak and unable "to *do*" (180).

And in spite of Isabel's desire to act and be independent, there are times when insecurity and underconfidence, fostered by inexperience and limited access to action, lead her to react instead of act, or to retreat into passivity or to seek external direction. When, for example, she leaves Osmond to be with her dying cousin, this act, while openly defiant of her husband and crucial in the context of her marriage, is significantly not the result of a bona fide decision. James says of her during her stay at Gardencourt after Ralph's death, "she lived from day to day, postponing, closing her eyes, trying not to think. She knew she must decide, but she decided nothing; her coming itself had not been a decision. . . . [S]he had simply started" (474). The tendency to lean or retreat is particularly evident in Isabel when she first meets Osmond and is awed by his refinement and sensibility. She keeps uncharacteristically quiet, watching him and trying to avoid seeming foolish or vulgar. One might well count this the reaction of any person in the first stages of love. But in a man, of course, self-effacement and passivity would be a handicap to success, whereas in a woman it is often, as by Osmond, deemed an attribute of ideal femininity and thus encouraged. Rebellion does flare up when Mme Merle praises this behavior—Isabel is not pleased that her self-effacement should be thought an improvement or an attraction (209). Nevertheless, the point is made that she can be immobilized by insecurity even though she values freedom and wishes to set her own standards.

Isabel does draw back when Osmond actually declares his love. She feels a "pang that suggested to her somehow the slipping of a fine bolt—backward, forward, she couldn't have said which." She retreats from "dread of having . . . to choose and decide"—to settle her fate. "What made her dread great," we are told, "was precisely the force which, as it would seem, ought to have banished all dread—the sense of something within herself, deep down, that she supposed to be inspired and trustful passion" (258). As with her other two suitors, Isabel would rather not be forced into this corner wherein she must choose between the slipping bolt—or loss of freedom—and what James calls "primitive need" (291), the need for security and sexual love, for a close personal attachment to a trusted, admirable, dependably strong man. The freedom-loving side of her answers Osmond, "Oh don't say that, please" (258). But later, the other side of her informs Ralph, when he implies that her projected marriage will be a "cage," that "if I like my cage, that needn't trouble you" (282).

One might suspect, at this point, that the duel between the two sides of Isabel's nature is over and that the party of independence has been vanquished. But a closer scrutiny reveals that what at first may appear to be near-total capitulation—her marriage—is actually Isabel's choice of as much independence as is consistent with emotional survival.

Isabel explains that she has "seen life"; and it does not look to be the "inviting expanse" she had judged it in the early days of her exploration of it. She has decided "one must choose a corner and cultivate that," because one cannot do anything so "general" as to explore the "whole field" (283); she has developed a sense that life is "vacant without some private duty that might gather one's energies to a point" (291). She tells Ralph that she is tired of *observing*, and James says that she had a need for an involvement which would enable her not only to observe and take but to *give* (291–92). These comments signal that she has discovered that she can remain single only at the price of living on the periphery. There is no place for her as a loved and involved being in her society outside of marriage, as she can see by observing the lives of the other women around her and by noting her own feelings. Unmarried, she will be doomed to the bleak role of observer and isolate, and she seeks to be an active participant, to throw herself into the world, as Ralph puts it (132).

Isabel is forced, by her need for emotional security and love, toward marriage, and the constraints upon her liberty inevitably consequent upon marriage. But it is no accident that she allows herself to love only where a modicum of liberty seems most likely to be hers and chooses a marriage which she believes will encroach as little as possible on her autonomy. She steadily avoids alliance with the persistent Warburton and Goodwood, allowing her passions to develop around the situation which she thinks will give her the most opportunity to act. She believes that she will have some scope with Osmond for her own independence, some "opportunity," some "occasion," that in being his "providence" she will be able to give as much as she will receive, that she will be a "contributor" coming to him with "charged hands" (351). In marrying him she will have not only the satisfaction of taking responsibility for Pansy (292), and of "launching" her husband (351), but a moral, if not a legal, power base. As she remarks to Ralph, when he tries to dissuade her from the marriage, the fact that Osmond is not rich is "just what I like him for" (287). Whereas Warburton and Goodwood are independently wealthy, Osmond is poor. She presumes she will have with him a freedom of action which is given not simply out of noblesse oblige but out of obligation, out of gratitude, because something is owed her in acknowledgment of her important—in fact, crucial—contribution to their joint welfare.

But Osmond turns out to be a "sterile dilettante" (286) who wishes his wife's mind to be his—"attached to his own like a small garden-plot to a deer park. . . . a pretty piece of property" (355). And Isabel has to choose once more between the two alternatives she permits herself to consider, neither of which allows her much liberty. She must choose whether to remain with her husband or escape with Goodwood.

The question now becomes whether this story is the story basically of the defeat or the victory of Isabel Archer, whether her progress through its pages ought to be reckoned a downhill or an uphill march. It is true that with her marriage Isabel changes. She becomes more patient and more cautious. She is dampened by the guilt produced by her conviction that her original self-effacement deceived Osmond, and she seeks to please him long after their disaffection has become evident to both. She is afraid of him, of entering into an actual act of deliberate disobedience. But she is more "afraid" of herself than of Osmond (412), as she tells Ralph. She knows that she can prove a formidable opponent rather than an obedient wife to Osmond and that she can fight his efforts to swallow her up in the mediocrity and ignobility she so clearly sees in him at last. As Isabel tells Henrietta when Henrietta warns her to leave Osmond before "the worst" comes and her "character gets spoiled," she is "taking very good care" of her character (410). She does not, she says, feel helpless, and remarks "there are many things I mean to do" (410). She has, as she finally admits to Ralph, been punished for her wish to look at life for herself (470) and to throw herself into it. But one has only to examine the very end of the book, asking the question why she refuses Goodwood's last offer, to know whether this book is the portrait of a woman whose desire for independence and autonomy is ultimately trampled down or triumphant.

Isabel returns to her husband partly because she holds her marriage vows sacred and believes she entered her contract with Osmond freely. No doubt she also views her promise to Pansy as a bond to be honored. But none of these considerations is enough to make her decide definitely, for, as she tells Ralph at Gardencourt, she does not know whether she will return.

What convinces her to go back is Goodwood's offer of sanctuary. When she sees the degree of resolution in Goodwood's expression, she has "a feeling of danger" (479). She listens to him "as she had never listened before," and it is with an effort that she answers him, asking how he proposes to help her. Goodwood then proceeds to make a case for the idea that Isabel, being unhappy, should trust him to remedy her situation. He tells her, "[Y]ou're afraid to go back. You're perfectly alone; you don't know where to turn. . . . Now it is therefore that I want you to think of *me*" (480). He is playing with all his weight on the idea of her helplessness, trying to appeal to her inclination to let herself be cared for, guided, taken responsibility for. When he asks, "[W]hy should you go back . . . ?" it is obvious that taking this tack has been a miscalculation. "To get away from *you*!" Isabel exclaims. She knows the full power of his love at last, but she refuses to choose the easy path, refuses the offer of the shoulder to lean upon. Goodwood then tries to appeal to her sense of justice by arguing that "a woman deliberately made to suffer is justified in anything in life," and he tempts her by implying that she is *afraid* to come with him. Isabel "gave a long murmur, like a creature in pain" (481); clearly she *is* tempted. "She had wanted help, and here was help. . . She believed just then that to let him take her in his arms would be the next best thing to her dying" (481). But note carefully the negativism of that last sentiment and the words with which James describes this belief and thus characterizes Goodwood's sexual appeal to Isabel: it was "a kind of rapture, in which she felt herself sink and sink" (481). The metaphors are all now connected to the idea of "sinking or swimming." Isabel "seemed to beat with her feet, in order to catch herself"; she beseeches Goodwood to do her "the greatest kindness of all. . . . to go away" (481). She continues, "As you love me, as you pity me, leave me alone!" (482). His response, predictably, is to do just the opposite. The metaphors continue—Isabel thinks "of those wrecked and under water following a train of images before they sink" while Goodwood kisses her, while she fights this last, and strongest, temptation to allow herself to be "possessed."

After she has felt to their highest intensity the fires of this freedom-consuming passion, Isabel is free. James says, "[S]he had not known where to turn; but she knew now. There was a very straight path" (482).

Isabel allows herself to love three men: Osmond—but only as long as he seems not only not to impinge upon but actually to offer space for the exercise of her liberty; her uncle, who "was one of those admirers who couldn't propose to marry her" (146); and Ralph, whom, when she perceives him to be possibly "on that tiresome list," she has "a sudden wish to strike . . . off" (286). Ralph she is able to love, finally, without reservation, as a brother, because she realizes that his illness makes him unable to reduce her autonomy. At no time does this woman, given by her society so little opportunity and encouragement for action, and by her own needs for love and security so little psychic room to nurture a spirit of independence, permit herself an outright choice of the easy and agreeable over her own liberty and selfhood, despite the fact that James has given her the ultimate excuse to do so—the lack of an alternative that will not be unspeakably difficult to endure.

The Portrait of a Lady is about Isabel's triumph, however Pyrrhic, and not her defeat, about her final upholding of her right to be free—although whatever freedom she has must be a small affair indeed and of small comfort to her except in the largest sense of her being able to approve of her choice and to be responsible for it. But that approval and responsibility make all the difference between the dignity of resistance and the smallness of surrender.

~ 1974 ~

What Can a Heroine Do? Or, Why Women Can't Write

JOANNA RUSS

1. Two strong women battle for supremacy in the early West.

2. A young girl in Minnesota finds her womanhood by killing a bear.

3. An English noblewoman, vacationing in Arcadia, falls in love with a beautiful, modest young shepherd. But duty calls; she must return to the court of Elizabeth I to wage war on Spain. Just in time the shepherd lad is revealed as the long-lost son of the Queen of a neighboring country; the lovers are united and our heroine carries off her husband and lad-in-waiting to the King of England.

4. A phosphorescently doomed poetess sponges off her husband and drinks herself to death, thus alienating the community of Philistines and businesswomen who would have continued to give her lecture dates.

5. A handsome young man, quite virginal, is seduced by an older woman who has made a pact with the Devil to give her back her youth. When the woman becomes pregnant, she proudly announces the paternity of her child; this revelation so shames the young man that he goes quite insane, steals into the house where the baby is kept, murders it, and is taken to prison where—repentant and surrounded by angel voices—he dies.

6. Alexandra the Great.

7. A young man who unwisely puts success in business before his personal fulfillment loses his masculinity and ends up as a neurotic, lonely eunuch.

8. A beautiful, seductive boy whose narcissism and instinctive cunning hide the fact that he has no mind (and in fact, hardly any sentient consciousness) drives a succession of successful actresses, movie produceresses, cowgirls, and film directresses wild with desire. They rape him.

AUTHORS DO NOT make their plots up out of thin air, nor are the above pure inventions; every one of them is a story familiar to all of us.[1] What makes them look so odd—and so funny—is that in each case the sex of the protagonist has been changed (and correspondingly the sex of the other characters). The result is that these very familiar plots simply will not work. They are tales for heroes, not heroines, and one of the things that handicaps women writers in our—and every other—culture is that there are so very few stories in which women can figure as protagonists.

Culture is male.[2] This does not mean that every man in Western (or Eastern) society can do exactly as he pleases, or that every man creates the culture *solus*, or that every man is luckier or more privileged than every woman. What it does mean (among other things) is that the society we live in, like all other historical societies, is a patriarchy. And patriarchies imagine or picture themselves from the male point of view. There is a female culture, but it is an underground, unofficial, minor culture, occupying a small corner of what we think of officially as possible human experience. Both men *and women* in our culture conceive the culture from a single point of view—the male.

Now writers, as I have said, do not make up their stories out of whole cloth; they are pretty much restricted to the attitudes, the beliefs, the expectations, and above all the plots, that are "in the air"—"plot" being what Aristotle called *mythos*; and in fact it is probably most accurate to call these plot patterns *myths*. They are dramatic embodiments of what a culture believes to be true—or what it would like to be true—or what it is mortally afraid may be true. Novels, especially, depend upon what central action can be imagined as being performed by the protagonist (or protagonists)—that is, what can a central character *do* in a book? An examination of English literature, or Western literature (or Eastern literature, for that matter) reveals that of all the possible actions people can do in fiction, very few can be done by women.

Our literature is not about women. It is not about women and men equally. It is by and about men.

But (you might object) aren't our books and our movies full of women? Isn't there a "love interest" or at least a sexual interest in every movie? What about Cleopatra? What about Juliet? What about Sophia Western, Clarissa Harlowe, Faye Greener, Greta Garbo, Pip's Estella, and the succession of love goddesses without whom film history would hardly exist? Our literature is full of women: bad women, good women, motherly women, bitchy women, faithful women, promiscuous women, beautiful women—

Plain women?

Women who have no relations with men (as so many male characters in American literature have no relations with women)?

Oddly enough, no. If you look at the plots summarized at the beginning of this article, and turn them back to their original forms, you will find not women but images of women: modest maidens, wicked temptresses, pretty schoolmarms, beautiful bitches, faithful wives, and so on. They exist only in relation to the protagonist (who is male). Moreover, look at them carefully and you will see that they do not really exist at all—at their best they are depictions of the social roles women are supposed to play and often do play, but they are the public roles and not the private women;[3] at their worst they are gorgeous, Cloudcuckooland fantasies about what men want, or hate, or fear.

How can women writers possibly use such myths?

In twentieth-century American literature there is a particularly fine example of these impossible "women," a figure who is beautiful, irresistible, ruthless but fascinating, fascinating because she is somehow cheap or contemptible, who (in her more passive form) destroys men by her indifference and who (when the male author is more afraid of her) destroys men actively, sometimes by shooting them. She is Jean Harlow, Daisy Faye, Faye Greener, Mrs. Macomber, and Deborah Rojack. She is the Bitch Goddess.

Now it is just as useless to ask why the Bitch Goddess is so bitchy as it is to ask why the Noble Savage is so noble. Neither "person" really exists. In existential terms they are both the Other, and the Other does not have the kind of inner life or consciousness that you and I have. In fact, the Other has no mind at all. No man in his senses ever says of himself *to himself*: I acted nobly because I am a Noble Savage. His reasons are far more prosaic: I did what I did because I was afraid, or because I was ambitious, or because I wanted to provoke my father, or because I felt lonely, or because I needed money, and so on. Look for reasons like that to explain the conduct of the Bitch Goddess and you will not find them; there is no explanation in terms of human motivation or the woman's own inner life; she simply behaves the way she does because she is a bitch. Q.E.D. No Other ever has the motives that you and I have; the Other contains a mysterious *essence* which causes it to behave as it does; in fact, "it" is not a person at all, but a projected wish or fear.

The Bitch Goddess is not a person.

Virgin-victim Gretchen (see number 5 above) is not a person. The faithful wife, the beautiful temptress, the seductive destroyer, the devouring momma, the healing Madonna—none of these are persons in the sense that a novel's protagonist must be a person and none is of the slightest use as myth to the woman writer who wishes to write about a female protagonist.

Try, for example, to change the Bitch Goddess–Male Victim story into a woman's story—are we simply to change the sex of the characters and write about a male "bitch" and a female victim? The myth still works in male-homosexual terms—Man and Cruel Youth—but the female equivalent is something quite different. Changing the sex of the protagonist completely alters the meaning of the tale. The story of Woman–Cruel Lover is the story of so many English ballads—you have the "false true lover" and the pregnant girl left either to mourn or to die, but you do not have—to indicate only some elements of the story—the Cruel Lover as the materially sumptuous but spiritually bankrupt spirit of our civilization, the essence of sex, the "soul" of our corrupt culture, a dramatization of the split between the degrading necessities of the flesh and the transcendence of world-cleaving Will. What you have instead, if the story is told about or by the woman, is a cautionary tale warning you not to break social rules—in short, a much more realistic story of social error or transgression leading to ostracism, poverty, or death. Moral: Get Married First.

No career woman, at least in literature, keeps in the back of her mind the glamorous figure of Daisy Faye, the beautiful, rich, indifferent boy she loved back in Cleveland when she was fighting for a career as a bootlegger. Reversing sexual roles in fiction may make good burlesque or good fantasy, but it is ludicrous in terms of serious literature. Culture is male. Our literary myths are for heroes, not heroines.

What can a heroine do?

What myths, what plots, what actions are available to a female protagonist?

Very few.

For example, it is impossible to write a conventional success story with a heroine, for success in male terms is failure for a woman, a "fact" movies, books, and television plays have been earnestly proving to us for decades. Nor is the hard-drinking, hard-fighting hero imagined as female, except as an amusing fluke—for example, Bob Hope and Jane Russell in *Paleface*. Nor can our heroine be the Romantic Poet Glamorously Doomed, nor the Oversensitive Artist Who Cannot Fulfill His Worldly Responsibilities (Emily Dickinson seems to fit the latter pattern pretty well, but she is always treated as the Spinster, an exclusively female—*and sexual*—role). Nor can a heroine be the Intellectual Born into a Philistine Small Town Who Escapes to the Big City—a female intellectual cannot escape her problems by fleeing to the big city; she is still a woman and Woman as Intellectual is not one of our success myths.

With one or two exceptions (which I will deal with later), all subliterary genres are closed to the heroine; she cannot be a Mickey Spillane private eye, for example, or one of H. Rider Haggard's adventure-story Englishmen who discover a Lost Princess in some imaginary corner of Africa. (She can be the Lost Princess, but a story written with the Princess herself as protagonist would resemble the chronicle of any other monarch and would hardly fit the female figure of Haggard's romances, who is—again—the Other.) The hero whose success in business alienates him from his family is not at all in the position of the heroine who "loses her femininity" by competing with men—*he* is not desexed, but *she* is. The Crass Businessman genre (minor anyway) is predicated on the assumption that success is masculine and a good thing as long as you don't spend all your time at it; one needs to spend the smaller part of one's life recognizing the claims of personal relations and relaxation. For the heroine the conflict between success and sexuality is itself the issue, and the duality is absolute. The woman who becomes hard and unfeminine, who competes with men, finally becomes—have we seen this figure before?—a bitch. Again.

Women in twentieth-century American literature seem pretty much limited to either Devourer/Bitches or Maiden/Victims. Perhaps male authors have bad consciences.

So we come at last to the question of utmost importance to novelists—What will my protagonist(s) do? What central action can be the core of the novel? I know of only one plot or myth that is genderless and in which heroines can figure equally with heroes; this is the Abused Child story (I mean of the Dickensian variety), and indeed many heroines do begin life as Sensitive, Mistreated Waifs. But such a pattern can be used only while the heroine is still a child (as in the first part of *Jane Eyre*). Patient Griselda, who also suffered and endured, was not a Mistreated Child but the adult heroine of a peculiar kind of love story. And here, of course, we come to the one occupation of a female protagonist in literature, the one thing she can do, and by God she does it and does it and does it, over and over and over again.

She is the protagonist of a Love Story.

The tone may range from grave to gay, from the tragedy of *Anna Karenina* to the comedy of *Emma*, but the myth is always the same: innumerable variants on Falling in Love, on courtship, on marriage, on the failure of courtship and marriage. How She Got Married. How She Did Not Get Married (always tragic). How She Fell in Love and Committed Adultery. How She Saved Her Marriage, but Just Barely. How She Loved a Vile Seducer and Eloped. How She Loved a Vile Seducer, Eloped, and Died in Childbirth. As far as literature is concerned, heroines are still restricted to one vice, one virtue, and one occupation. In the novels of Doris Lessing, an authoress concerned with a great many other things besides love, the heroines still spend most of their energy and time maintaining relations with their lovers (or marrying, or divorcing, or failing to achieve orgasm, or achieving it, or worrying about their sexuality, their men, their loves, and their love lives).

For female protagonists, the Love Story includes not only personal relations as such but bildungsroman, worldly success or worldly failure, career, the exposition of character, crucial learning experiences, the transition to adulthood, rebellion (usually adultery), and everything else. Only in the work of a few iconoclasts like George Bernard Shaw do you find protagonists like Vivie Warren, whose work means more to her than marriage, or Saint Joan, who has no "love life" at all. It is interesting that Martha Graham's dance version of Saint Joan's life turns the tale back into a Love Story, with Saint Michael (at one point, in the version I saw) inspiring Joan by walking astride her from head to foot, dragging his robe over her several times as she lies on her back on the stage floor.

How she lost him, how she got him, how she kept him, how she died for/with him. What else is there? A new pattern seems to have been developing in the last few years: female authors who do not wish to write Love Stories may instead write about heroines whose main action is to go mad—but How She Went Crazy will also lose its charm in time. One cannot write *The Bell Jar* or *Jane Eyre*, good as it is, forever.

A woman writer may, if she wishes, abandon female protagonists altogether and stick to male myths with male protagonists, but in so doing she falsifies herself and much of her own experience. Part of life is obviously common to both sexes—we all eat, we all get stomachaches, and we all grow old and die—but a great deal of life is not shared by men and women. A woman who refuses to write about women ignores the whole experience of the female culture (a very different one from the official, male culture), all her specifically erotic experiences, and a good deal of her own history. She falsifies her position both artistically and humanly: she is an artist creating a world in which persons of her kind cannot be artists, a consciousness central to itself creating a world in which women have no consciousness, a successful person creating a world in which persons like herself cannot be successes. She is a Self trying to pretend that she is a different Self, one for whom her own self is Other.

If a female writer does not use the two, possibly three, myths available to a she-writer, she must drop the culture's myths altogether. Is this in itself a bad thing? Perhaps what we need here is a digression on the artistic advantages of working with myths—that is, material that has passed through other hands, that is not raw-brand-new.

The insistence that authors make up their own plots is a recent development in literature; Milton certainly did not do it. Even today, with novelty at such a premium in all the arts, very little is written that is not—at bottom—common property. It's a commonplace that bad writers imitate and great writers steal. Even an iconoclast like Shaw "stole" his plots wholesale, sometimes from melodrama, sometimes from history, sometimes from his friends.[4] Ibsen owes a debt to Scribe, Dickens to theater melodrama, James to the ladies'-magazine fiction of his own time—nothing flowers without a history. Something that has been worked on by others in the same culture, something that is "in the air" provides a writer with material that has been distilled, dramatized, stylized, and, above all, clarified. A developed myth has its own form, its own structure, its own expectations and values, its own cues to nudge the reader. When so much of the basic work has already been done, the artist may either give the myth its final realization or stand it on its head, but in any case what he does will be neither tentative nor crude and it will not take forever; it can simply be done well. For example, the very pattern of dramatic construction which we take as natural, the idea that a story ought to have a beginning, a middle, and an end, that one ought to be led to something called a "climax" by something called "suspense" or "dramatic tension," is in itself an occidental myth—Western artists, therefore, do not have to invent this pattern for themselves.

Hemingway, whom we call a realist, spent his whole working life capitalizing on the dramatic lucidity possible to an artist who works with developed myths. The Bitch Goddess did not appear full-blown in "The Short and Happy Life of Francis Macomber"—one can find her in Fitzgerald—or Hawthorne, to name an earlier writer—or Max Beerbohm, whose *Zuleika Dobson* is certainly a Bitch Goddess, though a less serious one than her American cousins. "Macomber" is the ultimate fictional refinement out of the mess and bother of real life. Beyond it lies only nightmare (Faye Greener in West's *Day of the Locust*) or the half-mad, satiric fantastications Mailer uses to get a little more mileage out of an almost-exhausted pattern.

"Macomber" is perfectly clear, as is most of Hemingway's work. Nobody can fail to understand that Mrs. Macomber is a Bitch, that the White Hunter is a Real Man, and that Macomber is a Failed Man. The dramatic conflict is extremely clear, very vehement, and completely expectable. The characters are simple, emotionally charged, and larger than life. *Therefore* the fine details of the story can be polished to that point of high gloss where everything—weather, gestures, laconic conversation, terrain, equipment, clothing—is meaningful. (Compare "Macomber" with *Robinson Crusoe*, for example; Defoe is much less sure from moment to moment of what he wants to say or what it means.) One cannot stop to ask why Mrs. Macomber is so bitchy—she's just a Bitch, that's all—or why killing a large animal will restore Macomber's manhood—everybody knows it will—or why the Bitch cannot tolerate a Real Man—these things are already explained by the myth.

But this kind of larger-than-life simplicity and clarity are not accessible to the woman writer unless she remains within the limits of the Love Story. Again: what can a heroine do?

There seem to me to be two alternatives open to the woman author who no longer cares about How She Fell in Love or How She Went Mad. These are (1) lyricism and (2) life.

By "lyricism" I do not mean purple passages or baroque raptures; I mean a particular principle of structure.

If the narrative mode (what Aristotle called "epic") concerns itself with events connected by the chronological order in which they occur, and the dramatic mode with voluntary human actions which are connected both by chronology and causation, then the principle of construction I wish to call *lyric* consists of the organization of discrete elements (images, events, scenes, passages, words, what have you) around an unspoken thematic or emotional center. The lyric mode exists without chronology or causation; its principle of connection is *associative*. Of course no piece of writing can exist purely in any one mode, but we can certainly talk of the predominance of one element, perhaps two. In this sense of "lyric" Virginia Woolf is a lyric novelist—in fact, she has been criticized in just those terms—that is, "nothing happens" in her books. A writer who employs the lyric structure is setting various images, events, scenes, or memories to circling round an unspoken, invisible center. The invisible center is what the novel or poem is about; it is also unsayable in available dramatic or narrative terms. That is, there is no action possible to the central character and no series of events which will embody in clear, unequivocal, immediately graspable terms what the artist means. Or perhaps there is no action or series of events that will embody this "center" at all. Unable to use the myths of male culture (and apparently unwilling to spend her life writing love stories), Woolf uses a structure that is basically nonnarrative. Hence the lack of "plot," the repetitiousness, the gathering up of the novels into moments of epiphany, the denseness of the writing, the indirection. There is nothing the female characters can *do*—except exist, except think, except feel. And critics (mostly male) employ the usual vocabulary of denigration: these novels lack important events; they are hermetically sealed; they are too full of sensibility; they are trivial; they lack action; they are feminine (see Ellmann, "Phallic Criticism").

Not every female author is equipped with the kind of command of language that allows (or insists upon) lyric construction; nor does every woman writer want to employ this mode. The alternative is to take as one's model (and structural principle) not male myth but the structure of one's own experience. So we have George Eliot's (or Doris Lessing's) "lack of structure," the obviously tacked-on ending of *Mill on the Floss*; we have Brontë's spasmodic, jerky world of *Villette*, with a structure modeled on the heroine's (and probably author's) real situation. How to write a novel about a person to whom nothing happens? A person to whom nothing but a love story is *supposed* to happen? A person inhabiting a world in which the only reality is frustration or endurance—or these plus an unbearably mystifying confusion? The movement of *Villette* is not the perfect curve of *Jane Eyre* (a classic version of the female Love Story)—it is a blocked jabbing, a constant thwarting; it is the protagonist's constantly frustrated will to action, and her alternately losing and regaining her perception of her own situation (Millett 140–47). There are vestiges of Gothic mystery and there is a Love Story, but the Gothic mysteries turn out to be fakery and the Love Story (which occupies only the last quarter of the book) vanishes strangely and abruptly on the last page but one. In cases like these the usual epithet is "formless," sometimes qualified by "inexperienced"—obviously life is not like *that*; life is not messy and indecisive; we know what life (and novels) are from Aristotle—who wrote about plays—and male novelists who employ male myths created by a culture that imagines itself from the male point of view. The task of art—we know—is to give form to life—that is, the very forms that women writers cannot use. So it's clear that women can't write, that they swing wildly from lyricism to messiness once they abandon the cozy realms of the Love Story. And successes within the Love Story (which is itself imagined out of genuine female experience) are not important, because the Love Story is not important. It is a commonplace of criticism that only the male myths are valid or interesting; a book as fine (and well structured) as *Jane Eyre* fails *even to be seen* by many critics because it grows out of experiences—events, fantasies, wishes, fears, daydreams, images of self—entirely foreign to their own. As critics are usually unwilling to believe their lack of understanding to be their own fault, it becomes the fault of the book. Of the author. Of all women writers.

Western European (and North American) culture is not only male in its point of view; it is also Western European. For example, it is not Russian. Nineteenth-century Russian fiction can be criticized in much the same terms as women's fiction: "pointless" or "plotless" narratives stuffed with strange minutiae, and not obeying the accepted laws of dramatic development, lyrical in the wrong places, condensed in the wrong places, overly emotional, obsessed with things we do not understand, perhaps even grotesque. Here we have other outsiders who are trying, in less than a century, to assimilate European myths, producing strange Russian hybrids (*A King Lear of the Steppe, Lady Macbeth of Mtensk*), trying to work with literary patterns that do not suit their experiences and were not developed with them in mind. What do we get? Oddly digressive Pushkin. "Formless" Dostoevsky. (Colin Wilson has called Dostoevsky's novels "sofa pillows stuffed with lumps of concrete.") Sprawling, glacial, all-inclusive Tolstoy. And of course "lyrical" Chekhov, whose magnificent plays are called plotless to this very day.

There is an even more vivid—and tragic—example: what is an American black writer to make of our accepted myths? For example, what is she or he to make of the still-current myth (so prominent in *King Lear*) that Suffering Brings Wisdom? This is an old, still-used plot. Does suffering bring wisdom to Ellison's invisible man? When critics do not find what they expect, they cannot imagine that the fault may lie in their expectations. I know of a case in which the critics (white and female) decided after long, nervous discussion that Baldwin was "not really a novelist" but that Orwell was.

Critical bias aside, all artists are going to be in the soup pretty soon, if they aren't already. As a culture, we are coasting on the tag ends of our assumptions about a lot of things (including the difference between fiction and "propaganda"). As novelists, we are working with myths that have been so repeated, so triply distilled, that they are almost exhausted. Outside of commercial genres—which can remain petrified and profitable indefinitely—how many more incarnations of the Bitch Goddess can anybody stand? How many more shoot-'em-ups on Main Street? How many more young men with identity problems?

The lack of workable myths in literature, of acceptable dramatizations of what our experience means, harms much more than art itself. We do not only choose or reject works of art on the basis of these myths; we interpret our own experience in terms of them. Worse still, we actually perceive what happens to us in the mythic terms our culture provides.

The problem of "outsider" artists is the whole problem of what to do with unlabeled, disallowed, disavowed, not even consciously perceived experience, experience which cannot be spoken about because it has no embodiment in existing art. Is one to create new forms wholesale—which is practically impossible? Or turn to old ones, like Blake's Elizabethan lyrics and Yeats's Noh plays? Or "trivial," trashy genres, like Austen's ladies' fiction?

Make something unspeakable and you make it unthinkable.

Hence the lyric structure, which can deal with the unspeakable and unembodyable as its thematic center, or the realistic piling up of detail which may (if you are lucky) eventually add up to the unspeakable, undramatizable, unembodyable, action-one-cannot-name.

Outsiders' writing is always in critical jeopardy. Insiders know perfectly well that art ought to match their ideas of it. Thus insiders notice instantly that the material of *Jane Eyre* is trivial and the emotionality untenable, even though the structure is perfect. George Eliot, whose point of view is neither peccable nor ridiculously romantic, does not know what fate to award her heroines and thus falsifies her endings.[5] Genet, whose lyrical mode of construction goes unnoticed, is meaningless and disgusting. Kafka, who can "translate" (in his short stories only) certain common myths into fantastic or extreme versions of themselves, does not have Tolstoy's wide grasp of life. (That Tolstoy lacks Kafka's understanding of alienation and schizophrenia is sometimes commented upon, but that does not count, of course.) Ellison is passionate but shapeless and crude. Austen, whose sense of form cannot be impugned, is not passionate enough. Blake is inexplicable. Baldwin lacks Shakespeare's gift of reconciliation. And so on and so on.

But outsiders' problems are real enough, and we will all be facing them quite soon, as the nature of human experience on this planet changes radically—unless, of course, we all end up in the Second Paleolithic, in which case we will have to set about re-creating the myths of the First Paleolithic.

Perhaps one place to look for myths which escape from the equation Culture = Male is in those genres which already employ plots not limited to one sex—that is, myths which have nothing to do with our accepted gender roles. There seem to me to be three places one can look.

1. Detective stories, as long as these are limited to genuine intellectual puzzles ("crime fiction" is a different genre). Women write these; women read them; women even figure in them as protagonists. The slang name "who-dunit" neatly describes the myth: Finding Out Who Did It (whatever "It" is).

2. Supernatural fiction, often written by women (Englishwomen, at least)

during the nineteenth and the first part of the twentieth century. These are about the intrusion of something strange, dangerous, *and not natural* into one's familiar world. What to do? In the face of the supernatural, knowledge and character become crucial; the accepted gender roles are often irrelevant. After all, potting a twelve-foot-tall batrachian with a kerosene lamp is an act that can be accomplished by either sex, and both heroes and heroines can be expected to feel sufficient horror to make the story interesting. (My example is from a short story by H. P. Lovecraft and August Derleth.) However, much of this genre is as severely limited as the detective story—they both seem to have reached the point of decadence where writers are restricted to the reenactment of ritual gestures. Moreover, supernatural fiction often relies on very threadbare social/sexual roles—for example, aristocratic Hungarian counts drinking the blood of beautiful, innocent Englishwomen. (Vampire stories use the myths of an old-fashioned eroticism; other tales trade on the fear of certain animals like snakes or spiders, disgust at "mold" or "slime," human aggression taking the form of literal bestiality—lycanthropy—guilt without intention, the lex talionis, severe retribution for venial faults, supernatural "contamination"—in short, what a psychoanalyst would call the "archaic" contents of the mind.)

3. Science fiction, which seems to me to provide a broad pattern for human myths, even if the specifically futuristic or fantastic elements are subtracted. (I except the kind of male adventure story called Space Opera, which may be part of science fiction as a genre, but is not innate in science fiction as a mode.) The myths of science fiction run along the lines of exploring a new world conceptually (not necessarily physically), creating needed physical or social machinery, assessing the consequences of technological or other changes, and so on. These are not stories about men qua Man and women qua Woman; they are myths of human intelligence and human adaptability. They not only ignore gender roles but—at least theoretically—are not culture-bound. Some of the most fascinating characters in science fiction are not human. True, the attempt to break through culture binding may mean only that we transform old myths like Black Is Bad–White Is Good (or the Heart of Darkness myth) into new asininities like Giant Ants Are Bad–People Are Good. At least the latter can be subscribed to by all human races and sexes. (Giant ants might feel differently.)

Darko Suvin, of the University of Montreal, has suggested that science fiction patterns often resemble those of medieval literature.[6] I think the resemblance lies in that medieval literature so often dramatizes not people's social roles but the life of the soul; hence we find the following patterns in both science fiction and medieval tales:

I find myself in a new world, not knowing who I am or where I came from. I must find these out, and also find out the rules of the world I inhabit (the journey of the soul from birth to death).

Society needs something. I/we must find it (the quest).

We are miserable because our way of life is out of whack. We must find out what is wrong and change it (the drama of sin and salvation).

Science fiction, political fiction, parable, allegory, exemplum—all carry a heavier intellectual freight (and self-consciously so) than we are used to. All are didactic. All imply that human problems are collective, as well as individual, and take these problems to be spiritual, social, perceptive, or cognitive—not the fictionally sex-linked problems of success, competition, castration, education, love, or even personal identity with which we are all so very familiar. I would go even further and say that science fiction, political fiction (when successful), and the modes (if not the content) of much medieval fiction all provide myths for dealing with the kinds of experiences we are actually having now, instead of the literary myths we have inherited, which tell us only about the kinds of experiences we think we ought to be having.

This may sound like the old cliché about the Soviet plot of Girl Meets Boy Meets Tractor. And why not? Our current fictional myths leave vast areas of human experience unexplored: work, for one; genuine religious experience, for another; and above all, the lives of the traditionally voiceless, the vast majority of whom are women. (When I speak of the "traditionally voiceless," I am not pleading for descriptions of their lives—we have had plenty of that by very vocal writers; what I am talking about are fictional myths *growing out of their lives* and told by themselves for themselves.)

Forty years ago those Americans who read books at all read a good deal of fiction. Nowadays such persons read popularized anthropology, psychology, history, and philosophy. Perhaps current fictional myths no longer tell the truth about any of us.

When things are changing, those who know least about them—in the usual terms—may make the best job of them. There is so much to be written about, and here we are with nothing but the rags and tatters of what used to mean something. One thing I think we must know—that our traditional gender roles will not be part of the future, as long as the future is not a second Stone Age. Our traditions, our books, our morals, our manners, our films, our speech, our economic organization, everything we have inherited, tell us that to be a Man one must bend nature to one's will—or other men. This means ecological catastrophe in the first instance and war in the second. To be a Woman, one must be first and foremost a mother and after that a server of Men; this means overpopulation and the perpetuation of the first two disasters. The roles are deadly. The myths that serve them are fatal.

Women cannot write—using the old myths.

But using new ones—?

NOTES

[1] Number 3 is a version of *The Winter's Tale*; number 4 the biography of Dylan Thomas, as popularly believed; number 5 the story of Faust and Marguerite; and number 8 a slightly modified version of part of *Day of the Locust*. The others need no explanation.

[2] I am indebted to Linda Finlay, of the philosophy department of Ithaca College, for this formulation and the short discussion that follows it.

[3] I am indebted to Mary Uhl for the observation that Dickens's women are accurately portrayed as long as they are in public (where Dickens himself had many opportunities to observe real women) but entirely unconvincing when they are alone or with other women only.

[4] An overstatement. The plot of *Widowers' Houses* was a gift.

[5] In comparison with the organic integrity of Dickens's, I suppose.

[6] In conversation and in a paper unpublished as of this writing.

~ 1975 ~

Sylvia Plath's Children's Poems

MARY COHEN

RECENTLY, PARTICULARLY WITH the popularity of *The Bell Jar* in this country, Sylvia Plath has been called on to reveal the debilitations male society works on its talented women. Indeed, the novel does present a heroine whose madness is in part owing to—though not wholly caused by—the either/or, marriage-or-career, choice which alone is permitted her; the young woman who desires a full life of both creativity and emotional maturity very nearly dies for lack of hope that such fullness can be hers. In fact, it is not until Esther Greenwood meets a woman psychiatrist who is both successful and emotionally stable—and who neither forces Esther into accepting "safe" choices (shorthand or virginity) nor hopes to live vicariously through Esther's future successes—that the young woman is able to face the world beyond the bell jar.

I had read the novel, in the earlier English edition, at about the same time I read the *Ariel* poems—probably in 1966—and while I recognized many of the feelings Esther Greenwood expressed as true to the experience many young women met in college when they showed aspirations for more than hearth and home, I felt that, in the ten years between the events described in the novel and the writing of the novel itself, Plath had resolved in her own life the problems she had faced as a young woman. She had in fact been able to combine a career with motherhood, and her poetry written from the fullness of this period seemed to deal with other issues—both wider and deeper than those raised in *The Bell Jar*.

In 1969 Robert Bagg claimed that the *Ariel* poems were fired by an ardent feminism. At the time his article appeared, I remember thinking that his case did not seem really tenable. While it was true that in "Lady Lazarus" the poet threatens to come back and "eat men like air," I failed to see her singling out men and male forces as responsible for the horror she saw around her. Now, with the publication of the rest of Plath's mature poetry (*Crossing the Water*, a collection of largely transitional poems written between 1960 and 1961, and *Winter Trees*, poems written during the same time as the *Ariel* poems, were both published in 1971), a more complete assessment of Plath's thematic and technical development has been made possible; and, in fact, with the body of Plath's mature work before us, her growing feminism—quite different from the more typical resentments of the bright college girl denied prospects—becomes apparent.

One particularly interesting group of poems, those which record Plath's attitudes toward children, provide a telling example of her development. The "children's poems" (hardly poems *for* children, rather poems for which children provided the inspiration) demonstrate in little what happened in her poetry generally—a simple response gradually became more complex, as the poet examined herself and the world around her more critically. And, more important to this study, these poems reflect with increasing clarity her growing feminism.

Perhaps, before turning to the children's poems, it would be well to consider the progress that occurred between the early poems that appeared in *The Colossus*—the only book of poetry published while Plath was alive, one composed of poems written between 1956 and 1959—and *Ariel*, the first of the posthumous volumes, which appeared in 1965.

The *Colossus* poems, while effective, lack the tensions and complexity of the later work. For the most part, they are statements of single emotions or ideas: one poem, "The Colossus," describes the poet's wish to "rebuild" her dead father, while another, "Lorelei," expresses, somewhat romantically, her own desire for death; "Aftermath" records the disgust she feels for the onlookers at a local tragedy; "The Disquieting Muses" directs disgust toward herself. Poems like "Watercolor of Grantchester Meadows" or "The Thin People" reveal her sensitivity to menacing presences around her, but the menace is left vague, unspecified. Many early poems demonstrate a tendency several critics have noticed, that of giving life or human characteristics to inert or inhuman objects—"Mushrooms" is certainly one of the most enchanting, if disquieting, examples—but it is later, in poems like "Cut" (*Ariel*), that she will work out the converse of animation, by draining the life from herself. Perhaps the most curious point—at least it would seem so now—is that, to a large degree, these early poems show her searching for subjects: she describes a neighbor's pig ("Sow") or recounts the fanciful adventures of a bull ("The Bull of Bendylaw"), but she is far more cautious than she will be about entering private grounds, the richest source of her poetry.

To readers of *The Colossus*, then, the vibrant, angry voice which burst through in the *Ariel* poems must have seemed startlingly new. Suddenly the poet whirled before them—rabid at injustice, torn between love and hate, wrought with despair, and clamoring for vengeance. Her poetry seemed brimming with energy and charged by several, often conflicting, powerful emotions.

No doubt a number of things account for the changes—and, of course, many of these causes we will never know—but Ted Hughes points to her most important source of change, her daring to make the inward turning. In his brief annotated chronology of her work, Hughes points out the two or three poems from *The Colossus* in which, with hindsight, one can see Plath turning to her inner world (168). In these poems the poet began an investigation into the things which hurt her, an investigation continued in much of the poetry following her first volume. It was this search which helped her to see complex relationships between what had seemed—or, at least, had been represented in the earlier poetry as—simple or independent impulses.

Plath began writing her children's poems after the *Colossus* poems and, more especially, after the conception of her first child. Perhaps because we tend to stereotype poets, and because Plath has become "the poet of suicide," the note of joy in her work—admittedly a note not often heard—has won little attention. Yet her early children's poems do indeed reveal the unmistakable exhilaration she felt at being pregnant. The most frolicsome poem Plath was to write is "You're" (1960), in which she describes her unborn child in a series of exuberant metaphors:

> Clownlike, happiest on your hands,
> Feet to the stars. . . .
> O high-riser, my little loaf.
> Vague as fog and looked for like mail. . . .
> Snug as a bug and at home
> Like a sprat in a pickle jug.
> A creel of eels, all ripples.
> Jumpy as a Mexican bean.
> Right, like a well-done sum.
> A clean slate, with your own face on.

An even rarer occasion is "Metaphors for a Pregnant Woman" (1959), in which she delights in describing herself:

> I'm a riddle in nine syllables,
> An elephant, a ponderous house,
> A melon strolling on two tendrils. . . .
> I'm a means, a stage, a cow in calf.
> I've eaten a bag of green apples. . . .[1]

In "Morning Song" (1961), written after the birth of her first baby, the mood is one of awe, as Plath captures the mother's sense of wonder at having produced a separate, perfect being. She begins the poem by disclaiming all credit, explaining in Deist metaphor, "Love set you going like a fat gold watch." Later she insists, combining her sense of wonder with the realization that the child charts her own demise, that

> I'm no more your mother
> Than the cloud that distils a mirror to reflect its own slow
> Effacement at the wind's hand.

She mocks her own image—

> One cry, and I stumble from bed, cow-heavy and floral
> In my Victorian nightgown . . .

—but reveals her tenderness toward her child in the transformation of the night cries in the last few lines:

And now you try
Your handful of notes;
The clear vowels rise like balloons.

The initial line in which the poet refuses to believe or take credit for the wonder that is her baby sounds a typical note—that of self-deprecation—but the disclaimer stems from awe rather than bitterness or dislike; it is the closing lines, expressions of undeniable delight, that are unusual. In the course of another of the early poems one watches the poet's happy imaginings give way to dread. In "Child" (1960), after beginning with apparent blitheness, listing all the things she would like to have fill the child's eye—color, ducks, April snowdrops—the poet laments:

Pool in which images should be grand and classical
Not this troublous
Wringing of hands, this dark
Ceiling without a star.

The contrast between what is and what should be makes sad reflections.

There does seem to be a marked difference in the poems in which Plath contemplates her own children and those in which she considers more generally the fate of the innocents. The poems which revolve around her own children's actions—like "Morning Song," "Nick and the Candlestick" (1962), and, I suspect, even "Balloons," a poem written during the last week of the poet's life—are relieved by a note of hope or pleasure or playfulness unheard in almost any of her other poems.[2] Yet, after the very earliest poems, none of the children's poems is wholly free of the note of fear, a note which gradually intensifies.

As one studies the children's poems, it becomes apparent that allusions to the Christ child and to Mary came to have special value for Plath as she explored her hopes and fears for children; in fact, it is possible to trace in the poems which use this imagery the momentum of her growing despair. In "Heavy Women," a poem written in 1960 or 1961, Plath stands outside the poem and describes her sense of the menace bearing down on children of unsuspecting mothers. The poem begins innocently, even playfully, with a description of the heavy women, mothers of small children, pregnant again with the next child:

Irrefutable, beautifully smug
As Venus, pedestalled on a half-shell
Shawled in blond hair and the salt
Scrim of a sea breeze, the women
Settle in their belling dresses.
Over each weighty stomach a face
Floats calm as a moon or a cloud.

In the second stanza the poet describes the women as meditating "Devoutly as the Dutch bulb / Forming its twenty petals." If the poem were to end with the second stanza, the image would simply be one of women wrapped up in themselves, selves wrapped about unborn children; the poet would seem merely to be pillorying the smug self-absorption of childbearing women. But in the third stanza Plath turns the meaning; her point is rather that these women, now Mary figures, are unknowing Marys who do not hear what grinds down on them:

> Dusk hoods them in Mary-blue
> While far off, the axle of winter
> Grinds round, bearing down with the straw,
> The star, the wise grey men.

The familiar images associated with Christ's birth, evocative of hope and wonder, are transformed by harsh sounds and ominous description into something menacing both mothers and children.

The "wise grey men" reappear in "Magi" (1960 or 1961), a poem which renders the poet's conceptions of the disparity between the ideal and the real more effectively than the earlier poem "Child" had been able to do. In "Magi" the baby appears lively and healthy, and in obvious contrast to the menacing figures who attend her. The wise men surrounding the child are insensitive to the baby's actual presence, so intent are they on their abstractions—in fact, they themselves are "abstracts" as the poem constructs them:

> The abstracts hover like dull angels:
> Nothing so vulgar as a nose or an eye
> Bossing the ethereal blanks of their face-ovals.

In the next two stanzas Plath mocks their aloofness by making them the subjects of mundane or domestic comparisons—"Their whiteness bears no relation to laundry. . . . They're / The real thing, all right: the Good, the True—" but she refuses them "the Beautiful"; rather they are "Salutary and pure as boiled water," a homely image, yet one that is sterile, devoid of life. Consequently, they are "Loveless as the multiplication table." In contrast, the child is very much alive, and blissfully unaware of the men who attend her. (Curiously, the child attended by the Magi is a girl; this can probably be explained by the fact that Plath's first child was a girl, but the effect of the change is to shock us out of a historical view, that we are reading a poem about the Nativity, and to force us to see the miracle in every child, and the ever-lurking threat of sacrifice.) The poem continues:

> For her, the heavy notion of Evil
> Attending her cot is less than a belly ache.
> And Love the mother of milk, no theory.
> They mistake their star, these papery godfolk.
> They want the crib of some lamp-headed Plato.
> Let them astound his heart with their merit.
> What girl ever flourished in such company?

The poem would seem to mock the Magi's orientation successfully if it were not for the last line. The conclusion, especially when read in conjunction with the other poems which employ references to the Christ child and Mary, suggests the menace in their presence. Modern poets before Plath had tampered with traditional views of the Magi: Yeats robbed them of faith, Eliot of hope; but Plath turns them from mere witnesses to creatures more threatening, nearly diabolical. While no speaker is identified in the poem, "Magi" anticipates the laments of the Mater Dolorosa heard in later poems.

Late in 1962 Plath was to write one of the most ominous of the poems inspired by one of her own children: "Nick and the Candlestick" is a poem which continues the pessimism of "Heavy Women" and "Magi" in its beginning stanzas. Ostensibly describing the child's grim and threatening surroundings, the speaker actually makes us most conscious of her own horror. The house, to her a cave, becomes an "earthen womb" which drips tears "from its dead boredom"; she feels "Black bat airs / Wrap me, raggy shawls / Cold homicides"; they weld to her "like plums." The poet's first use of religious imagery is literally chilling:

> Even the newts are white,
> Those holy Joes.
> And the fish, the fish—
> Christ! They are panes of ice,
> A vice of knives,
> A piranha
> Religion, drinking
> Its first communion out of my live toes.

It isn't until the eighth stanza that Plath breaks from the imagery of cold and menace, when suddenly the speaker is startled by the sight of her child and wonders at his presence: "O love, how did you get here?" In lines reminiscent of "Child" she sees that "The blood blooms clean / In you, ruby," and laments, "The pain / You wake to is not yours." Then, even more abruptly, in the last four stanzas, the child having given her heart, her mood swings to one of exhilarating defiance:

> Let the stars
> Plummet to their dark address,
> Let the mercuric
> Atoms that cripple drip
> Into the terrible well. . . .

Her newfound strength stems from the final recognition of the poem:

> You are the one
> Solid the spaces lean on, envious.
> You are the baby in the barn.

Thus in "Nick and the Candlestick," for one rare moment, the Christ in her own son gives her joy and the reason to persevere. Plath herself most clearly explained the mixed mood of the poem, in a BBC broadcast, when she said of the poem: "A mother nurses her baby son by candlelight and finds in him a beauty which, while it may not ward off the world's ill, does redeem her share of it." Yet, in view of the verse drama *Three Women*, written only some months earlier, and the bleakly pessimistic poems of the last months, the exultant ending of "Nick" seems to be a sport. Joyful defiance was not a mood the poet could sustain. The guttering candle of the opening stanzas seems a truer image of the poet's mood than the profession of triumph at the end.

The miraculous child and the attendant dangers—the two motifs prominent in both "Magi" and "Nick and the Candlestick"—are amplified significantly in *Three Women*, a radio drama set in a maternity ward. The play's three speakers are a wife who bears a son, a secretary who miscarries, and a girl who must give up her baby girl for adoption. The first speaker reveals in positive terms what there is to live for; although in the course of the drama she takes us through the pain of childbirth, her final tone is one of joy:

> I am reassured. I am reassured.
> These are the clear bright colors of the nursery,
> The talking ducks, the happy lambs.
> I am simple again. I believe in miracles.

Yet her idea of the miraculous is *not* the exceptional. She loves her child because he is perfectly formed, healthy, and smiling; the ordinary is miracle enough. As the reader has come to suspect, no joy in the newborn exists without an attendant dread; here the mother senses a threat in the exceptional:

> I do not will him to be exceptional.
> It is the exception that interests the devil.
> It is the exception that climbs the sorrowful hill
> Or sits in the desert and hurts his mother's heart.
> I will him to be common,
> To love me as I love him,
> And to marry what he wants and where he will.

Presumably the exceptional child would be made the pawn of men, such as the Magi, who would use him somehow to further their ends; for this reason the mother asks that her child be allowed the common lot.

Because of its depiction of the hope a child can bring to a woman and, conversely, the devastation a woman suffers at the loss of a child, and because of its assertion that male destructiveness is to blame for such losses, *Three Women* stands as the single most important of Plath's ardently feminist (that is, man-hating or man-blaming) poems. The second speaker's words clarify what men are after; more significant, her speeches ground the charge, which becomes increasingly important to the poetry, that men are the source of destruction and pain in this world. It is *Three Women* which establishes the crucial link between Plath's feeling toward children and her feeling toward male society.[3]

From the imagery in "Magi" and the secretary's speeches it is possible to deduce what Plath sees as the heinous male qualities.[4] Both poems indict men

—and male gods—as life-sucking forces.[5] The men in these poems cannot respond to life in its manifest forms; rather they abstract "ideas" from what they see. In their world of ideas, cut off from living things, they become bent on power. Plath does not explain why men should be this way, except that they cannot warm to life itself. So their energy goes into building their designs for destruction: bulldozers, for general leveling, and guillotines for the resistant who seek to retain their "grossness," their unflattened, unlaundered selves. *Three Women* blames men for the brutality and oppression in the world and insists that women are still capable of enacting life's only miracle—perhaps its only hope of redemption—the creation of innocence.

It is important to see what point *Three Women* marks in Plath's development. The play, written in late spring or early summer of 1962, follows all of the children's poems discussed here (with the exception of "Nick and the Candlestick") and precedes the greater number of the *Ariel* poems. The poems written before *Three Women* gradually develop a pensive, even fearful note. The poet obviously delights in children and values their innocence above all else. She begins to take the measure of her opposition in *Three Women*, and from this point forward, men and male images take on increased power and an increasingly malevolent form. Consequently, in the poems which follow, one notices a falling away of hope and an intensification of the poet's rage because of it. Ultimately, the idea, voiced in *Three Women*, that the common child is safe, that only the exceptional child will fall subject to society's machinations, gives way to an increasingly hopeless belief that no child can escape.

The note of pessimism deepens in "Brasilia" (1962), a poem which resumes the use of Christian imagery. Here the poet speaks in the first person—in what has come to seem her own voice—as a mother who, unlike the heavy women, is aware of the forces which attend her in the hope of gaining her son. She draws the menacing figures vividly:

> Will they occur,
> These people with torsos of steel
> Winged elbows and eyeholes. . . .

and she imagines, for the first time, the horror awaiting her child:

> And my baby a nail
> Driven, driven in.
> He shrieks in his grease
>
> Bones nosing for distances.

The poem concludes with the speaker's wild plea:

> O You who eat
>
> People like light rays, leave
> This one
> Mirror safe, unredeemed

> By the dove's annihilation,
> The glory
> The power, the glory.

Since she longs for her baby to remain unredeemed and, so, remote from the realm which includes such abstract concepts as "power" and "glory," she asks that her child be "common." The passion of her plea, in contrast to the mother's unimpassioned statement of her wish in *Three Women*, suggests that it has become extraordinary, rather than common, for a child to be left to an ordinary, untrammeled life.

It is apparent in other poems as well—not just those dealing with children—that for Plath the promise of salvation has fallen away from the Christ story. While the poet, in "The Moon and the Yew Tree" (1962), equates Mary with tenderness, she lacks faith in her power to offer it; ultimately she "simply cannot see where there is to get to." Without hope, the sacrifice of the Christ child remains only sacrifice, without salvation. In "Mary's Song" (October or November 1962), the reader witnesses the final plummet to despair, as it is recorded in the children's poems; it is this poem which most precisely locates the poet's pain. The title of the poem suggests the Magnificat, Mary's song of praise and adoration, but the Magnificat's enumeration of the Lord's powers stands in stark contrast to the terror and despair of the modern song.[6] In this poem the poet offers some of her most painful images of unredeemed sacrifice; her hope for her own children—or for any child—gives way, as history is telescoped into a chronicle of relentless and meaningless sacrifice.

Plath's poem opens deceptively, seeming in its mundane statement to have little to do with Mary or with more troubling themes: "The Sunday lamb cracks in its fat"—a flat, domestic statement except, of course, for the suggestion of "Sunday lamb." As in so many of her other poems, Plath's consciousness here works on the ordinary until the simplest object becomes the source for countless comparisons and reveals much about the mind's way of traveling. In "Mary's Song," the trigger image—the Sunday roast—first assumes Christian significance through traditional language and imagery:

> The Sunday lamb cracks in its fat.
> The fat
> Sacrifices its opacity. . . .
>
> A window, holy gold.
> The fire makes it precious. . . .

The roasting lamb leads the speaker to a consideration of sacrificial fire and the sacrifice of Christ; but before a positive image is permitted to take shape, the conjunction of lamb and oven calls up the gas ovens used to incinerate the Jews. No sooner has the link between the Sunday roast and the sacrificial lamb been established than the mind races on, turning in midsentence to another fire, another sacrifice:

The same fire

Melting the tallow heretics,
Ousting the Jews.

The equation of Christ's crucifixion on Calvary, a lamb sacrificed to the fire, and the bodies of Jews sent to the incinerators is made later in the poem:

On the high

Precipice
That emptied one man into space
The ovens glowed like heavens, incandescent.

The equation is not a reassuring one, certainly; the whole notion of sacrifice is called into question. The symbolic sacrifice may turn "holy gold," but the actual sacrifices turn to ashes—"Mouth-ash, ash of eye." "They do not die" is a mockery of resurrection; the lives of the Jews are lost and the memory of this loss returns to obsess the poet. Finally, Mary, like the Madonna of many Renaissance paintings, is burdened with the knowledge of what will come:

It is a heart,
This holocaust I walk in,
O golden child the world will kill and eat.

Here the poet finds the locus of her despair; the force which will prevent her being "a wall, keeping the wind off" is all around her and ends the poet's hope for innocence. She walks through a holocaust, the collective human heart. For the poet without belief in salvation the Eucharist becomes a cannibalistic rite; all hope is driven from purgation, resurrection, and communion. She no longer pleads, as she did in "Brasilia," that this child be spared: no child will be spared.

In the children's poems, then, Plath moves from simple joy, to joy tinged with apprehension, and finally, to despair.[7] The growing complexity of vision in the children's poems as well as the increasing hopelessness parallels the development in Plath's poetry generally. Moreover, by working through this group of poems, one encounters the wellspring of her feminism, which in turn supplies much of the anger—hence the force—in the final poems.

Children provide Plath the only evident and continuing source of delight and of hope, a hope grounded on the possibility of a world which could learn to cherish their innocence. Gradually, however, hope is eroded by her growing conviction that women and children are forever bound to be victims of male oppression. In *Three Women* the poet had the secretary turn her anger on herself; in the later poems, however, the poet seems incapable of submerging her rage. In "The Applicant" (October or November 1962), Plath, in her disgust, exposes society's ugliness. The persona, here the voice of cruel authority, demands of a child, the bewildered applicant, "First are you our sort of a person?" then lists various prostheses the child might wear to show his kinship—in the words of the poem, "to show something is missing." Society cannot recognize its own deformities as deformities; rather, it demands that the new, healthy growth conform to its ruined image.

"Daddy" (also written in October or November 1962), one of Plath's most powerful poems, is fired by anger which wells in large part from the poet's conception of men and their will to destroy innocence. The change in her feelings toward her father is immediately apparent when one contrasts "Daddy" with the title poem of her first collection. In "The Colossus" the poet longs for her father, lamenting that, although she has attempted to mend and clean his immense, dead image, "I shall never get you put together entirely." The simple expression of longing in the early poem is a far cry from the complex of emotions sounded in "Daddy." Although the poet is contemptuous of herself for having consented to become a victim, the chief target in the poem is her father (and, at one point, her husband, whom she sees as continuing the pattern of oppression), who is subject to a scathing assault which ends on a triumphant note of defiance and renunciation: "Daddy, daddy, you bastard, I'm through." Read in conjunction with the children's poems, "Daddy" can be seen as the poet's realization that her own misery and guilt, even her attempts at suicide, stemmed from the deathhold of the dead father: ultimately the grown child blames "daddy" and his kind for stunting her once innocent, happy life.

One can learn a great deal about Sylvia Plath and her poetry by reading her children's poems chronologically and as a group. They help to correct the balance of our view of her by supplying new insights into her life's struggle: she was not simply hurtling herself toward death, as so many claim; she was fighting against the escape death offered because she had discovered something in the world worth preserving. Gradually, however, her belief that innocence might be preserved faltered, and she came to believe that, given the nature of things, the good—woman's capacity to re-create life, and the innocent lives that are formed—must fall victim to what is evil—men and "masculine" forces, which are power-hungry and destructive. This ultimate vision generated the many moods—the despair of "Mary's Song," the vituperative anger of "Daddy," the vengeance of "Lady Lazarus"—of her final and most powerful poems.

NOTES

[1] "Metaphors" was written early enough to be included in *The Colossus* and does appear in the British edition; it is included in the American edition of *Crossing the Water*.

[2] Hughes identifies poems for which their children, Freida and Nicholas, were the inspiration.

[3] Except for a 1,000-copy edition of *Three Women* published in 1968 by Turret Books, only excerpts of the poem had been available to readers before its appearance in *Winter Trees*.

[4] "Magi" presents the baby and the power-driven men in nearly equal balance. If the poem was in fact inspired by her own child, it would seem that Plath was able, as she was in "Nick and the Candlestick," to deny victory to the force which comes to seem the more powerful.

[5] In *Three Women*, the poet gives a painfully accurate portrait of a self-effacing woman: the secretary, who suffers most from male tyranny, is abject. Although she blames men for her loss, ultimately she believes she has been found wanting and turns on herself with loathing. She deems

herself unfit to bear children and powerless to assume any other meaningful position; in the end she resigns herself to becoming "a heroine of the peripheral."

[6]

> My soul doth magnify the Lord. . . .
> For he that is mighty hath done to me great things;
>   and holy is his name.
> And his mercy is on them that fear him
>   from generation to generation.
> He hath showed strength with his arm:
>   he hath scattered the proud in the imagination of
>   their hearts.
> He hath put down the mighty from their seats,
>   and exalted them of low degree.
>
> (Luke 1.46, 48–51)

[7] Admittedly the scheme is not perfect. "The Night Dances," written at approximately the same time as "Mary's Song" (October or November 1962), is an expression of delight, and "Balloons," written during the last week of her life, shows a touch of the old playfulness; but these poems, like "Nick and the Candlestick," were apparently prompted by the immediate actions of her own children, which helps to account for their unexpected temper.

~ 1977 ~

Middlemarch, *Daniel Deronda*, and Hegel's Master-Slave Relationship

SUSAN PECK MACDONALD

DURING THE DECADE in England in which John Stuart Mill, Elizabeth Gaskell, Trollope, Meredith, and scores of minor writers began to be newly interested in the lot of the married woman, George Eliot also turned her attention increasingly toward the young married woman (see Thomson, *Victorian Heroine*; see also Colby 256–302). In *Adam Bede* (1859) and *The Mill on the Floss* (1860), Dinah's, Hetty's, and Maggie's processes of self-development had been traced up to the point where they married or, through tragic circumstances involved in their self-development, failed to marry. By implication, marriage was a young woman's reward for having successfully reached psychological maturity. But the failings of the Casaubon and Lydgate marriages in *Middlemarch* (1871–72) and the Grandcourt marriage in *Daniel Deronda* (1876) demonstrate Eliot's new awareness that marriage itself presents social difficulties at least as complicated as those of adolescence and that the individual shortcomings a person reveals in the mating process (e.g., Dorothea's nearsightedness) only aggravate the complicated social problems within a marriage.

A problem implicit in the Victorian marriage was the inequality of men and women. In her 1855 essay "Margaret Fuller and Mary Wollstonecraft" Eliot had already shown her awareness of the dangers of ignorance in a woman like Rosamond:

> There is a notion commonly entertained among men that an instructed woman, capable of having opinions, is likely to prove an impracticable yoke-fellow, always pulling one way when her husband wants to go the other, oracular in tone, and prone to give curtain lectures on metaphysics. But surely, so far as obstinacy is concerned, your unreasoning animal is the most unmanageable of creatures, where you are not allowed to settle the question by a cudgel, a whip and bridle, or even a string to the leg. For our own parts, we see no consistent or commodious medium between the old plan of corporal discipline and that thorough education of women which will make them rational beings in the highest sense of the word. Wherever weakness is not harshly controlled it must *govern*. . . . (203)

She continues, again emphasizing how *men* are hurt by the ordinary social roles:

> Men pay a heavy price for their reluctance to encourage self-help and independent resources in women. The precious meridian years of many a man of genius have to be spent in the toil of routine, that an "establishment" may be kept up for a woman who can understand none of his secret yearnings, who is fit for nothing but to sit in her drawing-room like a doll-Madonna in her shrine. (204–05)

In different ways Casaubon's, Lydgate's, and Grandcourt's stories exemplify the dangers of inequality in marriage; Casaubon's and Grandcourt's deaths are hastened (if not caused) by their wives, and Lydgate dies relatively young after his professional career has been ruined on Rosamond's account. Dorothea, Rosamond, and Gwendolen, on the other hand, potentially or in fact can construct better lives for themselves after their husbands' deaths. Eliot's purpose, however, is not to reward wives and punish husbands. With her characteristic avoidance of simplistic explanations, Eliot does not present her married men as secure and happy in their roles while victimizing their wives; instead, she sees both men and women as sufferers in any social relationships that are based upon inequality or lack of consideration for others.

In reading *Middlemarch* we may be tempted to see the Casaubon and Lydgate marriages as antithetical, but despite our contrasting Dorothea's good intentions to Rosamond's mulishness, or Casaubon's pedantry to Lydgate's more vital research, Casaubon and Lydgate are alike in their initial expectations about marriage, and their wives are alike in initially accepting a kind of submission (see Harvey). In *Daniel Deronda* Grandcourt's supremacy is more extreme and sadistic, representing his conscious love of dominance rather than the unthinking and rather innocent acceptance of the social status quo which harms Lydgate and Casaubon. But the psychological ramifications of these three differing relations of mastery and submission are similar and are an important part of Eliot's continued fictional examination of egoism and of the ingredients of emotional or psychological health.

This pattern of mastery and submission and the gradual process by which the master loses his mastery so strongly resemble the master-slave relationship described in Hegel's *Phenomenology of the Spirit* (1807) that our understanding of the Casaubon, Lydgate, and Grandcourt marriages can be illuminated by a comparison to Hegel. Curiously, England was experiencing a new interest in Hegel at the time, stimulated by J. H. Stirling's *The Secret of Hegel* (1865). Before Stirling, English readers who did not know German had little opportunity to discover Hegel; a fragment of the *Logic*, translated by H. Sloman and J. Wallon (1855), and *Lectures on the Philosophy of History* (1857), translated by Eliot's friend John Sibree, were the only works available in English. But Eliot and her "husband" G. H. Lewes, of course, knew German. For her translations of two neo-Hegelian works, Strauss's *The Life of Jesus* (1846) and Feuerbach's *The Essence of Christianity* (1854), Eliot would necessarily have been aware of Hegel. In a letter of 1848 to John Sibree, she comments on an "*ideenvoll* observation of Hegel's," and in a letter of 1858 exhibits some sarcasm about people who cannot read Hegel in German (*Letters* 1: 247; 2: 511). Lewes, meanwhile, included a rather critical section on Hegel in his *History of Philosophy* (1841), but allowed him some "suggestive" ideas (qtd. in Muirhead 157).

After Stirling's *Secret*, in 1865, according to J. H. Muirhead, Hegel "arrived" and in the next decades was to become "a household word with the younger generation of students of philosophy" (171–73). Lewes was enough affected by this that for the fourth edition of his *History of Philosophy* he revised the sections on Hegel; in the preface he explains that the earlier forms of the section on Hegel were "very inadequately presented" and that "the length to which the chapters on Kant and Hegel extend is justified by the interest attached to these names" (v). The preface is dated December 1870, a time when Eliot was first working on Dorothea's story (Haight 431).[1] At this period we again find references to Hegel in Eliot's letters. In October 1870 she writes that Lewes has been spending his mornings with Hegel, and in November 1870 that he "has got so interested in various parts of his revision—reading and re-reading Leibniz, Hegel, and much of Kant, and being led on to alterations which he had not contemplated—that the business of this fourth edition is much more important than we had expected" (*Letters* 5: 118, 122). In March 1871 Lewes set out to visit Haslemere "but stayed in the waiting room of the station reading Hegel and overstayed the time of the train's starting, so had to return" (*Letters* 5: 140). Again in July 1871 she mentions Lewes's rewriting of the Hegel section (*Letters* 5: 169). So while Eliot does not, to my knowledge, refer to Hegel's *Phenomenology* or his master-slave relationship specifically, she did know something about Hegel and had him brought increasingly to her attention during the period when she was beginning *Middlemarch*.[2]

The essential elements of Hegel's master-slave relationship are that it is a dialectical process in which the master, by attempting to consolidate his position at the expense of the slave, ends by losing his mastery. Because Hegel is interested in the nature of the process (not just one application), it works in a variety of contexts. Marx, of course, later used it in a political and economic context. In a political context what is at stake is power or mastery, and the master-slave relationship, because it is a false or unhealthy relationship, results in the loss of power. But for Hegel it was more basically a social and psychological phenomenon related to the origins of one's sense of self. In a psychological context what is at stake is a healthy sense of self in a healthy relation to other equals or, on the other hand, the loss of self altogether.

Hegel's master-slave relationship is set forth in Section B of the *Phenomenology*, entitled "Self-Consciousness." In Section A, "Consciousness," he had explained the origins of consciousness in relation to our consciousness of external objects. But because each stage of consciousness comes to seem inadequate as it is fully worked out, it leads dialectically to a further stage wherein old inadequacies are resolved and new ones discovered. Section A ends with the subject-object problem of late eighteenth-century empiricism and with the Kantian solution, as Hegel saw it. The seeming gap between appearance and the supersensible world (Kant's phenomenon and noumenon) is closed by realizing that knowledge of the "other" is really knowledge of the self, hence "self-consciousness" (see also Findlay; Hyppolite).

Self-consciousness, in the Hegelian sense, is one's awareness of the self who does the knowing. In its first phase, "Desire," external objects lose their independent existence and exist for the sake of the subject desiring them. The end of this kind of desire is not the object itself but the reaffirmation of the subject's self-consciousness through his ability to impose his demands on it. Hegel's second stage of "Self-Consciousness" is the master-slave relationship in which the process takes place between two humans. What Hegel calls "Desire" is very much like what Eliot calls "egoism," and Eliot's characters begin at a stage much like the master-slave relationship in which the egoistic self enters upon social relationships. In a well-known passage in *Middlemarch* Eliot writes:

> We are all of us born in moral stupidity, taking the world as an udder to feed our supreme selves: Dorothea had early begun to emerge from that stupidity, but yet it had been easier to her to imagine how she would devote herself to Mr. Casaubon, and become wise and strong in his strength and wisdom, than to conceive with that distinctness which is no longer reflection but feeling—an idea wrought back to the directness of sense, like the solidity of objects—that he had an equivalent centre of self, whence the lights and shadows must always fall with a certain difference. (156–57)

Rosamond and Gwendolen are so stuck in this stage of egoism or narcissism that they are frequently seen in front of mirrors, reinforcing their sense of self by contact with an "other" who isn't an other (see Swann).

Hegel's master-slave relationship begins with the subject's realization that he needs recognition from an "other" that is not an object but a human self-consciousness like himself, what Eliot calls "an equivalent centre of self." It is thus an attempt to avoid solipsism, but it is egotistical and one-sided because it is an attempt to assert one's independence by forcing recognition from an "other" without in turn recognizing the same thing in the other—that is, without granting that the other also has an independent self. The result of the subject's refusal to grant to the other what he expects for himself is that he fails to gain what he wants—a secure sense of self or, in Hegelian terms, self-consciousness. Because his is a misdirected, or even perverted, enterprise, it results in solipsism, and because the solitary self has refused to grant selfhood to others, there are no others worthy to reinforce or recognize his own self-consciousness. The "other" has been degraded to the status of an object by the inadequacy of the relationship. The one-sidedness of the relationship makes it inherently unstable, and the master soon finds that the inexorable logic of the situation begins reducing his independence. Hegel writes:

> But for recognition proper there is needed the moment that what the master does to the other he should also do to himself, and what the servant does to himself, he should do to the other also. On that account a form of recognition has arisen that is one-sided and unequal.
>
> In all this, the unessential consciousness [the servant] is, for the master, the object which embodies the truth of his certainty of himself. . . . [J]ust where the master has effectively achieved rule, he really finds that something has come about quite different from an independent consciousness. It is not an independent, but

> rather a dependent consciousness that he has achieved. He is thus not assured of self-existence as his truth; he finds that his truth is rather the unessential consciousness, and the fortuitous unessential action of that consciousness. (*Phenomenology* 406; 1953 ed.)

In other words, because he has based his concept of self ("his truth") upon something (the servant) which he is simultaneously devaluing (something therefore "unessential"), the master's self-concept is also devalued.

Hegel next turns his attention to the servant when he writes that the "truth of the independent consciousness is accordingly the consciousness of the servant."[3] Having gained no recognition from the master, the slave is not indebted to, and is therefore independent of, the master. The slave slowly redeems himself from being a mere thing or object because, unlike the master, he must work and through work becomes aware of the independence of objects and ultimately the independent existence of his self. This is less relevant for our purpose with Eliot because Eliot's married women do not reach this stage or aspire to it.

What is most interesting about this point of resemblance between Hegel and Eliot is not so much Eliot's implicit analogy between women and slaves (which Mill also had used in his *Subjection*) or the implication that inequality in marriage may hurt both man and woman. What is interesting, first of all, is the point of contact between Hegel's and Eliot's psychological models, despite their difference in terminology. Eliot's interest in the destructive self-enclosure of egoism and the beneficial effect of sympathy (literally, feeling with the "other") is basically the same as Hegel's interest in the destructive effects of the master's refusal to recognize the "other" and the potentially beneficial effect of mutual recognition. In *Middlemarch* all the major characters are capable of both egoism and sympathy, but by *Daniel Deronda* there are two different kinds of relationships to choose from—the master-slave relationship of the egoists, Grandcourt and Gwendolen, or the equal and sympathetic relationship of the nonegoists, Daniel and Mirah. For both Hegel and Eliot, development of the proper sort of selfhood or self-consciousness must grow, paradoxically, out of a preliminary turning away from the self to the "other." For Eliot it becomes a process of first losing or forgetting the self in the other in order to find a larger self which, like Deronda's, can have fulfilling social relationships.

Secondly, the resemblance between Hegel and Eliot is interesting because of the similarity of their dialectical methods. Although a detailed exposition of Hegel's dialectic is outside the scope of this paper, we can first see some of its basic characteristics and then demonstrate it at work in the paradigmatic case of the master-slave relationship. J. N. Findlay explains that the dialectic is an attempt to overcome the limits of what Hegel calls the understanding (*Verstand*):

> The kind of thought characteristic of a formal deductive system is called by Hegel the thought of the Understanding, a thought characterized by great fixity and definiteness of notions, presuppositions and deductive procedures, as well as by an extreme stress on the distinctness and independence of one notion or principle from another. The Understanding, we may say, cuts off the corners of our ideas, all the fine penumbra by which they shade into other ideas, or imply them without

> plainly including them: it also checks the tendency of our ideas and principles to shift and transform themselves into other ideas and principles when faced with unwonted cases or questions. (57)[4]

The "Understanding" is suited for the deductive system of mathematics. The sense of causation we have, for instance, when one billiard ball hits another and causes the second one to move is predicated upon two distinct, independent, and essentially static billiard balls, neither of which has been altered by the contact even though their positions have changed. But if we think of biological rather than mathematical models—as both Hegel and Eliot did—we can see why the dialectic is a preferable method of explanation. In Hegel's preface to the *Phenomenology*, he often uses a biological analogy to describe his method:

> [Opinion] does not comprehend the difference of the philosophical systems in terms of the progressive development of the truth, but sees only the contradiction in this difference. The bud disappears as the blossom bursts forth, and one could say that the former is refuted by the latter. In the same way, the fruit declares the blossom to be the false existence of the plant, and the fruit supplants the blossom as the truth of the plant. These forms do not only differ, they also displace each other because they are incompatible. Their fluid nature, however, makes them, at the same time, elements of an organic unity in which they not only do not conflict, but in which one is as necessary as the other; and it is only this equal necessity that constitutes the life of the whole. (8)

Eliot also uses biological analogies, as in the following comment upon Gwendolen:

> For some of the goodness which Rex believed in was there. Goodness is a large, often a prospective word; like harvest, which at one stage when we talk of it lies all underground, with an indeterminate future: is the germ prospering in the darkness? at another, it has put forth delicate green blades, and by-and-by the trembling blossoms are ready to be dashed off by an hour of rough wind and rain. Each stage has its peculiar blight, and may have the healthy life choked out of it by a particular action of the foul land which rears or neighbours it, or by damage brought from foulness afar. (*Deronda* 48)

Biological phenomena like the growth of a plant or the complex social interrelationships of a group of animals are best explained in terms of modulation, modification, process, growth, and evolution rather than in terms of fixity and distinctness. While the Understanding imposes stability or fixity upon the material it examines, the dialectic is a method suited for recognizing and analyzing process or development or evolution. Findlay writes of Hegel's method that "the main contemporary importance of Hegel lies in his recognition of the 'open texture,' the unclear corners of all living notions, the fact that it is natural for them to move or develop in certain ways as soon as they are subjected to unwonted pressures" (22–23). Lewes, in his explanation of Hegel's dialectic, underlines this concern with process by speaking of "a principle of evolution from difference to difference, which differences are its moments." "Thus," he continues, "there is perpetual flux, nothing is ever fixed, definite, all is but the passing *moments* of the immanent movement'' (590).

Eliot's interest in development and evolution is thus shown by her use of a method like Hegel's. As they enter marriage, her characters are not static billiard balls with faults and virtues which will bounce off each other but remain unchanged in the process. Instead, they affect and are affected by each other dialectically. And of course they are affected by the roles of dominance and submission conventional to the Victorian marriage and by the potential for trouble inherent in those roles. The conflict inherent in the situation causes them to be constantly evolving toward different states within the relationship, rather than remaining static.

The ill-assortment begins with their view of their roles in marriage. Dorothea, ironically likening Casaubon to Milton, Locke, Bossuet, and other formidable great men, is looking for a superior. She egoistically endows Casaubon with all the qualities she would like to find in him and is, therefore, in no position to judge him. She begins in a position of reverence which is later to help poison their relationship.

Casaubon begins with what seems to be the perfect correlate for Dorothea's role; he accepts her adoration, expects to be in the superior position of father, teacher, or disciplinarian, and rejoices in her readiness to serve. He tells her, ''The great charm of your sex is its capability of an ardent self-sacrificing affection . . .'' (37). To him the two sexes are different, each with its characteristic excellence and its own role to play, but his role is to lead and hers to be a sort of appendage to him: he says she is ''adapted to supply aid in graver labours and to cast a charm over vacant hours'' (31–32).

The strain his role creates for Casaubon is that having initially cast himself, or been cast by Dorothea, in the role of superior, he cannot easily step outside his role because to meet Dorothea on any kind of equal plane would be an admission of defeat. We see this in Casaubon's fears as his imagination transforms Dorothea from an uncritical, ignorant girl into a ruthless and knowledgeable critic. The irony of Casaubon's situation soon becomes clear; instead of successfully reinforcing his sense of self with Dorothea's worship, he finds himself dependent upon her opinion of him and threatened by the loss of her worship: ''He had formerly observed with approbation her capacity for worshipping the right object; he now foresaw with sudden terror that this capacity might be replaced by presumption, this worship by the most exasperating of all criticism—that which sees vaguely a great many fine ends, and has not the least notion what it costs to reach them'' (149). Like Hegel's master, Casaubon has founded his self-esteem upon an inferior. But paradoxically if Dorothea really is inferior, then her opinion does not count, and although Casaubon wants to be recognized as a scholar, he cannot be so recognized except by someone competent to judge his scholarship. At the same time he is afraid of Dorothea's overcoming her ignorance and inferiority because he suspects he will then lose her good opinion. He cannot even accept her sympathy, for sympathy is a form of equality, and he fears that if she knows enough, she will begin to pity him. Thus, his initial superiority degenerates into a fear of her superiority in being able to pity him.

By the end of his life, which she hastens, Dorothea has become independent of his opinion while he is very much dependent on hers; his initial acceptance of inequality has led him from superiority to the reverse. At the end he is trapped in his egoism, like Hegel's master, unable to get outside himself because he had initially refused to accept the independence of the other. He has no clue to Dorothea's thoughts and can only imagine them from the shades of his own personality. In his mind he sees himself competing against the harsh criticisms of scholarly rivals, and projecting his values upon her, he supposes her estimation of him to be affected by a similarly competitive scheme wherein he must run ahead of his rivals or lose her esteem. He is trapped within his own values, thus, by projecting them onto Dorothea. He has created his own isolation and, in the end, dies alone.

Dorothea's own marital sufferings, while less severe than Casaubon's, are the correlate of his. From her initial position of reverence for him and discontent with herself, she moves, logically enough, toward wishing to emulate him. The first step out of her own inferiority is to try to understand him, but understanding is inconsistent, in this case, with admiration. Even with a far greater husband than Casaubon, Dorothea might have lost some of her admiration after coming to understand him, simply because understanding represents a kind of closeness or equality that admiration does not. A more secure husband (as Lydgate might have been) could have accepted understanding in the place of admiration, but Casaubon cannot.

In Dorothea's case, understanding leads to increased sympathy so that, by the end, she is psychologically healthier than Casaubon. She is like Hegel's slave in that she has been forced to recognize the existence of an "other" outside herself and has become more independent by so doing.

Lydgate's initial assumptions about marriage are similar to Casaubon's. Despite our greater liking for Lydgate, he, too, expected an inferior in his wife: "[H]e held it one of the prettiest attitudes of the feminine mind to adore a man's pre-eminence without too precise a knowledge of what it consisted in" (197). But he soon discovers the danger of adoration without understanding, for Rosamond, it turns out, dislikes medicine. She has married him because of his social superiority and yet does not particularly understand or respect what he thinks of as his superiority. As Lydgate says, "And to say that you love me without loving the medical man in me, is the same sort of thing as to say that you like eating a peach but don't like its flavour" (336).

Rosamond, of course, is clever enough to prevent Lydgate from seeing the flaws in his theory of marriage until it is too late; she is not willfully deceitful, but she knows that her role in the scheme is to admire without revealing the ignorance or ambition behind her admirations: "For Rosamond never showed any unbecoming knowledge, and was always that combination of correct sentiment, music, dancing, drawing . . . which made the irresistible woman for the doomed man of that date" (198). Rosamond is doing no more than performing perfectly what is asked of her; her ignorance of money is the logical correlate of her imprisonment in the home-sanctuary, and her carelessness with fact is the result of never being given responsibilities. Lydgate must pay heed to the facts of medicine because he will be held accountable for all he does, but the childlike woman of the home is encouraged in a variety of irresponsibilities. Rosamond's ability to admire Lydgate's professional ambition, without any sympathy for the substance thereof, is simply one case of her not needing to be logical in any of her thoughts or commitments.

So Lydgate discovers that Rosamond's respect for him is either superficial or nonexistent; the "shallowness of a waternixie's soul" (475) cannot give him the meaningful recognition which would strengthen his sense of purpose. He has tried to gain recognition from someone unworthy to give it, and so he finds himself looking "through less and less of interfering illusion at the blank unreflecting surface her mind presented to his ardour for the more impersonal ends of his profession and his scientific study, an ardour which he had fancied that the ideal wife must somehow worship as sublime, though not in the least knowing why" (428). Somewhat inconsistently, considering his early feeling that Dorothea was "too earnest" (69), Lydgate would now like to make contact with this "other" he has married because he senses how a reciprocal process of sympathy and understanding could replenish and revitalize him. Dorothea's sympathy after his disgrace does have this life-giving effect upon him, just as her sympathy has its momentary effect on the ordinarily unreachable Rosamond. But Rosamond's chilling "What can *I* do Tertius?" (434) is worlds away from Dorothea's passionate "Advise me—think what I can do—he has been all this life labouring and looking forward. He minds about nothing else" (432). Rosamond is self-enclosed and, ironically, independent. She does not care what Lydgate thinks of her, while he has come round to the position of wanting to reach her. She is trapped in herself, but he is trapped by her ability to frustrate all his best efforts. His initial desire for a "waternixie" wife thus comes back to haunt him. In wishing to have his way without discussing or explaining things to his partner, Lydgate finds he has chosen the very wife who is able to defeat his every command. Casaubon, similarly, had sought to protect himself from his fears but instead finds he has chosen a wife who brings those fears closer to him.

In a fuller and more brutal way, there is a similar reversal in *Daniel Deronda*. Grandcourt is far more assertive about his mastery and far less uneasy than Casaubon about the dangers of a relationship based upon inequality. His blindness to danger forces him to more and more extreme measures and, by dialectical logic, leads him to a crueler ending than either Casaubon or Lydgate.

Unlike *Middlemarch*, in which Casaubon's and Lydgate's supremacy seems clear at the beginning, *Daniel Deronda* begins one stage earlier and shows us the struggle for recognition between two would-be masters—Grandcourt and Gwendolen. But from the start, Grandcourt's advantages give him the upper hand. He has the crucial advantages of being a man and being wealthy, and he turns his languor into a weapon in the struggle for mastery. In their first conversation, at the archery meeting, the pauses between Grandcourt's replies cause

Gwendolen to wonder what he thinks of her, to wonder about him, and generally to feel more self-conscious then she usually does in conversation. John Blackwood described Gwendolen's "running mental reflections" as resembling "what passes through the mind after each move at a game . . ." (*Letters* 7: 182). All the qualities that cause Gwendolen to praise Grandcourt for being "not ridiculous"—his cold manners, his attention to propriety, his lack of spontaneity—all these constitute a competitive social game in which Grandcourt puts others at a disadvantage. He believes unquestioningly in the supremacy of his aristocratic values and manners, causing others to feel inferior as a result.

Gwendolen has quite as much determination to be master as Grandcourt, but the struggle is not decided on the basis of desire. Just as it was for Hegel's slave, fear is Gwendolen's weakness and later her strength. Fear is the quality which makes her open to Deronda's beneficial influence after the gambling scene at Leubronn, in the first chapter, and this same susceptibility, by making her initially weaker than Grandcourt, also makes her lose the initial struggle with him. By the time of the archery ball, Gwendolen has already begun to fear Grandcourt:

> If this situation had been described to Gwendolen half an hour before, she would have laughed heartily at it, and could only have imagined herself returning a playful, satirical answer. But for some mysterious reason—it was a mystery of which she had a faint wondering consciousness—she dared not be satirical: she had begun to feel a wand over her that made her afraid of offending Grandcourt. (88)

In the struggle Gwendolen is supported only by her high spirits and her belief in herself, but her susceptibility, fear, and lack of "cold artifice for the sake of enslaving" cause her downfall (310).

In the Hegelian paradigm, the slave, after failing to become master, prefers slavery to death (much as Gwendolen considers Grandcourt the lesser of two evils) and finds himself without recognition as an independent self, denied self-consciousness. From this negative position, he slowly works his way into a new state because of the inherent instability of the master-slave relationship. Eliot's handling of Gwendolen captures something of the negative stage when the self is not recognized. A great deal of the first book is concerned with Gwendolen's point of view. We move in and out of her mind, but we are often in her mind and know a great many of her thoughts. After the marriage, however, a partial withdrawal from her mind serves to convey the suppression of self Gwendolen is undergoing in her marriage. In her social appearances, she often seems to be merely a surface. Deronda, for instance, observes that the Grandcourts do not talk to each other at the New Year's Eve dance, and Gwendolen's face is blank until he approaches. When Grandcourt scolds her about the turquoise necklace, we are shown her imprisonment: she is "a white image of helplessness" and "she could not even make a passionate exclamation, or throw up her arms, as she would have done in her maiden days. The sense of his scorn kept her still" (337). Grandcourt seems to enjoy forcing Gwendolen to be a surface only (a "white image"), with no gestures to betray that there may be emotions behind the surface. As Grandcourt's wife, then, she is denied a self.

Somewhat later, Gwendolen considers carrying out Deronda's advice to interest herself in others by reading to enlarge her mind:

> But it was astonishing how little time she found for these vast mental excursions. Constantly she had to be on the scene as Mrs. Grandcourt, and to feel herself watched in that part by the exacting eyes of a husband who had found a motive to exercise his tenacity—that of making his marriage answer all the ends he chose, and with the more completeness the more he discerned any opposing will in her. And she herself, whatever rebellion might be going on within her, could not make up her mind to failure in her representation. (412)

Her identity is restricted to how she appears as Mrs. Grandcourt; there is no place for any independent life of her own, and the exigencies of being Mrs. Grandcourt prevent Gwendolen from cultivating herself in private.

The truth that the master-slave relationship tries to obscure is that our selves are not isolated and independent. Even when Grandcourt is not explicitly trying to coerce Gwendolen, the form of their relationship and the kind of person he is have their negative effects upon Gwendolen: "[T]he medium that now thrust itself everywhere before her view was this husband and her relation to him. The beings closest to us, whether in love or hate, are often virtually our interpreters of the world . . ." (506).

Gwendolen is in a worse position than Hegel's slave who finds that work is beneficial because it allows him to shape or affect something outside himself and, in so doing, to discover the self who shapes. While Hegel's slave is forced by the master to work, Gwendolen is forced by her master not to work. Having no work to do, as a man might, makes it much harder to become independent of Grandcourt:

> Gwendolen's inclination lingered over the project of the singing lessons as a sort of obedience to Deronda's advice, but day followed day with that want of perceived leisure which belongs to lives where there is no work to mark off intervals; and the continual liability to Grandcourt's presence and surveillance seemed to flatten every effort to the level of the boredom which his manner expressed: his negative mind was as diffusive as fog, clinging to all objects, and spoiling all contact. (441)

All this might seem to imply that Grandcourt is secure in his mastery, but such is not the case. Like Hegel's prototype wherein the master's mastery is essentially precarious and by its very nature likely to reverse itself, Grandcourt's seeming mastery is also precarious. Even before their engagement, when he seems most unperturbed, Grandcourt's pose has a potential weakness in his fear of rejection; Lush believes Grandcourt is kept from proposing by a "bitter objection to risk a repulse" (209). After the return from Leubronn, Grandcourt first sends a note, so that if Gwendolen intends to reject him, she will refuse seeing him without his actually proposing. After she accepts him, he sends the diamond ring by messenger because, as Gwendolen says, "He would rather make me put it on than ask me to let him do it" (232). These maneuvers to avoid rejection before the marriage are a hint that Grandcourt's power is not impregnable.

Grandcourt—like Casaubon, Lydgate, and the Hegelian prototype—is vulnerable because his feeling of superiority must be reinforced by others. This explains his initial tolerance of Deronda:

> Grandcourt did believe that Deronda, poor devil, who he had no doubt was his cousin by the father's side, inwardly winced under their mutual position; wherefore the presence of that less lucky person was more agreeable to him than it would otherwise have been. An imaginary envy, the idea that others feel their comparative deficiency, is the ordinary *cortège* of egoism; and his pet dogs were not the only beings that Grandcourt liked to feel his power over in making them jealous. (207–08)

Similarly his general contemptuousness, like Gwendolen's acting, requires an admiring audience:

> It is true that Grandcourt went about with the sense that he did not care a languid curse for any one's admiration; but this state of not-caring, just as much as desire, required its related object—namely, a world of admiring or envying spectators: for if you are fond of looking stonily at smiling persons, the persons must be there and they must smile—a rudimentary truth which is surely forgotten by those who complain of mankind as generally contemptible, since any other aspect of the race must disappoint the voracity of their contempt. (440)

Ultimately, then, he is not independent because his mastery depends upon recognition from others beneath him, but his contempt for them makes them a potentially hazardous foundation for his sense of self.

Another point on which Grandcourt is susceptible is his ability to understand others. Like all egoists—like Casaubon and Bulstrode, for instance—Grandcourt has a heightened sensitivity about topics which touch his egoism: "There was nothing that Grandcourt could not understand which he perceived likely to affect his *amour propre*" (223). Through this unusual acuity he later keeps Gwendolen in strict subservience. He instantly knows, for example, that Gwendolen's turquoise bracelet is some kind of symbol between Deronda and her in the scene when she suddenly reveals the bracelet. In social situations Grandcourt uses his mask of boredom to conceal a very keen attention to whether Gwendolen is conducting herself properly as his wife. But the very fact of this attention shows Grandcourt's incomplete mastery; he cannot simply relax in his position of power because he must continually reinforce it.

Furthermore, this keen understanding of what affects his amour propre has its own accompanying drawbacks. Grandcourt's highly developed and specialized form of perception has as its obverse side an utter insensitivity about whatever lies outside the framework of power relations he takes to be the reality of life. Whatever there is of ethical perception or feeling, unselfish concern for others, or high-mindedness, Grandcourt is blind to. On the subject of Gwendolen's feelings about Lydia, Grandcourt's understanding is characteristically limited:

> He had correctly divined one half of Gwendolen's dread—all that related to her personal pride, and her perception that his will must conquer hers; but the remorseful half, even if he had known of her broken promise, was as much out of his imagination as the other side of the moon. . . . Grandcourt's view of things was considerably fenced in by his general sense, that what suited him, others must put up with. There is no escaping the fact that want of sympathy condemns us to a corresponding stupidity. (448–49)

At first Grandcourt does not mind if Gwendolen talks "nonsense" with Deronda as long as she conducts herself properly; he "was not jealous of anything unless it threatened his mastery—which he did not think himself likely to lose" (241). But to the extent that Deronda converts Gwendolen to another and better view of human relationships, he frees Gwendolen from mental subservience to Grandcourt. And so ultimately all that Deronda is associated with—music, religion, unselfishness—is a threat to Grandcourt's mastery, and any thought of Gwendolen's that Grandcourt does not understand is just the sort of thought which can make her troublesome to him. Thus, all the "nonsense" which Grandcourt thinks has no bearing upon his mastery does have a bearing which he has been too shortsighted to realize.

The initial battle for supremacy is not followed by a period of stasis. The equilibrium begins to shift almost immediately because of the inherent instability of the master-slave relationship. Once reduced to subservience, Gwendolen is not so powerful an adversary that she can challenge Grandcourt directly; she is no longer trying to win a battle, just to survive, but that still compels her in directions Grandcourt does not like. The threat to him is seen less in her thoughts and actions than in the increasing harshness he resorts to in order to be sure of her.

A pattern begins to develop soon after their marriage: whenever Gwendolen makes any effort to be helped by Deronda or to find a larger life than that she shares with Grandcourt, he reasserts his mastery over her by preying upon her weakness—her care for appearances. Early in their marriage he can force her to wear the diamonds by telling her she must "appear decently" (321). As long as Gwendolen can see nothing more important in life than her social status, Grandcourt is often able to bring her back into line by criticizing her appearance or her manners. It is the narrowness of Gwendolen's ideals that Grandcourt uses to keep her in submission.

Similar incidents occur when Gwendolen uses her turquoise bracelet to signal to Deronda her contrition and her need for help and then at the musical party where Mirah sings. As several critics have pointed out, music in *Daniel Deronda* is an index of the characters' ability to feel and to get outside themselves (see Cirillo; Levenson). In talking to Deronda after Mirah has sung, Gwendolen is trying to take one further step toward that larger life Deronda, Mirah, and Klesmer enjoy. But when Grandcourt sees Gwendolen's obvious urgency in talking to

Deronda, he counters this new impulse of Gwendolen's without even commenting on it directly. Instead he simply announces that Lush will dine with them the next day. Since forcing Lush upon her revives her initial repulsion toward him and represents a broken promise on Grandcourt's part, this move is obviously a sign that Grandcourt is using more desperate measures with her, and thus a sign that he feels his mastery to be in danger.

The stakes are again increased when Gwendolen decides she wants singing lessons from Mirah. Grandcourt counters, once again, by preying on Gwendolen's fear of being ridiculous, saying. "[O]ne doesn't want to hear squalling in private" (442). Mortified, Gwendolen refers to Deronda's authority, meaning "to sling a small stone at her husband in that way" (442). Grandcourt, in turn, intimates that Mirah is Deronda's mistress. Gwendolen is stunned.

Grandcourt is trying a new tactic, no longer using Gwendolen's fear of vulgarity but playing on something even stronger in her. He thinks she is jealous of both Lydia and Deronda, and while he mistakes moral aversion for jealousy, he does at least understand that he is using much stronger weapons. Gwendolen recovers briefly after a visit to Mirah, but Grandcourt again crushes her by intimating that Mirah has lied. Yet he cannot stop there; he next tries his strongest weapon so far. He sends Lush to her with his will in order to force her to suffer Lush's vulgar arrogance, to remind her that she knew about Lydia before marrying him, and to threaten her with the insulting provisions of his will. Eliot's pairing of two illicit relationships here—the one, Grandcourt's maliciously imagined relationship between Mirah and Deronda, and the other, Grandcourt's relationship with Lydia—underscores how Grandcourt's severity comes always in reaction to Gwendolen's attempts to get outside her mental and marital prison. This particular effort of Grandcourt's fails because he has misunderstood Gwendolen's motives and because the relationship between Mirah and Deronda is constructed wholly out of the characteristics of Grandcourt's mind. His love of dominance extends not just to people's actions, for he seems to feel in this case that he can impose his view of reality upon Gwendolen, even to the extent of making her see a relationship between Mirah and Deronda that does not exist. But his power is partly illusory, and he is reacting rather than acting. He is beginning to fail because his shortsightedness keeps him from seeing that he is pushing her not into submission but into a desperation which will have its effect upon him.

At Gwendolen's first opportunity after this, she asks Deronda to come see her and tries to deceive Grandcourt. He, however, returns to find her in conversation with Deronda and announces that he is taking her yachting. At this point, he is still the master able to compel her to do what he wills, but he is having to take quite extreme measures to assure her compliance. He has to isolate her physically from all but himself in order to make certain she cannot escape the life he wants for her. Apparently his mastery is safe only in complete isolation.

This is doubly significant in Hegelian terms because the master-slave relationship is so bound up with the nature of self-consciousness and because recognition must come from others. Grandcourt's forcing Gwendolen into isolation on the yacht is, first of all, a direct threat to Gwendolen's emerging self. It means that there is no chance of her gaining recognition from anyone but Grandcourt (the servants, being slaves themselves, do not count), and Grandcourt is bent upon denying her selfhood. Second, it is an attempt to stabilize what, for Hegel, cannot be stabilized because the master cannot gain recognition from the slave without in turn granting the same to the slave. Her isolation is likely to become his.

Grandcourt does not succeed with his yachting scheme. Instead of reducing Gwendolen to submission, he only augments the turmoil within her, and a storm, reflective perhaps of her inner storm, drives them to land for repairs. On land they encounter Deronda, in what seems like an artistically awkward use of coincidence. But since Deronda represents the better form of human relationships which may evolve from the master-slave relationship, Grandcourt's fleeing Deronda in London only to find him in Genoa thus represents proof that the master cannot maintain his stranglehold on the slave. Accepting the inevitable, however, Grandcourt tries to force Gwendolen back into isolation (and submission) by going to sea again, this time in a sailboat.

Grandcourt's death is an externalising of the dialectical logic of the master-slave relationship. Throughout the novel the power struggle has been conveyed both through events and through imagery. Grandcourt's drowning is both event and image, the final objective correlative of the tendencies of the master-slave relationship. He has tried to deny the right kind of consciousness in Gwendolen, to isolate her from others, and to imprison her in herself. So when he is drowning, trapped and isolated in a foreign medium, Gwendolen is unable to get outside of herself to help him. Because Gwendolen sits in the boat seeing tortured images of her own soul and cannot get outside them soon enough to help Grandcourt, her isolation has become his. Like Hegel's prototypal master, Grandcourt ultimately cannot maintain self-consciousness because he has not recognized it in the other.

The full significance of the drowning is made clear only by seeing the boating incident in the context of imagery begun early in the novel. Initially the power relationship is described in terms of horse imagery. Gwendolen, at the beginning, loves nothing so much as the exhilaration of horseback riding, but from the first, there is an ambiguity about her riding which is in keeping with the other ambiguities about her. Although riding is a part of the desire for supremacy which the master-slave relationship involves, it is potentially also a way of forgetting oneself in exhilaration. But Gwendolen early in the novel refuses to choose the healthy options represented by Rex and Deronda; she chooses to do her horse riding with Grandcourt. Thus as she accepts Grandcourt's proposal, she is thrilled by looking out the window and seeing Grandcourt's two beautiful horses being led around slowly outside, according to his orders. To Gwendolen these two horses seem to be "symbols of command and luxury, in delightful contrast with the ugliness of poverty and humiliation at which she had lately been looking close" (226). It is typical of Grandcourt to parade his symbols, and typical of Gwendolen, at this point, to fail to see Grandcourt's manipulation of her. That the two horses are parading *together* seems to Gwendolen a sign that she need not become a slave in marriage, and the "command and luxury," as we know, are to be achieved by "making her gain out of another's loss" (334). Before marriage, we see Gwendolen, and she sees herself, as a rider of horses, a potential master, but all that changes with her marriage. Grandcourt sees her not as the rider but as the horse he will ride:

> From the very first there had been an exasperating fascination in the tricksiness with which she had—not met his advances, but—wheeled away from them. She had been brought to accept him in spite of everything—brought to kneel down like a horse under training in the arena, though she might have an objection to it all the while. On the whole, Grandcourt got more pleasure out of this notion than he could have done out of winning a girl of whom he was sure that she had a strong inclination for him personally. (237)

Soon Gwendolen also sees herself in this way. When she first puts on the diamonds, she says to herself, "He delights in making the dogs and horses quail: that is half his pleasure in calling them his. . . . It will come to be so with me; and I shall quail" (321). Grandcourt then observes to himself that she "answered to the rein" (321).

Gwendolen's deteriorating position is also shown through the associated image of the chariot. Early in the relationship with Grandcourt we are told, "Gwendolen wished to mount the chariot and drive the plunging horses herself, with a spouse by her side who would fold his arms and give her his countenance without looking ridiculous" (99–100). But during the engagement she feels "as if she had consented to mount a chariot where another held the reins" (243) and soon after that "the horses in the chariot she had mounted were going at full speed" (249).

These horse and chariot images of Gwendolen's and Grandcourt's relative positions are used again in the boating incident in which Grandcourt drowns. As they are about to go boating, Gwendolen warns him that it would be better for him to leave her at liberty, but Grandcourt "had the courage and confidence that belong to domination, and he was at that moment feeling perfectly satisfied that he held his wife with bit and bridle" (512). Once again she is the horse and he the rider. As Gwendolen sails out with him, she feels rage and sits like a "galley-slave" and a "prisoner" (523). Grandcourt "was naturally so at home on the sea that he could manage a sail with the same ease that he could manage a horse" (512).

This explicit connection between sea and horse, brief as it is, probably carries with it the traditional mythological association between Poseidon, lord of the sea, and the horses sacred to him, as well as the association between a boat which rides the waves and a chariot pulled by horses. Grandcourt, of course, is not a god over horses and waves; he merely thinks he is, and his punishment is fitting. Suddenly, in this novel where visions are creators, Gwendolen wishes his death and Grandcourt is struck by the sail he is so proud of having mastery over. To be saved he needs the rope. At this point the creatures he has proudly suppressed—Gwendolen, his horse, his boat—are symbolically overthrowing him and he no longer holds the reins. Gwendolen holds the rope (or rein) and fails to throw it to him because of the limitations he has helped impose on her. Symbolically, then, Grandcourt has caused his own death.

Drowning is the most fitting death for Grandcourt for several reasons. By subsuming the horse theme in the Poseidon myth, Eliot can show the master being overthrown by the creature he has enslaved. His isolation and enclosure in the water thus become an objective correlative of his solipsism. Since the rope which his creature cannot throw him is the rope he has used in indulging his love of dominance, the dialectical movement from his dominance to his overthrow is made to seem inevitable.

Furthermore the drowning is contrasted to Mirah's near drowning when Deronda saves Mirah as Gwendolen cannot save Grandcourt. Deronda can save Mirah because he is not self-enclosed. At the moment he sees her he "was forgetting everything else in a half-speculative, half-involuntary identification of himself with the objects he was looking at, thinking how far it might be possible habitually to shift his centre till his own personality would be no less outside him than the landscape . . ." (140). Eventually, Deronda's discovery of Mirah means his discovery of himself because through her he discovers Judaism and comes to know and accept his own past. With his discovery of himself comes that discovery of something larger than the self which Eliot would have us all aspire to. Thus Deronda is contrasted to Grandcourt in being able to recognize the independence of the "other," benefit reciprocally from the relationship, and in so doing enlarge his self-consciousness. Grandcourt, however, will not grant independence to another self and so is unable to be revitalized by relationships with others. He is isolated at the end, and Gwendolen is too self-enclosed to reach out to him. The ocean which swallows him is a fitting nemesis for one who has denied the healthful psychological process by which we move out of egoism into the larger life of social relations. The process is dialectical and made to seem inevitable; those who initially assume their own independence without recognizing an other's "equivalent centre of self" will lose their independence. Those who seek to become masters will become slaves.

NOTES

[1] According to Haight, Eliot began work on a story called "Miss Brooke" in early November 1870 and in December decided to combine it with the "Middlemarch" story already begun.

[2] In his *History of Philosophy*, Lewes refers to Hegel's *Phenomonology* a number of times.

[3] Hegel's terms were *Herr* and *Knecht*, which Baillie translated as "Lord" and "Bondsman," and Friedrich as "Master" and "Servant." I use the terms *master* and *slave* because they are most common.

[4] I do not use the terms *thesis, antithesis*, and *synthesis* because they are not used in Hegel's master-slave relationship, and, as Findlay explains, "The terms 'thesis,' 'antithesis,' and 'synthesis,' so often used in expositions of Hegel's doctrine, are in fact not frequently used by Hegel: they are much more characteristic of Fichte" (67).

AFTERWORD

What interests me most about this article now, fourteen years later, is that, even after winning the Florence Howe contest, it was never accepted for publication. I sent the article off to eight journals between 1976 and 1980, receiving rejections each time and frequently rewriting. Uncertain what might make the article more publishable, and isolated from either old boys' or emerging new girls' networks, I relied on clues from the rejection slips. One nineteenth-century journal thought the article too literary, another wanted to see evidence that Eliot read Hegel's *Phenomenology*, while a third complained that the article didn't illuminate Eliot's work. Several journals found it too narrow. In all this, the sentence that stands out most clearly in my memory at this distance came from a male *PMLA* reviewer in the days before submissions were read anonymously: "Dr. MacDonald will publish, but she should be less inclined to the case-making which the state of the profession unfortunately encourages."

Though I went on to write and publish other feminist criticism, this early rejection was perhaps crucial in turning me away from writing about literature and toward writing about writing. The questions that now preoccupy me lie in the domain of rhetoric: What are the conventions of different kinds of writing? How do novices discern those conventions and learn to imitate them? And what obstacles are there for novices trying to gain entrance to a discourse community?

In the case of my 1976 article, there were a number of obstacles. As literary history, it was unconventionally focused on indirect rather than direct influence (intertextuality, it might now conventionally be called). As literary analysis, it was unconventionally focused on extraliterary ideology. There was no established feminist discourse community yet. I was, indeed, "case-making," as the reviewer claimed—my case being that one sort of marriage is better than another and that the nineteenth-century roots of feminism include Eliot's neo-Hegelianism. But my "case" was hardly shocking and was so indirect, without explicit reference to emergent 1970s feminism, that the reviewer's peevishness today seems small-minded. Was it simply a case of an entrenched male reviewer discriminating against a threatening, upstart feminist? Not simply. The article was neglected partly because of its uneasy mixture of competing or not-yet-established conventions, but neglected also because as novice writer I did not know how to frame an article for my audience: what to make explicit and what not, how to mix textual explication and theory, how to make a case for the importance of what I was doing, or how, in short, to make my writing look acceptable to a discourse community.

Increasingly, I turned away from literary criticism because its standards seemed capricious to me; and, bearing nearly forgotten professional scars, turned toward rhetoric and composition, where the standards seemed more visible, explicit. I think it behooves all of us in literature or composition studies to make our discursive conventions more explicit to ourselves and to novices, if we are to grant access to novices.

University of California, San Diego

~ 1978 ~

Psyche Reborn: Tradition, Re-vision, and the Goddess as Mother Symbol in H. D.'s Epic Poetry

SUSAN STANFORD FRIEDMAN

OUT OF THE ashes of patriarchal culture, woman is giving birth to a new self, Adrienne Rich has written (''When We Dead'' 98; 1975 ed.) In H. D.'s epic poetry, the Goddess is an omnipresent force in that metamorphosis. As mother symbol, she guides the rebirth of the poet, her daughter. ''Write, write or die,'' Isis commands the aging poet in H. D.'s last poem, *Hermetic Definition*. To the poet-prophet of war-torn London in the *Trilogy*, the Goddess suddenly appears in a vivid dream, carrying the blank pages of a book yet to be written. Strangely, she comes with ''none of her usual attributes,'' without the Child. The ''Grand Mer'' of *Sagesse* whispers ''our simple mystery'' of love to her daughter, the poet, through the echo of a seashell. In *Helen in Egypt*, Helena frees herself from the burden of hatred when she realizes her identity with the Goddess and their mutual opposition to the ''*masculine* 'iron-ring of war.' '' Lilith, unjustly desecrated as a demon, is the prototype of woman-spirit incarnated throughout the ''processus'' of history in H. D.'s still-unpublished poem *Vale Ave*. Religious experience, the ''new sensation'' that ''sets the nerves quivering,'' is frequently a sign of the Goddess's ''Presence'' to the poet. ''The mother is the Muse, the Creator, and in my case especially, as my mother's name was Helen,'' H. D. writes (*Hermetic Definition* 7; *Trilogy* 97; *Sagesse*, in *Hermetic Definition* 75; *Helen* 55; *Vale Ave.; Tribute* xi).

Her name changes throughout the poems as H. D. fuses many of the protean forms of the ancient earth goddesses, but her core meaning for H. D. remains essentially the same. She is the female divine spirit embodying the power of regenerative mystical love in the midst of a fragmented, death-centered modern world. Protean forms of male divinity also figure significantly in H. D.'s poetry. Within the context of her whole religious-artistic philosophy, the female and male deities embody opposing aspects of the androgynous One. But for H. D., a woman poet in a culture where both gods and poets are male, the revelations of the Goddess have a special intensity and personal relevance. She serves as both muse and mother symbol for the woman poet in search of authentic identity and regenerative vision. Her manifestations in myth, dream, and religious experience transform the misogyny of patriarchal tradition and validate H. D. as woman, as poet. It is my purpose to outline where H. D. "discovered" the Goddess, how the Goddess functions in her poetic quest, and what light her mother symbol sheds on the creative potential of the bond between mother and daughter.

Paradoxically, H. D.'s intense immersion in the androcentric traditions of psychoanalysis and mysticism initiated her poetic creations of the Goddess as living symbol. She experienced these traditions as parallel quests whose revelations about the psyche and spiritual reality were similar, though their language was different (see Friedman, "Mythology"). With a dialectical approach to her materials, H. D. developed certain aspects in each overlapping tradition until she had created a woman's mythology antithetical to her source of inspiration.

H. D. was an analysand of Sigmund Freud for about five months during 1933 and 1934. *Tribute to Freud* documents the rich and wide-ranging influence Freud had on her poetic development as she learned from their sessions and his books how to translate the hieroglyphic script of the unconscious. One of the reasons H. D. gives for going to see Freud was for help in deciphering several occult experiences she had had in 1920 during her trip to Greece (39–56, 153–62). H. D. tells us that Freud viewed these visions as "dangerous symptoms" of an unresolved neurotic attachment to her mother (17, 30, 33, 39, 41, 44, 49, 123, 136). Paralleling what he had written about religious experience in general, Freud concluded that H. D. longed to fuse with her mother, to re-create the early period in infancy when the ego is as yet undifferentiated and cannot distinguish itself from the mother. H. D.'s buried infantile attachment to her mother had interfered with her achievement of "normal" womanhood and was threatening to destroy her ego's ability to distinguish between hallucination and reality. The route to "normal" femininity, in Freud's view, involved the young girl's transference of affection from her mother to her father. This transference is initiated by the girl's discovery of "her castration" and her belief that her genital "deficiency" is her mother's fault. Achievement of womanhood, Freud believed, was dependent on the young girl's "healthy" hostility toward and rejection of her mother—and, by extension, all other women—as her love object. Freud's general purpose in therapy, he had written elsewhere, was to strengthen the ego by weakening the hold of unconscious desires on the rational self. If forbidden or impossible unconscious wishes were brought to consciousness, their power to control behavior would disappear. In the context of H. D.'s analysis, he would help her recover and interpret the fragments of her dreams and visions so that the neurotic symptoms rooted in desire for union with her mother would disappear.[1]

As she did with many of Freud's value-laden biases, H. D. turned Freud's categories upside down—or right side up, if you will. She wanted access to the unconscious not to control it but to benefit from its inspiration and revelation (*Tribute* 71, 82–83). Out of the fragments of memory and dream, Freud had brought her mother back to life. She wrote in a letter to a friend, "I think people do actually come to us in dreams. I dream of my mother, simply confused dreams, mixed-up, that don't count—then one so clear and exact, with such perfect detail, that I KNOW that this time, I have actually been with her."[2] This recovery of her mother was a crucial step in her search for full womanhood, but not because she could then transfer her affection to a father symbol and men in general. Instead, this identification and bond with her mother freed her to explore the meaning of women's experience in a male-dominated world.

Freud's hypothesis that the childhood of the individual recapitulates the infancy of the human race presented H. D. with a formula that allowed her to link the patterns of her own unconscious with the patterns of all myth. In the world of dream and vision, the personal is the universal. Thereby her mother, as recalled in dream, is one version of the "Grand Mer," the prototypical mother of us all recorded in myth. Thereby her religious experiences were a contemporary manifestation of ancient matriarchal religions. Thereby H. D. understood that her extensive research into myths of the Goddess and mystical tradition was simultaneously an exploration of her own self as woman (see *Tribute* 12, 71, 73, Freud, *Civilization* 17, *General Introduction* 189, 209–23, *Future* 53).[3]

These equations gave structure and direction to H. D.'s fascination with the occult and heterodox religious traditions. In the late twenties and thirties, she actively used astrology, numerology, and tarot cards along with psychoanalysis to "read" her psyche and destiny. By the forties and fifties, this involvement expanded into spiritualism, Moravian mysticism, and the syncretist Kabbalah of a Frenchman, Robert Ambelain. Denis de Rougemont's *Love in the Western World* and Ambelain's books argued persuasively for H. D. that an underground mystical tradition has existed from the earliest times down through the present. Since H. D. was born and raised in her mother's tight-knit Moravian community in Bethlehem, Pennsylvania, she felt that her own personal history destined her to this syncretist tradition. These various forms of mysticism, nearly always persecuted by the dominant orthodox religions, differed sharply from the masculine monotheism of the established Judeo-Christian tradition. One important area of contrast for H. D. was the place of woman as symbol in the divine pantheon. The orthodox traditions created a masculine imagery of God and used this ideology to rationalize their belief in male superiority (see, e.g., Kramer and Sprenger; Eph. 5:22–33; 1 Tim. 2:8–15; 1 Cor. 11:3–15; H. R. Hays; Ruether). The mystical traditions, Ambelain and de Rougemont argue, posited a divine One (the En-Soph of the Kabbalah), a latent Whole that incorporated equally both masculine and feminine potential. The gods and goddesses of myth incarnate those dual principles. The dualism of masculine and feminine structures all manifest creation and governs all other dualisms such as light–dark, good–evil, positive–negative, spirit–flesh, active–passive, life–death, reason–intuition, rational–emotional, sun–moon (see, e.g., Ambelain 127–28; de Rougemont 65–69, 83–86, 118–19; 1956 ed.).

H. D.'s deep involvement in these traditions freed her from the imagery of patriarchal monotheism. Like her work with Freud, it brought her back to a mythic mother symbol and ultimately matriarchal religions. But for the Goddess to function as a symbol of mystical love, H. D. had to revise this syncretist tradition just as she did the psychoanalytical one. The dualisms of Gnosticism and the Kabbalah do indeed grant recognition to a Female Principle largely denied in orthodox traditions. But this dualistic mythology tends to equate the Female Principle with darkness, passivity, matter, evil, flesh, and death. Creation is a fall from perfection where the Male Principle, the spark of the divine, is shrouded in the flesh of the female (see de Rougemont 1956; Farwell; Meeks). Hardly a mythos to guide a woman's quest. To use these traditions, H. D. reversed and revised these dualisms. She re-valued the Female Principle and by the time she wrote *Helen in Egypt*, she associated the masculine with death, the machines of modern war, and technology (Freud's death instinct). The Goddess then embodied love (Freud's Eros), life, peace, and rebirth. Once having discovered the Goddess in mystical tradition, H. D. abandoned the androcentric lens of this tradition to develop her personal and mythic mother symbol into the cornerstone of her vision of salvation.

H. D.'s transformation of the largely negative mother symbol of mysticism into the Goddess who gives new life to her daughter the poet depends upon a paradoxical dialectic aptly described by Gershom Scholem, leading authority on the Kabbalah. All mysticism, he writes, "has contradictory or complementary aspects: the one conservative, the other revolutionary." The individual mystic has a unique vision of a formless divine whose expression is embodied in the symbolic language of the mystic's collective tradition. Scholem calls this interrelationship of the old and the new a "dialectic" that puts "new wine into old bottles" (5–25, esp. 7, 23). H. D.'s poetic mysticism operates on a similar dialectic, but with an important difference resulting from the fact that she was a woman within a male tradition. Like the traditional mystic, her mother symbol expressed the themes, imagery, and structures of psychoanalysis and mysticism. But the "individual," "revolutionary" aspect of her vision redefined the patriarchal bias of that tradition for women as a group. H. D. understood that since women have been reviled as a caste, the fate of individual transformation and transcendence is tied to the authenticity of cultural identity and symbol. The emerging self of women cannot be created in a purely individual dimension. Self-transformation is dependent upon the creation of a new group identity, a new mythology of womanhood. The Goddess appears in H. D.'s poetry to embody and inspire this process of re-vision, of revisionist mythmaking. She symbolizes both what has happened to women in patriarchal tradition and the potential of women to transcend the paralyzing definitions of "otherness." She is not so much a supernatural force outside women as a symbolic incarnation of the divine spark in women. The desecration of the Goddess in orthodox religions represents on a mythic scale the defilement of women in the historical dimension. The resurrection of the Goddess in H. D.'s poetry is linked with the transformation of women. She is the "*Bona Dea*" freed from the cage of the past:

she is not shut up in a cave
like a Sibyl; she is not

imprisoned in leaden bars
in a coloured window:

she is Psyche, the butterfly,
out of the cocoon.
(*Trilogy* 103)

This recognition of desecration and poetic re-vision of the mother symbol is a central theme in all of H. D.'s epic poems. As the daughter wonders in *Hermetic Definition*, "Astoroth . . . A star—a Star . . . Astoroth, you can not be malign / with so beautiful a name" and "Lilith . . . Lili—a flower—. . . Lilith, why do they call you a devil"? (17). These questions are explored in her long poems, each with its own special emphasis. Three of these poems, however, cover a representative spectrum; and at the risk of simplifying their extraordinary complexity, I would like to outline the role of H. D.'s mythical and personal mother symbol in the quest of the daughter.

The *Trilogy* records H. D.'s first real discovery of the Goddess in the context of religion; her messages give the poet-prophet the vision of spiritual reality that gives meaning to the modernist nightmare of World War II and the German Blitz of London. Discovery of the underlying apocalyptic pattern is linked to the poet's restoration of the mystery religions that centered on the Goddess. Like H. D.'s gradual recovery of her mother in analysis with Freud, the daughter-poet's return to the primal deity, the Goddess of matriarchal religions, is the result of a complex process that begins with immersion in the father symbols of divinity. The first poem of the *Trilogy* is dominated by the poet's search for the "Christos-image" and the divine father who appears at the end as Osiris ("O-Sire-Is") (54–57). In the second poem, *Tribute to the Angels*, the poet sees herself as a modern John whose "Revelations" transform the fire of death into the "Apocryphal fire" that must precede the new Jerusalem. "*I John saw*," H. D. writes, but her vision is a re-vision of biblical tradition, a "revolutionary" epiphany that transforms the Whore of Babylon into the Goddess of Salvation (see also Gubar, "Echoing Spell"). The poet's prayer to the seven masculine angels around God's throne is interrupted by the Goddess's sudden appearance to the poet: "I had been thinking of Gabriel, / of the moon-cycle, of the moon-shell, . . . how could I imagine / the Lady herself would come instead?" (92). The daughter must first understand how the mother has been defiled by misogynist monotheism:

. . . Knaves and fools

have done you wrong,
Venus, for venery stands for impurity

and Venus as desire
is venereous, lascivious. . . . (74)

In the alchemy of poetry, the daughter's words (logos) undo the patriarchal reduction of Venus to carnality and restore the matriarchal life-giving Goddess, "Star of the Sea, Mother":

> Now polish the crucible
>
> . . . .
>
> Swiftly re-light the flame.
> Aphrodite, holy name,
>
> . . . .
>
> return, O holiest one,
> Venus whose name is kin
>
> to venerate,
> venerator. (71, 75)

The daughter's purification of the mother symbol paves the way for dream, epiphany, and mystical revelation of the Goddess to the poet: the religious experience that both Freud and H. D. saw as her psychic fusion with her own mother. The personal and the mythic dimensions of mother and daughter overlapping, the Goddess comes first in dream just as H. D.'s own mother had returned so forcefully to her daughter (89–107). She appears once again in the poet's ecstatic vision of "resurrection reality" (80–87). Walking through the bombed-out city, the poet passes through a doorless frame and suddenly sees a charred may-apple tree flowering. Attribute of the Goddess, the tree does not symbolize the fall of man through woman's sin, as in Genesis. Instead, it incarnates the power of the Goddess to re-create life out of the ashes of death. Salvation comes not through the Son of God but through the Lady. Simultaneously echoing yet transforming masculine mythology, the refrain of *Tribute to the Angels* honors the power of the Goddess: "this is the flowering of the rood, / this is the flowering of the wood" (87, 110). Paradoxically, the Goddess's regenerative power is linked to her striking appearance without the Child. Instead she carries the "Book of Life" and embodies the mystical forces of love and logos in opposition to the contemporary reality of the "Sword." To give vision and new life to her daughter the poet, she must be transformed from the mother of God to the Goddess alone.

The Goddess, however, is a "revolutionary" vision not only as a female savior but also as a symbolic representation of the metamorphosis open to women. The alchemy of poetic vision that resurrects the Goddess can also restore the individual woman to authenticity. This process structures the quest of Helen to translate the hieroglyph of self in *Helen in Egypt*. H. D.'s Helen is a victim of the "mindbinding" Mary Daly has spoken of ("Prism"). She is "Helena, hated of all Greece," hated as a Pandora, a Greek Eve whose love for Paris starts the Trojan War (*Helen in Egypt* 2). The weight of androcentric judgment has been so great that Helen has repressed her memories of the war and imagined herself to have been transported innocently to Egypt by Zeus. Stesichorus, in his "Palinode," and Euripides, in his *Helen in Egypt*, had already written of Helen's innocence; she was really a chaste and virtuous wife brought to Egypt by Zeus while her phantom was sent to Troy. H. D.'s "Pallinode," or "defense," squarely confronts the patriarchal mythos by which women were either the chaste wife or booty of war, by which "the Command was bequest from the past / from father to son" (61). The fate of Helen's search for individual identity is tied to H. D.'s revisionist mythmaking, in which woman as cultural symbol is purified of misogyny and transformed into the force of love. Freed from shame, the "mindbinding" of patriarchal image, Helen spends the last two books of the epic exploring the three "phases" of the Goddess (Aphrodite, Thetis, Koré) who simultaneously embody Helen's self, H. D.'s mother, Helen, and the Grand Mer, mother of us all. The Mother Goddess, recovered for H. D. through psychoanalysis and mysticism, enables H. D. to transform woman's identity from "otherness" to authenticity. Having established this, H. D. could then go even further in her search to transcend dualism, to experience the interrelationships of love and death and the wholeness of the divine One.[4]

This transformation is tied ultimately to the capacity of women to write. The Goddess nearly always functions as a muse, for H. D.'s personae that she inspires are always implicitly or explicitly poets. The unconscious, H. D. learned from Freud, is the seat of all nonrational perception and is therefore the "fountainhead" of both religion and art (see, e.g., Freud, *Future, General Introduction* 384, "Relation"). The apocalyptic vision of rebirth brought by the Goddess in the *Trilogy* serves as inspiration for an art whose vision is religious and a religion whose language is art. "She must have been pleased / with the straggling company of the brush and quill / who did not deny their birthright," the poet says to the Lady (100). The "initiates born of one mother" are simultaneously poets and prophets who bring meaning to the catastrophes of the twentieth century. While there is no suggestion that these initiates in the *Trilogy* are all women, *Hermetic Definition* explicitly links the Goddess's function as muse to the capacity of the woman to write autonomously and without fear of male mockery or excessive male influence. The three-part poem records H. D.'s obsessions with two men—one as lover, one as poet—and her struggle to find her own "way."

Freedom from obsession comes appropriately through the metaphor of the woman poet giving birth as the human incarnation of the mother goddess. In the creative act, the daughter becomes the mother—the mother to her poem and to her autonomous self. "Ordered, ordained or controlled" by her muse Isis, this "pregnancy" and "birth" restore her identity as woman (*Hermetic Definition* 45). Many male writers have made the analogy between their own poetic creation and women's capacity to give birth. But in H. D.'s poem, this conventional metaphor takes on a new dimension of meaning. To create poems of hermetic vision that fuse the traditionally male functions of religion and art, she does not have to abandon her womanhood, as one critic has implied (see Riddel 449).[5] Instead, her creativity is rooted in her self as woman. When the dominance and scorn of the male world threatens that creativity, the Goddess as muse reveals herself in epiphany and religious experience to strengthen the woman poet and redirect her quest.

In H. D.'s poetry, the bond between the muse and poet reproduces the potentially creative tie between mother and daughter. But H. D.'s Goddess can function as inspirational mother symbol to her daughter the poet only after the mother figures of psychoanalytic and mystical tradition have been freed from their androcentric cage. If the mythic mother has to be transformed, what about H. D.'s real mother? In H. D.'s mythos, a single pattern structures the personal and the universal. Consequently H. D.'s dialectical interaction with the Goddess as cultural symbol parallels a revision of her relationship with her own mother. As H. D. remembers that relationship, her mother could only partially serve as inspirational muse and model to her daughter. The actual mother appears in H. D.'s writings as a woman full of warm life and laughter, whose artistic talents had been thwarted and her mind diverted by her identification with her husband, sons, and masculine culture in general. H. D.'s mother was an accomplished musician and painter who contrasted sharply with her scientist father, a well-known astronomer. To H. D., her parents embodied the choice she had to make between art and science (*Tribute* xii, xiii, 145). Failing in science and math (to the great disappointment of her father), H. D. chose to follow in her mother's footsteps. But this identification with her mother could not in itself free the daughter from the confines of a feminine destiny. As a victim of masculine culture herself, Helen Wolle was insecure and self-denigrating about her own considerable "gifts." H. D. remembers telling Freud that "painting reminded me of my mother. I told him how as children we had admired her painting and boasted to visitors, 'My mother *painted* that.' My mother was morbidly self-effacing" (*Tribute* 164). At another point she recalls her mother telling her "how when she was little and singing, her father said who is making all that noise. She was so hurt she never sang again." (*Gift* 32–33). Like many mothers, Helen Wolle was prevented by her own victimization from being a model of autonomy for her daughter. H. D.'s identification with her mother carried with it the destructive potential of becoming "morbidly self-effacing" and dependent on men for validation.

Her mother's internalization of masculine values took on their greatest intensity for the daughter in Helen Wolle's attitude toward her children. As the autobiographical *Gift* makes clear, H. D. believed that her mother did not recognize her daughter's artistic and psychic "gifts." This lack of awareness, H. D. later realizes, "was itself her [mother's] own sense of inadequacy and frustration carried a step further."[6] This negation of her self deepened to a rejection of her daughter. H. D. felt throughout her childhood that her mother openly favored her son Gilbert (*Tribute* 29, 33). Not a pretty or feminine child, the wild and strange Hilda was "an ugly duckling" to her mother (xi). In an attempt to get closer to her mother, H. D. had identified with her brother. "If I stay with my brother, become part almost of my brother, perhaps I can get nearer to *her*," she recalls (33). Freud explained H. D.'s longing for closeness with her mother as her desire to be a boy, her need to be important to her mother (120). Rejecting Freud's general hypothesis of penis envy as physiologically based, H. D. nonetheless expressed her longing to be in her brother's favored position. As fantasies that countered rejection, some of H. D.'s dreams recorded in the thirties recreate the child Hilda attempting to prove to her mother that she is special, more gifted or important than her brother (36–39, 119–23, 174–75). They are painful dreams which express the explosive ambivalence of mother–daughter relationships evident in such divergent works as George Eliot's *Mill on the Floss* and Rita Mae Brown's *Rubyfruit Jungle*.

Just as the Goddess of masculine tradition has symbolically embodied the "otherness" of woman, so the mother has often helped to perpetuate the dominant norms in her relationship with her daughter. Whether engaging in the practice of footbinding or the more subtle process of "mindbinding," the mother has sometimes acted on behalf of men to render her daughters physically or psychically wounded. The potentially creative bond of love and identification between mother and daughter has been distorted by patriarchal culture. To restore this bond as the center of her artistic and religious identity, H. D. had to transform her mother, just as she had revised the psychoanalytic and mystical traditions. The Goddess as inspirational mother symbol represents H. D.'s liberation of her mother from her imprisonment "in leaden bars / in a coloured window" of her Victorian context (*Trilogy* 103). So the mother who preferred her son over her daughter had to become the Goddess of the *Trilogy* who appears without her familiar male child. So the mother who did not recognize her daughter's "gift" had to become the Grand Mer who passes down the mysteries to her daughter in *Sagesse*. So the mother who was morbidly self-effacing about her own art had to appear as Isis, the Muse who commands her daughter to "Write, write or die." To be reborn as Psyche, the daughter must give birth to her own mother.

H. D.'s development of the Goddess as a projection of the mother–daughter bond and the creative capacity of women contains an underlying pattern that appears in other women authors as well. The rebirth of Psyche depends, first, upon a recognition of the androcentric roots of negative definition and, second, upon a subversive transformation of existing traditions that ultimately destroys their patriarchal base. The metamorphosis of self from "otherness" to authenticity is not a uniquely personal act, H. D.'s heroes understood. Women's quest for selfhood involves direct confrontation with the dominant cultural norms shaping the nature and destiny of women in general. Yet hidden within those norms often lie the seeds of potential antithesis. H. D. begins immersed in patriarchal imagery: Freud's psychoanalysis, mythological portraits of the "eternal feminine," and cultural designations of women as creators through motherhood alone. She uses these images to restore the bond with her mother, to resurrect the Goddess, to revise woman as a cultural symbol, and thus establish a valid dimension of woman's quest.

In this process of cultural transformation, the role of the artist is crucial. The Goddess is a Muse, "mother" to art as well as vision. Cultural tradition—its language, imagery, and theme—is the very medium of the artist's métier. Her revisionist mythmaking is "revolutionary" in more ways than Scholem intended, for her art is a creative act that helps establish a new cultural tradition. H. D.'s image for the poet in the *Trilogy* centers on the "worm"—the caterpillar who becomes a butterfly and the resurrection serpent who sheds its skin. Condensing a complex dialectical process into image, she writes of her companions in art: "We are . . . the carriers, the spinners" (24)—"carriers" of the old and "spinners" of the new. Out of the cocoon of the old "husk of self," the poet spins a new mythos that contains both continuity and metamorphosis.[7]

NOTES

[1] On religious experience, see Freud, *Civilization* 11–15. On the daughter's rejection of her mother, see his "Femininity." On Freud's rationalist purpose in therapy, see particularly his *An Outline* 62–63.

[2] 30 July 1941 letter to Viola Jordan. This correspondence, spanning some twenty-odd years, is part of the H. D. collection at the Beinecke Library, Yale University.

[3] Freud's formula also equated H. D.'s father with mythic male figures whose presence in H. D.'s poetry is also very real. But H. D.'s special emphasis on the Goddess is a very clear development of Freud's belief that the child's (and humanity's) attachment to the mother is primal.

[4] Helen also discovers the dialectical relationships of gods and goddesses, war and love, herself and Achilles. H. D.'s mythology of the Goddess is carefully interwoven with her search for father symbols and ultimately an androgynous One. For further discussion, see my "Creating a Women's Mythology."

[5] For a different view, see Vincent Quinn's discussion of the birth metaphor in "H. D.'s 'Hermetic Definition.' "

[6] A fortune-teller predicts that Helen Wolle will have a gifted child, but H. D.'s mother comments several times how strange it is that the prediction did not come true. Bypassing her own daughter, Helen's mother recognizes the "gift" in Hilda and passes on to her granddaughter the secrets of Moravian mysticism.

[7] A different version of this essay was delivered at MLA (1977) at Catherine F. Smith's Special Session on Epiphany, Apocalypse, and Vision in Writing by British and American Women. I am greatly indebted to Smith's exciting work on women and mysticism.

~ 1979 ~

Dancing through the Minefield: Some Observations on the Theory, Practice, and Politics of a Feminist Literary Criticism

ANNETTE KOLODNY

HAD ANYONE THE prescience, ten years ago, to pose the question of defining a "feminist" literary criticism, she might have been told, in the wake of Mary Ellmann's *Thinking about Women*, that it involved exposing the sexual stereotyping of women in both our literature and our literary criticism and, as well, demonstrating the inadequacy of established critical schools and methods to deal fairly or sensitively with works written by women. In broad outline, such a prediction would have stood well the test of time, and, in fact, Ellmann's book continues to be widely read and to point us in useful directions. What could not have been anticipated in 1969, however, was the catalyzing force of an ideology that, for many of us, helped to bridge the gap between the world as we found it and the world as we wanted it to be. For those of us who studied literature, a previously unspoken sense of exclusion from authorship, and a painfully personal distress at discovering whores, bitches, muses, and heroines dead in childbirth where we had once hoped to discover ourselves, could—for the first time—begin to be understood as more than "a set of disconnected, unrealized private emotions" (Geertz, "Ideology" 232). With a renewed courage to make public our otherwise private discontents, we saw that what had once been "felt individually as personal insecurity" came at last to be "viewed collectively as structural inconsistency" within the very disciplines we studied (Geertz, "Ideology" 204). Following unflinchingly the full implications of Ellmann's percipient observations, and emboldened by the liberating energy of feminist ideology—in all its various forms and guises—feminist criticism very quickly moved beyond merely "expos[ing] sexism in one work of literature after another" (Robinson, "Cultural Criticism" 51) and promised, instead, that we might at last "begin to record new choices in a new literary history" (Showalter,

Literature 36). So powerful was that impulse that we experienced it, along with Adrienne Rich, as much "more than a chapter in cultural history": it became, rather, "an act of survival" ("When We Dead" 90). What was at stake was not so much literature or criticism as such, but the historical, social, and ethical consequences of women's participation in, or exclusion from, either enterprise.

The pace of inquiry these last ten years has been fast and furious—especially after Kate Millett's 1970 analysis of the sexual politics of literature added a note of urgency to what had earlier been Ellmann's sardonic anger—while the diversity of that inquiry easily outstripped all efforts to define feminist literary criticism as either a coherent system or a unified set of methodologies. Under its wide umbrella, everything has been thrown into question: our established canons, our aesthetic criteria, our interpretative strategies, our reading habits, and, most of all, ourselves as critics and as teachers. To delineate its full scope would require nothing less than a book—a book that would be outdated even as it was being composed. For the sake of brevity, therefore, let me attempt only a summary outline.

Perhaps the most obvious success of this new scholarship has been the return to circulation of previously lost or otherwise ignored works by women writers. Following fast upon the initial success of the Feminist Press in reissuing gems such as Rebecca Harding Davis's 1861 novella *Life in the Iron Mills*, and Charlotte Perkins Gilman's 1892 *The Yellow Wallpaper*, published in 1972 and 1973, respectively, commercial trade and reprint houses vied with one another in the reprinting of anthologies of lost texts and, in some cases, in the reprinting of whole series. For those of us in American literature especially, the phenomenon promised a radical reshaping of our concepts of literary history and, at the very least, a new chapter in understanding the development of women's literary traditions. So commercially successful were these reprintings, and so attuned were the reprint houses to the political attitudes of the audiences for which they were offered, that many of us found ourselves wooed to compose critical introductions, which would find in the pages of nineteenth-century domestic and sentimental fictions some signs of either muted rebellions or overt radicalism, in anticipation of the current wave of "new feminism." In rereading with our students these previously lost works, we inevitably raised perplexing questions as to the reasons for their disappearance from the canons of "major works," and we worried over the aesthetic and critical criteria by which they had been accorded diminished status.

This increased availability of works by women writers led, of course, to an increased interest in what elements, if any, might comprise some sort of unity or connection among them. The possibility that women had developed either a unique or at least a related tradition of their own especially intrigued those of us who specialized in one national literature or another, or in historical periods. Nina Baym's recent *Woman's Fiction: A Guide to Novels by and about Women in America, 1820–1870* demonstrates the Americanists' penchant for examining what were once the best-sellers of their day, the ranks of the popular-fiction writers, among which women took a dominant place throughout the nineteenth century, while the feminist studies of British literature emphasized instead the wealth of women writers who have been regarded as worthy of canonization. Not so much building upon one another's work as clarifying, successively, the parameters of the questions to be posed, Sydney Janet Kaplan, Ellen Moers, Patricia Meyer Spacks, and Elaine Showalter, among many others, concentrated their energies on delineating an internally consistent "body of work" by women that might stand as a female countertradition. For Kaplan, in 1975, this entailed examining women writers' various attempts to portray feminine consciousness and self-consciousness not as a psychological category but as a stylistic or rhetorical device.[1] That same year, arguing essentially that literature publicizes the private, Spacks placed her consideration of a "female imagination" within social and historical frames, to conclude that, "for readily discernible historical reasons women have characteristically concerned themselves with matters more or less peripheral to male concerns," and she attributed to this fact an inevitable difference in the literary emphases and subject matters of female and male writers (*Female Imagination* 6). The next year, Moers's *Literary Women: The Great Writers* focused on the pathways of literary influence that linked the English novel in the hands of women. And, finally, in 1977, Showalter took up the matter of a "female literary tradition in the English novel from the generation of the Brontës to the present day" by arguing that, because women in general constitute a kind of "subculture within the framework of a larger society," the work of women writers, in particular, would thereby demonstrate a unity of "values, conventions, experiences, and behaviors impinging on each individual" as she found her sources of "self-expression relative to a dominant [and, by implication, male] society" (*Literature* 11).

At the same time that women writers were being reconsidered and reread, male writers were similarly subjected to a new feminist scrutiny. The continuing result—to put ten years of difficult analysis into a single sentence—has been nothing less than an acute attentiveness to the ways in which certain power relations—usually those in which males wield various forms of influence over females—are inscribed in the texts (both literary and critical) that we have inherited, not merely as subject matter but as the unquestioned, often unacknowledged *given* of the culture. Even more important than the new interpretations of individual texts are the probings into the consequences (for women) of the conventions that inform those texts. For example, in surveying selected nineteenth- and early twentieth-century British novels which employ what she calls "the two-suitors convention," Jean E. Kennard sought to understand why and how the structural demands of the convention, even in the hands of women writers, inevitably work to imply "the inferiority and necessary subordination of women" (164). Her 1978 study *Victims of Convention* points out that the symbolic nature of the marriage which conventionally concludes such novels "indicates the adjustment of the protagonist to society's values, a condition which is equated with her maturity." Kennard's concern, however, is with the fact that the structural demands of the form too often sacrifice precisely those "virtues of independence and individuality," or, in other words, the very "qualities we have been invited to admire in" the heroines (18; 14). Kennard appropriately cautions us against drawing from her work any simplistically reductive thesis about the mimetic relations between art and life. Her approach nonetheless suggests that what is important about a fiction is not whether it ends in a death or a marriage but what the symbolic demands of that particular conventional ending imply about the values and beliefs of the world that engendered it.

Her work thus participates in a growing emphasis in feminist literary study on the fact of literature as a social institution, embedded not only within its own literary traditions but also within the particular physical and mental artifacts of the society from which it comes. Adumbrating Millett's 1970 decision to anchor her "literary reflections" to a preceding analysis of the historical, social, and economic contexts of sexual politics (235–61), more recent work—most notably Lillian Robinson's—begins with the premise that the process of artistic creation "consists not of ghostly happenings in the head but of a matching of the states and processes of symbolic models against the states and processes of the wider world" (Geertz, "Ideology" 214). The power relations inscribed in the form of conventions within our literary inheritance, these critics argue, reify the encodings of those same power relations in the culture at large. And the critical examination of rhetorical codes becomes, in their hands, the pursuit of ideological codes, because both embody either value systems or the dialectic of competition between value systems. More often than not, these critics also insist upon examining not only the mirroring of life in art but also the normative impact of art on life. Addressing herself to the popular art available to working-class women, for example, Robinson is interested in understanding not only "the forms it uses" but, more important, "the myths it creates, the influence it exerts" ("Criticism—and Self-Criticism" 67). "The way art helps people to order, interpret, mythologize, or dispose of their own experience," she declares, may be "complex and often ambiguous, but it is not impossible to define" ("Criticism: Who Needs It?" 80).

Whether its focus be upon the material or the imaginative contexts of literary invention; single texts or entire canons; the relations between authors, genres, or historical circumstances; lost authors or well-known names, the variety and diversity of all feminist literary criticism finally coheres in its stance of almost defensive rereading. What Adrienne Rich had earlier called "re-vision"—that is, "the act of looking back, of seeing with fresh eyes, of entering an old text from a new critical direction" ("When We Dead" 90)—took on a more actively self-protective coloration in 1978, when Judith Fetterley called upon the woman reader to learn to "resist" the sexist designs a text might make upon her: asking her to identify against herself, so to speak, by manipulating her sympathies on behalf of male heroes, but against female shrew or bitch characters. Underpinning a great deal of this critical rereading has been the not-unexpected alliance between feminist literary study and feminist studies in linguistics and language acquisition. Tillie Olsen's commonsense observation of the danger of "perpetuating—by continued usage—entrenched, centuries-old oppressive power realities, early-on incorporated into language" (*Silences* 239–40), has been given substantive analysis in the writings of feminists who study "language as a symbolic system closely tied to a patriarchal social structure." Taken together, their work demonstrates "the importance of language in establishing, reflecting, and maintaining an asymmetrical relationship between women and men'' (Kramer et al. 646).

To consider what this implies for the fate of women who essay the craft of language is to ascertain, perhaps for the first time, the real dilemma of the poet who finds her most cherished private experience ''hedged by taboos, mined with false-namings.''[2] It also explains the dilemma of the male reader who, in opening the pages of a woman's book, finds himself entering a strange and unfamiliar world of symbolic significance. For if, as Nelly Furman insists, neither language use nor language acquisition is ''gender-neutral'' but is instead ''imbued with our sex-inflected cultural values''(184), and if, additionally, reading is a process of ''sorting out the structures of signification'' (Geertz, ''Thick Description'') in any text, then male readers who find themselves outside of and unfamiliar with the symbolic systems that constitute female experience in women's writings will necessarily dismiss those systems as undecipherable, meaningless, or trivial. And male professors will find no reason to include such works in the canons of ''major authors.'' At the same time, women writers, coming into a tradition of literary language and conventional forms already appropriated, for centuries, to the purposes of male expression, will be forced virtually to ''wrestle'' with that language in an effort ''to remake it as a language adequate to our conceptual processes'' (Stanley and Robbins 63). To all of this, feminists concerned with the politics of language and style have been acutely attentive. ''Language conceals an invincible adversary,'' observes the French critic Hélène Cixous, ''because it's the language of men and their grammar'' (887). But equally insistent, as in the work of Sandra M. Gilbert and Susan Gubar, has been the understanding of the need for *all* readers—male and female alike—to learn to penetrate the otherwise unfamiliar universes of symbolic action that comprise women's writings, past and present.[3]

To have attempted so many difficult questions and to have accomplished so much—even acknowledging the inevitable false starts, overlapping, and repetition—in so short a time, should certainly have secured feminist literary criticism an honored berth on that ongoing intellectual journey which we loosely term in academia ''critical analysis.'' Instead of being welcomed onto the train, however, we've been forced to negotiate a minefield. The very energy and diversity of our enterprise have rendered us vulnerable to attack on the grounds that we lack both definition and coherence, while our particular attentiveness to the ways in which literature encodes and disseminates cultural value systems calls down upon us imprecations echoing those heaped upon the Marxist critics of an earlier generation. If we are scholars dedicated to rediscovering a lost body of writings by women, then our finds are questioned on aesthetic grounds. And if we are critics, determined to practice revisionist readings, it is claimed that our focus is too narrow and our results are only distortions or, worse still, polemical misreadings.

The very vehemence of the outcry, coupled with our total dismissal in some quarters,[4] suggests not our deficiencies, however, but the potential magnitude of our challenge. For what we are asking be scrutinized are nothing less than shared cultural assumptions so deeply rooted and so long ingrained that, for the most part, our critical colleagues have ceased to recognize them as such. In other words, what is really being bewailed in the claims that we distort texts or threaten the disappearance of the great Western literary tradition itself[5] is not so much the disappearance of either text or tradition but, instead, the eclipse of that particular *form* of the text, and that particular *shape* of the canon, which previously reified male readers' sense of power and significance in the world. Analogously, by asking whether, as readers, we ought to be "really satisfied by the marriage of Dorothea Brooke to Will Ladislaw? of Shirley Keeldar to Louis Moore?" or whether, as Kennard suggests, we must reckon with the ways in which "the qualities we have been invited to admire in these heroines [have] been sacrificed to structural neatness" (14), is to raise difficult and profoundly perplexing questions about the ethical implications of our otherwise unquestioned aesthetic pleasures. It is, after all, an imposition of high order to ask the viewer to attend to Ophelia's sufferings in a scene where, before, he'd always so comfortably kept his eye fixed firmly on Hamlet. To understand all this, then, as the real nature of the challenge we have offered and, in consequence, as the motivation for the often overt hostility we've aroused should help us learn to negotiate the minefield, if not with grace, then with at least a clearer comprehension of its underlying patterns.

The ways in which objections to our work are usually posed, of course, serve to obscure their deeper motivations. But this may, in part, be due to our own reticence at taking full responsibility for the truly radicalizing premises that lie at the theoretical core of all we have so far accomplished. It may be time, therefore, to redirect discussion, forcing our adversaries to deal with the substantive issues and pushing ourselves into a clearer articulation of what, in fact, we are about. Up until now, I fear, we have only piecemeal dealt with the difficulties inherent in challenging the authority of established canons and then justifying the excellence of women's traditions, sometimes in accord with standards to which they have no intrinsic relation.

At the very point at which we must perforce enter the discourse—that is, claiming excellence or importance for our "finds"—all discussion has already, we discover, long ago been closed. "If Kate Chopin were *really* worth reading," an Oxford-trained colleague once assured me, "she'd have lasted—like Shakespeare"; and he then proceeded to vote against the English department's crediting a women's studies seminar I was offering in American women writers. The canon, for him, conferred excellence; Chopin's exclusion demonstrated only her lesser worth. As far as he was concerned, I could no more justify giving English department credit for the study of Chopin than I could dare publicly to question Shakespeare's genius. Through hindsight, I've now come to view that discussion as not only having posed fruitless oppositions but also as having entirely evaded the much more profound problem lurking just beneath the surface of our disagreement. That is, that the fact of canonization puts any work beyond questions of establishing its merit and, instead, invites students to offer only increasingly more ingenious readings and interpretations, the purpose of which is to validate the greatness already imputed by canonization.

Had I only understood it for what it was then, into this circular and self-serving set of assumptions I might have interjected some statement of my right to question why *any* text is revered and my need to know what it tells us about "how we live, how we have been living, how we have been led to imagine ourselves, [and] how our language has trapped as well as liberated us" (Rich, "When We Dead" 90). The very fact of our critical training within the structures imposed by an established canon of major works and authors, however, repeatedly deflects us from such questions. Instead, we find ourselves endlessly responding to the riposte that the overwhelmingly male presence among canonical authors was only an accident of history—and never intentionally sexist—coupled with claims to the "obvious" aesthetic merit of those canonized texts. It is, as I say, a fruitless exchange, serving more to obscure than to expose the territory being protected and dragging us, again and again, through the minefield.

It is my contention that current hostilities might be transformed into a true dialogue with our critics if we at last made explicit what appear, to this observer, to constitute the three crucial propositions to which our special interests inevitably give rise. They are, moreover, propositions which, if handled with care and intelligence, could breathe new life into now moribund areas of our profession: literary history (and, with that, the historicity of literature) is a fiction; insofar as we are taught how to read, what we engage are not texts but paradigms; and, finally, since the grounds upon which we assign aesthetic value to texts are never infallible, unchangeable, or universal, we must reexamine not only our aesthetics but, as well, the inherent biases and assumptions informing the critical methods which (in part) shape our aesthetic responses. For the sake of brevity, I won't attempt to offer the full arguments for each but, rather, only sufficient elaboration to demonstrate what I see as their intrinsic relation to the potential scope of and present challenge implied by feminist literary study.

1. *Literary history (and, with that, the historicity of literature) is a fiction.* To begin with, an established canon functions as a model by which to chart the continuities and discontinuities of, as well as the influences upon and the interconnections between, works, genres, and authors. That model we tend to forget, however, is of our own making. It will take a very different shape, and explain its inclusions and exclusions in very different ways, if the reigning critical ideology believes that new literary forms result from some kind of ongoing internal dialectic within preexisting styles and traditions or if, by contrast, the ideology declares that literary change is dependent upon societal development and thereby determined by upheavals in the social and economic organization of the culture at large.[6] Indeed, whenever in the previous century of English and American literary scholarship one alternative replaced the other, we saw dramatic alterations in canonical "wisdom."

This suggests, then, that our sense of a "literary history" and, by extension, our confidence in a "historical" canon is rooted not so much in any definitive understanding of the past as it is in our need to call up and utilize the past on behalf of a better understanding of the present. Thus, to paraphrase David Couzens Hoy, it becomes "necessary to point out that the understanding of art and literature is such an essential aspect of the present's self-understanding that this self-understanding conditions what even gets taken'' as comprising that artistic and literary past. To quote Hoy fully, ''this continual reinterpretation of the past goes hand in hand with the continual reinterpretation by the present of itself'' (166–67). In our own time, uncertain as to which, if any, model truly accounts for our canonical choices or accurately explains literary history, and pressured further by the feminists' call for some justification of the criteria by which women's writings were largely excluded from both that canon and history, we suffer what Harold Bloom has called ''a remarkable dimming'' of ''our mutual sense of canonical standards'' (*Map* 36).

Into this apparent impasse, feminist literary theorists implicitly introduce the observation that our choices and evaluations of current literature have the effect either of solidifying or of reshaping our sense of the past. The authority of any established canon, after all, is reified by our perception that current work seems to grow, almost inevitably, out of it (even in opposition or rebellion), and is called into question when what we read appears to have little or no relation to what we recognize as coming before. Were the larger critical community to begin to seriously attend to the recent outpouring of fine literature by women, this would surely be accompanied by a concomitant researching of the past, by literary historians, in order to account for the present phenomenon. In that process, literary history would itself be altered: works by seventeenth-, eighteenth-, or nineteenth-century women, to which we had not previously attended, might be given new importance as ''precursors'' or as prior influences upon present-day authors, while selected male writers might also be granted new prominence as figures whom the women today, or even yesterday, needed to reject. I am arguing, in other words, that the choices we make in the present inevitably alter our sense of the past that led to them.

Related to this is the feminist challenge to that patently mendacious critical fallacy that we read the ''classics'' in order to reconstruct the past ''the way it really was'' and that we read Shakespeare and Milton in order to apprehend the meanings they intended. Short of time machines or miraculous resurrections, there is simply no way to know, precisely or surely, what really was, what Homer intended when he sang, or Milton when he dictated. Critics more acute than I have already pointed to the impossibility of grounding a reading in the imputation of authorial intention, because the further removed the author is from us, so too must be her or his systems of knowledge and belief, points of view, and structures of vision (artistic and otherwise).[7] (I omit here the difficulty in finally either proving or disproving the imputation of intentionality because, inescapably, the only appropriate authority is unavailable: deceased.) What we have really come to mean when we speak of competence in reading historical texts, therefore, is the ability to recognize literary conventions which have survived through time—so as to remain operational in the mind of the reader—and, where these are lacking, the ability to translate (or perhaps transform?) the text's ciphers into more current and recognizable shapes. But we never really reconstruct the past in its own terms. What we gain when we read the ''classics,'' then, is neither Homer's Greece nor George Eliot's England *as they knew it* but, rather, an approximation of an already fictively imputed past made available, through our interpretive strategies, for present concerns. Only by understanding this can we put to rest that recurrent delusion that the "continuing relevance" of the classics serves as "testimony to perennial features of human experience" (Altieri 90). The only "perennial feature" to which our ability to read and reread texts written in previous centuries testifies is our inventiveness—in the sense that all of literary history is a fiction which we daily re-create as we reread it. What distinguishes feminists in this regard is their desire to alter and extend what we take as historically relevant from out of that vast storehouse of our literary inheritance and, further, feminists' recognition of the storehouse for what it really is: a resource for remodeling our literary history, past, present, and future.

2. *Insofar as we are taught how to read, what we engage are not texts but paradigms.* To pursue the logical consequences of the first proposition leads, however uncomfortably, to the conclusion that we appropriate meaning from a text according to what we need (or desire) or, in other words, according to the critical assumptions or predispositions (conscious or not) that we bring to it. And we appropriate different meanings, or report different gleanings, at different times—even from the same text—according to our changed assumptions, circumstances, and requirements. This, in essence, constitutes the heart of the second proposition. For, insofar as literature is itself a social institution, so, too, reading is a highly socialized—or learned—activity. What makes it so exciting, of course, is that it can be constantly relearned and refined, so as to provide either an individual or an entire reading community, over time, with infinite variations of the same text. It *can* provide that, but, I must add, too often it does not. Frequently our reading habits become fixed, so that each successive reading experience functions, in effect, normatively, with one particular kind of novel stylizing our expectations of those to follow, the stylistic devices of any favorite author (or group of authors) alerting us to the presence or absence of those devices in the works of others, and so on. "Once one has read his first poem," Murray Krieger has observed, "he turns to his second and to the others that will follow thereafter with an increasing series of preconceptions about the sort of activity in which he is indulging. In matters of literary experience, as in other experiences," Krieger concludes, "one is a virgin but once" (6).

For most readers, this is a fairly unconscious process, and, not unnaturally, what we are taught to read well and with pleasure, when we are young, predisposes us to certain specific kinds of adult reading tastes. For the professional literary critic, the process may be no different, but it is at least more conscious. Graduate schools, at their best, are training grounds for competing interpretive paradigms or reading techniques: affective stylistics, structuralism, and semiotic analysis, to name only a few of the more recent entries. The delight we learn to take in the mastery of these interpretive strategies is then often mistakenly construed as our delight in reading specific texts, especially in the case of works that would otherwise be unavailable or even offensive to us. In my own graduate career, for example, with superb teachers to guide me, I learned to take great pleasure in *Paradise Lost*, even though, as both a Jew and a feminist, I can subscribe neither to its theology nor to its hierarchy of sexual valuation. If, within its own terms (as I have been taught to understand them), the text manipulates my sensibilities and moves me to pleasure—as I will affirm it does—then, at least in part, that must be because, in spite of my real-world alienation from many of its basic tenets, I have been able to enter that text through interpretive strategies which allow me to displace less comfortable observations with others to which I have been taught pleasurably to attend. Though some of my teachers may have called this process "learning to read the text properly," I have now come to see it as learning to effectively manipulate the critical strategies which they taught me so well. Knowing, for example, the poem's debt to epic conventions, I am able to discover in it echoes and reworkings of both lines and situations from Vergil and Homer; placing it within the ongoing Christian debate between Good and Evil, I comprehend both the philosophic and the stylistic significance of Satan's ornate rhetoric as compared to God's majestic simplicity in book 3. But, in each case, an interpretive model, already assumed, had guided my discovery of the evidence for it (see Fish, "Normal Circumstances" 627–28).

When we consider the implications of these observations for the processes of canon formation and for the assignment of aesthetic value, we find ourselves locked in a chicken-and-egg dilemma, unable easily to distinguish as primary the importance of *what* we read as opposed to *how* we have learned to read it. For, simply put, we read well, and with pleasure, what we already know how to read; and what we know how to read is to a large extent dependent upon what we have already read (works from which we've developed our expectations and learned our interpretive strategies). What we then choose to read—and, by extension, teach and thereby "canonize"—usually follows upon our previous reading. Radical breaks are tiring, demanding, uncomfortable, and sometimes wholly beyond our comprehension.

Though the argument is not usually couched in precisely these terms, a considerable segment of the most recent feminist rereadings of women writers allows the conclusion that, where those authors have dropped out of sight, the reason may be due not to any lack of merit in the work but, instead, to an incapacity of predominantly male readers to properly interpret and appreciate women's texts—due, in large part, to a lack of prior acquaintance. The fictions which women compose about the worlds they inhabit may owe a debt to prior, influential works by other women or, simply enough, to the daily experience of the writer herself or, more usually, to some combination of the two. The reader coming upon such fiction, with knowledge of neither its informing literary traditions nor its real-world contexts, will thereby find himself hard-pressed, though he may recognize the words on the page, to competently decipher its intended meanings. And this is what makes the recent studies by Spacks, Moers, Showalter, Gilbert and Gubar, and others so crucial. For, by attempting to delineate the connections and interrelations that make for a female literary tradition, they provide us invaluable aids for recognizing and understanding the unique literary traditions and sex-related contexts out of which women write.

The (usually male) reader who, both by experience and by reading, has never made acquaintance with those contexts—historically, the lying-in room, the parlor, the nursery, the kitchen, the laundry, and so on—will necessarily lack the capacity to fully interpret the dialogue or action embedded therein; for, as every good novelist knows, the meaning of any character's action or statement is inescapably a function of the specific situation in which it is embedded (Fish, "Normal Circumstances" 643). Virginia Woolf therefore quite properly anticipated the male reader's disposition to write off what he could not understand, abandoning women's writings as offering "not merely a difference of view, but a view that is weak, or trivial, or sentimental because it differs from his own." In her 1929 essay "Women and Fiction," Woolf grappled most obviously with the ways in which male writers and male subject matter had already preempted the language of literature. Yet she was also tacitly commenting on the problem of (male) audience and conventional reading expectations when she speculated that the woman writer might well "find that she is perpetually wishing to alter the established values [in literature]—to make serious what appears insignificant to a man, and trivial what is to him important" (81; 1958 ed.). "The 'competence' necessary for understanding [a] literary message . . . depends upon a great number of codices," after all; as Cesare Segre has pointed out, to be competent, a reader must either share or at least be familiar with, "in addition to the code of language . . . the codes of custom, of society, and of conceptions of the world" (272–73) (what Woolf meant by "values"). Males ignorant of women's "values" or conceptions of the world will necessarily, thereby, be poor readers of works that in any sense recapitulate their codes.

The problem is further exacerbated when the language of the literary text is largely dependent upon figuration. For it can be argued, as Ted Cohen has shown, that while, "in general, and with some obvious qualifications . . . all literal use of language is accessible to all whose language it is . . . figurative use can be inaccessible to all but those who share information about one another's knowledge, beliefs, intentions, and attitudes" (9). There was nothing fortuitous, for example, in Charlotte Perkins Gilman's decision to situate the progressive mental breakdown and increasing incapacity of the protagonist of *The Yellow Wallpaper* in an upstairs room that had once served as a nursery (with barred windows, no less). But the reader unacquainted with the ways in which women traditionally inhabited a household might not have taken the initial description of the setting as semantically relevant; and the progressive infantilization of the adult protagonist would thereby lose some of its symbolic implications. Analogously, the contemporary poet who declares, along with Adrienne Rich, the need for "a whole new poetry beginning here" is acknowledging that the materials available for symbolization and figuration from women's contexts will necessarily differ from those that men have traditionally utilized:

> Vision begins to happen in such a life
> as if a woman quietly walked away
> from the argument and jargon in a room
> and sitting down in the kitchen, began turning in her lap
> bits of yarn, calico and velvet scraps,
>
> . . . .

pulling the tenets of a life together
with no mere will to mastery,
only care for the many-lived, unending
forms in which she finds herself.
(''Transcendental Etude'' 76–77)

What, then, is the fate of the woman writer whose competent reading community is composed only of members of her own sex? And what, then, the response of the male critic who, on first looking into Virginia Woolf or Doris Lessing, finds all of the interpretive strategies at his command inadequate to a full and pleasurable deciphering of their pages? Historically, the result has been the diminished status of women's products and their consequent absence from major canons. Nowadays, however, by pointing out that the act of ''interpreting language is no more sexually neutral than language use or the language system itself,'' feminist students of language, like Nelly Furman, help us better understand the crucial linkage between our gender and our interpretive, or reading, strategies. Insisting upon ''the contribution of the . . . reader [in] the active attribution of significance to formal signifiers'' (184), Furman and others promise to shake us all—female and male alike—out of our canonized and conventional aesthetic assumptions.

3. *Since the grounds upon which we assign aesthetic value to texts are never infallible, unchangeable, or universal, we must reexamine not only our aesthetics but, as well, the inherent biases and assumptions informing the critical methods which (in part) shape our aesthetic responses*. I am, on the one hand, arguing that men will be better readers, or appreciators, of women's books when they have read more of them (as women have always been taught to become astute readers of men's texts). On the other hand, it will be noted, the emphasis of my remarks shifts the act of critical judgment from assigning aesthetic valuations to texts and directs it, instead, to ascertaining the adequacy of any interpretive paradigm to a full reading of both female and male writing. My third proposition—and, I admit, perhaps the most controversial—thus calls into question that recurrent tendency in criticism to establish norms for the evaluation of literary works when we might better serve the cause of literature by developing standards for evaluating the adequacy of our critical methods.[8] This does not mean that I wish to discard aesthetic valuation. The choice, as I see it, is not between retaining or discarding aesthetic values; rather, the choice is between having some awareness of what constitutes (at least in part) the bases of our aesthetic responses and going without such an awareness. For, it is my view that insofar as aesthetic responsiveness continues to be an integral aspect of our human response system—in part spontaneous, in part learned and educated—we will inevitably develop theories to help explain, formalize, or even initiate those responses.

In challenging the adequacy of received critical opinion or the imputed excellence of established canons, feminist literary critics are essentially seeking to discover how aesthetic value is assigned in the first place, where it resides (in the text or in the reader), and, most important, what validity may really be claimed by our aesthetic "judgments." What ends do those judgments serve, the feminist asks; and what conceptions of the world or ideological stances do they (even if unwittingly) help to perpetuate? In so doing, she points out, among other things, that any response labeled "aesthetic" may as easily designate some immediately experienced moment or event as it may designate a species of nostalgia, a yearning for the components of a simpler past, when the world seemed known or at least understandable. Thus the value accorded an opera or a Shakespeare play may well reside in the viewer's immediate viewing pleasure, or it may reside in the play's nostalgic evocation of a once-comprehensible and ordered world. At the same time, the feminist confronts, for example, the reader who simply cannot entertain the possibility that women's worlds are symbolically rich, the reader who, like the male characters in Susan Glaspell's 1917 short story "A Jury of Her Peers," has already assumed the innate "insignificance of kitchen things."[9] Such a reader, she knows, will prove himself unable to assign significance to fictions that attend to "kitchen things" and will, instead, judge such fictions as trivial and as aesthetically wanting. For her to take useful issue with such a reader, she must make clear that what appears to be a dispute about aesthetic merit is, in reality, a dispute about the *contexts of judgment*, and what is at issue, then, is the adequacy of the prior assumptions and reading habits brought to bear on the text. To put it bluntly: we have had enough pronouncements of aesthetic valuation for a time; it is now our task to evaluate the imputed norms and normative reading patterns that, in part, led to those pronouncements.

By and large, I think I've made my point. Only to clarify it do I add this coda: when feminists turn their attention to the works of male authors which have traditionally been accorded high aesthetic value and, where warranted, follow Olsen's advice that we assert our "right to say: this is surface, this falsifies reality, this degrades" (45), such statements do not necessarily mean that we will end up with a diminished canon. To question the source of the aesthetic pleasures we've gained from reading Spenser, Shakespeare, Milton, and so on, does not imply that we must deny those pleasures. It means only that aesthetic response is once more invested with epistemological, ethical, and moral concerns. It means, in other words, that readings of *Paradise Lost* which analyze its complex hierarchal structures but fail to note the implications of gender within that hierarchy; or which insist upon the inherent (or even inspired) perfection of Milton's figurative language but fail to note the consequences, for Eve, of her specifically gender-marked weakness, which, like the flowers to which she attends, requires "propping up"; or which concentrate on the poem's thematic reworking of classical notions of martial and epic prowess into Christian (moral) heroism but fail to note that Eve is stylistically edited out of that process—all such readings, however useful, will no longer be deemed wholly adequate. The pleasures we had earlier learned to take in the poem will not be diminished thereby, but they will become part of an altered reading attentiveness.

These three propositions I believe to be at the theoretical core of most current feminist literary criticism, whether acknowledged as such or not. If I am correct in this, then that criticism represents more than a profoundly skeptical stance toward all other preexisting and contemporaneous schools and methods, and more than an impassioned demand that the variety and variability of women's literary expression be taken into full account, rather than written off as caprice and exception, the irregularity in an otherwise regular design. It represents that locus in literary study where, in unceasing effort, female self-consciousness turns in upon itself, attempting to grasp the deepest conditions of its own unique and multiplicitous realities, in the hope, eventually, of altering the very forms through which the culture perceives, expresses, and knows itself. For, if what the larger women's movement looks for in the future is a transformation of the structures of primarily male power which now order our society, then the feminist literary critic demands that we understand the ways in which those structures have been—and continue to be—reified by our literature and by our literary criticism. Thus, along with other "radical" critics and critical schools, though our focus remains the power of the word to both structure and mirror human experience, our overriding commitment is to a radical alteration—an improvement, we hope—in the nature of that experience.

What distinguishes our work from those similarly oriented "social consciousness" critiques, it is said, is its lack of systematic coherence. Pitted against, for example, psychoanalytic or Marxist readings, which owe a decisive share of their persuasiveness to their apparent internal consistency as a system, the aggregate of feminist literary criticism appears woefully deficient in system and painfully lacking in program. It is, in fact, from all quarters the most telling defect alleged against us, the most explosive threat in the minefield. And my own earlier observation that, as of 1976, feminist literary criticism appeared "more like a set of interchangeable strategies than any coherent school or shared goal orientation" has been taken by some as an indictment, by others as a statement of impatience. Neither was intended. I felt then, as I do now, that this would "prove both its strength *and* its weakness" ("Literary Criticism" 420), in the sense that the apparent disarray would leave us vulnerable to the kind of objection I've just alluded to, while the fact of our diversity would finally place us securely where, all along, we should have been: camped out, on the far side of the minefield, with the other pluralists and pluralisms.

In our heart of hearts, of course, most critics are really structuralists (whether or not they accept the label) because what we are seeking are patterns (or structures) that can order and explain the otherwise inchoate; thus we invent, or believe we discover, relational patternings in the texts we read which promise transcendence from difficulty and perplexity to clarity and coherence. But, as I've tried to argue in these pages, to the imputed "truth" or "accuracy" of these findings, the feminist must oppose the painfully obvious truism that what is attended to in a literary work, and hence what is reported about it, is often determined not so much by the work itself as by the critical technique or aesthetic criteria through which it is filtered or, rather, read and decoded. All the feminist is asserting, then, is her own equivalent right to liberate new (and perhaps different) significances from these same texts; and, at the same time, her right to choose which features of a text she takes as relevant because she is, after all, asking new and different questions of it. In the process, she claims neither definitiveness nor structural completeness for her different readings and reading systems, but only their usefulness in recognizing the particular achievements of woman-as-author and their applicability in conscientiously decoding woman-as-sign.

That these alternate foci of critical attentiveness will render alternate readings or interpretations of the same text—even among feminists—should be no cause for alarm. Such developments illustrate only the pluralist contention that, "in approaching a text of any complexity . . . the reader must choose to emphasize certain aspects which seem to him crucial" and that, "in fact, the variety of readings which we have for many works is a function of the selection of crucial aspects made by the variety of readers." Robert Scholes, from whom I've been quoting, goes so far as to assert that "there is no single 'right' reading for any complex literary work," and, following the Russian formalist school, he observes that "we do not speak of readings that are simply true or false, but of readings that are more or less rich, strategies that are more or less appropriate" (144–45).[10] Because those who share the term "feminist" nonetheless practice a diversity of critical strategies, leading, in some cases, to quite different readings, we must acknowledge among ourselves that sister critics, "having chosen to tell a different story, may in their interpretation identify different aspects of the meanings conveyed by the same passage" (Abrams 427).[11]

Adopting a "pluralist" label does not mean, however, that we cease to disagree; it means only that we entertain the possibility that different readings, even of the same text, may be differently useful, even illuminating, within different contexts of inquiry. It means, in effect, that we enter a dialectical process of examining, testing, even trying out the contexts—be they prior critical assumptions or explicitly stated ideological stances (or some combination of the two)—that led to the disparate readings. Not all will be equally acceptable to every one of us, of course, and even those prior assumptions or ideologies that are acceptable may call for further refinement and/or clarification. But, at the very least, because we will have grappled with the assumptions that led to it, we will be better able to articulate *why* we find a particular reading or interpretation adequate or inadequate. This kind of dialectical process, moreover, not only makes us more fully aware of what criticism is, and how it functions; it also gives us access to its future possibilities, making us conscious, as R. P. Blackmur put it, "of what we have done," "of what can be done next, or done again" (171),[12] or, I would add, of what can be done differently. To put it still another way: just because we will no longer tolerate the specifically sexist omissions and oversights of earlier critical schools and methods does not mean that, in their stead, we must establish our own "party line."

In my view, our purpose is not and should not be the formulation of any single reading method or potentially procrustean set of critical procedures nor, even less, the generation of prescriptive categories for some dreamed-of nonsexist literary canon.[13] Instead, as I see it, our task is to initiate nothing less than a playful pluralism, responsive to the possibilities of multiple critical schools and methods, but captive of none, recognizing that the many tools needed for our analysis will necessarily be largely inherited and only partly of our own making. Only by employing a plurality of methods will we protect ourselves from the temptation of so oversimplifying any text—and especially those particularly offensive to us—that we render ourselves unresponsive to what Scholes has called "its various systems of meaning and their interaction" (151–52). Any text we deem worthy of our critical attention is usually, after all, a locus of many and varied kinds of (personal, thematic, stylistic, structural, rhetorical, etc.) relationships. So whether we tend to treat a text as a *mimesis*, in which words are taken to be re-creating or representing viable worlds; or whether we prefer to treat a text as a kind of equation of communication, in which decipherable messages are passed from writers to readers; and whether we locate meaning as inherent in the text, the act of reading, or in some collaboration between reader and text—whatever our predilection, let us not generate from it a straitjacket that limits the scope of possible analysis. Rather, let us generate an ongoing dialogue of competing potential possibilities—among feminists and, as well, between feminist and nonfeminist critics.

The difficulty in what I describe does not escape me. The very idea of pluralism seems to threaten a kind of chaos for the future of literary inquiry while, at the same time, it seems to deny the hope of establishing some basic conceptual model which can organize all data—the hope which always begins any analytical exercise. My effort here, however, has been to demonstrate the essential delusions that inform such objections: if literary inquiry has historically escaped chaos by establishing canons, then it has only substituted one mode of arbitrary action for another—and, in this case, at the expense of half the population. And if feminists openly acknowledge ourselves as pluralists, then we do not give up the search for patterns of opposition and connection—probably the basis of thinking itself; what we give up is simply the arrogance of claiming that our work is either exhaustive or definitive. (It is, after all, the identical arrogance we are asking our nonfeminist colleagues to abandon.) If this kind of pluralism appears to threaten both the present coherence of and the inherited aesthetic criteria for a canon of "greats," then, as I have earlier argued, it is precisely that threat which, alone, can free us from the prejudices, the strictures, and the blind spots of the past. In feminist hands, I would add, it is less a threat than a promise.

What unites and repeatedly invigorates feminist literary criticism, then, is neither dogma nor method but, as I have indicated earlier, an acute and impassioned *attentiveness* to the ways in which primarily male structures of power are inscribed (or encoded) within our literary inheritance; the consequences of that encoding for women—as characters, as readers, and as writers; and, with that, a shared analytic *concern* for the implications of that encoding not only for a better understanding of the past but for an improved reordering of the present and future as well. If that *concern* identifies feminist literary criticism as one of the many academic arms of the larger women's movement, then that *attentive-*

ness, within the halls of academe, poses no less a challenge for change, generating, as it does, the three propositions explored here. The critical pluralism that inevitably follows upon those three propositions, however, bears little resemblance to what Robinson has called "the greatest bourgeois theme of all, the myth of pluralism, with its consequent rejection of ideological commitment as 'too simple' to embrace the (necessarily complex) truth" ("Dwelling in Decencies" 11). Only ideological commitment could have gotten us to enter the minefield, putting in jeopardy our careers and our livelihood. Only the power of ideology to transform our conceptual worlds, and the inspiration of that ideology to liberate long-suppressed energies and emotions, can account for our willingness to take on critical tasks that, in an earlier decade, would have been "abandoned in despair or apathy."[14] The fact of differences among us proves only that, despite our shared commitments, we have nonetheless refused to shy away from complexity, preferring rather to openly disagree than to give up either intellectual honesty or hard-won insights.

Finally, I would argue, pluralism informs feminist literary inquiry not simply as a description of what already exists but, more important, as the only critical stance consistent with the current status of the larger women's movement. Segmented and variously focused, the different women's organizations neither espouse any single system of analysis nor, as a result, express any wholly shared, consistently articulated ideology. The ensuing loss in effective organization and political clout is a serious one, but it has not been paralyzing; in spite of our differences, we have united to *act* in areas of clear mutual concern (the push for the Equal Rights Amendment is probably the most obvious example). The trade-off, as I see it, has made possible an ongoing and educative dialectic of analysis and proferred solutions, protecting us thereby from the inviting traps of reductionism and dogma. And so long as this dialogue remains active, both our politics and our criticism will be free of dogma—but never, I hope, of feminist ideology, in all its variety. For, "whatever else ideologies may be—projections of unacknowledged fears, disguises for ulterior motives, phatic expressions of group solidarity" (and the women's movement, to date, has certainly been all of these, and more)—whatever ideologies express, they are, as Geertz astutely observes, "most distinctively, maps of problematic social reality and matrices for the creation of collective conscience." And despite the fact that "ideological advocates . . . tend as much to obscure as to clarify the true nature of the problems involved," as Geertz notes, "they at least call attention to their existence and, by polarizing issues, make continued neglect more difficult. Without Marxist attack, there would have been no labor reform; without Black Nationalists, no deliberate speed" ("Ideology" 220, 205). Without Seneca Falls, I would add, no enfranchisement of women, and without "consciousness-raising," no feminist literary criticism nor, even less, women's studies.

Ideology, however, only truly manifests its power by ordering the *sum* of our actions.[15] If feminist criticism calls anything into question, it must be that dog-eared myth of intellectual neutrality. For, what I take to be the underlying spirit, or message, of any consciously ideologically premised criticism—that is, that ideas are important *because* they determine the ways we live, or want to live, in the world—is vitiated by confining those ideas to the study, the classroom, or the pages of our books. To write chapters decrying the sexual stereotyping of women in our literature, while closing our eyes to the sexual harassment of our women students and colleagues; to display Katharine Hepburn and Rosalind Russell in courses like The Image of the Independent Career Woman in Film, while managing not to notice the paucity of female administrators on our own campus; to study the women who helped make universal enfranchisement a political reality, while keeping silent about our activist colleagues who are denied promotion or tenure; to include segments like Women in the Labor Movement in our American studies or women's studies courses, while remaining willfully ignorant of the department secretary fired for her efforts to organize a clerical-workers' union; to glory in the delusions of "merit," "privilege," and "status" which accompany campus life in order to insulate ourselves from the millions of women who labor in poverty—all this is not merely hypocritical; it destroys both the spirit and the meaning of what we are about. It puts us, however unwittingly, in the service of those who laid the minefield in the first place. In my view, it is a fine thing for many of us, individually, to have traversed the minefield; but that happy circumstance will only prove of lasting importance if, together, we expose it for what it is (the male fear of sharing power and significance with women) and deactivate its components, so that others, after us, may literally dance through the minefield.[16]

NOTES

[1] In her *Feminine Consciousness in the Modern British Novel*, Sydney Janet Kaplan explains that she is using the term *feminine consciousness* "not simply as some general attitude of women toward their own femininity, and not as something synonymous with a particular sensibility among female writers. I am concerned with it as a literary device: a method of characterization of females in fiction" (3).

[2] See Adrienne Rich's discussion of the difficulty in finding authentic language for her experience as a mother in her *Of Woman Born* (15).

[3] In *The Madwoman in the Attic*, Sandra M. Gilbert and Susan Gubar suggest that women's writings are in some sense "palimpsestic" in that their "surface designs conceal or obscure deeper, less accessible (and less socially acceptable) levels of meaning" (73). It is, in their view, an art designed "both to express and to camouflage" (81).

[4] Consider, for example, Paul Boyers's reductive and inaccurate generalization that "what distinguishes ordinary books and articles about women from feminist writing is the feminist insistence on asking the same questions of every work and demanding ideologically satisfactory answers to those questions as a means of evaluating it" ("A Case against Feminist Criticism" 602). It is partly as a result of such misconceptions that we have the paucity of feminist critics who are granted a place in English departments which otherwise pride themselves on the variety of their critical orientations.

[5] Ambivalent though he is about the literary continuity that begins with Homer, Harold Bloom nonetheless somewhat ominously prophesies "that the first true break . . . will be brought about in generations to come, if the burgeoning religion of Liberated Woman spreads from its clusters of enthusiasts to dominate the West" (*Map* 33). He acknowledges that while something "as violent [as] a quarrel . . . would ensue if I expressed my judgment" on Robert Lowell and Norman Mailer, "it would lead to something more intense than quarrels if I expressed my judgment upon . . . the 'literature of Women's Liberation' " (36).

[6] The first is a proposition currently expressed by some structuralists and formalist critics; the best statement of the second probably appears in Georg Lukács, *Writer and Critic* (119).

[7] John Dewey offered precisely this argument in 1934 when he insisted that a work of art "is recreated every time it is esthetically experienced. . . . It is absurd to ask what an artist 'really' meant by his product: he himself would find different meanings in it at different days and hours and in different stages of his own development." Further, he explained, "It is simply an impossibility that any one today should experience the Parthenon as the devout Athenian contemporary citizen experienced it, any more than the religious statuary of the twelfth century can mean, esthetically, even to a good Catholic today just what it meant to worshipers of the old period" (108–09).

[8] A recurrent tendency in criticism is the establishment of false norms for the evaluation of literary works, notes Robert Scholes (131).

[9] For a full discussion of the Glaspell short story which takes this into account, see my "A Map for Rereading."

[10] These comments appear within Scholes's explication of Tzvetan Todorov's theory of reading.

[11] Indications of the pluralism that was to mark feminist inquiry were to be found in the diversity of essays collected by Susan Koppelman Cornillon for her early and ground-breaking anthology *Images of Women in Fiction*.

[12] Blackmur, of course, was referring to the way in which criticism makes us conscious of how art functions; I use his wording here because I am arguing that that same awareness must also be focused on the critical act itself. "Consciousness," he avers, "is the way we feel the critic's burden."

[13] I have earlier elaborated my objection to prescriptive categories for literature in "The Feminist as Literary Critic."

[14] "Ideology bridges the emotional gap between things as they are and as one would have them be, thus insuring the performance of roles that might otherwise be abandoned in despair or apathy," comments Geertz ("Ideology" 205).

[15] I here follow Fredric Jameson's view: "Ideology would seem to be that grillwork of form, convention, and belief which orders our actions" (*The Prison-House of Language* 107).

[16] Some sections of this essay were composed during the time made available to me by a grant from the Rockefeller Foundation, for which I am most grateful.

AFTERWORD

"Dancing through the Minefield" was composed as an assertion of sanity during one of the bleakest periods in my life. The essay began in 1977 as a series of random contemplations of the different shapes that feminist literary criticism was taking. It came together in 1978 as an attempt to codify some underlying assumptions then evident in feminist inquiry. The tone was intended to be celebratory, even as it was also meant to be cautionary: celebratory in the sense that so much extraordinarily good work had been produced in a relatively brief period, and cautionary because, as I knew all too personally, feminism in the academy was threatened, everywhere embattled in the 1970s. Indeed, the title metaphor was taken from one of my own recurring dreams: I was trying to negotiate a minefield, the dangers detonating all around me, my movements a frenzied dance of survival. The fact was, the minefield was also my waking experience: in 1975, following the denial of promotion (and, later, the denial of tenure), I had filed an EEOC discrimination complaint against the Department of English at the University of New Hampshire. By 1978, as I tried desperately to complete the essay, I was embroiled in a Title VII suit charging the school with anti-Semitism and sex discrimination.

What I lived with daily in 1978, therefore, was the threat that my career was over and that I, like so many others in that first generation of feminist critics, would be forced out of the academy. In the face of that threat, the essay was an attempt to leave something of myself behind, a statement of shared accomplishments.

What got left out of that shared vision—an omission that still grieves me—was the growing impact of lesbian criticism and the crucial importance of new work by and about minority women writers. Any reconsideration of the essay in the 1990s would have to account for the sharpened cultural critiques offered by these scholars and the challenge they successfully mounted to a moribund "American" literature canon.

If I were to write the essay today, I would be just as celebratory—having even more work to analyze and praise—and just as cautionary. My caution would probably be directed at the stunning impact of French-inspired inquiry, an inquiry that has taught us to deconstruct the assumptions and belief systems governing the world (or the world as text) but has yet to address any *re*construction of a belief system that would sustain active engagement in the world. If there is *only* text, and if the meanings of texts are inherently unstable, then on what faith, on what principle can we *act*? The instability of meaning, I would now insist, can be no justification for political disengagement. The minefield image that would govern the essay today, in short, would be the minefield of our own achievements and their implications.

Tucson, Arizona
January 1990

~ 1980 ~

The Domestic Alternative: Beyond Feminist Criticism

CORINNE DALE

FEMINIST CRITICS CHARGE that standard literary criticism too often considers male experience universal, thereby ignoring the female point of view and neglecting the literature which expresses the female sensibility. In fact, it is disconcertingly easy to find male sexual bias in literary criticism. For example, Leslie Fiedler, a favorite target for feminists, argues that in *The Scarlet Letter* Dimmesdale is "reduced . . . to feminine passivity," playing a "passive, feminine [role], his tremulous hand laid to his heart" (*Love and Death* 502–03). Clearly, the passive female stereotype invoked by Fiedler is denied within the novel itself by the sturdy, aggressive Puritan women as well as by Hester's own womanly assertiveness in defiance of societal pressure. On the other hand, feminist critics are themselves not immune to bias; those sympathetic to female characters sometimes paint equally distorted portraits. Betty H. Jones and Alberta Arthurs surely err when they describe Hester so transformed by her experience that she becomes the ideally pure and pious woman, whose "soul is flawless" (2, 9). Feminist critics are to be congratulated on what amounts to a liberation of literary criticism, but we must also take note of distortions arising from the special emphasis on the female point of view. For even as feminist critics have sensitized us to male bias, demanding a radical revision of criticism, they have themselves helped to perpetuate a sexually biased reading of American literature.

One of the most important contributions of feminist criticism is the uncovering of a body of writings which has been ignored, seemingly because of sexual bias. It is becoming clear that the writings of many women have been neglected because they do not derive from the masculine tradition which has informed so many American "master-pieces." Feminist critics have thus alerted us to the presence of American literary traditions which have been overlooked in the obsession with the American Adam, the frontier thesis, and other traditions which emphasize the individual. These traditions are more often than not assumed to be both male and peculiarly American. Women, we have learned, were themselves participating in a tradition which pertains to all human beings—the domestic tradition. Due to the insistence on a significant body of women's writings, however, domestic literature has been equated with women's literature, just as the American heroic tradition has been thought to be especially male. Each equation has a certain amount of truth to support it; but each also leads to a serious distortion of literature when applied too rigorously. Let us consider two examples of such distortions.

Theodore Gross discusses the American hero as an "exceptional man who seeks to realize an ideal" in opposition to authority (viii). Hester Prynne fits this standard definition of the heroic individual who resists society, if we can assume that Gross uses the term *man* in the generic sense. Yet Gross considers Dimmesdale to be the sole hero of Hawthorne's novel, stating that Hester never seeks to explore her sin and that she demonstrates "a moral weakness her lover never has." What is the source of Hester's weakness? She has become a feminist "and incurred an inevitable moral disintegration" (25). But Hawthorne himself points out that Hester reaches feminism through her investigation of her plight and dares to dream of a feminist ideal of personal, intellectual freedom which would have horrified the Puritan authorities.

Hester fares no better, however, with those feminist critics who call attention to what they see as a special female tradition. Nina Baym directly addresses the issue of male and female authors in her study of the domestic fiction written by women and read by women in unprecedented numbers in the 1820s through the 1870s. Contending that men could have written the stories of women so popular in that period, Baym asserts that in fact none did so, thus justifying her use of the term "woman's fiction" instead of "domestic fiction." Yet Hester's story fits the plot described by Baym as typical of this fiction—a story in which a young girl, deprived of traditional emotional and financial supports, develops a new self-awareness as she triumphantly makes her own way in the world. So far is Baym from considering the possibility of a male domestic tradition, however, that she continues by admitting that she has discovered no domestic novel which approximates the artistry of *The Scarlet Letter* (*Woman's Fiction* 11, 13–14).

I do not intend to deny the contributions made by Gross and Baym. On the contrary, I wish to point out how insidious sexual bias in literary criticism can be by illustrating its influence in the work of two influential critics. Between them, Hester is neither a truly American hero nor a domestic hero—and in both cases seemingly because *The Scarlet Letter* does not fit an unacknowledged criterion of gender. Like Baym, other critics too easily assume that domesticity is specifically a woman's concern, defining domestic fiction not simply as fiction about the home and the family but as fiction written by, about, and for women. In the reaction against the definition of American experience as male, many feminist critics have worked against their own goals, reinforcing the notion of gender-divided literary traditions and ultimately preventing domestic literature from taking its proper place in American literature. Now that we are beginning to recognize the validity of domestic writing as a significant tradition in American literature, we must also consider the matter of gender. This issue, which we have ignored for too long, has always biased the study of the domestic tradition and even the definition of domestic literature.

It is undeniable that a good deal of our domestic literature—and not merely sentimental fiction—is written by women. But it does not follow that domestic literature is written exclusively by women. Certainly, the individual experience of the writer, which is influenced and in some cases determined by that writer's gender, suggests the subjects and the values which she or he will choose to write about. Clearly also, the home has generally been considered to be the special province of the woman in our culture; it is not surprising that many of our great women writers were concerned with domestic subjects. But to argue, as Shulamith Firestone does in *The Dialectic of Sex*, that "the sex role system divides human experience" and that "men and women live in these different halves of reality" (165) is valid to a limited extent only. It is clearly not true that males have no experience with or commitment to domesticity. Yet many critics have proceeded as if male and female experience were discrete. Emily Stipes Watts praises Anne Bradstreet for her special use of household objects in her poetry (10), even though male Puritans also delighted in finding domestic metaphors for their relationship with God, whose providence was evident to them in the most common circumstances. Edward Taylor's "Huswifery" is an obvious example of poetry written by a man which relies on such common household objects as the spinning wheel to elucidate the relationship of God and Puritan. It is easy to excuse Watts's praise of Bradstreet as an overzealous feminist reading; still, she is working with a commonly accepted generalization that male literature stresses the freedom of the individual quest and thus is typically American, while female literature deals usually with domesticity (7).

In the nineteenth century, as in the Puritan society, men and women accepted gender stereotypes and wrote with a strong sense of their different roles. Men were thought to be peculiarly logical and materialistic, while women were considered to be emotional, pious, and submissive. Women's occupations, besides domestic duties, were those of seamstress, teacher, and writer; women were thus locked out of certain types of "male" experiences and strongly associated with the home. At the same time, as Ann Douglas and others have pointed out, women were considered to represent essential societal values—values which men as well as women were concerned with. *The Scarlet Letter*, along with Melville's *Pierre* and even Thoreau's *Walden*, shows that during the heyday of women's domestic fiction, males also dealt with domestic subjects. This fact has been obscured by the tendency to consider literature about the home and family to be domestic only when it is written by females. When males write about domesticity, their writing is typically discussed in terms of the frontier myth, the historical romance, the adventure story, or some other "masculine" tradition. Paradoxically, when someone such as William C. Spengemann does consider the domestic content of fiction written by males, this writing is still discussed as separate from women's writings. Thus, in documenting a dual tradition of adventure and domesticity in American literature, Spengemann relegates novels by women to the subcategory of sentimental fiction, which he defines as fiction dealing with the emotions of an ''exiled heroine'' (88). Spengemann thus suggests that domestic literature has been dominated by men, a reversal of the usual identification of domestic and female writers. But at the same time, he subclassifies the literature according to the gender of the author.

The second unnecessary restriction of domestic literature is implied in Spengemann's definition of the sentimental novel as well as in Baym's description of domestic fiction as fiction about the experiences of a heroine; both identify a subset of literature which is about a woman as well as by one. *The Scarlet Letter*, as I have suggested, is about a young woman's growing self-awareness; but Hawthorne is equally concerned with the minister's degeneration, both moral and physical. This degeneration, moreover, is also a domestic story; the focus is on Dimmesdale's denial of Hester and Pearl and the consequences of that denial—for Dimmesdale as well as for Hester. Neither character lives a solitary life. Dimmesdale becomes a great social and religious leader, while Hester, Dimmesdale's female counterpart, also becomes a leader in the community, a social and spiritual adviser, especially for troubled women. Yet *The Scarlet Letter* is not usually considered to be about family but to be another ''typical'' American story of quest for individual freedom in which the domestic functions merely as the rejected alternative.

Other great American novels of this period more clearly fit the paradigm of the hero who rejects the domestic in order to seek an individual goal. Critics acknowledge that male writers often value the home and family as the rejected alternative which casts in relief the lonely and courageous search of the protagonist. Thus, in *Moby-Dick*, Ahab tragically rejects the vision of home suggested to him by Starbuck in order to continue his compulsive search for the white whale. Ishmael and Queequeg's friendship, projected in terms of marriage, also provides a domestic counterpoint to Ahab's isolation. Significantly, however, critics often deemphasize the domestic aspects of such male relationships. Fiedler, apparently struck by Melville's humorous suggestions of homosexuality in Ishmael and Queequeg's marriage, focuses on the homosexual implications in other male pairs, deemphasizing the domestic aspects of such male friendships as that of Jim and Huck Finn (''Come Back''). Yet Jim's paternal instruction of Huck in the joys and sorrows of family love is essential to Huck's growing moral stature and, to a great extent, accounts for the reader's dissatisfaction with Huck's final betrayal of Jim and his rejection of family as he lights out for the territory.

While many readers will object to Fiedler's interpretation, most will agree with Nina Auerbach's distinction between male and female communities. She states that the male community is typically structured by the quest which is important to specific individuals in contrast to the female community which is structured by community spirit and thus is truly domestic (*Communities* 17). Ahab's crew have indeed pledged themselves to Ahab's personal quest; nevertheless, their communal dedication is featured in such chapters as ''A Squeeze of the Hand,'' in which Ishmael blissfully squeezes the hands of his companions together with the whale sperm in a transport of fellow-feeling. As the crew of the *Pequod* illustrates, the two types of community which Auerbach defines as male and female are not always mutually exclusive and not necessarily gender-divided traditions.

The male domestic community in *Moby-Dick* is no anomaly in American fiction. A significant portion of American fiction focuses on domestic communities which are patriarchal or even exclusively male rather than female-dominated. For example, in the mid-nineteenth century, during the same period when feminine domestic fiction gained such great popularity, plantation fiction was developing in the South. This fiction depends on the domestic significance of the plantation as an extended family community. As a matter of fact, when the distinction between "domestic fiction" and "plantation fiction" is closely examined, it becomes evident that plantation fiction is a type of domestic fiction. William R. Taylor notes that plantation novels are closely allied to the "so-called 'domestic novel'—the sentimental novel of the home and family." But Taylor continues to refer to two separate traditions even though his discussion of plantation novels suggests that they fit his definition of the domestic novel, and, more important, that we can benefit from considering plantation fiction from a domestic angle. Taylor, moreover, supports the strong association of women with domesticity when he asserts that both plantation novelists and domestic novelists give women the dominion of the home, citing John Pendleton Kennedy's *Swallow Barn* as evidence (167).

Actually, many plantation writers, especially male writers such as Kennedy, create patriarchal plantation communities in which the matron, although praised, is either absent or too busy to make more than a token appearance. *Swallow Barn*, the first plantation novel, typically allows the plantation matron only a brief appearance, during which she is introduced as the soul of industry; throughout the rest of the novel, the plantation is dominated by the planter himself. William Gilmore Simms, the most popular antebellum southern novelist, sets up an all-male domestic community in his widely read novel *Woodcraft*. Women are gleefully excluded from this community, which is described as a paradigm of domestic and social harmony. William Faulkner and many other modern Southern writers continue the long tradition of patriarchal plantation communities in such novels as *Absalom! Absalom*! In that novel, Thomas Sutpen, the inverse of Ahab, seeks his personal fulfillment in the establishment of a family dynasty, but he is destroyed because he views the home as an abstract symbol of success without truly valuing his family. When we learn to recognize the domestic content of such fiction as this—written by and about males—we can begin to see that the domestic tradition is part of the mainstream of American literature.

It may be that the key to an understanding of domestic literature, however, is the question of audience. For whom was domestic fiction written? Most critics accept the idea that quest fiction and domestic fiction (by which is usually meant male and female literatures) oppose each other in terms of values as well as in subject matter. Critics stress that domestic fiction, particularly the domestic fiction of the 1820s through the 1870s, was written for women, emphasizing that this literature was not part of the male-dominated tradition of sophisticated letters. And it is true that this fiction demonstrates a modest feminism in its stories of women who triumph over men and achieve financial and emotional independence. It also seems clear that the feminine domestic fiction of this period affirmed values commonly held by women and allowed them a forum for airing their grievances: the domestic values of familial love, mutual service, and communal harmony are usually upheld even though the home often falls far short of the domestic ideal, a situation which precipitates the action and carries an incipient feminist message (Baym, *Woman's Fiction* 27).

It is important to remember, however, that domestic values do not appeal to women alone but to the culture as a whole. Too often we assume that domestic values are equated with the values of society, in particular social stability, religious piety, and conventional morality—those values which are rejected by the American hero. In a recent study of frontier women, Julie Roy Jeffrey confesses, "My original perspective was feminist; I hoped to find that pioneer women used the frontier as a means of liberating themselves from stereotypes and behaviors which I found constricting and sexist" (xv–xvi). In the course of her investigation, Jeffrey recognizes her bias, but she remains disappointed in the results of her research because she continues to equate liberation with the frontier and to perceive the home as intrinsically restrictive. Specifically, Jeffrey accepts the view of the frontier as a place of liberation from domestic restrictions. Yet it is more reasonable to view the pioneers, both men and women, as people attempting to domesticate the frontier, not to flee domesticity. To equate domesticity with repression is as limiting, finally, as identifying the home with feminine fulfillment.

A corollary to this identification of the home with restrictive social conventions is the belief that women's domestic novels are often considered to be poor literature because they are subversive of the "masculine" values of materialism (Jones and Arthurs 3) and of individuality, a value which has proven dear to the American Adam and to male-dominated criticism. It is doubtful that critics have rejected women's fiction for its opposition to masculine values, however. According to nineteenth-century sexual stereotypes, masculine values are commercial and materialistic. In opposition to the male world of the marketplace, the home—often but not always presided over by a woman—is frequently upheld as the domestic ideal. But frontier fiction opposes these masculine values just as much as domestic fiction does. In fact, both traditions work against forces which have always seemed threatening to Americans—obsessive ambition, crass materialism, and greed for power and wealth. Just as the individual may escape down the open road from an alienating society, the same individual may find comfort and purpose in the family. Huck Finn, at least, had a difficult time making up his mind whether he wanted to be adopted by a family on the shore or whether he wanted to find happiness by himself in the territory. Often the women of Clemens's novel are considered to have been "cast immutably as grim-faced 'sivilization' on the shore" (Auerbach, *Communities* 28); but Mary Jane and her sisters, distraught over the breakup of the slave family, teach Huck a good deal about domestic love. Their values are certainly not the same as the values of "sivilization." The home can thus represent a domestic alternative to the wilderness for the individual who wishes to reject a corrupt society.

The domestic alternative, then, should not be considered a woman's tradition, even though much and perhaps most domestic literature is written by women. Domestic literature, especially domestic literature written by and about women, may have had and may continue to have a special message for a female audience; such novels may even constitute a subcategory of domestic literature. But domestic literature also asserts important values of the American culture, values which constantly undergo reexamination and which continue to concern us today.

Modern critics demand equal treatment for women's writings. Nevertheless, by insisting that domestic literature is women's literature or that women's literature is domestic literature, many call for a separate but equal position, not true integration. Some claim that women's domestic literature is actually more American than men's literature, since it was written for a popular audience, instead of for a male intellectual elite (Wasserstrom 129–31). Others claim that women's domestic literature transcends the limitations of "masculine literature" by appealing to universal values (Watts 176): these support the standard view that the male tradition of the quest is peculiarly American. Still, fiction written by women will never be equal so long as it is considered to be a separate tradition.

In fact, there is no more reason to accept the notion that American literature is exclusively frontier or quest literature than there is to split American literature along lines of gender. What could be more American than plantation literature or than pioneer literature, both of which are focused on the home? What about the literature of black Americans, in which so often the family provides a cohesive center of order and of emotion? What about the literature asserting the communal values of Native Americans? Surely these traditions are just as peculiarly American as the frontier tradition is. Can we maintain that *Light in August* is the story of Joe Christmas but not the story of Lena Grove? Is the ending of that novel somehow not truly American since it concludes with the vision of a family rather than an individual traveling down an open road?

It would be foolish to suggest that gender does not profoundly influence experience. I do not contend that the sex of the writer or of the protagonist or of the audience is meaningless in literature. On the contrary, it is necessary for critics to recognize how gender relates to literature if we are to understand literature as a reflection of human, and not just male, experience. It is logical to suppose that male and female visions of domesticity will differ. Females, especially those who participate directly in domestic tasks, such as cooking and clothing manufacture, not to mention childbirth and nursing, perceive domesticity from a different angle from males, particularly those who experience domesticity basically as physical comfort and as a symbol of moral and religious piety. The impact of sexual stereotyping must also be felt in domestic fiction: the writer who projects a male domestic hero clearly must deal with problems of characterization which do not affect the characterization of a female domestic hero.

I do contend, however, that the popular concept of gender-based literary traditions is, to a large extent, in the eye of the critic and that this critical bias has blinded us to some significant problems of characterization and structure as well as to the purpose, effect, and value of much domestic fiction. I also contend that domestic fiction—that is, fiction about the home and family, whether written by, about, and for women *or* men—is a true American tradition. Like the quest tradition, the domestic tradition has its roots in European and especially in British literature, but this tradition has also been transformed by the American experience so that it speaks directly to our needs as well as to universal concerns.

Some feminists are currently calling for "androgynous" literary criticism—that is, criticism which recognizes the value of both male and female ideals. This concept used to be called "humanism," with the difference that "humanism" suggests a whole rather than stressing division by gender. It appears that the new emphasis on gender may be necessary, since we have allowed it to bias our reading without recognizing its influence. Still, the desired end is a humanistic reading of our literature. The response of Mark Twain's Jim to the biblical story of Solomon may serve to illustrate the point. Refusing to accept the conventional wisdom that Solomon was the wisest of all men, Jim considers Solomon's most famous judgment the "beatenes' notion in de worl'." No one with only one or two children is going to be so wasteful as to threaten to chop a baby in two, Jim points out. He further suggests that anyone with any gumption would simply shine around among the neighbors and find out who that child belongs to. As readers, we share Huck's frustration: Jim simply cannot be made to see the point. At the same time, however, we are bound to admire Jim's critical response, his highly developed humanistic—and domestic—sensibility.

AFTERWORD

I wrote the preceding essay ten years ago as an attack on critical assumptions about gender-based traditions in American literature. Specifically, I sought to demystify the American Adam/frontier myth and to demonstrate that domestic writing was being defined as a feminine corollary to that male tradition. I called attention to the fact that even feminist critics were making assumptions about author, reader, and subject based on their acceptance of an authoritative and often inaccurate reading of American literature as the heroic quest for individual freedom outside the home.

Today, it is difficult to remember how completely the myth of the American Adam dominated our reading of American literature. Women's writings, too, are no longer presumed to be sentimental projections of home and family. Critics now recognize that no authoritative reading exists. No American Eve has arisen to take her place in the critic's American Eden. Indeed, as feminist readers, our strength, and our frustration, is our continuing criticism of ourselves—feminists re-reading feminists.

Nevertheless, we still are likely to base readings on unexamined assumptions about gender: we still are influenced by the notion that males write about questing individuals while females write about community. Our need to describe women's writing with reference to women rather than to men remains; our desire to affirm a women's literary tradition continues. These strong impulses motivate the good work that is being done—rescuing woman-authored texts and articulating women's textual accomplishments. But this work, paradoxically, demands an accurate reading of male-authored fiction.

More feminist readings of male-authored texts are essential. We cannot understand the influence of gender by examining female-authored texts in isolation. As I argued ten years ago, Anne Bradstreet's subjective treatment of her home and family can be understood well only when we acknowledge the domestic imagery of male Puritans, such as the spinning wheel of Edward Taylor. The domestic is still a neglected motif in male-authored American literature, a motif that can be uncovered by critics open to nontraditional readings.

The gender of the author, too, must be acknowledged as only one aspect of signature. The current examination of women's language and narrative structure is proving extremely fruitful. But modern fictions by women that subvert traditional narrative and linguistic structure are not functions of gender alone. Eudora Welty is not only a woman, after all, but also a white, middle-class, twentieth-century American, and so on, and a descendant of the modernists.

Our challenge today is to attend to signature, reader, and subject in all their complexity. As feminist critics, we can meet the challenge only after recognizing and laying to rest the critical tyrants of the past. As for the American Adam, *in pace requiescat*!

Nashville, Tennessee
January 1990

~ 1981 ~

Archetype and Structure: On Feminist Myth Criticism

CYNTHIA A. DAVIS

MANY STUDENTS, AND teachers, of feminist criticism first come to the field through courses like Images of Women in Literature. The typology that emerges from such courses often illuminates relationships among female literary characters of different periods, gender definitions, and symbolic structures in myth and literature. Thus many feminist critics would like to use mythic patterns and categories as referents for the study of literature. But the approach has drawbacks, for myth criticism seems to posit a fixity of pattern and image incompatible with a feminist understanding of gender and power relations. The feminist critic must find a way to reconcile the two approaches.

Jungian notions of archetypes are especially troublesome. Archetypal theory does seem to describe enduring and fundamental patterns in myth, culture, and literature; Joseph Campbell's descriptions of the hero myth, for example, can be quite useful for discussions of narrative, theme, and form. But Jungian explanations of such recurrence include the "liturgical pronouncements about The Masculine and The Feminine" that critics like Lillian S. Robinson find "harmful to a coherent and fruitful reading of 'the literature of women' " ("Dwelling in Decencies" 884). The Jungian position insists that a recurrent female image like the mother, in all its variations, is so powerful and constant that it must be the manifestation of an archetype, "an inward image at work in the human psyche" whose effect "may be followed through the whole of history" (Neumann 3). That is, while the particular image varies with culture and personal experience, appearing as Terrible Mother here, Good Mother there, the archetype underlying or represented by the image is "inborn . . . identical in all men [sic]" 9.1: 3).[1] And this archetype corresponds not only to universal psychic structures; it also corresponds to the "feminine principle which was and is . . . the mainspring of woman, controlling both her physical life and her inner psychological being" (Harding 29). Thus to delineate the archetype is to grasp not just a reality of which woman may be the symbol but what she *is* in the deepest way. Such a view certainly seems to lock women into the constricting roles that a feminist critic is bound to question, the categorical identification of woman with matter and Eros, man with spirit and Logos.

Fortunately, critiques of Jungianism have begun to alter those assumptions and offer adjusted views of archetypes. One major criticism has been of the Jungian identification of man's "internal image" of woman with the "feminine principle" that "controls" an actual woman and with her own self-image. C. G. Jung's definition of archetype stresses its distinction from its representative image: "The archetype is essentially an unconscious content that is altered by becoming conscious . . . archetypes are not determined as regards their content, but only as regards their form and then only to a very limited degree" (9.1: 6, 155). Why, then, insist that because a psychic reality—or a relation to the world—often takes a female image, it must be female in an absolute sense? It is as if, having explained that archetypal images of fire as life principle suggest "a kind of *phlogiston theory*" (9.2: 394), Jung were to go on to insist that the phlogiston theory is literally true.

The basic problem arises, as Carol Christ points out, because "Jungians do not distinguish between the 'feminine' as a compensatory aspect of the male experience and the feminine as the primary mode of experience in women" ("Some Comments" 67). The attributes of "the feminine" in Jungian theory are largely the attributes of the not-self—nature, the environment—and of the hidden self—the unconscious and irrational elements of the psyche. Man naturally would image those qualities in what is inevitably different—woman, always his Other. (One should notice, however, that there is a whole complex of images serving this function—depths, interiors, and various natural objects included—and Jungians tend to subsume all under the heading of the feminine.) Thus in the Jungian model, the male psyche, primarily conscious and logical, has a "compensatory aspect" that takes symbolic female form; and this personification, his "anima," can be "projected" into the external world—that is, onto real or imaginary women. This model is appealing in its grasp of the symbolic quality of otherness and of the need to project onto others qualities and functions concealed in the self. So when Jung postulates that for women the hidden self would take the form of a male "animus," the reversal seems logical. But Jung takes that reversal of image to mean that the female psyche is itself little more than an upside-down version of the male. Jung says, "Woman is compensated by a masculine element and therefore her unconscious has, so to speak, a masculine imprint. . . . The animus corresponds to the paternal Logos just as the anima corresponds to the maternal Eros" (9.2: 29). The anima, the embodiment of the male's other self, moves over to become the female's primary self; and "the male projection of the feminine is [assumed to be] the same as a woman's projection of her own selfhood" (Christ, "Some Comments" 68). Whereas Jung elsewhere observes that the intense meaning of a figure like the mother does "not come from the mother herself, but rather from the archetype projected upon her" (9.1: 159), the model of male and female psyches equates the gender images with the archetypal principles they may embody.

Jung further asserts that for a man the anima takes "significant form" in a single image which still has the dual possibilities of the archetype; the animus, however, appears "as a plurality of persons." He explains the difference as due to man's greater capacity for generalization: "[H]is world consists of a multitude of co-ordinated factors, whereas her world, outside her husband, terminates in a sort of cosmic mist" (7: 332, 338). Emma Jung more perceptively explains the plurality of the animus as due to "the more diversified field of man's activity" in the world; but she too accepts the "forms of relationship" that unify the anima as both man's perception of woman and woman's own sense of self: "it is part of feminine nature to serve man as a mirror" (28, 65). Recognition of the secondary nature of woman in the Jungian perspective clarifies this formulation, which assumes woman's existence as dependent on role definition (as anima or primary self) and man's as beyond outside definition. Variety is impossible to a nature conceived primarily as not-man, though dualism of function is possible. (Sherry Ortner has explained how the "polarized ambiguity" of the female image results from her placement outside the "human" sphere.) Even when the not-man is the perceiving self, she cannot control and generalize sufficiently to create a single significant representation of what lies outside her.

The pernicious effects of such a conflation of hidden self and not-self, of reality and image, woman and not-man appear in the obtuse interpretations Jungians can offer when bemused by gender. Critics like Christine Gallant may want to argue that "archetypes are quite neutral in value and certainly not behavioral roles to be followed" (90), but Jungians have often used them in very prescriptive ways. Joseph Henderson's explanation that an intellectual woman's dream of decapitation obviously "meant she was ready" to be a "more submissive" woman is not unusual (129–30); Jung himself remarked that "in women . . . Eros is an expression of their true nature, while their Logos is often only a regrettable accident" (9.2: 29). This rigid allotment of male and female qualities can lead to tortuous reasoning, like his explanation of male intellectual pettiness: "Men can argue in a very womanish way, too, when they are anima-possessed and have thus been transformed into the animus of their own anima" (9.2: 29)—that is, when man is himself, he is Logos; only the domination of a female entity can explain intellectual failure.

Such assumptions can create the kinds of problems in literary analysis that Lee R. Edwards shows in Erich Neumann's study *Amor and Psyche*. Psyche, Edwards says, is clearly defined as an archetypal hero by "the controlling matrices" of character, action, and relationship ("Labors" 35); but Neumann is too concentrated on Psyche's gender to accept her universal significance. He insists on assuming that "Psyche as a female character necessarily indicates woman's link to the unconscious, while Amor as a male character is, conversely, and with equal necessity, representative of masculinity's greater consciousness. . . . In his reading he claims that Psyche is the representative of the female archetype; in reality, she is for him merely the projected anima of patriarchal culture" ("Labors" 40). Judith Fetterley offers a similar correction of perspective in her discussions of American versions of myth and their interpretations. Though not Jungian, she too makes a distinction between male projections of "the feminine" and female conceptions of the self. Acceptance of the male orientation as "universal,'' she shows, has blinded critics to its implications; agreement that woman is the anima, her nature Eros, allows the critic to move from abstract theme to characterization without fully seeing the effect of one on the other. Fetterley points out, for example, that because most Hawthorne critics discuss ''The Birthmark'' as an exposition of the dangers of idealization without questioning the identification of woman with matter, they miss Hawthorne's analysis of the mechanisms of hostility displaced and disguised as purification (22–33). Similar limits can be seen in current myth criticism. For example, critics studying John Barth's versions of the hero myth tend to accept Barth's earth-mother figures and therefore the implication that the women characters' ''freedom'' consists of taking on yet another anima function (see Tilton; Tatham). Thus they ignore the way that Barth's incorporation of the myth into the theme of subjective relativism exposes the hidden biases of that position, and the way his flattening of perspective is a consequence of those biases (see C. A. Davis).

Christ points out that Jungian concepts of gender are drawn mostly from ''myth and literature created by males'' and that when that androcentricity is understood, the definition of the eternal feminine can be quite useful in analyzing patriarchal culture (''Some Comments'' 66, 68). The feminist critic can use the archetypes and mythic parallels to explain the use of women as projections and symbols and the perspective and themes implied by those forms. Emma Jung says, ''[T]he anima . . . represents the feminine personality components of the man and at the same time the image he has of feminine nature in general, in other words, the archetype of the feminine'' (46). Seeing that link without accepting the male appropriation of female reality can offer important clues about what is repressed or excluded (by author and/or characters) by projection onto women characters. Such an approach can enhance other studies of women characters as well. Anne Robinson Taylor has found, for example, that the female narrators of male authors often reflect the writer's inner life in an especially direct way. The point here is not just that a feminist archetypal criticism can show the male orientation of myth; it can also, by observing the author's version of that orientation, explore important concerns about self and world. Application of feminist distinctions between anima and female self provides an opening for central analyses of theme, characterization, point of view, and narrative consciousness.

The difficulties increase, however, in applying the archetypes to literature by women and/or to women as central characters. The Jungian view appropriates power and thought to the male self, as opposed to the ''undeveloped, childlike, or primitive character'' of the feminine mind (Emma Jung 16). The female is thus cut off from the conscious choices of selfhood. How can the androcentric model be corrected to allow for women's psychic development? One's first impulse might be to assume the male model with simple corrections for gender. Edwards suggests that possibility, emphasizing the universality of the hero and the ''timeless and acultural'' nature of mythic patterns of selfhood (''Labors'' 44). Annis Pratt similarly asserts that Jungian theories, ''if turned upside down to admit of women as human participants in the quest for identity and rebirth experience, are helpful in the elucidation of the psychomythological development of the female hero'' (''Archetypal Approaches'' 3). This might at first seem to mean simple role reversal: if the equation of anima with female and animus with male consciousness is dropped, then the woman's animus could, like the man's anima, embody the deep realities of the psyche that she projects onto the opposite sex. Male symbology would embody the woman's not-self, all that the feminine is for a man. Fuller recognition of the animus as ''an erotic *other* or male-figure'' would, as Pratt points out, eliminate some of the contradictions in Jung's theory of the androgynous self (7). But simple reversal does not create a myth adequate to the female psychic experience. Though the process of psychic development takes the familiar forms of quest, descent, and rebirth for both male and female, the terms of that development are modified by gender.

To understand just how they are modified, we must look not to male myths and anima figures but to female-centered and female-created myths. Many feminist writers are studying those forms. Mary Daly's analyses of myth dis-cover stories of female selfhood and repression concealed in familiar myths (*Beyond God; Gyn/Ecology*). Susan Gubar similarly explores the Demeter myth's special significance for women writers (''Mother''). Susan Friedman's work on H. D. shows how the poet ''utterly transforms the psychoanalytic and mythological traditions she works within'' by a woman-centered perspective (''Creating a Women's Mythology''). And Carol Christ's studies of woman's spiritual quest conclude that it typically involves ''participation and union of a nonpersonal core of the self with the whole,'' as opposed to a male hero's conquest of the not-self (''Margaret Atwood'' 327; see also *Diving Deep*).

Such work shows woman-centered myths, heretofore obscured by male culture and male transmission of myth. Observation of archetypal forms formerly neglected—like animus figures and mystical union with the not-self—can help transform the paradigms by which we grasp literary meanings. But in order to conduct the search, we must uproot the idea of the eternal feminine. To do so may, paradoxically, tie the archetype more closely to image. Extending the Jungian differentiation ''between the archetypal and the personal aspects of the anima'' (Emma Jung 86) may help eliminate the equation of woman with anima. But it still allows, as Naomi Goldenberg notes, a proclamation of ''the proper experience of women''—womanhood outweighing woman. Thus she suggests that Jungians should ''equate image with archetype. . . . All imaginal activities, all images, could then be understood as archetypes to the degree that they move things and partake of what we might want to call 'numinosity.' *Archetypes therefore would refer to the imaginal or religious process itself rather than to past documents of that process*'' (449). Such an approach is less an abolition of Jungian theory than an elimination of its inconsistencies; treatment of the archetype as image would accommodate Jung's idea of its ''affinity with physical phenomena'' and his explanation that it is ''altered'' by entering into consciousness (7: 152; 9.1: 6), rather than lurking behind the image in pure state. The critic could then see Psyche's quest, for example, as heroic without either demanding that it match the male quest exactly or forcing on it an absolute model of the feminine. Gender's effect on archetype could be considered without reducing all women to anima.

Other theories of myth might seem to offer fewer problems to the feminist because they avoid the "liturgical pronouncements" about gender as absolute and inherited idea. Further, despite their many differences, ritual, functionalist, and later structuralist myth theories all tend to emphasize the whole narrative over the isolated image. This would seem especially promising for discussion of the effect on the whole of individual variations in point of view and character—for example, the nature of female quest narratives.

Unfortunately, most critics working with myth structure have failed to see these possibilities and so have been quite limited in their perceptions. Writers like Philip Wheelwright, Joseph Campbell, and—preeminently—Northrop Frye have indeed rejected the Jungian definition of archetype as rooted in the collective unconscious, preferring to ignore questions of source and speak simply of "persistent patterns of human thought and expression" that should be understood "on their own terms as far as possible instead of imposing extrinsically oriented interpretations upon them" (Wheelwright 55). The idea of the archetype, then, is derived from observation rather than deterministic theory; the critic can observe the forms in myth and show their relation to literature. Carol Christ works in something like this mode when she compiles observations of female quest narratives. The problem with many of these writers, however, is that their insistence on divorcing form from content and context, their evasion of questions of source, make them especially prone to unwarranted assumptions about the meaning of archetypes and especially blind to their own extensions of that meaning. Consider, for example, this passage from Northrop Frye:

> The material world is in a way feminine to the perceiver; it is the body which receives the seed of his imagination, and the works of the imagination which are the artist's children are drawn from that body. We think of Nature as feminine, and so she is. . . .
>
> The worship of a female principle, therefore, specifically a maternal principle, is not imaginative and is only possible to natural religion. (74–75)

These comments, no doubt based on observation of many mythic tales, are soaked in questionable assumptions, of which the most fundamental is that all artists, even all perceivers, are male (see also Smith 259). Joseph Campbell displays a similar blind spot when, in a book that does include examples of female heroes, he still says without qualification: "Woman, in the picture language of mythology, represents the totality of what can be known. The hero [described as 'he'] is the one who comes to know" (*Hero* 116). Because they do not take into account that most of the tales they study are created and transmitted by males, because they allow the generalization to overtake the fact (e.g., the occasional female hero), and above all because they never question the equation of male with universal (notice Frye's interchangeable "we"/"he"/"the artist" and his confident "and so she is"), they end up with another version of Jung's "liturgical pronouncements" about the feminine. They are thus often unable to discuss the limitations of the myth or its possible variations. In *The Masks of God: Occidental Mythology*, Campbell does sometimes take account of social shifts:

> The patriarchal point of view is distinguished from the earlier archaic view by its setting apart of all pairs-of-opposites—male and female, life and death, true and false, good and evil—as though they were absolutes in themselves and not merely aspects of the larger entity of life. (26–27)

In this he anticipates Daly's discussions of submerged female myth. But most of his work assumes the male perspective as universal.

The arrival of structuralism, then, might seem to hold out hope for a more rigorous approach. Claude Lévi-Strauss and followers retain the empirical approach so appealing to writers like Campbell, collecting all the versions of a myth in order to discuss it; and they display a similar preoccupation with form. In "The Structural Study of Myth," Lévi-Strauss insists that a myth's meaning is not in its "isolated elements" but in "the way those elements are combined"; the "bundles of . . . relations" constituting myth display the binary nature of human thought by the "progressive mediation" between exaggerated oppositions (174, 175, 188). This theory is appealing; the notion of binary thought seems quite fruitful for understanding gender as potent symbol. And Lévi-Strauss's formula for mythic inversions can be a tool for discussing male/female versions of parallel stories: indeed, his discussion of the "Ash-Boy" and "Cinderella" tales suggests such questions (190). By studying the way that a change in terms necessitates transformations in the whole structure, Lévi-Strauss promises to overcome the separation of form and content that produces so many problems in the Jungian analysis. He has been reticent about the way to distinguish just which "terms" are elements in the transformation and which may be superficial details. But gender certainly seems important enough to be part of the significant "bundles of relations."

Still, the literary critic will have difficulties using the theory. Lévi-Strauss insists that "the myth [consists] of all its versions" (181). While this does away with the search for a "true" version, it is troublesome in its rejection of any distinction between oral and written, primitive and sophisticated, literary and nonliterary versions. It would equate, for example, Joyce's *Ulysses* with an oral version of the Ulysses story (see Munz 23). Further, Lévi-Strauss, like Frye and company, is resolutely ahistorical, insistent that the "conceptual structures" of the human mind do not change, that "these forms are fundamentally the same for all minds—ancient or modern, primitive or civilized." Thus, while myth versions may change, the laws of their transformation do not, and so the myth itself remains. The interest of the analyst is in the fundamental oppositions and mediations in their permutations—not in the history of the myth, the psychology or history of the individual teller, or the circumstances of production of the individual version. History can be used "for cataloguing the elements" of the structure (Lévi-Strauss, *Savage Mind* 262), not for explaining its meaning.

Thus the structuralist and related versions of myth analysis offer both possibilities and new problems for the feminist literary critic. On the one hand, feminist critics are reluctant to ascribe absolute meaning to an individual image, much more inclined to define meaning within the context of patterns and relations than Jungians. They see myth, as Wheelwright puts it, as neither an enactment of the collective unconscious nor "a fiction imposed on one's already given world, but . . . a way of apprehending that world. Genuine myth is a matter of perspective first, invention second" (150). (Lévi-Strauss's schemata are a way of defining the principles of that perspective.) This view introduces important issues about the nature of human perception and conflict as well as individual psychic experience. On the other hand, the absolute divorce of form and meaning from historical and material contexts (and this is true of structuralist literary critics as well as anthropologists) limits the discussion of any myth or version of it, often produces hidden assumptions about meaning, and may confuse meaning by refusal to see the consequences of choice of terms. Lee Edwards remarks that the choice of a woman hero is, in concrete social and historical terms, the choice of a "marginal" character whose heroism therefore has new dimensions; neither Frye's view of woman as nature/environment nor Lévi-Strauss's formula of "inversion" seems able to take in such dimensions.

The weaknesses of all such "universal" views of myth show why most feminist critics choose to treat myth in literature (as in culture) as *tradition*. Consciousness of myth as transmitted through history, custom, and literature can allow the critic to distinguish between different meanings for the "same" story or figure. The role of the earth mother, for example, can be a liberating model for women, encouraging a sense of power and natural connection (as in Margaret Atwood's *Surfacing*); or it can be part of the paralyzing definition of woman as anima. Consideration of that difference requires exploring the relation between myth and mythos, archetype and social context.

In *The Masks of God: Creative Mythology*, Joseph Campbell explains that "creative mythology"—that is, mythic forms in literature and other art created by individuals—arises from an individual "experience of value": "Thus it corrects the authority holding to the shells of forms produced and left behind by lives once lived" (7). The nature of myth is in its combination of concrete situation and timeless pattern; the critic's task, especially with literature, is to find the point of intersection, to see what terms the myth takes in each incarnation. Lee Edwards's view of the Psyche myth recognizes that the "acultural" reading is difficult because "we are dealing with a tale embedded in a male-dominated culture"; in that context, Psyche's heroism is complicated by her womanhood, making her "a marginal being who adapts the ritual process to her own unique ends" ("Labors" 48). That reading offers a model for the myth critic aware of social pressures on the myth. The special significance of the female hero is not her representation of the Jungian feminine mode—a type primarily important in a male hero's story—but the effect her gender has, as both physical and social reality, on the terms of the myth. Gender is linked to social relations in the world that supplies concrete images. That meaning may well be in conflict with traditional associations, as in the Psyche story; Nina Baym shows another sort of conflict in Cooper's work, in which the women characters' traditional power as "Dark Ladies" is drained away by their reduction to a form of social exchange ("Women"). Thus neither Jungian absolutism nor identification of gender as exchangeable term is sufficient to explain the many versions of myth.

Such considerations are, of course, important for discussing all literary myths, but especially so in the study of women writers, who bear a complex relation to the traditional female image. The woman is always Other in the male myth, unpossessable but needed, capable of dual effects, allowing and threatening the man's sense of identity. The woman novelist enters a literature and culture rooted in this myth, in which gender relations are the parable for human relations to the outer world, in which *human* means "male." In this realm, "the mythic proportions of woman are recognizable and real; it is only the human dimensions that are patently false" (Gornick 144). But in a very real sense, the received versions of myth are the structures the writer has to work with; to step completely out of one's culture is impossible. The woman writer can add the "human dimension" by identifying with the mythic female in a way that men cannot; thus the resurrection of myths that center on women, like Demeter and Helen, or that stress women's closeness to nature. On the other hand, the woman writer lives in a culture that uses those types against actual women, displacing onto them all the qualities most feared even while draining them of significance or independent power. Thus any attempt to work with traditional myth or to invent a new myth involves a complex relation to female images and indeed to the whole narrative.

The need to affirm and simultaneously to subvert traditional myth, along with more obvious social pressures, may produce what Gilbert and Gubar describe as the "palimpsestic" technique, in which apparently traditional forms—marriage stories, male narrators, Gothic novels—are undermined by hidden "codes" of image and reference, "meanings hidden within or behind the more accessible, 'public' content of their works" (*Madwoman* 72). They speak, of course, of nineteenth-century writers, who were perhaps more narrowly confined; twentieth-century writers can create more overtly liberated stories—not least because they have the examples of those foremothers. But the kind of coding Gilbert and Gubar study was necessitated not only by outmoded literary fashion. The great weight of tradition and culture is still androcentric; the female author still faces the problem of May Sarton's Mrs. Stevens: what can the Muse mean for a woman artist? How can she find her own way of doing what has been defined as a male activity? The adaptation of the fundamental myth is the real question beneath apparently more superficial formal tinkering; and the hidden patterns of feminine experience and perception must be revealed both in new forms and in versions of old ones. Thus in the search for patterns not "accessible" to a "public," androcentric consciousness can go on even as new forms are created. (Perhaps the failure to adapt critical approaches to this perception explains why so many feminist—or just female—writers are accused of "formlessness" by reviewers: the patterns they explore have been invisible to traditional culture.)

Such observations are essential to the reconciling of image to archetype that myth critics must do. Whatever its basis—Jungian, structuralist, historical—myth criticism cannot ignore either gender or its social definition. The myth's perspective and limits must be defined; and its manifestation in particular literary forms must be linked to the individual and social context that produced them. Otherwise, we have only a schema, not a way to understand its realization.

NOTE

[1] The volume number (or volume and part numbers) is followed by a colon and the paragraph number.

AFTERWORD

Since this essay was written, in 1980, feminist literary theory and criticism have grown into a rich and wide-ranging body of knowledge. I will not attempt to review the scholarship that now addresses the issues in this essay. I would just observe that the correction and counteranalysis of patriarchal myth that the essay calls for have indeed developed, along two main avenues.

One, exemplified by Annis Pratt's work, continues to uncover mythic structures with special meaning for women. This approach explores the consequences of women's marginality by asking what happens to the patriarchal story when woman is the hero, or how the story looks from the point of view of characters other than the male actor. Perhaps most important, though, it also unveils different stories, ones with the potential for decentering patriarchal myth and making women no longer marginal but central: the tales of Demeter/Koré, Psyche, and others that constitute a repressed tradition for women.

The second approach, exemplified in the continuing scholarship of Sandra Gilbert and Susan Gubar, also explores the mythic consequences of women's marginality, but with much more attention to context. Gilbert and Gubar focus on the production and transmission of myth as text and tradition. In so doing, they reveal the artistic manipulation of mythic structures that forms a literary tradition.

This is essential work. Many of the current debates in religion, literature, and culture center on the relation between the literal images of particular myth and its compelling meaning (the debate over gender and the priesthood is only one obvious example). Recently, the great popularity of Joseph Campbell's public-television interviews demonstrated the public hunger for a deeper meaning to experience; yet it showed once again the inadequacy of the ahistorical approach.

The understanding of myth and gender as embedded in historical context is just beginning. Feminist critics have laid the foundation for a new understanding of myth that can make it adequate to women as well as men.

Washington, DC
July 1990

~ 1982 ~

Pope and Sexual Difference: Woman as Part and Counterpart in the "Epistle to a Lady"

ELLEN POLLAK

> [M]en act and women appear. *Men look at women. Women watch themselves being looked at. This determines not only most relations between men and women but also the relation of women to themselves. The surveyor of woman in herself is male: the surveyed female. Thus she turns herself into an object—and most particularly an object of vision: a sight.*
>
> *John Berger,* Ways of Seeing

SCHOLARS HAVE BEEN attentive to Pope's use of the commonplace eighteenth-century analogy between the arts of poetry and painting in his "Epistle to a Lady." Indeed, as Robert J. Allen has pointed out, the figure of the "sister arts" is at the very heart of the structure of Pope's text, which—in a manner not unusual in the genre of the literary character—conceives a series of verbal descriptions of women in terms of visual portraiture (81–83; see also Ault, ch. 5; Hagstrum 100–06, 236–41; Price 59–63; Brownell; Brower 267). Addressing his poem to his friend Martha Blount, whom he means to dissociate from the general failings of her sex, Pope takes his dedicatee and reader on a tour of a gallery of paintings in which several "nymphs" assume a variety of historical poses and costumes and in which the poet-guide himself at times assumes the role of portraitist.

What critics have not explored in any sustained way, however, is precisely how the poetry-painting metaphor that links the "sister arts" in "To a Lady" interacts with the subject of the poem itself—which is not simply women but, more specifically, their characterlessness. It is the nature of that interaction that my reading here will seek to analyze. The concept of character was protean in the eighteenth century, the term having current and historical associations not only with a particular literary genre, but with the techniques of writing, hieroglyphics, engraving, coin making, and painting as well. These associations have been enumerated elsewhere.[1] What I shall be looking at particularly here is the way Pope taps the fluid meanings of this term as a central binding force in his linking of verbal and visual modes of representation in order to establish (what would seem to be rather antithetical in a character essay) the notion of female characterlessness. Although this apparent contradiction does function as an important structural paradox in Pope's work, I shall argue that it has a certain ideological consistency in terms of the author's implicit metaphorization of the female as a work of art. Martha, I shall suggest, is objectified here both as a sign of her own insignificance and as a medium for Pope's self-reference. Ultimately, we can gain access to Pope's central metaphoric gesture in this text only by bringing into the range of critical inquiry the conventional ideological imperatives regarding gender that it inscribes. Although previous readings have often fruitfully mined the personal and historical contexts of Pope's poem, in a number of important cases the sexual ideology that informs its tropes and themes has been obscured. When this context is brought into relief, the terms of Pope's personal tribute to Martha Blount are rendered problematic at the least; indeed, the portrait of Martha Blount itself, which has traditionally been taken as an affectively "positive" rendering of a woman, may be read as well and perhaps more fundamentally as the vehicle for a conception of the female as a lack. Having no meaning in herself, woman here is at best a part and counterpart of man, whom she at the same time mirrors and completes.[2]

I

Pope's literary tribute to Martha Blount is the portrait of a woman in a portrait gallery looking at images of women. Mirrors within mirrors. But who, to borrow a term from the epigraph to my text, is the surveyor of this work? Whose image is being reflected in the mirrors?

The poem is built around the assertion of a dominant distinction: Martha is not like most other women. Pope wants to expose the vanity of women who hide behind the flattering forms of art, who make themselves (or affect to have themselves made) into objects of vision, sights; and he accomplishes this end by showing his reader, through irony, how incompletely (how defectively) most women substantiate the forms that they inhabit. As satirist, he refuses to dress his subjects in the lies of panegyric; he will strip them to their imperfect "natural parts."[3] He will, he says, draw women as they are, not as they appear. Indeed the very essence of his sketches—of these characters without character—will be generated at the point of difference between seeming and being, at the point at which we know these dazzling presences are empty, signs of absences, of lacks. Encouraged to dissemble, women are not at all as they appear:

> Bred to disguise, in Public 'tis [they] hide;
> There, none distinguish 'twixt [their] Shame or Pride,
> Weakness or Delicacy; all so nice,
> That each may seem a Virtue, or a Vice. (203–06)

Only the muted presence of a Martha, Pope insists, can signify a female authenticity. Her reserve is the mark of a genuine presence ("to dazzle let the Vain design, / To raise the Thought and touch the Heart, be thine!" [249–50]);

toasts and queens who flaunt their graces go down "unregarded"—things (252). Most women are impostors; Martha eschews all affection. Unencumbered by assumed identities, she is offered by Pope not as an object, a painted surface, but in the flesh, as what Irvin Ehrenpreis has called "a living being" (164), as proof that woman can be other (more) than lack.

What I shall argue here is that (like the distinction in the *Rape* between coquette and prude, or between Belinda and what Clarissa says Belinda ought to be [see Pollak, "Rereading"]) the distinction that Pope exploits as the rhetorical fulcrum of this text is, on his own terms, false—a distinction without a difference. There are limits to the way Pope can intelligibly represent Martha's singularity as a woman; indeed, in his very reverence for her "difference" from the inferior sameness of "other women," he reinscribes her status both as object and inferior.[4] In his hall of mirrored sights, Martha may on the most manifest level constitute an invisible "naked presence," but in the margins of this satire on woman as artifact she too stands framed, her flesh made text, within the terms of a discourse that can render woman only as negation. Further, not only is the distinction between the "living" Martha and her transmuted female counterparts collapsed within Pope's text, but both she and they operate finally as unacknowledged hieroglyphs of man—pretexts for the ultimately disembodied presence of Martha's poet. Standing beside his subject like a shadow, Pope does essentially all the talking in this text, which nonetheless presents itself as but a moment in an ongoing dialogue; Martha mostly silently looks on. The very statement that provides the point of departure for the work (that " 'Most Women have no Characters at all' ") is remote, having been uttered by her "once," in another place, another time. Moreover, this comment—which Pope appropriates both as and for his own—is a slip of Martha's tongue, words she has "let fall" in spite of herself. When Martha speaks, her voice is not her own.

Pope's text denies "character" to women in a more fundamental sense than even its own ironies would suggest. Metaphorically bridging the gap between verbal and visual modes of representation by his use of this key term, Pope establishes an essentially unitary structure of sexual difference—an economy of gender in which woman is not other in an irreducible, but only in an appropriated, sense. She is not the sign of a separate, autonomous otherness, is not a subject, an end in herself, but is "his other," the not-man that by opposition gives identity (gives "character") to man. Pope's sketches here contribute to the evolving genre of literary "characters," but they draw as well on other eighteenth-century senses of the term. Although *character* was used figuratively in painting to refer to what distinguishes a thing from something else, it was defined most "literally" as a written or inscribed symbol, a signifying mark (see Coleman 23–29). Pope exploits the first of these two meanings quite openly in his assertion that women, having no characters, are essentially alike; but by implicitly asserting woman's indistinguishability from man, his text also activates the more literal definition of the term. For despite the poet's claim in his "Argument" that he is representing female character "as contradistinguished from the other Sex," Pope's women remain in the most basic sense unsignified ("uncharactered") as such—the paradox of Martha's invisible corporeality itself concretizing woman's lack of access to the structures of either literal or visual representation in the form of an affirmation.[5] Women, in short, are occasions here for Pope's self-reference; he—the poet—has and is the last word in this essay about them (292).

The constitutive difference between Martha and Pope's "others" is elaborated in terms of their relative unity. Most women are scattered; in life and in art, they inhabit many poses, many frames. Made of "Matter too soft" to bear the "lasting mark" of consistent character, they are impossibly, infinitely changeable. Indeed, their fleeting essences seem to defy representation. The hopelessly confusing and shifty nature of "the sex" challenges the abilities not only of the painter, who by "Some flying stroke" (154) must "Catch, ere she change, the Cynthia of this minute" (20), but of the satirist as well. How is one to pin a woman down? "Woman and Fool are two hard things to hit, / For true No-meaning puzzles more than Wit" (114–15). Outside meaning and outside form, the reality of "normal" women is too slippery, too intractable, to compose.

By contrast, Martha has equanimity. Unlike her foils, she is contained, it would appear, within herself. She has good sense, good humor, and exquisite self-control (257–68). Demonstrating the composure of a saint, she is herself a composition. She may be composed:

> Heav'n, when it strives to polish all it can
> Its last best work, but forms a softer Man;
> Picks from each sex, to make its Fav'rite blest,
> Your love of Pleasure, our desire of Rest,
> Blends, in exception to all gen'ral rules,
> Your Taste of Follies, with our Scorn of Fools,
> Reserve with Frankness, Art with Truth ally'd,
> Courage with Softness, Modesty with Pride,
> Fix'd Principles, with Fancy ever new;
> Shakes all together, and produces—You.
> (271–80)

A delightful composite, Martha warrants the specificity of direct address, the privilege of a personal pronoun. Created "in exception to all gen'ral rules," she is announced as quintessentially herself (see Keener 76–77).[6]

Thus while Martha clearly stands in a state of grace with respect to the moral sanctions of Pope's text, her foils appear to be moral exiles, embodiments of uncontrolled sexuality and anarchic individualism who manifestly threaten social order. But Pope's organizing distinction begins to deconstitute itself precisely at this point. For the very characteristic of unmitigated self-love that unites "most women" in a narcissistic uniformity also keeps them constantly doubling back on themselves in self-defeat, so that female threat to the social order is always defused in Pope by providential design. Narcissa's moral emptiness may have some sinister implications—she may all but "stew a child"—but finally her viciousness "hardly" effects any serious damage and, like Atossa's "Heav'n-directed" wealth (150), even lends itself to some inadvertent good (she "Gave alms at Easter, in a Christian trim / And made a Widow happy, for a whim" [53–58]).[7]

Pope's misogyny and philosophic optimism, in short, intersect at the point where women, who have fundamentally negative value, are fundamentally impotent. Whether we consider the essentially frivolous affectation of the early portraits (29–51) or the "impotence of mind" with which those with pretensions to intellect try speciously to rationalize irrational behavior (69–100), Pope's "evil" women are pathetic and self-thwarting. Even Atossa, whose rage actually aspires to achieve subversive force, is undermined by her own "Spirit," her own desire. Female deviance in Pope always finally comes back to lend support to the stability of the discourse that excludes it. Indeed, far from being outside the law that houses Martha, Pope's female grotesques are generated by it and in turn sustain it.[8]

In Pope's textual (and sexual) economy, solipsistic reasoning is the accomplice to an essentially specular, narcissistic womanhood. A woman's ruling passion is her pleasure; her thirst for power is but a function of her desire (207–18). The poet's famous lines disclaiming the fault in female pleasure (209–13) merely parody what has already been depicted—in the portraits of Sin in State, Philomedé, and Flavia—as the typically female self-justifying tautology. By an obstinate error of thought, woman legitimizes her own desire in her own mind by deftly misconstruing her injunction to please men ("and where the lesson taught / Is but to please, can Pleasure seem a fault?"). Inverting the syntax of the cultural imperative, she asserts herself in opposition to an inexorable law of gender that defines her as an object of male desire. But inexorable means fixed. A woman may seek to assume subjectivity, to insert herself as subject into an economy that denies her any presence on those grounds, but inevitably her desire will be recuperated by the masculine prerogative she usurps.

Indeed, the masochism of a woman's pleasure in Pope is fatally inscribed: "Yet mark the fate of a whole Sex of Queens! / Pow'r all their end, but Beauty all the means" (219–30). The dreadful spectacle of "Ghosts of Beauty" gliding "round and round" the sites of their former pleasures (haunting "the places where their Honour dy'd" [242]) is Pope's image of the circularity of a female desire that can never be fulfilled, of a pleasure that consumes itself even in the moment of gratification.[9]

As representative of the "good woman," Martha differs from her satirical counterparts in the manifest condition of her desire. Her "true charm" as a woman who *plays by* the system and reaps the rewards of her submission is being asserted as an alternative to the specious charms of those who simply *play* the system, exploiting (or trying to exploit) their status as sexual objects in order to ascertain the blandishments of power. While "most women" aspire to reverse the natural grammar of desire, Martha, the poet tells us, "has her humour most, when she obeys" (264).

Pope exploits a subtle but telling pun in the term "humour." The paradox reduces contradiction, but it is not clear where the slack of difference is taken up. A congruence is being asserted between the principles of individual desire and conformity to a law outside the self. Martha's "humour," read as will or personal whim, is most gratified when she follows the desire of another, of a man. Certain fixed social relations are implied: a husband has control over the will of his wife; in order to get what she wants, she must do what he says.

But *humour* also means "Good-humour" (292) or "Temper" (257), that saintlike quality of mind that we know Martha, as every woman should, possesses. Embodying an intrinsic motivation to please, the line asserts, Martha "really is" most happy when she obeys. Her will—indeed her wish—is his command, and her good humor is most sustained by her obedience. She obeys freely, voluntarily.

In other words, the statement works two ways: Martha's good humor may be most nourished, but it is also most exercised, by the necessities of submission. Two counterstatements operate side by side: Martha has no original desire, no pleasure that originates in her; she has such desire, but has resigned it or has pushed it underground. But, as Pope's irony suggests and as Clarissa's warning in 1717 had made quite clear, there is agreement even within these discontinuous texts. Resignation is a functional requirement of feminine good humor, which covers and ameliorates loss: "What then remains, but well our Pow'r to use, / And keep good Humour still whate'er we lose?" (*Rape* 29–30). Moreover, whichever sense we settle on at a given moment—whether we read Pope's line as positing female masochism (a natural coincidence of obedience and desire in a woman) or as valorizing female virtue as a dynamic social relation in which woman's desire capitulates to phallocratic law—the ultimate implication for Pope's rendering of Martha is the same. By collapsing the difference between female obedience and humor, Pope effectually effaces the autonomous desire of his "subject." Martha is esteemed because, both like and unlike other women, she is not "other," because her pleasure has been elided with the imperatives of a masculine pleasure, because essentially her will is not her own.

Analysis of this pun shows further erosion of the enabling distinction of Pope's text. Martha is "other" than the "others," but only within the limits of a hierarchy of sexual difference in which the female term is not primary but derived. Her specificity as a female systematically effaced, Martha is valued as a metonymic substitute for man. For woman, says Pope, whether she remains discreetly hidden inside the law or flamboyantly transgresses its boundaries, inhabits a place of nonmeaning. She has "No-meaning" in herself (115); she is a lack.

Indeed, in Pope's system, incomprehensibility is valorized as a woman's "proper pleasure." A woman's perfection is in her imperfection, she is "Fine by defect" (44). Even Martha's charm—the mark of female nature at its "best"—is the result of a "Contradiction" (270). Like the women she is so blessedly unlike, she too "defies definition," is "indescribable" (Keener 72, 76), so that her very singularity is the basis of her sameness with "the sex." In both fine and foolish women, it is nonidentity, insignificance that appeals; it seduces the moralist and disarms the critic ("Woman and Fool are two hard things to *hit*" [emphasis added]). "Women," wrote Pope in his *Thoughts on Various Subjects*, "as they are like riddles in being unintelligible, so generally resemble them in this, that they please us no longer when once we know them" (10: 558). Unintelligibility is the condition of female charm.

Is Pope's tribute to Martha Blount, then, a compliment or not? The poet's note to line 215 suggests the possibility of conscious equivocation:

> William Ayre . . . records a complaint made to Pope about these lines by a "Lady whose name for Virtue . . . has been conspicuous . . . and who in her Youth was thought one of the handsomest Women of Quality." Pope replied, "Madam, I must intreat of you to observe, that I only say:
>
> But every WOMAN is at Heart a Rake. This in no Way affects your Ladyship, who was an Angel, when you were young, and now advancing into Life, are almost already become a Saint." The complainant "was Woman enough to be pleas'd with the Compliment."

The very protest here, in its lack of modesty, invites the poet's scorn. But the passage may sustain a variant reading: a "good woman" is impossible to find. Indeed, being woman and not woman, a Lady is a radical contradiction—a fine occasion for the play of Popeian wit. The exceptional woman is positively valued because she cannot be named. Divinity, sainthood, ladyship are all euphemisms that, applied to woman, affirm the very lack that they obscure. This is the greatest paradox of all: Martha is being etched by a discourse that situates her outside the law of intelligibility. But, as the portraits of recuperated female deviancy show, in Pope's mythic economy those outside are also in. The margins Miss Blount inhabits occupy the same conceptual space on which the "characters" of Narcissa and Atossa have been drawn.

II

"To a Lady" is Pope's second Moral Essay. On the characters of women, it is a companion piece to Pope's first epistle on the characters of men, but it "looks forward" in the series, too, by virtue of the central economic metaphor it exploits. Representing women as gold, it is Pope's prelude to two subsequent epistles on the use of riches.[10] But if "To a Lady" is best understood within the frame of the three related poems that surround it, that literary context itself needs to be considered in light of the organizing structures of the larger, ideological context of which it is in turn a part.[11] An examination of the role of gender in conditioning the meaning of this text can help us to identify the limits of purely formalist interpretations of it as well as of some important readings that attend to its biographical and allusive contexts without inquiring into the sexual values that informed them.

For Rebecca Parkin, who produced one of the most distinguished New Critical readings of the poem, Pope's interpenetrating paradoxes are the basis of the complexity of his work. I would argue that, on the contrary, these paradoxes only create the illusion of complexity. Indeed, as I have tried to show, their interpenetration is possible precisely because the difference that they entertain is false, so that the opposing terms they postulate can readily be mutually exchanged. The illusion of complexity (the illusion of a difference where there is none) is actually a sophisticated rhetorical strategy for obscuring an ideological simplicity, for bifurcating a premise that is singular and not, as Parkin argues, "polysemantic." In one sense, to be sure, my reading and the New Critics' do concur; they both attribute a certain integrity, or unity, to Pope's work. But the condition of being "well-wrought" is hardly a guarantee of ideological innocence, and the acontextual character of most formalist treatments of "To a Lady" seems worthy of analysis itself.

Ideological context has been obscured as well by those critics whose approach has been in other important ways contextual. Indeed, one of the most interesting interpretations of the poem is by a critic who not only seeks to read it in terms of the context of Pope's life and entire canon but who also specifically endeavors to explain the relationship between "To a Lady" and the other Moral Essays. This is Thomas Edwards, who finds a pessimism in "To a Lady" that is absent from the other poems in the series. To Edwards, the redemptive force of Pope's affection for Martha Blount at the end of epistle 2 seems tenuous beside the enormously powerful portrayal of hopelessness that occurs earlier in the poem, in the lines on the death of dowagers. By contrast to the "potent myth of a beautiful and harmonious relationship between man and his environment" established in "Cobham," "Bathurst," and "Burlington," "To a Lady" seems to "linger ominously on the possibility that the positive potential of experience is gravely limited." It thus threatens to disrupt the Augustan "pattern of meaning" that organizes the Moral Essays as a whole (77).

Edwards explains this discrepancy in tone in terms of Pope's personal development. By the time "To a Lady" was written, the poet's "anxious, 'modern' concern about the working of mutability" was waging an increasingly intense conflict with the Augustan optimism that informed his earlier work (2). "To a Lady" is finally a "poetic triumph that remains Augustan," but it represents a triumph under stress (17).

The limitation of this explanation consists in its bypassing of gender as a determining factor in the meaning of Pope's text. What Edwards takes at face value (and thus tacitly sanctions by failing to analyze) is the rhetorical strategy by which Pope makes woman in this poem stand as the universal equivalent of a genderless humanity even as he displaces postlapsarian experience onto her alone. In other words, his poem exploits the specificity of female existence as somehow peculiarly representative of the "human condition," but only in order to reinforce the pastoral myth of man's beautiful and potent relation to the world; these countertexts are part of one idea. Thus when Edwards reads "To a Lady" as evidence of Pope's concern with the futility of human existence, when he fails to see the extent to which this concern is in fact being mitigated by being projected onto women, he mistakes a part for the whole. Reading Pope's "generic She" (I use the term as the feminine variant of that familiar masculine pronoun, the "generic He" that also includes woman within man) as a sign of transparent presence, he elevates the second Moral Essay—conceptually an extension, a part, a prop of all the others—to the status of an ontologic threat.

But far from being a point of stress within the Popeian quartet, this poem functions to alleviate stress by neutralizing difference within the very discourse that gives Pope's Moral Essays unity. Rather than straining the optimistic neoclassicism of the series, "To a Lady" reiterates the standard, classical identification of woman with the body, circumstance, necessity.[12] The connection is implicit (if not acknowledged) in Parkin's observation that the women in this text are embedded in the vicissitudes of time. But it emerges too in the operation of the broader symbolic system by which Pope's women are unformed "Matter," inert, unfruitful, useless "things" (3, 112, 252). Indeed, it is by their very exclusion from the permanence of form, by bearing the symbolic burden of mutability, that Pope's women tie Cobham, Bathurst, and Burlington to life and to the productive realm of possibility.

Male virtue (a redundancy if read etymologically) is, in the Popeian text, active and generative: seminal. And the passages saluting the masculine figures celebrated by the Moral Essays are thick with the language of power and positive action: the Man of Ross "enabled to pursue," empowered to "supply"; Burlington encouraged to "proceed," "make," "erect," "repair," "restore"; and Bathurst urged to "teach us," "to value," "T'enjoy"—all verbs that require an object to build upon. Spacks's striking observation of both the general paucity of verbs and the relatively frequent use of the imperative form of the verb "to see" in "To a Lady" offers an interesting comparison to Pope's verb usage here (*Argument* 165). Masculine virtue, what Pope calls "Sense," consists in co-operating with natural design, but it is no mere passive conformity, as Edwards's discussion of the negative example of Sir Balaam makes quite clear. Balaam may have all the trappings of Puritan virtue—"self-denial, mechanical piety, and economic solidity"—but to Pope "This is moral vacuity . . . ; Balaam's career is the saga of the creation of evil *ex nihilo*. If 'virtue' is only a restraint and not a positive impulse, it is helpless in the face of worldly temptation, and Balaam's financial success brings disaster" (60). As Pope had established parenthetically in the story of Cotta's son, "what to shun will no great knowledge need, / But what to follow, is a task indeed" ("Bathurst" 201–02).

If we read Pope's epistles paratactically—as Edwards does, ignoring the internal hierarchy of gender—Martha, whom Pope applauds for avoiding the pitfalls of female viciousness, ought to partake of active virtue too. But the condition of her goodness, like Balaam's, is restraint. Only the withholding generosity of Phoebus (who denies her "the Pelf / Which buys [her] sex a Tyrant o'er itself" [287–88]) can protect her from the corrupting love of wealth. (Note the recuperative optimism here: even female corruption "buys into" a system of its own suppression.) Further, while the address to Bathurst appeals to its subject's dynamic, responsible powers of mediating between the extremes "Of mad Good-nature, and of mean Self-love" (227–28), the lines to Martha praise her as a fait accompli of mediation, a blended, finished "work" whose charm and moral perfection are stasis itself. The reward for her goodness is not, as for the Man of Ross, in the active "ends of being," but is passively contingent on the blandishments of men: by the patronage of Apollo she is protected from herself; by the patronage of Pope, she is immortalized and blessed (281).

Neither is Martha's "sense" a function of rational cognition, though it does bespeak a passive *re*-cognition of her proper social "place." In men, reason is an enabling force, a source and precondition of power and of purpose:

Two Principles in human nature reign;
Self-love, to urge, and Reason, to restrain;

. . . .

Self-love, the spring of motion, acts the soul;
Reason's comparing balance rules the whole.
Man, but for that, no action could attend,
And, but for this, were active to no end;
Fix'd like a plant on his peculiar spot,
To draw nutrition, propagate, and rot;
Or, meteor-like, flame lawless thro' the void,
Destroying others, by himself destroy'd.
(*Essay on Man*, epistle 2, lines 53–66)

Pope's image of "human nature" sans reason here sounds very much like Atossa's and Silia's "impotence of mind" (the female variant of the "God within the mind" [*Essay on Man*, epistle 2, line 204]). But by collapsing the distinction between obedience and desire in Martha, Pope has effectually eliminated the ground on which reason can perform its intermediary, regulatory function of steering between the extremes of mad good nature and mean self-love. Reason, like action, has redemptive force in men; but a woman can have "sense" only to the extent that she retreats from public view and camouflages her impotence by never presuming to judge or act.[13]

Pope's paratactic presentation of sexual "character," which treats each gender within the rhetorical frame of its "own" text, helps throw his readers off the scent of the implied hierarchical relation between these frames. Thus Edwards reads epistle 2 as through a telescope, drawing it forward from its peculiarly recessed position within the Moral Essays to a plane of value equivalent to the others. And Pope would seem to encourage the parallel reading. Consider, for example, these two passages from *An Essay on Man* and the "Epistle to Cobham" juxtaposed to the two apparent echoes from "To a Lady" which follow:

This light and darkness in our chaos join'd,
What shall divide? The God within the mind.
Extremes in Nature equal ends produce,
In Man they join to some mysterious use;
Tho' each by turns the other's bound invade,
As, in some well-wrought picture, light and shade,
And oft so mix, the diff'rence is too nice
Where ends the Virtue, or begins the Vice.
(epistle 2, lines 203–10)

Our depths who fathoms, or our shallows finds,
Quick whirls, and shifting eddies, of our minds?
Life's stream for Observation will not stay,
It hurries all too fast to mark their way.
In vain sedate reflections we would make,
When half our knowledge we must snatch, not take.
("Cobham" 29–34)

Come then, the colours and the ground prepare!
Dip in the Rainbow, trick her off in Air,
Chuse a firm Cloud, before it fall, and in it
Catch, ere she change, the Cynthia of this minute.
(17–20)

Pictures like these, dear Madam, to design,
Asks no firm hand, and no unerring line;
Some wand'ring touch, or some reflected light,
Some flying stroke alone can hit 'em right:
For how should equal Colours do the knack?
Chameleons who can paint in white and black?
(151–56)

Pope makes a number of analogous statements about men and women in these passages, and even uses some of the same metaphors from nature and art in doing so; but he does not therefore offer equivalent examples of "universal truths" about human nature. In men, as in women, vice and virtue are often mixed beyond recognition and, in the shifting stream of life, it is difficult to pin either male or female character down. These inferred assertions do not contradict anything that Pope actually says, but they leave many additional implications out. Stable moral categories do exist in the larger Popeian universe. "Fools!" the passage from *An Essay on Man* continues,

who from hence into the notion fall,
That Vice or Virtue there is none at all.
If white and black blend, soften, and unite
A thousand ways, is there no black or white?
(211–14)

Indeed, there is; and women's relation to this continuum of value is different from men's. Female "vice" and "virtue" are plotted along an entirely different axis from the one whose extremes are identified by Pope as white and black or light and shade. Woman moves in a world of hues and mixed colors, not values—a world of rainbows, chameleons, and reflected light, where she is most virtuous when she is most "in the shade." Only by rhetorically dislocating "To a Lady," by creating the illusion of a contextual vacuum, can Pope pretend to draw moral distinctions between women without effectually denying the tenet of their undifferentiated amorality.

III

For all her variability, woman in Pope's text invariably functions at once as a sign of her own lack and as an alibi for the primacy of a masculine presence. She may usurp fictitious identities, may even pretend—like Atossa—to the tyrannical force of masculinity and burn herself out in the very passion by which she resists annihilation; or she may disappear "ladylike" inside the contours of another subjectivity; but identity is finally conferred on her only within the terms of a hegemonic coupling in which she is both a part and mirror, or counterpart, of a presence not her own.

Clearly, within this implicit structure of sexual difference, women cannot logically be distinguished from one another on the basis of intrinsic worth; for every woman's value, by definition, is conditional, is ontologically dependent on the exteriority of her relation to the law of a privileged masculine term.

Nonetheless, despite the very logic of the structures he exploits, Pope does poetically assert the efficacy of distinguishing on these grounds. His very poetry enables the illogic, exploiting a range of rhetorical strategies for stabilizing the contradiction between his simultaneous assertion and denial of intrinsic female worth. And nowhere, perhaps, is this contradiction naturalized in so condensed a form as in the controlling economic metaphor of his poem, the identification of women with gold. Bringing the contextual force of moral epistles 3 and 4 into play at the point of its juncture with the force of bourgeois sexual myth, this metaphor at once discloses and conceals Pope's underlying objectification of the female as both an ornament and a means of production within the institution of bourgeois marriage.

The first to point to the pervasiveness of the gold metaphor in "To a Lady" was Geoffrey Keogh, whose note on its significance is worth quoting at length not only because it effectively explicates some of the implications of the figure but also because of its ready acceptance of the analogy's complimentary intent:

> The central metaphor of the first four lines . . . depends on the original Greek meaning of *character* (the stamped image on a coin), which only later acquired the meaning of stereotype and habitual characteristic. Unlike the sturdy alloy of a circulating coin which will resist wear, women are a more noble metal. They are pure gold, hence do not circulate; rather they are hoarded as domestic treasure, or like jewelry serve as an adornment. . . . Unlike slaves and men of the world, their service is voluntary rather than for hire. Hence their soft matter (flesh) will never bear the branded mark of a fugitive slave. Unlike the graven images of the deified emperors on coins of the empire, they are less distinguished by the lineaments of their features than by their color. . . .
>
> The metaphor of painting and portraiture dominates this epistle, after which Pope goes on to describe men in terms of money and gold. Unlike men, women are not all of a stamp, inflexible and unchanging; they are rather as full of subtle shadows as a fine oil painting.

Keogh reads the image as conferring on woman a unique and distinctly female kind of excellence; it makes her superior to men in some respects. But context is, as always, of the essence and, like Edwards, Keogh disregards aspects of the very context he invokes. The poems to Bathurst and Burlington do not "describe men in terms of money and gold" so much as in terms of the way they use those forms of wealth. Moreover, Pope's views on the character of luxurious, inactive wealth are for the most part unequivocally negative; in "Bathurst" hoarded riches are virtually scatologically portrayed:

> Wealth in the gross is death, but life diffus'd,
> As Poison heals, in just proportion us'd:
> In heaps, like Ambergrise, a stink it lies,
> But well-dispers'd, is Incense to the Skies.
>
> (233–36)

Implicit in the manifestly complimentary statement that women are made of a purer and more precious metal than men, in other words, is a latent message that they are for that very reason more corrupt. Only "Use," the proper dispersion of property, has the power to purify riches and give value to material wealth by turning it to productive, wholesome ends: "'Tis Use alone that sanctifies Expence / And Splendor borrows all her rays from Sense" ("Burlington" 179–80). As Edwards remarks in his gloss on Pope's lines from "Bathurst" on "commodious Gold," "gold is dangerous because it lacks more identity" (52). It derives value only by virtue of " Man's " ability to transform it into something needful to "human" life.

Thus, insofar as women in "To a Lady" are "uncharactered," and so "do not circulate" as autonomous entities (confined to private life, they have no public function in society, nor do they perform any practical, public service), they are identified with gold in its primitive, inactive state and are thereby associated with unfruitful, decadent wealth (domestic treasure) and useless art ("artful to no end," they are not only impotently cunning but merely ornamental). They are a sort of filthy lucre unmediated by industrious or rational enterprise, a storehouse of unrealized possibility turned in upon itself that, like the uncreated matter of Milton's cosmos, is recognizable by its formlessness and made manifest by its anticreative force.[14]

Only circulation within a masculine economy (in both the libidinal and market senses of that term) can confer value on a woman. Only coupling with a masculinity that would efface her even in the moment of embrace can bring woman into the realm of the proper, property. Martha, the "truly esteemable" woman, is gold but, oddly, a gold refined of its "dazzle," a blend of "soft" and "hard" qualities, an alloy of womanhood and masculinity.

Here the full constellation of relationships between marriage, female chastity, and property in the eighteenth century comes into active play. By the turn of the century, marriage had become a woman's "calling"—a substitute, in the middle and upper-middle classes, for the more active forms of economic function performed by women in a precommercial age.[15] Within bourgeois culture, woman's prescribed economic role was the almost exclusively passive and intermediary one of vessel in the continuance of masculine property. Marriage enclosed female sexuality within a neutralizing institutional sanction even as, through its enshrinement of the laws of conjugal chastity, it transformed that sexuality into a vehicle for enlarging and perpetuating wealth. More completely in this period than ever before, female chastity in marriage was identified with property, its violation with disrupting the legitimate perpetuity of the masculine estate.[16]

Thus, though Martha is composed, "within herself," hers is not the containment of self-possession. Finding power in submission, freedom in necessity, her quintessential "selfhood" is but a function of her "belonging" to a desire not her own. Combining the virtues of wifehood, motherhood, submission, and chastity is, paradoxically, the mark of Martha's sameness with "the sex." For she is no more an id/entity, no more intrinsic to herself, no more unmixed or less impure than Pope's adulterous and vicious scattered women. Content to be a social satellite (the image of the moon simultaneously evoking the Miltonic conception of "reflected light" and Diana, goddess of chastity), she is still riches; and though she is not promiscuously, she is nevertheless properly, "dispers'd."

Martha's maternal and wifely status is a feature of special critical interest since, in point of fact, Pope's friend was both single and childless. By and large, the critical explanation for this selective falsification of Pope's subject (who, curiously enough, is still read as an emblem of authenticity) has been discretion, chivalry; Pope sought to "protect the maiden lady of his poem." Only the association of Martha with Diana through the image of the moon provides a hint of a historical spinsterhood (Ehrenpreis 165–66).[17]

Although it is probably accurate to say that in some sense Pope's poem does enable the ideological contradiction by which his "disguised" heroine represents "the real," it still seems worth inquiring about the terms that condition that contradiction. And indeed, the inconsistency can be accounted for by reference to a prescriptive intertext.[18] Given the exigencies of the ideological content of his text, as well as its at least patent design as a personal compliment, Pope was obliged to represent his heroine as fulfilling all the most important features of a socially sanctioned feminine ideal. Only a text that conformed to the terms of bourgeois myth by valorizing chastity within marriage while evading the necessity of condoning the "superannuated" virginity of a single woman could constitute a readerly tribute within the conventions of eighteenth-century sexual codes.[19] Since the myth did not fit the woman to whom he sought to pay a tribute both consistent and complete, Pope quite simply made the woman fit the myth, leaving as little manifest trace as possible in his text of the violence by which the fact of the historical Martha is effaced.

Indeed, so complete and so proficient is Pope's mastery of a discourse in which woman is both logically and ontologically denied, in which the notion of female identity is absent altogether, that Pope's "good" and "evil" women are equivalently conceived as variants of men. The very formula that encodes Martha's positive "femininity" as a moderation, muting, or canceling of femaleness by maleness encodes unmediated femaleness as "masculine," as rakish and tyrannical, as the usurpation of a subjectivity that is always, by definition, male.

Martha's "softness" is not the errant softness of indefinite outlines nor the overrefinement of unmuted gold, but she is still matter. If her virtue is in her tractability, in the fact that her contours can be molded, what Ehrenpreis calls the "roundedness" of her heroinism is not the roundedness of a "living being" but rather of a sculpted, polished Galatea (164). For even as she is scripted as the incarnation of Pope's positive values, she is crypted in the "living corpus" of his text.[20] Her body fetishistically cloaked in borrowed lunar light, she is celebrated as an object/means of masculine fulfillment, mute inspiration, muse of a poet's thoughts, a male's desire ("To raise the Thought and touch the Heart be thine!"). In chilling exchange for that rare service, entombment in Pope's verse extends her life: "Be this a Woman's Fame, with this unblest, / Toasts live a scorn, and queens may die a jest" (281–82). And if crypted, cryptic too. Anonymous "Lady," faceless pronoun, buried in the indeterminacy of direct address even as she is personalized by the candor of a private interchange, undeciphered hieroglyph, she is "charactered" both as woman and the artifact of man.[21]

NOTES

[1] See especially Patrick Coleman. The standard work on the early genre of the character is Benjamin Boyce's *The Theophrastan Character in England to 1642*; see also by Boyce *The Character Sketches in Pope's Poems*. Paul Korshin makes numerous helpful references to character in *Typologies in England 1650–1820*. I am indebted to him for sharing with me a portion of his work in progress on characters.

[2] One important and persuasive essay that does consider the poem in the context both of antifeminist satire and of the conventions of eighteenth-century womanhood is Felicity Nussbaum's "Pope's 'To a Lady' and the Eighteenth-Century Woman." The most recent and direct challenge to the link that Nussbaum and some eighteenth-century writers have suggested between "To a Lady" and earlier antifeminist satire is by Howard D. Weinbrot in *Alexander Pope and the Traditions of Formal Verse Satire* (189–98). Nussbaum further explores the subject of women in Pope's poetry in *The Brink of All We Hate*, which appeared as this essay was going to press. Neither the "Epistle to a Lady" nor *The Rape of the Lock*, Nussbaum argues there, "is finally misogynist, but each is ambiguous and complex in its use of eighteenth-century conventions and commonplaces about the sex" (140). My argument in the present essay is that, ultimately, even the ambiguities and complexities of Pope's use of sexual convention have a certain underlying ideological coherence and consistency. Some of my other differences with Nussbaum will be elaborated below. Carole Fabricant also has some fascinating points to make about Pope and pictorialism in "To a Lady" in "Pope's Portraits of Women."

[3] I use *The Twickenham Edition of the Poems of Alexander Pope*, vol. 2, *The Rape of the Lock*; vol. 3.1, *An Essay on Man*; and vol. 3.2, *Epistles to Several Persons*. The passage from "Epistle to a Lady" referred to above occurs in vol. 3.2, p. 65, lines 185–90. All future references to Pope's poems will be indicated parenthetically by line number in my text.

[4] Nancy K. Miller offers a more extended discussion of the recuperation of the exceptional woman in eighteenth-century texts in *The Heroine's Text*.

[5] I am influenced here by Peggy Kamuf's description of the specularity of Rousseau's *Letters to d'Alembert* in "Rousseau's Politics of Visibility."

[6] Critics have noted the unusual intimacy of address that characterizes this poem—unusual especially in Pope's poems of this period. See Brower (266, 275) and Griffin (124–25).

[7] Both Nussbaum ("Pope's 'To a Lady' " 453) and Patricia Meyer Spacks (161) have commented on the essentially figural nature of Pope's "realism"; but both, to my mind, are also inclined to give undue force to the potential for evil embodied in Pope's negative portraits: "The series of portraits add up to a preliminary judgmental definition of women . . . as dangerous in their moral weakness" (Spacks 162); and "Woman, distinct from man and in inevitable conflict with him, wields her power for the forces of disorder and even chaos" (Nussbaum 452). Both readings seem to me to underplay the extent to which Pope's satire repeatedly neutralizes the threat of sexual difference by denying it an identity of its own. In other words, as I shall be arguing here, Pope's women are not so much "immoral" as amoral.

[8] I differ in emphasis here from Spacks, who notes the "deepening sinister implications" of female deviance in Pope's opening sequence of portraits. Although there do seem to be arcs of increasing intensity in the sketches, there is also (as Spacks herself has beautifully shown) an inverse relationship between the intensity and scope of female influence in this poem. I cannot agree therefore that Atossa's violent attitude toward social hierarchy ever convincingly threatens its existence. Spacks justly, and very usefully, locates Pope's women irretrievably inside relationship. But I do not see that status as the basis of woman's threat to social order; on the contrary, as I shall argue presently, I see it as the very condition of her inability to act (Spacks 159–62).

[9] The image is itself latently erotic. Indeed, it reminds one of the autoerotic hovering of the sylphs (*Rape* 1.44), who embrace women when women reject men (1.67–68). Since the sylphs are the spirits of dead coquettes, projections or externalizations of Belinda's own psychic life, their embraces (sylph embraces) are really self-embraces, and the function of the erotic dream that Ariel conjures over the sleeping Belinda's head is to stoke the maiden's sense of self-importance (1.35). And just as Belinda's autoerotic pleasure is associated with sterility in Pope's message that the overzealous defense of beauty is a fruitless enterprise, so this image in "To a Lady," which conflates the death

of beauty/pleasure with the birth of pleasure (the death of honor), equates unattached female sexuality with futility and death. Brower (275–77) has noted the thematic and stylistic links between this passage in "To a Lady" and Pope's genealogy of the sylphs in *The Rape of the Lock*.

[10] My reference to the poem's thematic "anticipation" of epistles 3 and 4 is based on its final placement in the series. In fact, of the four Moral Essays, "To a Lady" was written last. It was placed second in the series several weeks before Pope's death.

[11] For an extended discussion of the textual history of the Moral Essays that also argues the importance of reading the four epistles in the light of their interrelatedness (though to a somewhat different end than I argue for it here), see Miriam Leranbaum, chapters 1 and 3.

[12] For discussion of the classical identification of women with necessity, and in particular with what Pope himself calls "private life" (200), see, for example, Jean B. Elshtain, chapter 1; and Susan Okin, parts 1 and 2.

[13] Indeed, Martha's "virtue" resembles the "fix'd virtue" of the Stoics more than it does the rational, active "virtue" Pope admires in men (see *Essay on Man*, epistle 2, lines 101–04).

[14] Milton also associates women with that "precious bane," "ribs of Gold" (*Paradise Lost* 1.690–92). For an interesting analysis of the Augustan satirists' view of women as inherently anticreative, see Susan Gubar's "The Female Monster"; see also my comment on Gubar's article. For an excellent analysis of the association between rationality and industry implicit in eighteenth-century political theory, see C. B. Macpherson.

[15] A more extended discussion of middle- and upper-class women's gradual withdrawal from direct forms of economic activity in the late seventeenth and early eighteenth centuries can be found in Alice Clark. Natalie Zemon Davis offers a useful analysis of the strengths and limits of Clark's work in her review article.

[16] As Dr. Johnson observed of female chastity, "all property depends upon it" (Boswell 2: 457). By exacerbating the damaging effects of bastardy on the lineal descent of family wealth, the new types of marriage settlements introduced in the seventeenth century helped intensify social anxiety over the chastity of wives. For fuller discussion of such changes in property law, see H. J. Habakkuk.

[17] Noting that editions of "To a Lady" prior to the "death-bed" of 1744 read "Sighs for a Sister" in line 260, instead of "Sighs for a Daughter," F. W. Bateson, editor of the Twickenham text, writes: "[No] doubt the reference had been too obvious and had started gossips talking." The historicism of Ehrenpreis's and Bateson's practical explanation for the terms of Martha's "virtue" finds a common ground with my more formal analysis in the realm of social ideology, which affects both life and art.

[18] Consider, for example, the parallel between Pope's lines describing Martha's "Temper" (257–68) and these lines advising a lady how to use "*Art* . . . and a skilful *Hand*" in dealing with an ill-tempered husband in Halifax's popular conduct book for women, *The Lady's New Years Gift, or, Advice to a Daughter*: "You are dextrously to yield every thing till he beginneth to cool, and then by slow degrees you may rise and gain upon him: Your *Gentleness* well timed, will, like a Charm, dispel his Anger ill placed; a *kind Smile* will *reclaim* when a *shrill pettish Answer* would provoke him" (Savile 14).

[19] The concept of the "superannuated virgin" is from Richard Allestree's *The Ladies Calling*, another very widely read conduct book that remained influential well into the eighteenth century.

[20] For several recent analyses of the inscription of the female body as text, see Kamuf, *Fictions*; Vickers; Gubar, " 'Blank Page.' "

[21] I would like to thank Mary Poovey and Julia Epstein for reading and offering suggestions on an earlier draft of this essay.

AFTERWORD

When "Pope and Sexual Difference" won the Florence Howe Prize in 1982, it was part of a book-length work in progress—*The Poetics of Sexual Myth: Gender and Ideology in the Verse of Swift and Pope*—that would be published in 1985 by the University of Chicago Press as part of Catharine R. Stimpson's Women in Culture and Society series. Thus, as the record shows, I have been well nurtured by the feminist academy. Thank goodness for that.

How little I still knew in 1982 about the trouble I was getting myself into by undertaking a feminist reading of (some would say by "taking on") the two most canonical male poets of the English eighteenth century. Perhaps I should have known when, after sending word of the prize to the distinguished editor of a distinguished literary journal that by then had had my piece for some six weeks, I received this curt reply:

> Dear Professor Pollak: Please accept our warmest congratulations on your award. Since the information can have no conceivable bearing on our reader's judgment, I shall refrain from passing it along to him.

Surely I should have suspected when, some six weeks after that, the same editor regretfully rejected the essay, which one reader found to be "a distortion, rather than a different perspective. It presses its language onto the poem, rather than opening it up." I've often wondered about that image. It rather reminds me of a note I received from a male colleague thanking me for giving him a copy of my book. "I greatly look forward to getting into it—if you can overlook the sexual implication."

Since those early days—before reviews—I've come to terms with the backhanded compliment. One reviewer says I "grapple womanfully" with Swift. Another, who seems to half admire the "aggressively cerebral" way I write, finds himself at a loss for words to describe my book: "If I were certain that the author would take it as a compliment, I would use the adjective 'seminal.' " Oh, well. I suppose it's all preferable to the female reviewer who cites my primary concern with the condition of women as a sign of my narrowness and my naive ordering of priorities. (For a discussion of the controversy surrounding my work and that of another scholar of the eighteenth century, Laura Brown, see Markley.)

I've come to terms with the backhanded compliments, because I know they're not inevitable. And I know *that* because of the Women's Caucus for the Modern Languages, because of the Chicago series, and because of journals like *Studies in English Literature*, which originally published "Pope and Sexual Difference" and helps to celebrate the Women's Caucus now by giving me permission to reprint my essay here.

You might say the Women's Caucus has sustained me by giving me, fairly early in my career, a second—an alternative—reality against which to measure myself and my experience as a woman and a feminist in the academic world. Paradoxical as it may seem, it has helped me keep my sanity by giving me a *dual* academic identity; instead of simply a lunatic on the fringe, I'm a prize-winner as well as a fanatic. And that, in the end, has really mattered. The other sh–– simply reminds me why I'm here.

East Lansing, Michigan
February 1990

~ 1983 ~

The Virgin Shapeshifter: Melville's Quarrel with Maids

FAYE M. LENARCIC

READERS HAVE LONG been aware of Melville's misogynistic attitude toward women. Much commentary has been devoted to the biographical details of the author's relationships with his mother, his wife, and other female relatives and friends. The reader learns, for example, that Melville had contempt for the female reader, evidenced in his amazement that Sophia Hawthorne was capable of understanding and enjoying *Moby Dick*. Again, his scorching commentary upon attending a reading by Fanny Kemble Butler reveals a man who held firm beliefs about the traditional role of women. On this occasion he found the speaker "so unfemininely masculine that had she not, on unimpeachable authority, borne children, I should be curious to learn the result of a surgical examination of her person in private" (Leyda 288). Biographical data on the relationship between Herman and Lizzie, particularly the recent publication of the Kring and Carey letters, shed further light on the Melvilles' deeply troubled marriage. When the reader recalls that Melville often challenged Lizzie, in an attempt to humiliate and demean her for her supposed lack of intelligence, it comes as no surprise that this woman, perhaps with bitter irony, appeared at a costume picnic in 1855 as Cypherina Donothing, continually adding up cyphers to find the sum, but failing each time: She "was one of the most successful characters of the day, although she did nothing well" (Leyda 507).

That Melville's domestic troubles furnish clues to his hostility toward his fictional castrating females has been well documented (see Crowley). To date, critical attention has focused on the shrewish wives in tales like "I and My Chimney" and "Jimmy Rose," on the comic phallic posturings of the narrator in "Cock-a-Doodle-Do," or on the domineering mother in *Pierre*. Although Melville's hostility and castration fears are obvious in these works, the comic tone often serves to defuse the real hostility of the narrator, and these narrators ultimately achieve at least modest victories over their antagonists. The chimney remains intact, the wallpaper keeps its roses, the cock lives on in the narrator's memory, and Mrs. Glendinning is punished with insanity and death.

Melville's deepest anxieties toward women are not revealed in his depiction of nagging shrews. Nor is it necessary to speculate at length on his flawed relationships with wife and mother in order to arrive at an understanding of his misogynistic views. One need only examine the female characters and references to the female nature scattered throughout the long career of Melville to discover the real threat which women pose for the author. It is woman in her role as fallen Eve, the Circean enchantress, the archetypal femme fatale which threatens the body and soul of narrator and author alike. It is the inevitable discovery of the rampant sexuality inherent in the female which haunts Melville and causes his heroes to flee, even unto death, from the seductive embrace. Moreover, this power of sexuality is destructive to both male and female. The femme fatale is "fatal" in the sense both of being death dealing and destined to play out endlessly her "fated" role on earth. No woman is exempt from this destiny, and therein lies the nightmare for Melville and his heroes. Each innocent and modest maiden is discovered to be a shapeshifter. Beneath her asexual, nunlike exterior lurks the passionate, destructive sexuality of the temptress. Within every Yillah there abides a Hautia, and it is this discovery that devastates Melville's protagonists and best explains the author's fear of, repulsion toward, and occasional sympathy for his fictional females.

Although critics like Leslie Fiedler and D. H. Lawrence have outlined Melville's difficulties in portraying meaningful heterosexual relationships, and although commentators like Charles Haberstroh have effectively demonstrated Melville's fear of sexual surrender and "his bewilderment generally over the idea of physical involvement with women" (*Melville and Male Identity* 60), such criticism has generally focused on the women in *Mardi* and *Pierre*. As a result, the persistent and consistent theme of Melville's disenchantment and hostility toward the virgin shapeshifter has not yet been satisfactorily demonstrated. This paper proposes to present evidence of Melville's lifelong treatment of the power of sexuality to transform the innocent maiden into the fatal woman. This theme is present in the very early "Fragment from a Writing Desk," continues through the novels, takes on nightmarish proportions in "The Tartarus of Maids," and persists, albeit with diminished intensity, in the late poetry.

Leon Howard sees Melville's second "Fragment from a Writing Desk" as evidence of a "high spirit to whom the joke was not bitter" (15). Although the fragment does contain humor, there is more than a suggestion of bitterness in the romantic youth's first discovery of woman as shapeshifter. The treatment of Inamorata and the Youth by Martin Pops is more satisfactory, and supports my own reading of the fragment. Pops notes that Inamorata "is Melville's first portrait of the tantalizing *femme fatale*, who, after a series of literary transformations, eventuates in the seductive Isabel who fatally arouses Pierre" (27).[1] In the sketch, the narrator ironically portrays himself as a man of the world, and deems it impossible that he could be "outgeneraled, routed, defeated, by a mere rib of the earth." The battle imagery is appropriate here, as is the reference to Eve. The naive and self-inflated narrator is most assuredly "outgeneraled" by the deceptively innocent temptress. Inamorata knows her man, and predicts in her note to him that he will "incontinently" follow the bearer. He does so follow, "plunging ahead like an infuriated steed," as he approaches Inamorata's bower. He momentarily feels "an agony of apprehension" and repents the "inconsiderate haste which had hurried [him] on" (268). He pursues the love goddess, however, and enters her "shrine," where he perceives her as a divine apparition, dressed in "a flowing robe of the purest white" (270). The Youth's mistaken impression of her as representative of purity and innocence is evidenced when he "prostrates" himself before her "sweet Divinity." As Pops notes, this woman combines the image of Holy Virgin with that of seductive Eve. What the Youth has ignored is that on top of her pure white robe she wears a sash "of pink satin, on which were broidered figures of Cupid in the act of drawing his bow" (270). Too late, the Youth discovers the perils of mistaken identity. As the fires of her eyes enflame his "soul," he acknowledges her passionate nature and falls at her feet. The divine woman has metamorphosed into a "fair mortal," and the final joke is on the duped narrator. The love goddess is deaf and dumb, and the Youth flees from her "with a wild cry of agony" (271). Inamorata is only the first of Melville's many enchantresses whose sexuality sends the heroes fleeing in terror, and the Youth becomes the prototype of all the later Melvillean males who learn to their horror that virginal robes of the purest white are inevitably tainted by Eve's "crimson zone."

The threat of female sexuality is tempered by the joys of idyllic love in *Typee*. Long regarded as the projection of Melville's fantasies, *Typee* celebrates maidens who are young, sensuous, and "void of artificial restraint" (77). The primitive sexuality of the Typeean "nymphs" proves irresistible to the "bachelor sailors." As the mermaids swim out to meet the incoming ship, with their "jet-black tresses streaming over their shoulders, and half-enveloping their otherwise naked forms," the men are "captured" by "these artless creatures" (14). Yielding to these feminine charms, the crew proceed to unleash their "unholy passions" (15). While the narrator doesn't harshly condemn either the nymphs or their "prisoners," he does exhibit some guilt at leading these "poor savages" into vice, and accuses the crew members of "debauchery." He also cannot bring himself to describe the "abandoned voluptuousness" of the island girls.

While Tommo is attracted to these maids, he has mixed feelings of admiration and repulsion at their overt display of female sexuality. When the girls exhibit a "prying inquisitiveness" concerning the bodies of Toby and Tommo, the two men are "outraged at their familiarity" and shocked at their "overstepping the due limits of female decorum" (77). Later, the narrator is reconciled to the maidens' lack of embarrassment and declares that one of his chief amusements is "bathing in company with troops of girls" (131).

Ideal male and female relationships abound in the land of Typee, where polyandry is the norm and sexual jealousy is unknown. The men on the island generally allow the women "every possible indulgence," yet even primitive males are aware of the mysterious and potentially dangerous powers of the female. Strict "taboos" are enforced against women who approach the male retreat known as "Bachelor's Hall," which must remain "secure from female intrusion" (189). Most important, females must never approach the holy ground. Death is the "dreadful penalty that secured the Hoolah Hoolah ground from the imaginary pollution of a woman's presence'' (92). Although the narrator describes the natives' fears as ''imaginary,'' the fact remains that ''civilized'' men in Melville are just as suspicious of feminine ''pollution.''

There is little to say about Tommo's relationship with Fayaway, the most ''beauteous nymph'' of all the fair maidens. She is obviously a fairy princess, as her name suggests.[2] A dark maiden with blue eyes, Fayaway is the ''very perfection of female grace and beauty'' (85). Tommo is enchanted by her, but never exhibits any real passion or abiding sentiment for her. He describes himself rather blandly as her ''declared admirer,'' and feels, when he is with her, as if he has been ''transported to some fairy region, so unreal did everything appear'' (134). As Edwin Haviland Miller points out, Tommo's romantic interlude with Fayaway is never convincing because of ''Melville's embarrassment in sentimental, heterosexual situations.'' Tommo ''only pretended to fall in love with Fayaway, who is a creampuff out of sentimental novels transferred to an exotic setting'' (130). It is evident that when an opportunity to escape presents itself, Tommo leaves Fayaway, who is ''speechless with sorrow,'' without a backward glance. Because this ''perfect'' fantasy woman remains static, she does not play the role of woman as shapeshifter and is therefore not threatening to Tommo. In *Typee*, Melville has created an isolated valley where the hero, if endangered by cannibals, is at least immune to the dangers of ''man-eating'' women.

The theme of the pure maiden transformed is not, however, entirely absent from Melville's first novel. Significantly, Tommo's account of the missionary's wife and the Queen of Nukuheva occurs before he enters the fantasy world of the Typee valley. The two anecdotes wherein these women are described serve as humorous yet ominous reminders to the reader that both savages and civilized men alike are threatened and disillusioned by female sexuality. The two brief stories are similar to parables in structure and meaning. The missionary's wife, a ''white woman,'' is initially regarded by the natives as ''some new divinity.'' They are curious about her, yet in awe of this strange white goddess. They attempt to ''pierce the sacred veil of calico'' in which she is ''enshrined,'' in order to ''ascertain'' her ''sex.'' When the divine goddess is revealed to be a mere mortal woman, the natives' ''idolatry was changed into contempt'' (6). In disgust, the natives strip her of her garments and warn her against further ''deceits.'' Although the holy man's wife symbolizes covert sexuality, ultimately her true nature is revealed as, once again, the maiden is transformed into the sexual female, and the natives experience the disillusion typical of Melville's male characters.

The anecdote that follows recounts the overt sexual behavior of an Island Queen. Unlike the missionary's ''lady,'' this woman is not shy ''of exhibiting her charms'' (7). She is paradoxically described as ''the fair person of his dark-complexioned spouse'' and makes a ludicrous appearance to the ship's company. She is habited in ''a gaudy tissue of scarlet cloth,'' her bare legs are covered with spiral tattoos, and she wears a ''fanciful turban of purple velvet, figured with silver sprigs, and surmounted by a tuft of variegated feathers'' (8). This parody of a pagan fertility goddess is unreservedly aggressive in her sexuality. She approaches an ''old salt'' and proceeds to undress him to examine his tattoos.

Worse yet, she proudly throws up her skirts and exhibits her tattooed posterior to the shocked onlookers. At this, the seasoned seamen are "aghast" and tumble over each other in their haste to flee "the scene of so shocking a catastrophe" (8). Significantly, neither natives nor sailors can abide the sight of the sexual female without expressing their horror and contempt. The Queen of Nukuheva and the missionary's wife are but two manifestations of the single shape-shifter—the maiden transformed. The only difference between the two women is that the "civilized" one camouflages her true nature, while the primitive Queen openly acknowledges her sexuality.

Leon Howard, Charles Haberstroh ("Melville, Marriage and *Mardi*"), and others have read *Mardi* as a commentary on the early years of Melville's marriage. The biographical approach stresses the anxieties the newlywed husband felt as he tried to establish himself as an economically solvent author and as an independent male surrounded by family members, most of whom were females. Although the biographical approach is a fruitful one, there is also much evidence that in *Mardi* Melville continued his fearful and hostile attack on woman as shapeshifter. At least one commentator has noted that Hautia and Yillah "are but two expressions of the same person" (Travis 92).[3] This notion is supported by several key episodes scattered throughout the novel which serve as warnings to Taji of the danger he is courting.

The episode concerning Annatoo and Samoa is the first warning Taji receives. Their disastrous marriage provides evidence of the maiden transformed into a combination of Fatal Woman and shrew. Once upon a time Annatoo had been lovely and innocent, but her "first virgin bloom had departed, leaving nothing but a lusty frame and a lustier soul" (69). Once awakened to her true nature as sexual being, she is open to the many unpleasant side effects of the sexually awakened woman. She becomes vain, decks herself out with "brass baubles," and mourns that "there was none to admire her but Samoa her husband" (75). Her advances toward old Jarl indicate her lasciviousness and also her deception of Samoa, who remains blind to her flirtations: "She would give him sly pinches, and then look another way, innocent as a lamb" (114). The Fatal Woman is capable of disguising herself as the innocent maiden when this suits her purpose. Annatoo is finally punished by the author for her deceptions when she is struck in the forehead by a block and "swallowed up in the whirlpool under our lea" (117). Because Annatoo is an obvious shrew and only a parody of the seductress, the narrator comically dismisses her as relatively harmless.

Soon after Annatoo goes to her death, Yillah appears on the scene. Taji jumps at the chance to save the "beautiful maiden" and "hotly" swears that he will deliver the captive at all costs. Melville's choice of the verb "hotly" is appropriate, since Taji soon acknowledges that he has committed a murder "perhaps, for a selfish purpose; the companionship of a beautiful maid" (135). Before he even sees Yillah, then, the "innocent maid" has caused Taji to commit murder. The prize he gains appears "like a saint from a shrine," with her snow-white skin and "blue, firmament eyes" (137). It is significant that old Jarl does not share Taji's enthusiasm for this "idol." The experienced sailor looks upon Yillah as "an Ammonite syren, who might lead me [Taji] astray" (147). Although some critics have interpreted Jarl's reaction as jealousy at this intrusion into bachelors' paradise, his wisdom in judging Yillah as a siren is later borne out.

The relationship between Yillah and Taji is blissful for a time, while they both maintain their illusions of being divine. Both are adored as semideities by island natives, yet gradually the two lovers perceive themselves "dwarfing down to mortals" (159). The pure white maiden is in the process of being transformed into a siren, as a result of carnal knowledge. She becomes "pensive" and "lost in reveries," and Taji grows "uneasy." Symbolically, the Incognito now appears on the scene, and this "unknown," disguised being completes the transformation of the maiden. Immediately before Yillah vanishes, Taji's perception of her changes, evidenced in the new imagery he uses to describe her. He is "enchanted" now by Yillah: "[D]ay by day did her spell weave round me its magic, and all the hidden things of her being grew more lovely and strange" (193). In these words Taji is revealing more than he knows. He will later discover that his earlier dim suspicions about his motives for "saving" Yillah were correct. He has deceived himself by seeing Yillah as the divine maiden, the virgin captive. Blinded by his own carnal lust, he has been duped by woman as shapeshifter. Rather than rescuing an innocent maiden, he has himself been captured by the "real" Yillah—personified in the siren Hautia. Because Taji cannot surrender his dream of pure, sexless love, he is repulsed and frightened by Yillah in her transformed state.

The messengers of Hautia, bearing their symbolic flowers, serve as yet another warning to the blind quester. The "meaning" of the various flowers is interpreted for Taji by the poet Yoomy, and one of the poems composed by Yoomy functions as a clear warning to the unheeding Taji:

> Oh! royal is the rose,
> But barbed with many a dart;
> Beware, beware the rose,
> 'Tis cankered at the heart.
>
> Sweet, sweet the sunny down,
> Oh! lily, lily, lily down!
> Sweet, sweet, Verbena's bloom!
> Oh! pleasant, gentle, musky bloom!
>
> Dread, dread the sunny down;
> Lo! lily-hooded asp;
> Blooms, blooms no more Verbena;
> White-withered in your clasp.
> (268)

The royal rose in the poem symbolizes Hautia, and the sweet lily represents Yillah. The lily is traditionally associated with purity and modesty, while the rose of the poem has two possible meanings. The usual "rose" is a symbol of beauty, while the "glorious moss-roses numberless" signify "Pleasure without Alloy" (see M. R. Davis). Yoomy's warning is to beware the "cankered" heart of the rose, which is hidden from view by sweet "lily down." That is, the "white" Yillah is merely the deceptive outside of the "barbed" Hautia, and the latter will cause the former to "wither" in one's clasp.

When Taji finally succumbs to the temptations of the "wild witch," he commits himself to follow her, though the lure be death. At this point Taji suspects some connection between Yillah and Hautia and comments that the two are connected "in some mysterious way," as he admits that he has "conflicting emotions" toward the temptress. After hearing Mohi's account of Ady and Rea, wherein the innocent maid is captured by the dark-eyed seductress, Taji finally understands that "in some wild way, Hautia has made a captive of Yillah, in some one of her black-eyed maids, the blue-eyed One was transformed" (649). Unable, however, to face the reality of his dream vision in her present incarnation, Taji heaps scorn upon the "snake," "vipress," and "shining monster" who has made him a "victim" (652). This refusal to accept the dark earth-woman and thereby also possess the pure, white Yillah has been termed "adolescent" by one critic (see Carpenter 272). Indeed, Taji's fleeing in terror from the maiden transformed suggests that the Fatal Woman as death is preferable to woman as "fated" sexuality.

The theme of the virgin shapeshifter next appears, although only briefly, in *Redburn*. The hero's initiation into experience requires that he learn about the perils of female sexuality and the deceptions of maidens. Three linking episodes convey this message to the naive hero. After Redburn observes the squalor and depravity of Liverpool, he escapes for an afternoon in the country, where he encounters "three adorable charmers" living in a gardenlike environment. Recalling Hautia's "moss-roses," the reader is immediately on guard when the maidens are described with their "six red cheeks, like six moss-roses, hanging from the casement" (213). Redburn is enchanted by these three "Peris, three Houris," and is especially taken with one of them, "the most beautiful rosebud I had yet seen in England" (213). As the girls sit across the table from him, eating buttered muffins, Redburn "wished I was a buttered muffin myself." This humorous and innocent remark is ironic when examined literally. Does the naive Redburn really wish to be devoured by these three "Peris"? Melville spares him this fate, however, and Redburn escapes the "charmers," who merely "ravish" him in his dreams.

Soon after this episode Redburn meets Harry Bolton and is spirited off to London, where the Edenic bower of the three charmers is transformed into the "bower of Babylon." When Redburn realizes that he may be ensconced in a brothel, he feels his "face burning with embarrassment" and is "ill at heart" (231). The place seems "infected" and "crawling with lizards." The dread which Redburn experiences when confronted with evidence of female sexuality is typical of Melville's heroes. Sexuality is attractive only when it is hidden beneath an exterior of purity and innocence, as seen in the "three charmers." Overt sexuality is consistently repulsive to Melville's males.

The final stage in Redburn's education into the mysteries of the shapeshifter occurs on board the ship on the way home. One of the steerage passengers, a tailor, is tyrannized by his coquettish wife, who is reminiscent of the three charmers in appearance: "Young and handsome; just such a beauty as farmers'-boys fall in love with; she had bright eyes, and red cheeks, and looked plump and happy" (265). Appearances are deceiving, however, because the attractive charmer is another Annatoo. She dominates her husband and makes a fool of him by using her sexual charms. When she looks "bewitchingly up at him, with her irresistible eyes," the poor man cannot resist her (266). These three episodes, taken together, function as an allegorical warning to both Redburn and the reader: never trust beautiful and innocent young maidens. Beneath their exteriors lurks the lust of the whore; marry such a one, and she will bewitch you with her sexual charms and thus rule over you. As in *Typee* and the Annatoo story, Melville treats the theme with humor. By the time we next meet the "adorable charmer," in *Pierre*, however, Melville's vision of the Fatal Woman has become terrifying indeed.

Many critics see *Pierre* as Melville's most autobiographical work and identify the fictional characters with their real-life models as follows: Lizzie becomes Lucy, Mary Glendinning is based on Maria Melville, Glen Stanly is likened to Herman's orphaned cousin Stanwix, and so on (see E. H. Miller; Murray). According to this reading, the novel depicts the author's ambivalent feelings toward both mother and wife, exemplified in Pierre's simultaneous feelings of attraction and repulsion toward incestuous love. Regardless of what Melville initially intended to do, the novel again portrays the innocent hero's initiation into the mysteries of female sexuality and his subsequent disillusionment with the virgin transformed. In this work Isabel is Fatal Woman at her most destructive; because of her all three main characters must die in the end.

In his seminal article on Melville's and Hawthorne's dark and fair ladies, Frederic Carpenter asserts that in *Pierre*, "even more clearly than in *Mardi*, the blonde becomes the symbol of goodness, the dark the symbol of evil. Once again the idea of innocence is associated with the blonde, the idea of passion with the dark" (259). While initially the two women do seem to be polar opposites, by the end of *Pierre* the distinctions have become blurred when the "good" and "bad" angels are confused in Pierre's mind, and the two angels join forces to destroy the hero.

Although Lucy is at least once described as "delicious bait" for the marriage trap set by Mrs. Tartan, Pierre is never seriously threatened by this innocent girl. He confesses that he is "entirely willing to be caught, when the bait is set in Paradise, and the bait is such an angel," but Lucy is entirely too "ethereal" to cast the spell of sexual desire on Pierre (28). In fact, Pierre can't even imagine conjugal relations with this "heavenly fleece," who would most likely "dissolve" on contact. While Pierre himself is portrayed as innocence personified in the early chapters, Melville does hint that he has one "fatal" flaw. His "one little uncelestial trait" is his "bountiful appetite" (16). It is this "excellent appetite" which predisposes him to the fleshly attractions represented by Isabel and permits him to "murder" his first love.

From the outset, Isabel is described in the language of enchantment. The mystery of Isabel for Pierre "possessed all the bewitchingness of the mysterious vault of night, whose very darkness evokes the witchery" (142). The analogy between sex and death is drawn here and prefigures the "fatal" joining of the lovers in the final scene. The transformation of the long-suffering "sister" into the Fatal Woman occurs in a later scene, although as the consummate shape-shifter, Isabel is able to play the two roles simultaneously. As Pierre gazes into her "wonderful transfigured eyes," he momentarily perceives her changed attitude as "the work of an invisible enchanter. Transformed she stood before him; but her gentler sex returned to Isabel at last . . ." (160). Thus, even before brother and sister actually admit their incestuous desires, it is evident that Isabel is not simply a sibling in Pierre's eyes.

Whether or not Pierre and Isabel ever literally consummate their "marriage" has long been debated.[4] The answer is probably unimportant, since we do know that they desire one another physically and that admitting these feelings results in major changes in their relationship. When the "terrible self-revelation" of their mutual passion is understood, "then they changed; they coiled together, and entangledly stood mute" (192). After this moment of revelation, both characters "change" in dramatic fashion (see Kellner). It is no longer possible for Pierre to perceive Isabel as his innocent, long-lost sister, and Isabel herself now takes on more characteristics of the Fatal Woman. When she learns of Lucy's impending arrival, she becomes jealous and distraught. She compares Lucy to a "good angel" and herself to the "other," dark angel, and threatens to "murder" Lucy with "one look" (313). The admission of his passionate feelings also has a destructive effect on Pierre. Interestingly, once Isabel is "transformed" before his eyes, Pierre seems to lose his desire for her. Like Taji, Pierre is both attracted and repulsed by female sexuality, and he now "involuntarily" draws back from her touch. He escapes from both virgin and seductress by spending much of his time alone in his room, writing madly. Ashamed and terrified of his own sexuality and that of Isabel, Pierre no longer understands which woman is his "good" and which is his "bad" angel. The distinction between the two women becomes blurred, as the shape-shifting continues. The powerful Isabel is now "entirely fluid" and passive with Pierre, while the "nun-like" Lucy shows "wonderful strength" in her sweetness and amazing "inflexibility in one so fragile" (237). All is confusion in Pierre's troubled mind, and his only solution is found in the violence of murder and suicide. His final words to both virgin and seductress are bitter ones: "Ye two pale ghosts, were this the other world, ye were not welcome. Away!—Good angel and Bad angel both!—For Pierre is neuter now!" (360). Once again a Melvillean hero has been "done in" by the virgin transformed. Although his own "appetites" have predisposed him to Isabel's seductive charms, his destruction is brought about by the confusing and contradictory manifestations of woman as shapeshifter.

There is some indication of a change in Melville's attitudes toward women between the completion of *Pierre* and the writing of the short fiction. Yet despite the humorously ironic pose struck by the narrators, the tales of the fifties contain much resentment of the dominating woman. Undoubtedly Melville's own domestic situation served to turn his attention from the image of the siren to the image of the shrew and the woman as fertility principle. During this time Melville's wife produced four children in six years; thus "it is not difficult to suspect that her husband had begun to regret his own fertility, and to have much on his mind the machine-like aspect of human reproduction'' (Dillingham 202). Although Melville's hostility toward female sexuality during this time is still apparent, it is tempered now with some sympathy for the Fatal Woman, who, after all, is not responsible for her predestined lustful nature and who, in fact, often suffers herself as a result of her sexuality. The theme of the virgin transformed takes on new dimensions now, as the author explores the horrors of female sexuality in his nightmare vision of a descent into a literal hell of virginal women.

''The Paradise of Bachelors and the Tartarus of Maids'' has occasioned much controversy among Melville critics. Some readers maintain that Melville is contrasting the carefree lives of the bachelors with the painful realities of the maids' existence (see Eby). Others read the first work ironically, asserting that the author is condemning the bachelors for leading shallow, uncommitted lives, while his deepest sympathies lie with the unfortunate maids (see Browne). Beryl Rowland perceptively traces the ambivalence of both reader and author toward these bachelors to Melville's humorous tone, which makes the values deliberately confusing: ''The ironic undertone which pervades the whole tale makes it impossible to know how seriously we are to regard the degeneracy with which he charges the present-day representatives of the Templars'' (39). An examination of certain key passages may shed some light on this puzzling story.

Melville's early description of the Benedick tradesmen provides an interesting contrast to his bachelors. These men, representing the average, careworn married inhabitant of the outer world of London, are ''sick with the din and soiled with the mud of Fleet Street'' (202). As they hurry through life, ''with ledger-lines ruled along their brows, thinking upon rise of bread and fall of babies,'' they foreshadow the overworked maids of the ''Tartarus.'' These men serve as a warning to the narrator of the sufferings attendant upon the male who has fallen into the ''trap'' of marriage. The tale of the original Templars serves as another warning to the narrator. Their history is described as a ''sad'' one. Ruined by the phallic ''worm of luxury'' which gnawed at their ''monastic vow'' and led to their moral degeneration into ''rakes,'' these forefathers of the modern bachelors provide another object lesson on the dangers of sexuality. The Templars' acquisition of sexual knowledge, then, has resulted in the present effeminacy of their descendants, who have stopped exercising their phallic ''steeds and lances'' and now only exercise their mouths in conversation and eating. That sexual indulgence can lead to effeminacy has already been demonstrated by Donjalolo in *Mardi*. Although Melville is undeniably satirizing these placid gentlemen, his derision is certainly mild. Compared with the lives of the Benedick tradesmen, the bachelors' lot is an easy one. Secure from the horrors of marriage and the lures of sirens, these men are exempt from life's greatest pains.

The question, of course, is how much Melville blames these bachelors for leading lives exempt from pain and trouble. It is significant that the author does not accuse these men of pretending that illness, cruelty, poverty, and injustice are nonexistent. What he resents them for is not having ''wives or children to give them an anxious thought.'' The ''pain'' these bachelors escape from is ''those twinges of their consciences touching desertion of the fireside'' (209).

This specific accusation can only be read as thinly disguised envy on the narrator's part. The reader recalls that this same narrator is "the last lingerer" at the banquet and speaks with regret and nostalgia of transient bachelor freedoms: "But fine though they be, bachelors' dinners, like bachelors' lives, can not endure forever" (210). Since some of the actual bachelors present have clung to the single state well into old age, the implication here is that the author is reminiscing about his own transformation from carefree bachelor to married Benedick tradesman. It is unlikely that Melville is referring to the literal mortality of the bachelors. If these bachelors lead shallow, uncommitted lives, their simple pleasures are nonetheless very attractive to the narrator, who can barely drag himself away from this "paradise."

Although commentators disagree on "The Paradise of Bachelors," no such controversy exists about "The Tartarus of Maids." No one has yet argued that this portrait of hell is really Melville's ironic praise of female sexuality or the joys of motherhood. There is no humor in this nightmare tale of fear and revulsion at female sexuality and its dire consequences for both men and women. The narrator's castration fears have been well documented by Beryl Rowland and others and are best exemplified when the narrator's blood "curdles" as the girls ply the "whet stone up and down the sword-blade" during the paper-making process. The narrator, like Taji and Pierre before him, is a prime target for the castrating female because of his own sexual desires. The male's horror of his own drives is evident when he loses control of his horse and plunges through the grim "Black Notch" and into the "Devil's Dungeon." This feeling of being "out of control" reminds the narrator of being "in a runaway London omnibus" (213).

Once the narrator is inside the mill, his attention turns away from his own fears as he observes the maids at their work. In a brief parable of the virgin transformed, Melville clearly describes the shape-shifting process: "I looked upon the first girl's brow, and saw it was young and fair; I looked upon the second girl's brow, and saw it was ruled and wrinkled. Then, as I still looked, the two—for some small variety to the monotony—changed places; and where had stood the young, fair brow, now stood the ruled and wrinkled one" (215). Although the transformation is sudden, the moral is clear. The young, fair virgin is a deceiver; although she is more victim than willing participant in the sexual process, her visible appearance is changed through sexual awareness. She becomes "ruled" by her sexuality and loses all innocence. Beneath the pale, blank faces of these virgins, then, lurks the omnipresent "Blood River" of female sexuality.

Although horrified by the evidence of female sexuality which surrounds him, the narrator is capable of feeling some sympathy for these unfortunate slaves of sex: "Round and round here went the enormous revolutions of the dark colossal water-wheel, grim with its one immutable purpose" (216). The Fatal Woman is herself a victim of fate, bound by her biological destiny to obey the cycle of nature. The implication is that the virgin's transformation is inevitable, yet the sympathy elicited by the thought is only partial.

Melville's mixed emotions of sympathy and contempt are again evident when he describes the girls as "slaves" to the iron animal of male sexuality and notes that they serve their master "mutely and cringingly as the slave serves the Sultan" (216). Again, the maids are compared to "so many mares haltered to the rack" (217). Rowland notes that mares "were popularly believed to be so lascivious that they might be impregnated by the wind, and to be so acquiescent that, unlike other animals, they would receive the male at any time" (403). While the image of each maid being sentenced to death by the "erected sword" might elicit more sympathy, this sentiment is immediately stifled by the suggestion that the girls are, after all, responsible for their fate and perhaps deserve their punishment. The girls, Melville tells us, are "their own executioners; themselves whetting the very swords that slay them" (218). There is, perhaps, an obscene pun on the word "whetting"; at any rate, the blame reverts to the maids again, who inspire uncontrollable lust in the male. That death and suffering are just punishments for the fallen Eve is not a new idea, and there does seem to be some hint of doing penance for sins in Melville's treatment of these maids. When the narrator questions why the girls are so "sheet-white," the "cruel-hearted" Cupid replies that the constant "handling [of] white sheets" makes them so "sheety" (218). Marvin Fisher has pointed out that the word "sheet" at one time referred to performing penance, originally for fornication (89).

Ultimately, the narrator's feelings of "awe" at the gestation process are overshadowed by his feelings of horror and revulsion.[5] The machinery of birth, the symbolic female sex organs, strike "strange dread into the human heart, as some living, panting Behemoth might" (221). Upon learning that the workers are "all maids," the narrator is filled with a "strange emotion" and "involuntarily" bows low in "pained homage to their pale virginity" (222). That the homage is "involuntary" and "pained" is significant. The narrator's reluctance to pay tribute to the sexual female is understandable in light of his "monstrous dread" of her and in light of Melville's hostility toward the virgin transformed. Most likely, the "homage" takes the form of a deep regret that "pale virginity" inevitably disguises rampant sexuality. A like sentiment appears in "The Paradise of Bachelors," where the narrator regrets that bachelors' lives "can not endure forever."

The final sentiments in the two stories, however, are very different. While the narrator "lingers" in bachelor heaven, he "shoots through the pass" in the second story, eager to escape from this hell of female sexuality. If the two stories offer any evidence that Melville's attitude toward the sexual female has mellowed, the change is slight enough. As victims of their fate, the maids command some sympathy and are not as hostilely treated as is Hautia, for example. Yet, as "their own executioners," the maids are not completely blameless. Fear and suspicion of the "pale virgin" still hold sway in Melville's heart.

Nearly forty years after writing the diptych, Melville returned to the theme of the virgin shapeshifter in his late poetry. In 1891, "After the Pleasure Party" appeared in his *Timoleon* volume. Because this poem is uncharacteristic of Melville in the use of a woman as narrator, many readers have speculated that she is merely a disguise for Melville himself and that the poem is an autobiographical account of the author's conflict between his sexual and artistic drives (e.g., W. B. Stein). Other critics, like Leon Howard, maintain that the poem "has no superficial autobiographical significance at all" (334) yet are at pains to explain why Melville departed from his lifelong pattern of using only male personae. Perhaps the answer to this question lies in Melville's desire to offer irrefutable evidence of the virgin transformed. He had dealt with this theme in every imaginable way but one during his career; yet Inamorata, Hautia, Isabel, the maids of Tartarus were all described by male narrators. What better way to lend credence to his belief that within each virgin lives a lustful counterpart than to elicit firsthand testimony from woman herself? Urania's "confession," topped off by the warning to all virgins from the poet himself, becomes Melville's strongest statement on woman's "fatal" sexuality.

The epigraph to the poem, spoken by the male god of love, warns all virgins against attempting to deny the "tempests" of passion. The final lines of the poem echo this male warning, and, together, the epigraph and final speech provide a male framework for this female confession. As Urania begins to speak, her words echo other Melvillean virgins from the past. Fate has aided love in ambushing the unsuspecting "pale" virgin, just as fate ambushed Isabel and the maids of Tartarus. Urania has led a "cloistral" life, reminiscent of the "nun-like" Lucy, yet she is aware, at last, that inevitably "one's sex asserts itself" ("After the Pleasure Party" 213). This knowledge ("what all may ween") comes later to her than to others, despite her advanced intellectual powers. The "all" who know this already includes the earlier pale virgins in the Melville canon. The juxtaposition of "cold obstruction" and "blaze," "fires," and "flame" and "terrace chill" in stanzas 5 and 6 recalls the cold/hot imagery in "The Tartarus of Maids" and looks forward to similar fire/ice paradoxes in the Rose poems. For Urania, and for Melville, sexuality can be described only in contradictions.

Urania, ambushed by love, has passionate desires for a young man who is apparently enamored of a "peasant girl." Once awakened sexually, like Isabel, Urania experiences the pangs of shame and also "envy and spleen." She is vitriolic in her attack on the peasant maid, accusing her of being a deceiver. The "adorable charmer" is in reality a "cheat," full of "wiles" which she hides under a "mien how meek." Again, the reader recalls Melville's earlier attacks on the virgin as shapeshifter. When these same sentiments are spoken by a woman who is herself a shapeshifter, the effect is dramatic. Urania admits, however, that it is her "pain" which instigates her "belittling" remarks. Her jealousy knows no bounds, for she would gladly undergo any transformation in order to win her loved one's heart. She is ready to renounce all her "starry lore" and become the "veriest wanton" if need be. She curses again the fate that will not "set free / This sexless bound in sex," recalling once more Melville's paradoxical virgin transformed. Yet her "self-illusion" of being able to "sustain" herself without love is gone forever, and she is "chilled" by the truth: "Shivers yon bramble above the vale, / And disillusion opens all the shore." These lines recall the "frost-bitten" narrator of "Tartarus," who is also "chilled" by disillusion in that virgin hell.

Urania tries a final time to escape her torment by praying to the Virgin Mary, and "half-resolves" to become a nun, but cannot do this. At last she invokes the "armed Virgin" Athena, asking her for relief from sexual "strife," but to no avail. The Melville reader knows that the virgin, once transformed, can never return to the innocent state. The shapeshifter can change in only one direction. The male narrator now speaks, and his concluding remarks confirm the "fondness" of Urania's appeal for deliverance from passion. Her lesson has universal applications, for her example teaches all women that it is futile for them to deny their very nature. "Anatomy is destiny" for Urania, and for "Virgins everywhere." If Melville is less hostile and less accusatory toward women in his later years, he is still preoccupied with female sexuality.[6]

Melville's final treatment of this theme occurs in the Rose poems, dedicated ironically to his wife, who is hailed not as a rose but as the "Madonna of the Trefoil." A double irony is present here when the reader recalls that Lizzie was apparently allergic to roses and suffered from "rose-fever" for weeks at a time. William Stein believes that the dedication to "Winnifred" is irrelevant:

> Coming as an afterthought, the dedication has been taken to control the inspiration of the entire volume—a kind of floral bouquet of love. Actually it was a necessary subterfuge! Its affectations of feeling have nothing in common with the thematic patterns of the poetry. (152)

It is true that the poems do not seem to be in any sense personal statements of love from husband to wife. Although some of the poems celebrate joy, peace, love, and even sexuality, "darker views are constantly asserting themselves" (Shurr 189). To the last, Melville's attitudes toward women and female sexuality are contradictory and ambivalent. The mood of these poems is not "totally idyllic" (Shurr 184). Although Melville no longer flees in terror from the virgin transformed, his quarrel with maids is only partially resolved. If the "melting mood" is upon him in his old age, the "chill" is present too. Since Melville uses roses to symbolize many diverse qualities in these poems, my treatment will be limited to those poems in which roses are specifically connected with women and sexuality.

The poem "Hearth Roses" is perhaps the most "personal" of the Rose poems. Addressed to a loved one, the poem describes the aging poet's hopes that the passion of his old age may "vie with Hearth-Roses" (*Collected Poems* 296). The sweet-smelling embers of the sugar-maple logs are compared to the rose in its last bloom and, by analogy, to the passion of the aging lovers. By using sexual imagery in "bed," "Garden of Fire," "musk," and "expire," the poet makes clear that he is describing a sexual rather than a spiritual union. This is one of those poems which have led critics to see in Melville's final works his "acceptance of life . . . his contentment with mortality, his genuine love for Elizabeth . . ." (Howard 317). In "The Vial of Attar," the rose is specifically identified with a beloved woman. The death of Lesbia's lover in pagan times was especially crushing because there was no belief in a reunion in the afterlife. When the fires of passion turned into "cold ashes," the bereaved lover was inconsolable. In the second stanza the "Rose's lover" imagines that his love is superior to the purely physical passion of Lesbia, since, when the woman dies, he will be "solaced" by the memory of her "essence" and will not grieve. His belief that their love is somehow more ethereal than physical is shown to be a delusion, however, as he finally admits that "there is nothing like the bloom." The poet, like Lesbia, recognizes that "love is physical chemistry, not spiritual affinity" (W. B. Stein 223).

"The Rose Farmer" has generally been read as an autobiographical account of Melville's career as a writer, and this has led to conflicting views about the poet's seeming choice of the rose over the attar (see Shurr; W. B. Stein). The biographical controversy apart, "The Rose Farmer" offers a playfully satiric view of women and suggests that if Melville does not take these "roses" seriously, at least he no longer is terrified of the sexuality they represent. The first two stanzas assert the paradoxical nature of the rose as beautiful yet "prickly." The narrator has inherited a "pleasure-ground," a "garden" of beauty, and must decide how best to cultivate this garden. The roses eavesdrop on the poet's conversation with the rose farmer and periodically react to the men's words. When the farmer brags that "my darlings cluster to caress me," his "rose-seraglio" overhears his "fond" remark and disapproves. The women-roses in the poem are vain, jealous, and easily upset, but the experienced farmer, "long time versed / In roses husbanded by him," knows the way to flatter their vanity and ensure their loyalty. When he advises the poet to enjoy the "brief delight" of plucking his roses, since the supply of buds is endless, every rose there "bridles aloft the passionate head" in anger and resentment at being thus trivialized. They are likened in their jealousy to a polygamous Mormon's first wife, who resents being supplanted by subsequent wives. The farmer recovers his advantage, however, by reassuring the roses who resent such callous usage that their "evanescence is the charm!" He maintains that their fleeting beauty "lured the sons of God below." The vain and shallow roses miss the satire and are "flattered" to think that they "are adored" by "angelic sweethearts overhead." Perhaps this passage suggests that women must at least maintain the illusion that they have spiritual worth as well as sexual charms. Certainly, when Yillah, Urania, and the others are forced to acknowledge their sexuality, they are "shamed" and resentful at being reduced to "slaves" of sex. The rose farmer, then, enjoys the transient pleasures provided by his rose-women and doesn't worry about their "transcendental essence." Unlike the earlier Melville, the farmer has no illusions about the nature of women and thus suffers no pain when he sees them in their true form as "fair daughters of Eve."

Perhaps the lean Parsee who quests after "quintessential bliss" represents Melville in his desire to maintain the purity of the virgin ideal. Ironically, this Parsee, in his denial of the rose itself (sexuality), actually "scimiters the living rose!" William Stein has equated the Parsee with "pathologial hatred of sexual woman," and his insight is profound here, recalling Melville's hatred and destruction of his earlier virgins transformed. The "L'Envoi" indeed suggests that the poet has become "wiser" in his attitude toward both the "roses" and the damsels they represent.

Although these Rose poems do suggest that Melville has become reconciled to female sexuality, there are other, contradictory statements found in the following poems. "Amoroso" can easily be read as another poem celebrating the joys of sexuality and the "wintry" love of old age. The poet's delight in sexual puns is evident in his references to "mossed in furs all cosey" and "a huntsman ever ruddy," while the Moss-Rose itself represents "Pleasure without Alloy." The problem with this interpretation lies in the fire/ice imagery so often found in Melville's treatment of sexuality. The poem does not, in conventional fashion, equate snow and cold with lack of passion and fire with passionate love. Rather, the entire relationship between Rosamond and the poet is paradoxically a hot/cold affair. In this "plighted pair" the "chill" of the virgin Queen Diana is "bonded" with the "flame" of the lover. Although fire and ice share "one purity" in the poem, the Moss-Rose still has a "cheek like ice":

> To feel your cheek like ice,
> While snug the furs inclose—
> This is spousal love's device
> This is Arctic Paradise,
> And wooing in the snows!

It is tempting to read these lines ironically, to mean that wedded love has paired Melville's ubiquitous "chill" virgin with a more ardent spouse, resulting in a cold paradise indeed. Or, alternately, the "cheek like ice" may suggest the virgin shapeshifter, whose "snug . . . furs inclose" her hidden sexuality, the "Moss-Rose." At any rate, the pairing of fire/ice images results here in an ambiguous description of "wooing in the snows."

William Shurr probably oversimplifies "Under the Ground" as a poem about cut roses being placed in an old tomb to keep them fresh so that they can later adorn a wedding (197). Although William Stein's interpretation more nearly agrees with my own, he asserts that Melville is here arguing "that ill-advised prudery corrupts instinctive pleasures" (205), an assertion that is questionable. Stein rightly sees the "dewy chaplets" as young virgins whose chastity must be preserved for their wedding night by locking them in a safe "vault." However, although the narrator "marvels" at this "inhuming" of roses, he has not yet heard the boy's explanation for the necessity of such an entombment. The future bridegroom wants his roses to "keep their bloom." The key to the poem lies in the last line: "Yea, we the rose entomb." The meaning here seems to be, "Indeed, we *must* entomb the rose" or, in colloquial jargon, "You'd better believe we entomb the rose!" If this interpretation is sound, the poem recalls Melville's lifelong suspicion and fear of the virgin's hidden lustful nature.

If Melville, in his "melting mood," is now condemning the patriarchal insistence on the virgin bride, then he has indeed completely reversed his lifelong position on the deceptively dangerous virgin. This supposition is less credible when we examine "The Ambuscade," where the poet is clearly restating his usual position. The "meek" virgin here recalls the "nun-like" Lucy, the "cloistered" Urania, and the "snow-white Yillah" from earlier works. Her outer garments are "seemly" apparel for her "pale passionless" purity, yet her nunlike demeanor is merely a temporary illusion. The fire/ice imagery suggests the central paradox of Melvillean women. The frosty purity is only a "May-snow," guarding the "slumbering germ" of passion which will flower with time into "Amor's burning rose." While William Stein accuses this maiden of "unconscious coquetry," of concealing her charms in an effort to "ambush" an unsuspecting lover (206), it is apparent that the virgin herself will be the victim of Amor's ambush, recalling the erotic awakening of Urania. Once again, Melville evokes the image of the maiden transformed by passion, the virgin shapeshifter. He no longer, however, damns her for her transformation; if Melville has become reconciled to female sexuality, this reconciliation is partly a final acceptance of the *inevitability* of "Amor's burning rose."

Biographical and critical commentators agree that Melville had obvious difficulty dealing with his fictional and real-life women. Richard Chase has commented that Melville can seldom picture a woman without terror, while Charles Haberstroh suggests that "because Melville made no attempt to understand women, they remained for him a fortress of perilous approach" (*Melville and Male Identity* 66). Because the "hard facts about Melville's sexual needs and the extent of their fulfillment are blessedly non-existent" (A. Stein 11), the wise Melville reader will stop short of drawing parallels between the author's real-life sexual problems and the fears, hostility, and anger he projects onto his sexually awakened fictional females. The fact remains that in his late poetry, despite some evidence that Melville accepted women, or at least stopped blaming them for their sexuality, he never really resolved his quarrel with maids. He could never quite forgive his virgin shapeshifters for shattering his youthful dream of the pure-white Yillah.

NOTES

[1] Martin Pops notes the transformation of the demythologized maiden from "divine" to mortal status and the similarities between Lucy and Isabel.

[2] "Fay" derives from the French *fae* (fairy), or one of the fates.

[3] I am indebted to Mildred Travis for her suggestion that Yillah and Hautia are the same person, perhaps representing the two faces of Venus.

[4] Henry Murray, for example, believes that Isabel remains "physically unattainable," while Robert Kellner argues that Pierre and Isabel do have sexual relations.

[5] According to Edwin Haviland Miller, "birth was always a painful subject to a man who idealized bachelor heroes" (184).

[6] Melville does hint here that females are not themselves to blame for their "fatal" flaw.

AFTERWORD

Reactions to my winning the 1983 Florence Howe Award were varied and informative. I was delighted, upon request, to provide copies of my paper to two Melville scholars. I was most gratified to receive a congratulatory note from Annis Pratt on my "solid, detailed, and scholarly" work. I was, of course, pleased to have a section on Melville's poetry accepted for publication.

Other responses were less positive. While rejecting the essay as "a shade too polemical," one editor acknowledged that it was "well-researched and well-written." I appreciated his comments because they indicated close and careful attention to the text and also because he raised several questions about the similar hostility found in Hawthorne's works. These questions prompted me to analyze Hawthorne more carefully and to contrast clearly the two authors' treatment of female sexuality in my dissertation.

I was amused at another rejection letter, this from a highly touted journal, one of whose readers misread most of my essay. He complained that I found "only mysogeny [sic] in Melville," rather than the contradictions and ambiguity that I did uncover. This reader also assumed that I was male: Lenarcic is "overly selective in evidence that he can use" and he is "excessively opinionated."

After these brief forays into the world of traditional publications, I turned my attention to the more pressing matter of using the Melville paper, in lengthened form, as a central chapter in my dissertation, "The Emergence of the Passionate Woman in American Fiction, 1850–1920." While Melville's heroes *are* hostile toward female sexuality, this hostility is grounded in real terror of the destructive force of passion for both sexes. Hawthorne, by contrast, is more accepting of woman's carnality. He clearly blames his heroes for imposing on powerless women impossible angel/whore polarities. Characters like Beatrice Rappaccini and Georgiana Aylmer are portrayed as victims of males who project their own sexual fears onto women. Hawthorne reserves his fear and ambivalence for women like Hester and Zenobia, who, as a result of their sexual transgressions, assert their intellectual independence from conventional society. Unlike Melville, Hawthorne can forgive his heroines their sexuality, but he is threatened by the accompanying intellectual freedom and power of these New Women who venture where "other women fear to tread."

My research also led me to conclude that women authors feared the seducer as much as men feared the seductress. The solution for authors like Mary Wilkins Freeman, Elizabeth Stuart Phelps, Sarah Orne Jewett, and Charlotte Perkins Gilman lay in deemphasizing the sexuality of their heroines, who often opt for celibacy in order to achieve selfhood and career satisfaction. For example, a fascinating comparison with Melville's "Paradise of Bachelors" can be found in Phelps's *Old Maid's Paradise* and *Burglars in Paradise*, in which male lovers are depicted as enticing, if unwelcome, "burglars" in a comfortable world of celibate women. Similarly, Gilman's *Herland* portrays a feminist utopia in which sexual attraction is unknown, men are nonexistent, and children are produced by parthenogenesis. It was not until the turn of the century that authors, primarily women like Chopin, Gertrude Atherton, and Wharton, were able to demand both sexual satisfaction from men who viewed them as equals and the autonomy to pursue careers and personal goals.

My winning entry in the 1983 Florence Howe contest was the incentive I needed to pursue my interest in Melville. It led to a dissertation on the much broader topic of male and female attitudes toward female sexuality during the nineteenth century. I feel I have now come full circle, back to the Women's Caucus for the Modern Languages for publication of my original paper. I am very pleased to be in the company of other feminist writers, some of whom are, undoubtedly, "a shade too polemical" for traditional journals.

Herkimer, New York
January 1990

~ 1984 ~

Reading Ourselves: Toward a Feminist Theory of Reading

PATROCINIO P. SCHWEICKART

Three Stories of Reading

1. In his presidential address to the 1982 MLA Annual Convention, Wayne Booth tells a story that is "perhaps close enough to our shared experience to justify the telling." His concern is to offer a "myth" that might enable us "to dramatize not just our inescapable plurality but the validity of our sense that [as teachers and scholars of literature and composition] we belong together, somehow working on common ground" ("Arts and Scandals" 313).

Once upon a time there was a boy who fell in love with books. When he was very young, he heard over and over the legend of his great-grandfather, a hard-working weaver who so desired knowledge that he figured out a way of working the loom with his legs, feet, and one hand, leaving the other hand free to hold a book, and who worked so steadily in that crooked position that he became permanently crippled. The boy heard other stories about the importance of reading. Salvation, he came to believe, was to be found in books. At the age of six, he read his first *real* book (*The Wizard of Oz*) and was rewarded by his great-aunt Manda with a dollar.

When the boy grew up, he decided to become a teacher of "litcomp." His initiation into the profession was rigorous, and there were moments when he nearly gave up, but gradually, "there emerged from the trudging a new and surprising love, a love that with all my previous reading I had not dreamed of: the love of skill, of craft, of getting clear in my mind and then in my writing what a great writer had got right in his work" (315). Eventually, the boy, now grown, got his doctorate, and after teaching for thirteen years in small colleges, he returned to his graduate institution to become one of its eminent professors.

Booth caps his narration by quoting from *The Autobiography of Malcolm X*. It was in prison that Malcolm learned to read:

> For the first time I could pick up a book and now begin to understand what the book was saying. Anyone who has read a great deal can imagine the new world

> that opened. Let me tell you something: from then until I left that prison, in every free moment I had, if I was not reading in the library, I was reading on my bunk. . . . [M]onths passed without my even thinking about being imprisoned. In fact, up to then, I never had been so truly free in my life. (qtd. in Booth 317)

"Perhaps," says Booth, "when you think back now on my family's story about great-grandfather Booth, you will understand why reading about Malcolm X's awakening speaks to the question of where I got my 'insane love' [for books]" (317).

2. The ellipsis in the Malcolm X passage quoted by Booth roused my curiosity. What exactly, I wondered, had been deleted? What in the original exceeded the requirements of a presidential address to the MLA? Checking, I found the complete sentence to read: "Between Mr. Muhammad's teachings, my correspondence, my visitors—usually Ella and Reginald—and my reading, months passed without my even thinking about being imprisoned" (173). Clearly, the reference to the leader of the notorious Black Muslims is the dissonant phrase, and it suggests a story of reading very different from Booth's. Here is how Malcolm X tells it. While serving time in the Norfolk Prison Colony, he hit upon the idea of teaching himself to read by copying the dictionary:

> In my slow, painstaking, ragged handwriting, I copied into my tablet everything on that first page, down to the punctuation marks. . . . Then, aloud, to myself, I read back everything I'd written on the tablet. . . . I woke up the next morning thinking about these words—immensely proud to realize that not only had I written so much at one time, but I'd written words that I never knew were in the world.

After copying the dictionary, Malcolm X began reading the books in the prison library. "No university would ask any student to devour literature as I did when this new world opened to me, of being able to read and *understand*." What did he read? What did he understand? He read Gregor Mendel's *Findings in Genetics*, and it helped him to understand "that if you started with a black man, a white man could be produced; but starting with a white man, you never could produce a black man—because the white chromosome is recessive. And since no one disputes that there was but one Original Man, the conclusion is clear" (173, 175).

He read histories, books by Will Durant and Arnold Toynbee, books by W. E. B. Du Bois and Carter G. Woodson, and he saw how "the glorious history of the black man" had been "bleached" out of the history books written by white men:

> [My] eyes opened gradually, then wider and wider, to how the world's white men had indeed acted like devils, pillaging and raping and bleeding and draining the whole world's non-white people. . . . I will never forget how shocked I was when I began reading about slavery's total horror. . . . The world's most monstrous crime, the sin and the blood on the white man's hands, are almost impossible to believe. (175)

He read philosophy—the works of Schopenhauer, Kant, Nietzsche, and Spinoza, and he concluded that the "whole stream of Western Philosophy was now wound up in a cul-de-sac'' as a result of the white man's ''elaborate, neurotic necessity to hide the black man's true role in history.'' Malcolm X read voraciously, and book after book confirmed the truth of Elijah Muhammad's teachings. ''It's a crime, the lie that has been told to generations of black men and white both. . . . Innocent black children growing up, living out their lives, dying of old age—and all of their lives ashamed of being black. But the truth is pouring out of the bag now'' (181).

Wayne Booth's story leads to the Crystal Ballroom of the Biltmore Hotel in Los Angeles, where we attend the protagonist as he delivers his presidential address to the members of the Modern Language Association. Malcolm X's love of books took him in a different direction, to the stage of the Audubon Ballroom in Harlem, where, as he was about to address a mass meeting of the Organization of Afro-American Unity, he was murdered.

3. As we have seen, an ellipsis links Booth's story of reading to Malcolm X's. Another ellipsis—this time not graphically marked—signals the existence of a third story. Malcolm X's startling reading of Mendel's genetics overlooks the most rudimentary fact of human reproduction: whether you start with a black man or a white man, without woman, you get *nothing*. An excerpt from Virginia Woolf's *A Room of One's Own* restores this deleted perspective.

The heroine (call her Mary, says Woolf) goes to the British Museum in search of information about women. There she discovers to her chagrin that woman is, ''perhaps, the most discussed animal in the universe'':

> Why does Samuel Butler say, ''Wise men never say what they think of women''? Wise men never say anything else apparently. . . . Are [women] capable of education? Napoleon thought them incapable. Dr. Johnson thought the opposite. Have they souls or have they not souls? Some savages say they have none. Others, on the contrary, say women are half divine and worship them on that account. Some sages hold that they are shallower in the brain; others that they are deeper in consciousness. Goethe honoured them; Mussolini despises them. Wherever one looked men thought about women and thought differently. (26–30)

Distressed and confused, Mary notices that she has unconsciously drawn a picture in her notebook, ''the face and figure of Professor von X. engaged in writing his monumental work, *The Mental, Moral, and Physical Inferiority of the Female Sex*:

> His expression suggested that he was labouring under some emotion that made him jab his pen on the paper as if he were killing some noxious insect as he wrote, but even when he had killed it that did not satisfy him; he must go on killing it. . . . A very elementary exercise in psychology . . . showed me . . . that the sketch had been made in anger.

Nothing remarkable in that, she reflects, given the provocation. But ''how explain the anger of the professors? . . . For when it came to analysing the impression left by these books, . . . there was [an] element which was often present and could not be immediately identified. Anger, I called it. . . . anger disguised and complex, not anger simple and open'' (31–32).

Disappointed with essayists and professors, Mary turns to historians. But apparently woman played no significant role in history. What little information Mary finds is disturbing: "Wife-beating, I read, was a recognized right of a man, and was practiced without shame by high as well as low." Oddly enough, literature presents a contradictory picture:

> If woman had no existence save in fiction written by men, we would imagine her to be a person of utmost importance; very various; heroic and mean; splendid and sordid; infinitely beautiful and hideous in the extreme; as great as a man, some think even greater. But this is woman in fiction. In fact, as Professor Trevelyan points out, she was locked up, beaten and flung about the room. (44–45)

At last, Mary can draw but one conclusion from her reading. Neither male professors, nor male historians, nor male poets can be relied on for the truth about women. Woman herself must undertake the study of woman. Of course, to do so, she must secure enough money to live on and a room of her own.

Booth tells his story, we recall, within the framework of a professional ritual. It is intended to remind us of "the loves and fears that inform our daily work" and of "what we do when we are at our best." He hopes that it shows, if not a unity, then enough of a "center" "to shame us whenever we violate it." The principal motif of the myth is the hero's insane love for books and the way this develops with education and maturity into "critical understanding," which Booth defines as that synthesis of thought and passion which should replace, "on the one hand, sentimental and uncritical identifications that leave minds undisturbed, and on the other, hypercritical negations that freeze or alienate." Booth is confident that the experience celebrated by the myth is archetypal:

> Whatever our terms for it, whatever our theories about how it happens or why it fails to happen more often, can we reasonably doubt the importance of the moment, at any level of study, when any of us—you, me, Malcolm X, my great-grandfather—succeeds in entering other minds, or "taking them in," as nourishment for our own? (317–18)

Now, while it is certainly true that something one might call "critical understanding" informs the stories told by Malcolm X and Virginia Woolf, they fill this term with thoughts and passions one would never suspect from Booth's definition. From the standpoint of the second and third stories of reading, Booth's story is utopian. The powers and resources of his hero are equal to the challenges he encounters. At each stage he finds suitable mentors. He is assured by the people around him, by the books he reads, by the entire culture, that he is right for the part. His talents and accomplishments are acknowledged and justly rewarded. In short, from the perspective of Malcolm X's and Woolf's stories, Booth's hero is fantastically privileged.

"Utopian" has a second meaning, one that is by no means pejorative, and Booth's story is utopian in this sense as well. In overlooking the realities highlighted by the stories of Malcolm X and Virginia Woolf, Booth's story anticipates what might be possible, what "critical understanding" might mean for everyone, if only we could overcome the pervasive, systemic injustices of our time.

Reader-Response Theory and Feminist Criticism

Reader-response criticism, as currently constituted, is utopian in the same two senses. The different accounts of the reading experience that have been put forth overlook the issues of race, class, and sex and give no hint of the conflicts, sufferings, and passions that attend these realities. The relative tranquillity of the tone of these theories testifies to the privileged position of the theorists. Perhaps, someday, when privileges have withered away or at least become more equitably distributed, one or the other of these theories will ring true. Surely we ought to be able to talk about reading without worrying about injustice. But for now, reader-response criticism must confront the disturbing implications of our historical reality. Paradoxically, utopian theories that elide these realities undermine the utopian impulses that inform them.

In fact, the obvious question of the significance of gender has already been explicitly raised, and—this testifies to the increasing impact of feminist criticism as well as to the direct ideological bearing of the issue of gender on reader-response criticism—not by a feminist critic but by Jonathan Culler, a leading theorist of reading.[1]

> If the experience of literature depends upon the qualities of a reading self, one can ask what difference it would make to the experience of literature and thus to the meaning of literature if this self were, for example, female rather than male. If the meaning of a work is the experience of a reader, what difference does it make if the reader is a woman? (42)

Culler's survey of reader-response theory is instructive, for it enables us to anticipate the direction reader-response theory might take when it is shaken from its slumber by feminist criticism. According to Culler, the different models (or "stories") of reading that have been proposed are all organized around three problems. The first is the issue of control: Does the text control the reader, or vice versa? For David Bleich, Norman Holland, and Stanley Fish, the reader holds controlling interest. Readers read the poems they have made. Bleich asserts this point most strongly: the constraints imposed by the words on the page are "trivial," since their meaning can always be altered by "subjective action." To claim that the text supports this or that reading is only to "moralistically claim . . . that one's own objectification is more authoritative than someone else's" (112). At the other pole are Michael Riffaterre, Georges Poulet, and Wolfgang Iser, who acknowledge the creative role of the reader but ultimately take the text to be the dominant force. To read, from this point of view, is to create the text according to *its* own promptings. As Poulet puts it, a text, when invested with a reader's subjectivity, becomes a "subjectified object," a "second self" that depends on the reader but is not, strictly speaking, identical with him.

Thus reading "is a way of giving way not only to a host of alien words, images and ideas, but also to the very alien principle which utters and shelters them. . . . I am on loan to another, and this other thinks, feels, suffers and acts within me" (43).[2] Culler argues persuasively that regardless of their ostensible theoretical commitments, the prevailing stories of reading generally vacillate between reader-dominant and text-dominant poles. In fact, those who stress the subjectivity of the reader as against the objectivity of the text ultimately portray the text as determining the responses of the reader.

The second question prominent in theories of reading is closely related to the first. Reading always involves a subject and an object, a reader and a text. But what constitutes the objectivity of the text? What is "in" the text? What is supplied by the reader? Again, the answers have been equivocal. On the face of it, the situation seems to call for a dualistic theory that credits the contribution of both text and reader. However, Culler argues, a dualistic theory eventually gives way to a monistic theory in which one or the other pole supplies everything.

The third problem identified by Culler concerns the ending of the story. Most of the time, stories of reading end happily. "Readers may be manipulated and misled, but when they finish the book their experience turns into knowledge . . . as though finishing the book took them outside the experience of reading and gave them mastery of it." However, some critics—Harold Bloom, Paul de Man, and Culler himself—find these optimistic endings questionable and prefer instead stories that stress the impossibility of reading. If, as de Man says, rhetoric puts "an insurmountable obstacle in the way of any reading or understanding," then the reader "may be placed in impossible situations where there is no happy issue, but only the possibility of playing out the roles dramatized in the text" (Culler 79–82).

Such have been the predominant preoccupations of reader-response criticism. Before indicating how feminist critics could affect the conversation, let me consider an objection. A recent essay by Elaine Showalter suggests that we should not enter the conversation at all. During its early phases, she claims, the principal mode of feminist criticism was "feminist critique," which was counter-ideological in intent and concerned with the feminist as *reader*. Happily, we have outgrown this necessary but theoretically unpromising approach. Today the dominant mode of feminist criticism is "gynocritics," the study of woman as *writer*, and this has put us in the position of developing a feminist criticism that is "genuinely woman-centered, independent, and intellectually coherent" ("Feminist Criticism" 247–50).

But why should the activity of the woman writer be more conducive to theory than the activity of the woman reader? If it is possible to formulate a basic conceptual framework for disclosing the "difference" of women's writing, surely it is no less possible to do so for women's reading. The same difference, be it linguistic, biological, psychological, or cultural, should apply in either case. In addition, what Showalter calls "gynocritics" is in fact constituted by feminist *criticism*—that is, *readings*—of female texts. Thus the relevant distinction is not between woman as reader and woman as writer but between feminist readings of male texts and feminist readings of female texts, and there is no reason why the former could not be as theoretically coherent (or irreducibly pluralistic) as the latter.

At the same time, there are good reasons for feminist criticism to engage reader-response criticism. Both dispute the fetishized art object—the "Verbal Icon"—of New Criticism, and both seek to dispel the objectivist illusion that buttresses the authority of the dominant critical tradition. Feminist criticism can have a real impact on reader-response criticism, since, as Culler has noticed, it is but a small step from the thesis that the reader is an active producer of meaning to the conclusion that there are many different kinds of readers and that women—because of their numbers if for nothing else—constitute an essential class. Reader-response critics cannot take refuge in the objectivity of the text or even in the idea that a gender-neutral criticism is possible. They can continue to ignore the implications of feminist criticism only at the cost of incoherence or intellectual dishonesty.

It is equally true that feminist critics need to question their allegiance to text- and author-centered paradigms of criticism. Feminist criticism, we should remember, is a mode of praxis. The point is not merely to interpret literature in various ways; the point is to *change the world*. We cannot afford to ignore the activity of reading, for it is here that literature is realized as praxis. Literature acts on the world by acting on its readers.

To return to our earlier question: What will happen to reader-response criticism if feminists enter the conversation? It is useful to recall the contrast between Booth's story and those of Malcolm X and Virginia Woolf. Like Booth's story, the "stories of reading" that currently make up reader-response theory are mythically abstract and appear, from a different vantage point, to be by and about readers who are fantastically privileged. Booth's story had a happy ending; Malcolm's and Mary's did not. For Mary, reading meant encountering a tissue of lies and silences; for Malcolm it meant the verification of Elijah Muhammad's shocking doctrines.

Two factors—gender and politics—suppressed in the dominant models of reading gain prominence with the advent of a feminist perspective. The feminist story will have at least two chapters. The first will be concerned with feminist readings of male texts, the second with feminist readings of female texts. In addition, in this story, gender will play a prominent role as the locus of political struggle. The story will speak of the difference between men and women, of the way the experience and perspective of women have been systematically and fallaciously assimilated into the generic masculine, and of the need to correct this error. Finally, it will identify literature—the activities of reading and writing—as an important arena of political struggle, a crucial component of the project of interpreting the world in order to change it.

Feminist criticism does not approach reader-response criticism without preconceptions. Actually, feminist criticism has always included substantial reader-centered interests. In the next two sections of this paper, we will review these interests, first with respect to male texts, then with respect to female texts. In the process, we will uncover some of the issues that might be addressed and clarified by a feminist theory of reading.

The Female Reader and the Literary Canon

Although reader-response critics propose different and often conflicting models, by and large, the emphasis is on features that do not vary with the nature of the reading material. The feminist entry into the conversation brings the nature of the text back into the foreground. For feminists, *how* we read depends on *what* we read. More specifically, the feminist inquiry into the activity of reading begins with the realization that the literary canon is androcentric and that this has a profoundly damaging effect on women readers (see Showalter, "Women" 855; L. Edwards, "Women" 226).

To put the matter theoretically, androcentric literature structures the reading experience differently depending on the gender of the reader. For the male reader, the text serves as the meeting ground of the personal and the universal. Whether or not the text approximates the particularities of his own experience, he is invited to validate the equation of maleness with humanity. The male reader feels his affinity with the universal, with the paradigmatic human being, precisely because he is male. Consider the famous scene of Stephen's epiphany in *A Portrait of the Artist as a Young Man*:

> A girl stood before him in midstream, alone and still, gazing out to sea. She seemed like one whom magic had changed into the likeness of a strange and beautiful seabird. Her long slender bare legs were delicate as a crane's and pure save where an emerald trail of seaweed had fashioned itself as a sign upon the flesh. Her thighs, fuller and softhued as ivory, were bared almost to the hips, where the white fringes of her drawers were like feathering of soft white down. Her slateblue skirts were kilted about her waist and dovetailed behind her. Her bosom was a bird's, soft and slight, slight and soft, as the breast of some dark plumaged dove. But her long fair hair was girlish: and touched with the wonder of mortal beauty, her face. (195)

A man reading this passage is invited to identify with Stephen, to feel "the riot in his blood" and, thus, to ratify the alleged universality of the experience. Whether or not the sight of a girl on the beach has ever provoked similar emotions in him, the male reader is invited to feel his *difference* (concretely, from the girl) and to equate that with the universal. Relevant here is Lévi-Strauss's theory that woman functions as currency exchanged between men. The woman in the text converts the text into a woman, and the circulation of this text/woman becomes the central ritual that establishes the bond between the author and his male readers.

The same text affects a woman reader differently. Judith Fetterley gives the most explicit theory to date about the dynamics of the woman reader's encounter with androcentric literature. According to Fetterley, notwithstanding the prevalence of the castrating bitch stereotype,

> the cultural reality is not the emasculation of men by women, but the *immasculation* of women by men. As readers and teachers and scholars, women are taught to think as men, to identify with a male point of view, and to accept as normal and

> legitimate a male system of values, one of whose central principles is misogyny. (xx)

The process of immasculation does not impart virile power to the woman reader. On the contrary, it doubles her oppression. She suffers

> not simply the powerlessness which derives from not seeing one's experience articulated, clarified, and legitimized in art, but more significantly, the powerlessness which results from the endless division of self against self, the consequence of the invocation to identify as male while being reminded that to be male—to be universal—. . . is to be *not female*. (xiii)

A woman reading Joyce's novel of artistic awakening—in particular, the passage quoted above—will, like her male counterpart, be invited to identify with Stephen and therefore to ratify the equation of maleness with the universal. Androcentric literature is all the more efficient as an instrument of sexual politics because it does not allow the woman reader to seek refuge in her difference. Instead, it draws her into a process that uses her against herself. It solicits her complicity in the elevation of male difference into universality and, accordingly, the denigration of female difference into otherness without reciprocity. To be sure, misogyny is abundant in the literary canon (see Rogers). It is important, however, that Fetterley's argument can stand on a weaker premise. Androcentricity is a sufficient condition for the process of immasculation. (For another reading of the Joyce passage, see Howe, "Feminism" 262–63.)

Feminist critics of male texts, from Kate Millett to Judith Fetterley, have worked under the sign of the "resisting reader." Their goal is to disrupt the process of immasculation by exposing it to consciousness and by disclosing the androcentricity of what has customarily passed for the universal. However, feminist criticism written under the aegis of the resisting reader leaves certain questions unanswered, questions that are becoming ripe for feminist analysis: Where does the text get its power to draw us into its designs? Why do some (not all) demonstrably sexist texts remain appealing even after they have been subjected to thorough feminist critique? The usual answer—that the power of male texts is the power of the false consciousness into which women as well as men have been socialized—oversimplifies the problem and prevents us from comprehending both the force of literature and the complexity of our responses to it.

Fredric Jameson advances a thesis which seems to me to be a good starting point for the feminist reconsideration of male texts: "The effectively ideological is also at the same time necessarily utopian" (*Political Unconscious* 286). This thesis implies that the male text draws its power over the female reader from authentic desires, which it rouses, then harnesses to the process of immasculation.

An illustration is in order. Consider Lawrence's *Women in Love* and, for the sake of simplicity, concentrate on Birkin and Ursula. Simone de Beauvoir and Kate Millett have convinced me that this novel is sexist. Why does it remain appealing to me? Jameson's thesis prompts me to answer this question by examining how the text plays not only on my false consciousness but also on my authentic liberatory aspirations—that is to say, on the very impulses that drew me to the feminist movement.

The trick of role reversal comes in handy here. If we reverse the roles of Birkin and Ursula, the ideological components (or at least the most egregious of these—e.g., the analogy between women and horses) stand out as absurdities. Now, if we delete these absurd components while keeping the roles reversed, we have left the story of a woman struggling to combine her passionate desire for autonomous conscious being with an equally passionate desire for love and for other human bonds. This residual story is not far from one we would welcome as expressive of a feminist sensibility and, interestingly enough, a novel Lawrence might have written—namely, the proper sequel to *The Rainbow*.

My affective response to the novel Lawrence did write is bifurcated. On the one hand, because I am a woman, I am implicated in the representation of Ursula and in the destiny Lawrence has prepared for her: man is the son of god, but woman is the daughter of man. Her vocation is to witness his transcendence in rapt silence. On the other hand, Fetterley is correct that I am also induced to identify with Birkin and that, in so doing, I am drawn into complicity with the reduction of Ursula, and therefore of myself, to the role of the other.

However, the process of immasculation is more complicated than Fetterley allows. When I identify with Birkin, I unconsciously perform the two-stage rereading described above. I reverse the roles of Birkin and Ursula, and I suppress the obviously ideological components that in the process show up as absurdities. The identification with Birkin is emotionally effective because, stripped of its patriarchal trappings, Birkin's struggle and his utopian vision conform to my own. To the extent that I perform this feminist rereading *unconsciously*, I am captivated by the text. The stronger my desire for autonomous selfhood and for love, the stronger my identification with Birkin, and the more intense the experience of bifurcation characteristic of the process of immasculation.

The full argument is beyond the scope of this essay. My point is that *certain* (not all) male texts merit a dual hermeneutic: a negative hermeneutic that discloses their complicity with patriarchal ideology and a positive hermeneutic that recuperates the utopian moment which is the basis of their emotional power.[3]

Reading Women's Writing

Showalter is correct that feminist criticism has shifted emphasis in recent years from "critique" of (primarily) male texts to the study of women's writing. Of course, the interest in women's writing has not entirely effaced the critical study of patriarchal texts.[4] As feminist criticism shifted its emphasis to the study of women's writings, "feminist critique" shifted its focus from androcentric literature to the androcentric critical strategies that have pushed women's writings to the margins of the literary canon (see Showalter, "Double Critical Standard"; Ohmann; Baym, "Melodramas").

The deep symbiotic relationship between the androcentric canon and androcentric modes of reading is well summarized by Kolodny:

> *Insofar as we are taught how to read, what we engage are not texts but paradigms*. . . . [I]nsofar as literature is itself a social institution, so, too, reading is a highly socialized—or learned—activity. . . . [W]e read well, and with pleasure, what we already know how to read; and what we know how to read is to a large extent dependent upon what we have already read (works from which we've developed our expectations and learned our interpretive strategies). What we then choose to read—and, by extension, teach and thereby "canonize"—usually follows upon our previous reading. (88–89, in this volume)

We are caught, then, in a rather vicious circle. An androcentric canon generates androcentric interpretive strategies, which, in turn, favor the canonization of androcentric texts and the marginalization of gynocentric ones. To break this circle, feminist critics must fight on two fronts—for the revision of the canon to include a significant body of works by women, and for the development of the reading strategies consonant with the concerns, experiences, and formal devices that constitute these texts. Of course, to succeed, we also need a community of women readers, qualified by experience, commitment, and training, who will enlist the personal and institutional resources at their disposal in the struggle.[5]

The critique of androcentric reading strategies is essential, for it opens up some ideological space for the recuperation of women's writing. Turning now to this project, we observe, first, that a large volume of work has been done and, second, that this endeavor is coming to look even more complicated and more diverse than the criticism of male texts. Certainly, it is impossible in the space of a few pages to do justice to the wide range of concerns, strategies, and positions associated with feminist readings of female texts. Nevertheless, certain things can be said. The remainder of this section will focus on an exemplary essay: "Vesuvius at Home: The Power of Emily Dickinson," by Adrienne Rich. My commentary looks forward to the articulation of a paradigm that illuminates certain features of feminist readings of women's writing.

I am principally interested in the rhetoric of Rich's essay, for this represents an implicit commentary on the process of reading women's writing. Feminist readings of male texts are, as we have seen, primarily resisting. The reader assumes an adversarial or at least detached attitude toward the material at hand. In the opening pages of her essay, Rich introduces three metaphors that proclaim a very different attitude toward her subject:

> The methods, the exclusions, of Emily Dickinson's existence could not have been my own; yet more and more, as a woman poet finding my own methods, I have come to understand her necessities, could have served as witness in her defense. (158)

> I am traveling at the speed of time, along the Massachusetts Turnpike. . . . "Home is not where the heart is," she wrote in a letter, "but the house and adjacent buildings." . . . I am traveling at the speed of time, in the direction of the house and buildings. . . . For years, I have been not so much envisioning Emily Dickinson as trying to visit, to enter her mind through her poems and letters, and through

> my own intimations of what it could have meant to be one of the two mid-nineteenth century American geniuses, and a woman, living in Amherst, Massachusetts. (158–59)
>
> For months, for most of my life, I have been hovering like an insect against the screens of an existence which inhabited Amherst, Massachusetts between 1830 and 1886. (158)
>
> . . . Here [in Dickinson's bedroom] I become again, an insect, vibrating at the frames of windows, clinging to the panes of glass, trying to connect. (161)

A commentary on the process of reading is carried on silently and unobtrusively through the use of these metaphors. The first is a judicial metaphor—the feminist reader speaks as a witness in defense of the woman writer. Here we see clearly that gender is crucial. The feminist reader takes the part of the woman writer against patriarchal misreadings that trivialize or distort her work.[6]

The second metaphor refers to a principal tenet of feminist criticism: a literary work cannot be understood apart from the social, historical, and cultural context within which it was written. As if to acquiesce to the condition Dickinson had imposed on her friends, Rich travels through space and time to visit the poet on her own *premises*. She goes to Amherst, to the house where Dickinson lived. She rings the bell, she goes in, then upstairs, then into the bedroom which had been "freedom" for the poet. Her destination, ultimately, is Dickinson's mind. But it is not enough to read the poet's poems and letters. To reach her heart and mind, one must take a detour through "the house and adjacent buildings."

Why did Dickinson go into seclusion? Why did she write poems she would not publish? What is the meaning of these poems about queens, volcanoes, deserts, eternity, passion, suicide, wild beasts, rape, power, madness, the demon, the grave? For Rich, these are related questions. The revisionary rereading of Dickinson's work is of a piece with the revisionary rereading of her life:

> I have a notion genius knows itself; that Dickinson chose her seclusion, knowing what she needed. . . . She carefully selected her society and controlled the disposal of her time. . . . Given her vocation, she was neither eccentric nor quaint; she was determined to survive, to use her powers, to practice necessary economies. (160)
>
> To write [the poetry that she needed to write] she had to enter chambers of the self in which
>
> Ourself, concealed—
> Should startle most—
>
> and to relinquish control there, to take those risks, she had to create a relationship to the outer world where she could feel in control. (175)

The metaphor of visiting points to another feature of feminist readings of women's writing—namely, the tendency to construe the text not as an object but as the manifestation of the subjectivity of the absent author—the "voice" of another woman. Rich is not content to revel in the textuality of Dickinson's poems and letters. For her, these are doorways to the "mind" of a "woman of genius." Rich deploys her imagination and her considerable rhetorical skill to evoke "the figure of powerful will" who lives at the heart of the text. To read Dickinson, then, is to try to visit with her, to hear her voice, to make her live *in* oneself and to feel her impressive "personal dimensions."[7]

At the same time, Rich is keenly aware that visiting with Dickinson is *only* a metaphor for reading her poetry, and an inaccurate one at that. She signals this awareness with the third metaphor. It is no longer possible to visit with Dickinson; one can enter her mind through her poems and letters only as one can enter her house—through the back door out of which her coffin was carried. In reading, one encounters only a text, the trail of an absent author. Upstairs, at last, in the very room where Dickinson exercised her astonishing craft, Rich finds herself again "an insect, vibrating at the frames of windows, clinging to panes of glass, trying to connect." But though "the scent is very powerful," Dickinson herself is absent.

Perhaps the most obvious rhetorical device employed by Rich in this essay, more obvious even than her striking metaphors, is her use of the personal voice. Her approach to Dickinson is self-consciously and unabashedly subjective. She clearly describes her point of view—what she saw as she drove across the Connecticut Valley toward Amherst (ARCO stations, McDonald's restaurants, shopping plazas, as well as "light-green spring softening the hills, dogwood and wild fruit trees blossoming in the hollows") and what she thought about (the history of the valley, "the scene of Indian uprisings, religious revivals, spiritual confrontations, the blazing-up of the lunatic fringe of the Puritan coal," and her memories of college weekends in Amherst). Some elements of her perspective would have been alien to Dickinson—ARCO and McDonald's; others would establish their affinity—the sight of dogwood and wild fruit trees in the spring and, most of all, the experience of being a woman poet in a patriarchal culture.

Rich's metaphors together with her use of the personal voice indicate some key issues underlying feminist readings of female texts. On the one hand, reading is necessarily subjective. On the other hand, it must not be wholly so. One must respect the autonomy of the text. The reader is a visitor and, as such, must observe the necessary courtesies. She must avoid unwarranted intrusions—she must be careful not to appropriate what belongs to her host, not to impose herself on the other woman. However, reading is at once an intersubjective encounter and something less than that. By reading Dickinson, one may enter her mind, feel her presence. But at the same time, the text is a screen, an inanimate object. Its subjectivity is only a projection of the subjectivity of the reader.

Rich suggests the central motivation, the regulative ideal, that shapes the feminist reader's approach to these issues. If feminist readings of male texts are motivated by the need to disrupt the process of immasculation, feminist readings of female texts are motivated by the need "to connect," to recuperate or formulate—it comes to the same thing—the context, the tradition, that would link women writers to each other, to women readers and critics, and to the larger community of women. Of course, the recuperation of such a context is a necessary basis for the nonrepressive integration of women's point of view and culture into the study of a humanities that is worthy of its name.[8]

Feminist Models of Reading: A Summary

As we noted in an earlier section, mainstream reader-response theory is preoccupied with two closely related questions: Does the text manipulate the reader, or does the reader manipulate the text to produce the meaning that suits her own interests? What is "in" the text? How can we distinguish what it supplies from what the reader supplies? These questions refer to the subject-object relation that is established between reader and text during the process of reading. A feminist theory of reading also elaborates this relationship, but for feminists, gender is crucial—the gender inscribed in the text as well as the gender of the reader. Hence the feminist story has two chapters, one concerned with male texts and the other with female texts.

The focus of the first chapter is the experience of the woman reader. What do male texts *do* to her? The feminist story takes the subject-object relation of reading through three moments.

The phrasing of the basic question signals the first moment. Control is conferred on the text: the woman reader is immasculated by the text. The feminist story fits well, at this point, into Wolfgang Iser's framework. Feminists insist that the androcentricity of the text and its damaging effects on women readers are not figments of their imagination. These are implicit in the "schematized aspects" of the text. The second moment, which is similarly consonant with the plot of Iser's story, involves the recognition of the crucial role played by the subjectivity of the woman reader. Without her, the text is *no-thing*. The process of immasculation is latent in the text, but it finds its actualization only through the reader's activity. In effect, the woman reader is the agent of her own immasculation.[9]

Here we seem to have a corroboration of Culler's contention that dualistic models of reading inevitably disintegrate into one of two monisms. Either the text and, by implication, the author, or the woman reader is responsible for the process of immasculation. The third moment of the subject-object relation—ushered in by the transfiguration of the heroine into a feminist—breaks through this dilemma. The woman reader, now a feminist, embarks on a critical analysis of the reading process, and she realizes that the text has power to structure her experience. Without androcentric texts she will not suffer immasculation. Moreover, her recognition of the power of the text is matched by her awareness of her essential role in the process of reading. Without her, the text is nothing—it is inert and harmless. The advent of feminist consciousness and the accompanying commitment to emancipatory praxis reconstitutes the subject-object relationship within a dialectical rather than a dualistic framework, thus averting the impasse between the "dualism of narrative" and the "monism of theory" described by Culler. In the feminist story, the breakdown of Iser's dualism indicates neither a mistake nor an irreducible impasse but the possibility of *choosing* between two modes of reading. The reader can submit to the power of the text, or she can take control of the reading experience. The recognition of the existence of the choice suddenly makes visible the normative dimension of the feminist story: she *should* choose the second alternative.

Now what does it mean for a reader to take control of the reading experience? First of all, she must do so without forgetting the androcentricity of the text or its power to structure her experience. In addition, it is not, as in Iser's model, simply a matter of selecting among the concretizations that the text allows. Recall that a crucial feature of the process of immasculation is the woman reader's bifurcated response. She reads the text *both* as a man and as a woman, and in either case, the result is the same: she confirms her position as other. Taking control of the reading experience means reading the text as it was *not* meant to be read—in fact, reading it against itself. Specifically, one must identify the nature of the choices proffered by the text and, equally important, what it precludes—namely, the possibility of reading as a woman *without* putting oneself in the position of the other or, equivalently, the possibility of reading so as to affirm womanhood as another, equally valid paradigm of human existence.

All this is easier said than done. It is important to realize that reading a male text, no matter how virulently misogynist, could do little damage if it were an isolated event. The problem is that within patriarchal culture, the experience of immasculation is paradigmatic of women's encounters with the dominant literary and critical traditions. A feminist cannot simply refuse to read patriarchal texts, for they are everywhere and they condition her participation in the literary and critical enterprise. In fact, by the time she becomes a feminist critic, a woman has already read numerous male texts—in particular, the most authoritative texts of the literary and critical canons. She has introjected not only androcentric texts, but also androcentric reading strategies and values. By the time she becomes a feminist, the bifurcated response characteristic of immasculation has become second nature to her. The feminist story stresses that patriarchal constructs have objective as well as subjective reality; they are inside and outside the text, inside and outside the reader.[10]

Because patriarchal constructs have psychological correlates, taking control of the reading process means taking control of one's reactions and inclinations. Thus a feminist reading—actually a rereading—is a kind of therapeutic analysis. The reader recalls and examines how she would "naturally" read a male text in order to understand and therefore undermine the subjective predispositions that had rendered her vulnerable to its designs. Beyond this, the pervasiveness of immasculation necessitates a collective remedy. The feminist reader hopes that other women will recognize themselves in her story and join her in her struggle to transform the culture.[11]

"Feminism affirms women's point of view by revealing, criticizing and examining its impossibility" (637). Had we nothing but male texts, this sentence from Catherine MacKinnon's brilliant essay on jurisprudence could serve as the definition of the project of the feminist reader. The significant body of literature written by women presents feminist critics with another, more heartwarming task: that of recovering, articulating, and elaborating positive expressions of women's point of view, of celebrating its survival in spite of the formidable forces that have been ranged against it.

Unlike the first chapter of the feminist story of reading, which is centered on a single heroine—the woman reader battling her way out of a maze of patriarchal constructs—the second chapter features two protagonists—the woman reader and the woman writer—in the context of two settings. The first is judicial—one is standing witness in defense of the other. The second is dialogic—the two women are engaged in intimate conversation.

The judicial setting points to the larger political and cultural dimension of the project of the feminist reader. Feminist critics may well say with Harold Bloom that reading always involves the "art of defensive warfare" (*Kabbalah* 126). What they mean by this, however, would not be Bloom's individualistic, agonistic encounter between "strong poet" and "strong reader" but something more akin to "class struggle." Whether concerned with male or female texts, feminist criticism is situated in the larger struggle against patriarchy.

The importance of this battle must not be underestimated. However, feminist readings of women's writing open up space for another, equally important critical project—namely, the articulation of a model of reading that is centered on a female paradigm. While it is still too early to present a full-blown theory, the dialogic aspect of the relationship between the feminist reader and the woman writer suggests the direction that such a theory might take. As in all stories of reading, the drama revolves around the subject-object relationship between text and reader. The feminist story—exemplified by the Adrienne Rich essay discussed in the section "Reading Women's Writing"—features an intersubjective construction of this relationship. The reader encounters not simply a text but a subjectified object—the "heart and mind" of another woman. She comes into close contact with an interiority—a power, a creativity, a suffering, a vision—that is *not* identical with her own. The feminist interest in construing reading as intersubjective encounter suggests an affinity with Poulet's (rather than Iser's) theory. Moreover, as in Poulet's model, the subject of the literary work is its author, *not* the reader:

> A book is not only a book; it is a means by which an author actually preserves [her] ideas, [her] feelings, [her] modes of dreaming and living. It is a means of saving [her] identity from death. . . . To understand a literary work, then, is to let the individual who wrote it reveal [herself] to us *in* us. (46)

For all this initial agreement, however, the dialogic relationship the feminist reader establishes with the female subjectivity brought to life in the process of reading is finally at odds with Poulet's model. For the interiorized author is "alien" to Poulet's reader. When he reads, he delivers himself "bound hand and foot, to the omnipotence of fiction." He becomes the "prey" of what he reads. "There is no escaping this take-over." His consciousness is "invaded," "annexed," "usurped." He is "dispossessed" of his rightful place on the "center stage" of his own mind. In the final analysis, the process of reading leaves room for only one subjectivity. The work becomes "a sort of human being" at "the expense of the reader whose life it suspends" (47).[12]

Note that the metaphors of mastery and submission, of violation, of control, so prominent in Poulet's essay, are entirely absent in Rich's essay on Dickinson. In the paradigm of reading implicit in her essay, the dialectic of control (which shapes feminist readings of male texts) gives way to the dialectic of communication. Reading is a matter of "trying to connect" with the existence behind the text.

This dialectic also has three moments. The first involves the recognition that genuine intersubjective communication demands the duality of reader and author (the subject of the work). Because reading removes the barrier between subject and object, the division takes place *within* the reader. Reading induces a doubling of the reader's subjectivity, so that one can be placed at the disposal of the text while the other remains with the reader. Now this doubling presents a problem, for, in fact, there is only one subject present—the reader. The text—the words on the page—have been written by the writer, but meaning is always a matter of interpretation. The subjectivity roused to life by reading, while it is attributed to the author, is nevertheless not a separate subjectivity but a projection of the subjectivity of the reader. How can the duality of subjects be maintained in the absence of the author? In an actual conversation, the presence of the other preserves the duality. One must still assimilate and interpret her utterances, so that we still have the introjection of the subject-object division as well as the possibility of hearing only what one wants to hear. But in a real conversation, the other person can interrupt, object to an erroneous interpretation, provide further explanations, change her mind, change the topic, or cut off conversation altogether. In reading, there are no comparable safeguards against the appropriation of the text by the reader. This is the second moment of the dialectic—the recognition that reading is necessarily subjective. The need to keep it from being *totally* subjective ushers in the third moment.

In the feminist story, the key to the problem is the awareness of the double context of reading and writing. Rich's essay is wonderfully illustrative. To avoid imposing an alien perspective on Dickinson's poetry, Rich informs her reading with the knowledge of the circumstances in which Dickinson lived and worked. She repeatedly reminds herself and her readers that Dickinson must be read in light of her *own* premises, that the "exclusions" and "necessities" she endured and, therefore, her choices were conditioned by her own world. However, Rich's sensitivity to the context of writing is matched by her sensitivity to the context of reading. She makes it clear throughout the essay that her reading of Dickinson is necessarily shaped by her own experience and interests as a feminist poet living in the twentieth-century United States. The reader also has her own premises. To forget these is to run the risk of imposing them surreptitiously on the author.

To recapitulate, the first moment of the dialectic of reading is the recognition of the necessary duality of subjects. The second is the realization that this duality is threatened by the author's absence. In the third moment, the duality of subjects is referred to the duality of contexts. This moment marks the realization of reading as a mediation between author and reader, between the context of writing and the context of reading.

Although feminists have always believed that objectivity is an illusion, Rich's essay is the only one, as far as I know, to exhibit through its rhetoric the necessary subjectivity of reading coupled with the equally necessary commitment to reading the text as it was meant to be read. The third moment of the dialectic is apparent in Rich's weaving—not blending—of the context of writing and the context of reading, the perspective of the author and that of the reader. The central rhetorical device effecting this mediation is her use of the personal voice. As in most critical essays, Rich alternates quotes from the texts in question with her own commentary, but her personal voice marks a difference. Her strategy has two functions. First, the personal voice serves as a reminder that her interpretation is informed by her own perspective. Second, it is an essential feature of her tactful approach to Dickinson—a gesture warding off any inclination to appropriate the authority of the text as a warrant for the validity of the interpretation. The interpretation is presented as an *interpretation*; its claim to validity rests on the cogency of its arguments, *not* on the authorization of the text.

Rich accomplishes even more than this. She reaches out to Dickinson not by identifying with her but by establishing their affinity. Both are American, both are women poets in a patriarchal culture. By playing this affinity against the differences, Rich produces a context that incorporates both reader and writer. In turn, this common ground becomes the basis for drawing the connections which, in her view, constitute the proper goal of reading.

One might ask, Is there something distinctively female (rather than "merely feminist") in this dialogic model? While it is difficult to specify what "distinctively female" might mean, there are currently very interesting speculations about the way males and females conceive of themselves and of their relations with others. The works of Jean Baker Miller, Nancy Chodorow (*Reproduction*), and Carol Gilligan suggest that men define themselves through individuation and separation from others, while women have more flexible ego boundaries and define and experience themselves in terms of their affiliations and relationships with others. Men value autonomy, and they think of their interactions with others principally in terms of procedures for arbitrating conflicts between individual rights. Women, on the other hand, value relationships and are most concerned in their dealings with others to negotiate between opposing needs so that the relationship can be maintained. This difference is consistent with the difference between mainstream models of reading and the dialogic model I am proposing for feminist readings of women's writing. Mainstream reader-response theories are preoccupied with issues of control and partition—how to distinguish the contribution of the author/text from the contribution of the reader. In the dialectic of communication informing the relationship between the feminist reader and the female text/author, the central issue is not of control or partition but of management of contradictory implications of the desire for relationship (one must maintain a minimal distance from the other) and the desire for intimacy (up to and including a symbiotic merger with the other). It could be argued that

Poulet's model is also preoccupied with these issues. However, it is significant that in his model, the prospect of a close rapport with another provokes both excitement and anxiety. Intimacy, while desired, is also felt as a threat to one's integrity. For Rich, on the other hand, the prospect of merging with another is problematical but not threatening.

Let me end with a word about endings. Dialectical stories look forward to optimistic endings. Mine is no exception. In the first chapter, the woman reader becomes a feminist, and in the end she succeeds in extricating herself from the androcentric logic of the literary and critical canons. In the second chapter, the feminist reader succeeds in effecting a mediation between her perspective and that of the writer. These "victories" are part of the project of producing women's culture and literary tradition, which in turn is part of the project of overcoming patriarchy. It is in the nature of people working for revolutionary change to be optimistic about the prospect of redirecting the future.

Culler observes that optimistic endings have been challenged (successfully, he thinks) by deconstruction—a method radically at odds with the dialectic. It is worth noting that there is a deconstructive moment in Rich's reading of Dickinson. Recall her third metaphor: the reader is an insect "vibrating at the frames of windows, clinging to the panes of glass, trying to connect." The suggestion of futility is unmistakable. At best, Rich's interpretion of Dickinson might be considered as a "strong misreading" whose value is in its capacity to provoke other misreadings.

We might say this—but must we? To answer this question, we must ask another: What is at stake in the proposition that reading is impossible? For one thing, if reading is impossible, then there is no way of deciding the validity of an interpretation—the very notion of validity becomes problematical. Certainly it is useful to be reminded that the validity of an interpretation cannot be decided by appealing to what the author "intended," to what is "in" the text, or to what is "in" the experience of the reader. However, there is another approach to the problem of validation, one that is consonant with the dialogic model of reading described above. We can think of validity not as a property inherent in an interpretation but as a *claim* implicit in it. An interpretation, then, is not valid or invalid in itself. Its validity is contingent on the agreement of others. On this view, Rich's interpretation of Dickinson, which she frankly acknowledges to be conditioned by her own experience as a twentieth-century feminist poet, is not necessarily a misreading. In advancing her interpretation, she implicitly claims its validity. That is to say, to read a text and then to write about it is to seek to connect not only with the author of the original text but also with a community of readers. To the extent that she succeeds and to the extent that the community is potentially all-embracing, her interpretation has that degree of validity.[13]

Feminist reading and writing are alike grounded in the interest of producing a community of feminist readers and writers and in the hope that, ultimately, this community will expand to include everyone. Of course this project may fail. The feminist story may yet end with the recognition of the impossibility of reading. But this remains to be seen. At this stage I think it behooves us to *choose* the dialectical over the deconstructive plot. It is dangerous for feminists to be overly enamored of the theme of impossibility. Instead, we should strive to redeem the claim that it is possible for a woman, reading as a woman, to read literature written by women, for this is essential if we are to make the literary enterprise a means for building and maintaining connections among women.

NOTES

[1] Wayne Booth's essay "Freedom of Interpretation" is another good omen of the impact of feminist thought on literary criticism.

[2] Poulet's theory is not among those discussed by Culler. However, since he will be useful to us later, I mention him here.

[3] In *Women and the Demon*, Nina Auerbach employs a similar—though not identical—positive hermeneutic. The tension between the positive and negative feminist hermeneutics is perhaps most apparent when one is dealing with the "classics." See, for example, Carol Neely, "Feminist Modes of Shakespeare Criticism."

[4] It is equally true that "gynocritics" has always been on the feminist agenda. *Sexual Politics* contains not only the critique of Miller, Lawrence, and Mailer that had earned Millett such notoriety but also her wonderful rereading of *Villette*.

[5] For an excellent account of the way in which the feminist "interpretive community" has changed literary and critical conventions, see Jean Kennard, "Convention Coverage: Or, How to Read Your Own Life."

[6] Susan Glaspell's story "A Jury of Her Peers" revolves around a variation of this judicial metaphor. The parable of reading implicit in this story has not been lost on feminist criticism. See Annette Kolodny, "A Map for Rereading" (460–63).

[7] There is a strong countertendency, inspired by French poststructuralism, which privileges the appreciation of textuality over the imaginative recovery of the woman writer as subject of the work. See, for example, Mary Jacobus, "Is There a Woman in This Text?" especially the concluding paragraph. The last sentence of the essay underscores the controversy: "Perhaps the question that feminist critics should be asking is not 'Is there a woman in this text?' but rather: 'Is there a text in this woman?' "

[8] I must emphasize that although Rich's essay presents a significant paradigm for feminist readings of female texts, it is not the only such paradigm. An alternative is proposed by Caren Greenburg in "Reading Reading."

[9] Iser writes:

> As we read there occurs an artificial division of our personality, because we take as a theme for ourselves something we are not. Thus, in reading there are two levels—the alien "me" and the real, virtual "me"—which are never completely cut off from each other. Indeed, we can only make someone else's thoughts into an absorbing theme for ourselves provided the virtual background of our personality can adapt to it. (67)

The process described above is formally similar to the bifurcated response of the woman reader to androcentric texts. Add the stipulation that the alien "me" is a male who has appropriated the universal into his maleness, and we have the process of immasculation described in the section "The Female Reader and the Literary Canon."

[10] The pervasiveness of androcentricity drives feminist theory beyond the individualistic models of Iser and of most reader-response critics. Something akin to Stanley Fish's "interpretive community" has to be incorporated into the feminist story. See Fish, *Is there a Text in This Class*?

[11] It is, perhaps, important to point out that although the woman reader is the "star" of the feminist story of reading, this does not mean that men are excluded from the audience. On the contrary, it is hoped that on hearing the feminist story, they will be encouraged to revise their own stories to reflect the fact that they too are gendered beings and that, ultimately, they will take control of their inclination to appropriate the universal at the expense of women.

[12] As Culler points out, the theme of control is prominent in mainstream reader-response theory. Poulet's story is no exception. The issue of control is important in another way. Behind the question of whether the text controls the reader or vice versa is the question of how to *regulate* the profession. If the text is controlling, then there is no problem—we can simply refer to the authority of the text. But if the text is not necessarily controlling, then how do we constrain readers and critics (i.e., our students and colleagues)? How can we rule out "off-the-wall" interpretations? Fish's answer is interesting to feminist critics. The constraints, he says, are exercised not by the text but by the institutions within which literary criticism is situated. It is but a small step from this idea to the recognition of the necessarily political character of literature and criticism.

[13] The approach that I am suggesting here draws on Jurgen Habermas's definition of truth and validity as a claim implicit in an assertion and redeemable through discourse, specifically in the unconstrained discourse of an "ideal speech situation." Within this view, the emphasis shifts from the specification of conditions for the validity of propositions, to the specification of conditions for the process of validation—the warrant for truth is domination-free discourse. See "Wahrheitstheorien." I am indebted to Alan Sobel's unpublished translation.

~ 1985 ~

Milton's Daughters: The Education of Eighteenth-Century Women Writers

BETH KOWALESKI-WALLACE

THE TELEVISION SHOWS of my childhood presented many examples of benevolent patriarchs: from Robert Young to Fred MacMurray, these men counseled befuddled women and children alike and rarely erred in the advice they gave. We remember their trademarks—cardigan sweaters, pipes, libraries discreetly lined with titleless books. Not all of us had fathers like these, but in their symbolic capacity these men served as "Father" to us all, for, in the words of Dorothy Van Ghent: "[U]nder our anciently inherited patriarchal organization of the family . . . our 'fathers' are not only individual fathers but all of those who have come before us—society as it has determined our conditions of existence, and the problems we have to confront" (147–48). These television fathers of the late 1950s and 1960s were but distant reincarnations of earlier stereotypes—the benevolent patriarchs of the great eighteenth-century novels—and Van Ghent elaborates on the significance of these figures. But the "father imago" identified by Van Ghent was never static. Goldsmith's satiric rendering of Dr. Primrose answers Fielding's affable Squire Allworthy, while Richardson and Jane Austen harshly critique the expensive consequences of irresponsible fatherhood. Nonetheless, the eighteenth-century novel is characterized by its persistent adherence to the myth of the benevolent patriarch, the belief that, in the best of all possible situations, a strong, generous father figure—selfless, wise, and competent—provides a coherent worldview. His dependents willingly and lovingly entrust their lives to his care, believing that only he can channel their energies to constructive ends.

Eighteenth-century literary biography reiterates the preoccupation with the benevolent patriarch by providing examples of men-centered women, "daddy's girls," among them Elizabeth Carter, Hannah More, Maria Edgeworth, and Fanny Burney. In her exploration of the last writer's dependency on her father, Patricia Spacks uncovers a "dynamic of fear" which demands the father's presence as guardian for morality for Burney (*Imagining a Self* 161). Yet Burney's early diaries intimate the extent to which her father resembled lover more often than judge for the adolescent girl. In one revealing passage, the young author (age twenty-six) describes a trip to her father's inner sanctum to receive his verdict on her first literary production. Unmistakably sexual overtones surface as daughter Fanny anticipates her father's response:

> I was almost *afraid—& quite* ashamed to be alone with him—but he soon sent for me to his little gallery cabinet—& then with a significant smile that told me what was coming, & made me glow to my forehead with anxious expectation, he said, "I have read your Book, Fanny—but you need not blush at it—it is full of merit—it is really extraordinary." I fell upon his neck with heart-beating emotion, and he folded me in his arms so tenderly that I sobbed upon his shoulder—so delighted was I with his precious approbation. But I soon recovered to a gayer pleasure more like his own. (Ms. 658)[1]

Given the innuendos of the passage—the embarrassment at exposure to her father's "gaze," the revealing blush, the climax involving increased pulse rate followed by tender caresses—one might well make the case that Burney wrote the novel to "seduce" her father and that she succeeded. Not literally, of course, though in psychoanalytic terms the scene is rife with meaning. Burney is a bit old to play out the oedipal conflict here, but her presentation of the novel to her father may be interpreted as a substitute for her sexual presence, while her father's approval of her text compensates for the sexual union they will never achieve. On a more literal level, in choosing to court her father's approval by imitating his masculine literary discourse, Burney represses the feminine discourse associated with her stepmother and, presumably, with her dead mother as well. Her stepmother encourages Fanny's skill with the needle, while her father teases her into writing. If she wrote *Evelina* to seduce her father, she did so only because she had been previously seduced by what he had to offer.[2]

Like Fanny Burney, many eighteenth-century literary women allowed themselves to be seduced by a masculine literary discourse and by the benevolent patriarch who was the bearer of that language. Literary daughters are special kinds of daughters, women who adapt themselves to both a familial and a literary hierarchy. The terms of the family romance suggested by modern psychoanalysis might be used metaphorically to describe the daughter's apprenticeship to her father's patriarchial literary tradition. Willingly forsaking her literal mother, the woman writer accepts her place in a literary heritage that is not her own and does not express her interests. The psychological dependencies generated by this situation are poignant. At the age of thirty-seven, Maria Edgeworth felt that without her father she would "sink into that nothing from which he raised me" (qtd. in Butler 207). For Elizabeth Carter, Maria Edgeworth, and Fanny Burney, the choice of the patriarchal literary tradition was facilitated, perhaps even necessitated, by the death of the real mother. For Hannah More, the real mother appears to have been inconsequential, while her father represented an entire erudite tradition inaccessible through her mother. At her father's knee she heard stories of classical heroes, told first in their original languages, then in translation. But her father also stopped teaching her mathematics when he grew "frightened at his own success" (Roberts 1: 18).

Such anecdotes remind us that the benevolent patriarch achieves his recognized status as moral guardian only upon the willing submission of his daughters to his superior "wisdom." The myth of the benevolent patriarch is generated *on both sides* according to the needs of both parties, as Dorothy Dinnerstein's analysis suggests. She explains that "patriarchy remains a refuge that we are afraid to dismantle. We feel that the reign of the early mother is waiting for us just outside its walls; and besides, we must balance our dislike of constraint against our fears of freedom" (189). Women, then as now, gravitated toward their fathers to escape their mothers' claustrophobic embrace or, more important perhaps, the claustrophobic life history the mother bore with her. In this way a historical understanding of woman's position enhances the relational models proposed by psychoanalytic theories. With this point in mind, in this essay I wish to explore two questions. How did the myth of the benevolent patriarch continue to be particularly salient in an age of supposedly diminishing patriarchalism? In what ways were literary daughters complicitous in the perpetuation of that myth? In answer to these questions I will argue for the centrality of a particular educational paradigm. In the second part of my essay I will suggest ways in which one woman writer, Hannah More, structured her career in response to the presence of the myth of the benevolent patriarch.

In his detailed account of the evolving family structure in the eighteenth century, Lawrence Stone finds evidence for the decline of patriarchy in changing property settlements and in the decline of family prayers. According to Stone, new attitudes toward death and increased attention given to personal and bodily privacy mark the ascendancy of "affective individualism" (239–58). But Stone here limits patriarchal power to its external manifestations. In the words of Michel Foucault, Stone examines the "mechanism of power" from a distance, ignoring its "capillary form of existence, the point where power reaches into the very grain of individuals, touches their bodies and inserts itself into their actions and attitudes, their discourses, learning processes and everyday lives" (*Power* 39). As the literature testifies, during the eighteenth century the patriarch continued to exercise just such "capillary" forms of power. In particular, he was able to maintain his control over his family through the instruction of his children. By educating them into the ways of deference and obedience, the patriarch assured his own paternal authority while establishing familial loyalties among members. Yet this process was most often implemented without any visible signs of coercive power.

The great educational text for the eighteenth century was John Locke's *Some Thoughts upon Education*, in which the philosopher posited the best method to assure parental authority through nontyrannical means. As Jay Fliegelman has noted in another context:

> The great challenge of eighteenth-century politics, familial and national, was to make authority and liberty compatible, to find a surer ground for obligation and obedience than "the fear of the rod." If imperiousness and severity create in men a slavish temper and a dissembled obedience that awaits but the right moment to

> throw off all restraint, force must be replaced by reasonableness, the imposition of absolute will with the creation of shared values. (14)[3]

Although historians have long recognized the implications of Lockean psychology for eighteenth-century political life, the special consequences of the popularization of Locke's educational theories for the female child have received virtually no attention.

But substitute "women" for "men" in the Fliegelman quotation above, and a new series of questions appears. What would have been the impact of Lockean pedagogy designed to inculcate familial and political allegiances in a young girl? How might the noncoercive exercise of paternal authority—the creation of a sense of "shared values"—have affected her developing sense of individuality, of a self free to express its independent needs and interests? Locke certainly intended his theories to be applied to female children, as he acknowledged in a letter to Mrs. Clarke: "Since therefore I acknowledge no difference of sex in your mind relating . . . to truth, virtue and obedience, I think it well to have nothing altered [in his text] from what is [writ for the son]" (Axtell 344). That Locke's text was extraordinarily popular is well documented (see Plumb xvii; see also checklist of printings, Axtell 98–104), and Fliegelman traces modified Lockean tenets as they appeared in well-known conduct books, such as Dr. Gregory's *A Father's Legacy to His Daughters*. Because records reflecting actual parental schemes for home education—especially of daughters—are almost nonexistent, the traces of Locke's pedagogical paradigm must be discerned elsewhere, in family correspondence or memoirs, for example, or in the very terms in which the grown woman continues to address her father.[4] To isolate Locke's text is not to suggest that it alone initiated the "myth of the benevolent patriarch" but rather to emphasize the ways in which one enormously popular pedagogical current contributed to that ideology. In this view, actual curriculum is less important than pedagogical method or attitude. Although the women under discussion may have been exposed to different educational materials during their formative years, they shared a central educational experience under their fathers' authority.

The key elements of Locke's plan, especially as they are relevant to the female child, are threefold. First, Locke's parents are naturally benevolent; they are neither tyrants nor are they ignorant of their child's desires. Locke assumes a great deal of natural affection, even leniency. "Parents, being wisely ordain'd by Nature to love their Children, are very apt, if Reason watch not that natural Affection very warily, are apt, I say, to let it run into Fondness. They love their little ones, and 'tis their Duty: But they often, with them, Cherish their Faults too" (Axtell 130). The parent must struggle against such faults—the child's natural obstinacy or willfulness in particular—in order to foster the child's sense of discipline. Locke's second point follows: a sense of filial obligation must be *created*. Advocating the early establishment of parental authority, Locke recognizes the potency of parental power, provided that the power is not merely physical. The exercise of mere physical power corrupts the child and encourages a violent temper. More important, mere physical power soon loses its effectiveness: "For I am very apt to think that *great Severity* of Punishment does very little Good; nay, great Harm in Education . . . whatsoever *Rigour* is necessary, it is more to be used, the younger Children are, and having by a due Application, wrought its Effect, it is to be relaxed, and changed into a milder Sort of Government" (Axtell 146–47).

Locke's "milder Sort of Government" amounts to a psychological manipulation of the child's natural affections, a seduction of the child's loving predisposition. The parent begins early to win the child's allegiances in order to assure a lifetime of loyalty. Thus Locke's third important assertion is that only by imprinting upon the child's mind first by means of "fear and awe," and later by means of "Love and Friendship," will the parent rest secure in the child's continuing loyalties. The child's fear of the tyrannical father might provoke "a counterfeit Carriage" and a "dissembling outside" of loyalty and obedience, but habits "woven into the Very Principles of Nature" will truly influence the child's life and establish the necessary political allegiances (Axtell 146). Locke stresses the importance of such psychological imprinting; it must be "begun early, and inflexibly kept to, till *Awe* and *Respect* be grown familiar, and there appears not the least Reluctancy in the Submission, and the ready Obedience of their minds" (Axtell 147). Locke's position may be summarized as follows:

> If therefore a strict Hand be kept over Children *from the Beginning*, they will in that Age be tractable and quietly submit to it, as never having known any other: And if, as they grow up to the Use of Reason, the Rigour of Government be, as they deserve it, gently relaxed, the Father's Brow more smooth'd to them, and the Distance by Degrees abated; his former Restraints will increase their Love, when they find it was only a Kindness to them, and a Care to make them capable to deserve the Favour of their Parents, and the Esteem of every Body else. (Axtell 146)

Although Locke's proposed plan applies to governance by both parents, it should be clear that his educational paradigm serves the patriarchal structure particularly well. It assures no mere obedience, but thorough dedication to the value system under which one grows to political maturity. Locke views the family as a model for the state, and his ultimate goal is the ongoing security of the existing social contract. The mother's role in such a process is tangential. She can back up the father or, as was the case in the lives of many strong intellectual women, she can withdraw from the process altogether.[5] Locke's scheme is consonant with relational models proposed by modern psychoanalytic theories, the cornerstone of his program being the establishment of "fear and awe." Young girls are especially susceptible to such emotions when being tutored by their fathers because of their perception of the fathers' disproportionate status in the domestic setting.

Contemporary feminist psychoanalytic theory suggests a deeper drama of preoedipal identity and boundary confusion likely to result from the female child's early exposure to her father's tuition under Locke's rubric. Loyalty to the father's value system results in unconscious tensions, most notably confusion about one's self-worth as a woman. In the words of one contemporary feminist, in order to identify with the father, "the daughter must give up her own preoedipal tie to the mother, and often take on the father's contemptuous devaluation of and contemptuous attitude for the mother and, by extension, for women as a group" (Flax 37; see also Chodorow, *Reproduction*, chs. 6–8). Memoirs, diaries, and letters of literary women from the period intimate the unresolved conflict continually being replayed. Many literary women suffered debilitating headaches. Elizabeth Carter, for example, encountered the first of her lifelong headaches when, despite her father's conviction that she had no talent for languages, she taught herself Latin and Greek (Pennington 1: 7–9). Hannah More and Maria Edgeworth shared her symptom. At other times extreme self-deprecation or infantile dependencies suggest the continuing psychological crisis generated by early dependencies on paternal approval.

Locke's paradigm assumes that the educating father always acts in his child's best interest, but this point is arguable when the child is female. In Locke's scheme contractualism replaces patriarchalism, yet the contract doesn't necessarily serve the daughter's interests—that is, her right to independent self-development.[6] The Lockean paradigm putatively establishes moral and physical independence, but, in fact, its emphasis on "normative values" precludes the female child's development of the capacity to imagine a discourse existing outside the prevailing social structure.[7] Locke's paradigm particularly frustrates the female child's self-definition because of the context in which the tuition occurs: the father insists that he is acting as her own best friend in her own best interests. In Dr. Gregory's version of this:

> A father's zeal for his daughter's improvement, in whatever can make a woman amiable, with a father's quick apprehension of the dangers that too often arise, even from the attainment of that very point, suggest his admonitions, and render him attentive to a thousand little graces and little decorums which would escape the nicest moralist who should undertake the subject on uninterested speculation. . . . You will hear, at least for once in your lives, the genuine sentiments of a man who has no interest in flattering or deceiving you. (143)

Eternally vigilant, with an eye to every potential danger that besets the female sex, the Lockean father anticipates his daughter's every step and serves her truly where others would falsely seduce her. Rebellion becomes impossible in a situation where there exist no obvious signs of tyranny or repression but only the gentle reassurance of love, friendship, an amatory disinterestedness.

The significance of Locke's educational paradigm lies in its establishment of a paternal presence, a particular attitude or pose against which the child finds it difficult to assert herself, as Maria Edgeworth's correspondence with her father illustrates. Reading Richard Edgeworth's letters to his daughter, one is struck by the claustrophobic atmosphere generated by the father's solicitude. Marilyn Butler notes that Maria liked to refer to herself as "little i" in her letters. On one occasion, having written to thank her father for a present of £500, she received the following reassurances from him:

> I gave you £500 to make you independent for Subsistence—I think every grown up person should by degrees be rendered independent as to the necessaries of life—I shall always keep you dependent upon me for a degree of Esteem, affection entertainment & Sympathy that you will find difficult to obtain from any but a husband & to a good husband I will make over all my rich possessions in your heart—I am therefore under no apprehension of losing you & you may *sew* my name to my Bond without offending your *Heart* or *Understanding*—that is your antithesis you know.

Citing this letter out of context, Butler does not explain the ways in which Edgeworth felt her ''Heart'' and her ''Understanding'' antithetical. Later in her biography Butler remarks that Edgeworth's attitudes as a grown woman writer reflect the decade in which her father grew to intellectual maturity (102–03, 266).[8] Sandra M. Gilbert and Susan Gubar make this same point in other terms: ''Maria Edgeworth solved this problem of what we have been calling 'the anxiety of female authorship' by writing as if she were her father's pen'' (*Madwoman* 151). This lifetime commitment to her father's values and ideals, even when those values were in conflict with her own, issues from Edgeworth's early experiences under her father's tuition. The dependency that Butler re-creates (though she herself does not find it problematic) comes in part from the father's Lockean pose, reflected in the letter above. Edgeworth's psychological dependencies are exacerbated by her financial dependencies; it should be of little wonder that she should repeatedly articulate a discourse not her own, given the circumstances under which her father tutored her.

Nonetheless, despite the extreme efficacy of the Lockean educational paradigm, the ambivalence and even anger felt by father-dependent women is sometimes manifested in unpredictable ways. For example, in *Evelina* Fanny Burney's protagonist is involved in the struggle to obtain for herself the status, wealth, and marriage partner she desires. She must assert herself against an aristocratic father, who initially refuses to recognize her legitimacy; at the same time she must come to terms with the absence of her mother, who died before the story began. The course she chooses is passive-aggressive, full of actions which appear innocent but which in fact strike out at the offending parties responsible for her vulnerability and dependency. As she faces the father who denies her legitimacy, she evokes the ghost of her dead mother; her father claims this confrontation ''set[s] his brain on fire'' (372). In interpreting this scene, Mary Poovey explains that Evelina, in her symbolical position as her deceased mother, ''serves as the agent for both humbling and punishing her father'' (26). But the question of Evelina's legitimacy only substitutes metaphorically for the larger issue of her independent sexual presence, and Burney's protagonist may be said to exorcise the author's own hostilities toward the father who refused to recognize his daughter's mature sexual identity.

The following comment by Fanny Burney in her *Memoirs of Dr. Burney* betrays the unresolved ambivalence remaining as she reminisces about the ways in which her father educated her:

> The second child, Frances, was the only one of Mr. Burney's family who was never placed in any seminary and never was put under any governess or instructor whatsoever. Merely and literally self-educated, her sole emulation for improvement, and sole spur for execution, were her unbounded veneration of the character, and affection for the person of her Father; who nevertheless had not, at the time, a moment to spare for giving her lessons, or even for directing her pursuits. (d'Arblay 1: 197–98)

In words that curiously echo Evelina's own (for example, "I have often thought my fate particularly cruel, to have but one parent, and from that one to be banished forever"), Burney suggests that, as her teacher, her father was continually absent yet always present; he taught her nothing and he taught her everything. His mere presence as her father was enough to inspire her development. Here we see a dynamics of dependence at work, as well as the subversion of the independent self. Fanny Burney had legitimate reasons to complain of her father's inconstant attentions, but since paternal existence gives shape and meaning to her own life, to speak directly of his failings would be to undermine the grounds for her own identity. Writing as a grown, married woman, Fanny Burney still stands in fear and awe of her father and refuses to question outwardly whether he served her own best interests. But the presence of her mother's ghost in the early pages of those memoirs reminds us of Burney's failure to achieve some resolution with her father. As she begins the massive task of sorting her father's papers, she searches for traces of her dead mother's life—she hopes in turn to find some explanation for her own. But her father's papers yield no such evidence; she finds him "laconic almost to silence" on the subject of his feelings for her mother—and Burney is reminded once more that the price for her father's support was some critical aspect of her own feminine experience, some aspect that only her dead mother might have addressed (qtd. by Hemlow 449). If Burney's work in the last years of her life reflects some ongoing, unanswered anxiety, this is because a father's love can never adequately fulfill the primary need for a mother's unqualified support and feminine nurturing. Years after that first paternal seduction, Burney's desire must be seen as unsatisfied.

In contrast to Burney, who returns again and again to her relationship with her father, Hannah More disencumbered herself of her real father only to involve herself in a series of paternal seductions that resolve themselves in neat symmetry. If she first courted the clergyman who gave her a sixpence for reciting her catechism so prettily, she last surrendered her heart to the ultimate benevolent patriarch, the Evangelical Christ. More had always been attracted to older, intellectual men whose interests resembled her father's. At sixteen she contrived to meet the elder Thomas Sheridan, who was lecturing in Bristol. A little later she "formed an acquaintance" with a popular astronomer named James Ferguson and a linen draper named Peach, who had been a friend of Hume. Similar tutorial friendships followed with Dr. John Langhorne and Sir James Stonehouse. Her fixation with older men was exacerbated by a love affair at twenty-three with a man almost twenty years her senior. Her fiancé postponed the wedding three times before her sisters insisted that she break the engagement and arranged for an annuity of £200 in recompense. With this money Hannah More moved to London, but this severance ironically precipitated another string of father-daughter relationships. From 1773 to 1785 More's closest friends were David Garrick and Horace Walpole, both of whom were considerably older than she. One modern biographer wryly summarizes More's social connections: ''Hannah wrote lovely obituaries for several wives but appears to have had no earlier interest in them'' (Hopkins 26; see also Hopkins, chs. 4–10; Roberts 1: 37; H. Thompson; M. G. Jones).

Like Dorothea Brooke, who envisions herself playing daughter to Casaubon's Milton, Hannah More cast herself as a self-styled ''daughter of Eve'' to any number of literary men. Upon arriving in London, she made pilgrimages to great literary fathers—Sir Joshua Reynolds, Sir Edmund Burke, and, of course, Samuel Johnson. Her sister records the first visit to the author of *Rasselas*: ''Not finding Johnson in his little parlour when we came in, Hannah seated herself in his great chair, hoping to catch a little ray of his genius; when he heard it, he laughed heartily and told her it was a chair on which he never sat'' (Roberts 1: 37). For the modern feminist, the scene is both comic and distressing. If More's obsequiousness is painfully obvious, so too is her eagerness to usurp Johnson's ''seat.'' Her choice of the wrong chair signals her inability to perceive the true sources of Johnson's genius and her own great distance from them. Nonetheless, the sisters continue to believe that Johnson and More share a particular rapport. When Hannah receives some notice for the publication of her first poem, the sisters believe that the seduction is mutual, and one sister writes home in jest that ''if a wedding should take place before our return, don't be surprised,—between the mother of Sir Eldred [More's poetic protagonist] and the Father of my much-loved Irene; nay, Mrs. Montague says, if tender words are the precursors of connubial engagements, we may expect great things, for it is nothing but 'child,' 'little fool,' 'love,' and 'dearest' '' (Roberts 1: 46).

In this transparent joke, we can perceive the ''lovesickness'' at the heart of the literary daughter. Although the tone of the passage is clearly playful, it insinuates that in order to be embraced by literary patriarchy, a daughter must first ''give birth to'' literary production. Literary motherhood transforms Hannah More from daughter to wifely equal; ''tender words are the precursors of connubial engagements'' in more ways than one. Yet the terms of endearment marking the literary marriage remind the daughter of her persistently subordinate position: More remains a ''child'' or ''little fool'' to Johnson. In addition, although according to More's sisters the young aspiring female author is now ''married'' to patriarchal literary tradition, her text still suffers from dubious paternity—no literary father gives her works the canonical legitimacy she craves. Her own poems remain the ''bastardized'' derivations of more successful male literary productions. The romance between a literary daughter and patriarchal tradition remains unsatisfactory, as becomes even clearer in More's relationship to Milton, the only literary father capable of supplanting Johnson.

In her journals Hannah More records that she provoked Johnson's ire only on one occasion, when he corrected her for a glib citation of that ''horribly wicked'' book *Tom Jones* (Roberts 1: 101). More contradicts herself, however, when she later describes a quarrel with Johnson over the genius of John Milton (Roberts 1: 125), and More's worship of Johnson pales alongside her greater reverence for Milton. More's debt to the epic poet is apparent from the beginning of her career. In her very first published work, four young girls go in search of an absent mother who bears the name of Milton's muse, Urania. Many of More's early texts, her "Sacred Dramas" in particular, rehearse Miltonic themes and styles; More often seems aware of the extent and depth of her reliance on Milton. In the 1801 preface to the first edition of her *Complete Works*, she candidly confesses the presence of "either plagiarisms in [her own work], of which [she] was not aware, or coincidences which will pass for plagiarisms." She continues: "Blending with the new judgment of the critic, the old indignation of the poet, who of us in this case is not angry with those *who have said our good things before us*?" (*Complete Works* 1: xiii–xiv). Certainly, as More suggests, this posture is not original—Chaucer similarly complained that the literary field had been "picked over" before his arrival (The Legend of Good Women 61–80)—but in More's case the statement rings true. In her introduction to the "Sacred Dramas" she laments the lack of inspiration to transport her to Milton's heights; nonetheless, she casts her project in Miltonic terms. Boldly restating Milton's opening invocation, she proposes to "sing / The ways inscrutable of heav'n to man." Her epigraph for "Moses," taken from *Paradise Lost*, as well as her footnotes to the poem, suggest her awareness of her proximity to Milton's territory, but her self-conscious, childlike imitation flounders so that Milton's presence only serves to illuminate the thinness of More's own offerings.

More appears content to rest in her subordinate position at the feet of Milton's greatness. In *Strictures on the Modern System of Female Education*, her identification with Milton's real daughters becomes manifest; in defending Milton's character as a father, she implicitly defends her own father as well. Milton, according to More, merely enforced the "strict domestic regulations of his age" in having his daughters read Greek and Latin to him (*Complete Works* 7: 174). She overlooks the point of this biographical anecdote: Milton's daughters were said not to have understood the languages they read. In denying it a hardship "that an affectionate child" amuse an afflicted parent, More obscures the significance of the story: Milton's daughters are emblematic of all Miltonic daughters who participate in a literary tradition they do not comprehend.

But a patriarchal literary tradition demands only compliance, not comprehension from its daughters. More's defense of Milton includes her implicit concession to patriarchal hierarchies. The key to this concession is her belief that the daughter's energies require circumscription, as well as her corresponding conviction that, like Eve, woman yields subjection with "coy submission, modest pride and sweet reluctant amorous delay." To Horace Walpole she writes, "To be unstable and capricious, I really think, is but too characteristic of our sex; and there is perhaps no animal so much indebted to subordination for its good behavior as woman" (Roberts 1: 427). Reflecting the human perception of woman's "monstrousness" traced by Dinnerstein and others, the view of woman as a power less transcendent of nature than her male counterpart, More subscribes to the myth that patriarchal authority controls the potential for chaos and protects woman from the primitive forces of war within her. Like Fanny Burney, she stands in fear and awe of the father (in this case Milton) who claims to serve her interests best.

For Hannah More, patriarchal literary tradition, exemplified in the works of Milton, provides an important defensive strategy against her own anxiety about "woman's nature." That is, as a woman, More fears being identified with the forces of mortality and mutability associated with Mother Nature—and she views the Christian image of womanhood as an important improvement over previous, misogynist stereotypes. In being "daughter to God and Man," Milton's first woman is no longer daughter to her Mother Nature. More's preoccupation with this connection led her in 1808 to create her own version of Milton's Eve in her didactic novel *Coelebs in Search of a Wife*. Her female protagonist, Lucilla Stanley, is given a tender conscience designed to protect her from a female vanity and to make her more acceptable to the men around her. But so conscientious is this latter-day Eve that she is incapacitated by persistent doubts about her own self-worth. In her own words: "Nothing humbles me more than compliments; for when I compare what I hear with what I feel, I find the picture of myself drawn by a flattering friend so unlike the original in my heart, that I am more sunk by my own consciousness of the want of resemblance, than elevated that another has discovered it. It makes me feel like an impostor" (*Works* 2: 407). The price this ideal daughter pays for her father's approval is her susceptibility to what we call "the impostor syndrome." The "original in [her] heart" to whom she refers is both the sense of her true, "fallen" self and some image of her persistent resemblance to her mother Eve. More's portrait serves to remind us of the ongoing "dis-ease" experienced by all daughters who attempt to repress their mothers' images within themselves in order to sustain their fathers' approval.

For Hannah More herself, a successful literary career as a "daughter of Eve" entailed an ongoing battle with profound self-doubt and fears of inadequacy, as well as devastating illnesses that appear to have had their origins in a nervous sensibility. In correspondence with John Newton in 1796, she wrote of God's "unpromising and unworthy instruments," intimating that she felt herself among them: "It always gives me the idea (if the idea is not too low and familiar) of a great author writing with a very bad pen" (Roberts 1: 476). If More allowed God to replace other literary fathers, she found his demands no less challenging. More's humble stance constituted her defense mechanism against a continuing sense of inadequacy experienced as she began to write *Strictures on the Modern System of Female Education*, her most influential work. Debilitating headaches threatened the work's completion. One letter to William Wilberforce warrants quoting at length:

> I was attacked with one of my violent spasms in my head on the Saturday night. . . . This pain continued almost intolerable during two days and two nights, and left my nerves in a high state of irritation. On Monday, being alone, I fell down from the place where I was sitting in a fainting fit. I dashed my face against the corner

> of a stone wall, and lay a long time without giving any signs of life. My sisters found me in a posture which must soon have suffocated me,—with my face frightfully disfigured, and the floor sprinkled with blood. There was a strong contest between life and death, but it pleased my merciful God to raise me up. (Roberts 2: 23)

Despite such violent attacks, Hannah More lived a long and productive life. Throughout the later years of her life, she was able to formalize her suffering by projecting a radical alliance between politically marginal woman and a martyred, emasculated god. The Christian god to whom she apprenticed herself in the last phase of her career was not the dramatic patriarch of the Old Testament but a domesticated, benevolent Christ, one who, like Locke's benevolent patriarch, teaches primarily by example. Yet the history of More's career exemplifies the arduous psychological struggle that confronted any eighteenth-century literary woman who chose consciously to embrace her father's value system, repressing her own connections with her real mother in the process. Such literary daughters experienced both an emotional and intellectual coercion. The illnesses they all seem to have shared were only symptomatic of their deeper struggles with a psychological "dis-ease" about the extent to which they betrayed their inner selves in the process of embracing their fathers' values.

If we examine the lives of these literary daughters in a broad historical perspective, we see that women educated under the Lockean paradigm paid the price of their own autonomy. In the terms of Gerda Lerner's definition they were able to define neither themselves nor the values by which they lived (161–62). The institutional arrangements they found "to order their environment along with their needs" were neither adequate nor totally satisfactory. Most important, exploiting Lerner's definition further, we find that these women never moved out of that world "in which one is born to marginality, bound to a past without meaning, and prepared for a future determined by others." The circumstances under which they grew to intellectual maturity offered neither freedom of choice nor of action. Despite the occasional glimpse of a feminist insight, these women were neither aware of a "meaningful past" nor free to shape their own futures.

It should go without saying that the beginning of a consciousness Lerner identifies for us must come out of some positive identification with our mothers, for to deny their voices is to deny the possibilities for change within ourselves. Most of us recognize aspects of the literary daughter's complicity. The autonomy described by Lerner is an ideal rarely achieved by women who have had the mixed experience of growing up in a patriarchal family. To strive for autonomy is to recognize first that "father doesn't always know best," despite our deepest psychological impulses to believe the contrary. The seduction of the literary daughter continues today, in academic circles and elsewhere. It may be difficult, in Dinnerstein's terms, to confront those residual fears of our mothers, or to endure the images of their own painful life stories found within ourselves. But we have no choice; without such struggles we are condemned to be "daddy's girls"—condemned, that is, to live under the weight of a patriarchal tradition we ourselves have helped to perpetuate.[9]

NOTES

[1] Compare Burney's retelling of the event in Madam d'Arblay, *Memoirs of Dr. Burney*, under "Publication of Evelina," where the third-person narration considerably alters the immediacy of the event.

[2] For anecdotes concerning the tension between Dr. Burney's and her stepmother's views of Fanny's writing, see Anne Raine Ellis. I am not unaware of the resonance of this term for a critic like Jane Gallop, who uses recent French feminist criticism to develop a different kind of argument about seduction; see especially her *The Daughter's Seduction* (70–79). To cite Gallop's own distinction, the American feminist tends to be interested in a "self" ("a center, a potentially autonomous individual"); however, the French feminist often pursues a "subject" ("a place in language, a signifier that is already alienated in an intersubjective network"). See Gallop, "Psychoanalysis and Feminism" (106). My interest in this paper is with the former; as will become clearer in the course of my argument, I am interested primarily in using the term "seduction" as a metaphor to describe the subversion of the autonomous self. And yet it may conveniently describe the psychoanalytic process as well.

[3] I have found Fliegelman's reading of Locke most influential for its insistence that "Locke's concern here [in the pedagogical essay] is not with circumscribing paternal authority, but with rendering it more effective by making it noncoercive" (13).

[4] Presumably, plans for women's education in the home were rarely schematic enough to yield such records. Although sons were more often educated according to set programs, a father might abandon such a program when convenient. Richard Edgeworth, for example, originally planned to educate his son using Rousseau's theories, but when a new scientific project absorbed his attention, the son was sent to a Catholic seminary (see Butler 37, 44). Thus, even for sons, discrepancies between theory and practice often occurred.

[5] The history of Hannah More's mother exemplifies this situation. Biographers speculate on her social origins, which appear to have been humbler than her husband's. Roberts describes Grace More as "a young woman of plain education, the daughter of a creditable farmer, but endowed, like [her husband], with a vigorous intellect" (15), but in this story about a household of five daughters, little more is heard of the mother's opinions or sentiments. The daughters imitated their father's choice of a profession in establishing a school. It is surely not coincidental that in Hannah More's first adult work, a play entitled *The Search after Happiness*, four girls seek the advice of an absent mother figure.

[6] On the Lockean contract, see Gordon Schochet, *Patriarchalism in Political Thought*. To his credit, Locke carefully distinguishes between Eve's subjection to Adam as *divine law* and as *human custom*: "God, in this text [Gen. 3.16], gives not, that I see, any Authority to *Adam* over *Eve*, or to men over Wives, but only fortels what should be the Womans Lot, how by his Providence he should order it so, that she should be subject to her husband, as we see that generally the Laws of Mankind and customs of Nations have ordered it so; and there is, I grant, a Foundation in Nature for it." So in the end, Eve's interests cannot be said to be considered by Locke; his true focus in this passage remains, of course, disproving that Adam had any divine monarchical right. See John Locke, *Two Treatises of Government* (192).

[7] Compare Fliegelman:

> Neither Locke nor Rousseau believed that daughters should be encouraged to the same spirit of independence as their male counterparts. . . . [W]hereas sons were freed from parental dependence by the development of autonomous reason, daughters, whose virtue must always have a protector, were to find a similar liberation through marriage. (126)

This is one of the rare occasions on which Fliegelman mentions Locke's text in relation to women's situation. The passage depends on Rousseau for its support; no quotation from Locke explains this assertion. We can legitimately question whether marriage ever provided a daughter's liberation from the psychological dependencies generated within the family structure.

[8] For a relevant discussion of the ways in which economic dependence can thwart a daughter's independent thinking, see Virginia Woolf's discussion of female ''influence'' in the first part of *Three Guineas*.

[9] I would like to acknowledge and thank both the National Endowment for the Humanities and the American Council of Learned Societies for their generous support enabling me to research and write this essay.

~ 1986 ~

Feminism and Deconstruction: Reconstructing the Elegy

CELESTE M. SCHENCK

THE FEMALE ELEGIST would be likely to agree with Bernard in Virginia Woolf's *The Waves* that "nothing that has been said meets our case"; she, like Bernard, has "no ceremonies" with which to write a poetry for the dead, "only private dirges and no conclusions, only violent sensations, each separate" (157). Women poets from the first refuse or else rework the central symbolisms and procedures of elegy mainly, I think, because the genre itself excludes the feminine from its perimeter except as muse principle or attendant nymph. The funeral elegy is, from its inception in the poetry of Theocritus and his followers, Bion and Moschus, a resolutely patriarchal genre: a song sung over the bier of a friend-forebear in order both to lay the ancestor to rest and to seize the pipes of pastoral poetry from his barely cold hands, it is modeled on archaic initiation rituals of a younger man by an elder. Its locus classicus is the initiation of an obvious greenhorn by father Socrates in Plato's pastoral dialogue, that "prose idyll" the *Phaedrus* (Cody 23). In modern poems, the Freudian model of sons succeeding their poetic fathers by violent means replaces the Greek homosexual pattern, but in all cases the elegiac initiation scene is a masculine one: since classical times, the elegy functions as a ritual hymn of poetic consecration during the course of which a new poet presents himself as heir to the tradition. The masculine elegy is, from the moment Moschus announces he will sing for his master Bion, above all a vocational poem.[1]

It is no wonder, then, that Anne Bradstreet has such difficulty negotiating her elegy for Sir Philip Sidney: the muses actually upbraid her for aspiring to write elegy (probably because it implies succession of the singer), seize her pen, and almost prevent her from finishing the poem:

> How to persist, my muse is more in doubt;
> Which makes me now with Sylvester confess,
> But Sidney's Muse can sing his worthiness.
> The Muses' aid I craved; they had no will
> To give to their detractor any quill;

With high disdain, they said they gave no more,
Since Sidney exhausted all their store.
They took from me the scribbling pen I had,
(I to be eased of such a task was glad)
Then to revenge this wrong, themselves engage,
And drave me from Parnassus in a rage. (191)

Nor, in light of Bradstreet's "anxiety of authorship" (Gilbert and Gubar, *Madwoman* 49), is it surprising that in her "In Honour of Du Bartas" she should retreat into silence and "leave thy praise to those shall do thee right" (194). She could only echo his praises adequately had she "an Angels voice, or *Bartas* [own] pen." Interestingly enough, the only famous person Bradstreet succeeds in eulogizing is Queen Elizabeth, in an elaborate panegyric to a female power "that is not regulated and controlled by men" (Martin 19). Early female elegists deplore their own inadequacies rather than the patriarchal constraints of the form: "The more I say, the more thy worth I stain, / Thy fame and praise is far beyond my strain," writes Bradstreet of Sidney (190). But a female elegist might also feel that as yet nothing had been articulated that might speak to her case. As Anne Finch would have it in "The Losse," elegiac literary traditions are inadequate to inscribe *her* grief: "She wou'd her tongue, to the sad subject force, / But all great passions, are above discourse" (23). Katherine Philips, in "Orinda upon Little Hector Philips," does not trust herself with the task of elegy, but she also suggests covertly that the loss of her son exceeds elegiac convention: "Tears are my Muse and sorrow all my art, / So piercing groans must be thy elegy" (Bernikow 59–60).

To "meet the case" of a feminine elegiac, one would need to raise and answer the following questions: (1) How do women poets understand the elegiac task? (2) How do they invert or suspend traditional elegiac procedures? (3) Which of the elegy's rigorously prescribed conventions do they choose to undo or deconstruct? (4) What sorts of poetic solutions emerge in women's funeral poetry that might be termed "reconstructive" of the genre? Having invoked the methodology of deconstruction by my deployment of its terms, I intend to address, by way of conclusion, its relevance to a feminist rereading of the genre. The elegy here will be pressed into service as an occasion for exploring both the methodological similarities of feminism and deconstruction and the ultimate ideological incompatibility of that all-too-ambivalent alliance.[2]

The masculine elegiac is from the first a gesture of aspiring careerism. Theocritus's legacy to Vergil, in the form of a corpus of idylls, was an established tradition of announcing one's literary appearance by a ritual donning of shepherd's weeds. The pastoral elegy, the most vatic form within an apprenticeship genre,[3] is primarily a poetry of ambition, focusing as it does on issues of literary succession and poetic potency. William Empson, tongue in cheek, calls elegy (the metaphor is particularly apt) "the trigger of the literary man's biggest gun," because beneath the surface of an occasion-poem is often a subtext of ruthless ambition (58). By ritually celebrating the death of a fellow poet—in Vergil's fifth eclogue, Mopsus is specifically called *diuina poeta* and rewarded for poetically marking his "master's" passing—a poet separates himself from the forebear and simultaneously prepares to take his place. The most important convention of elegy is the deification of the dead one in a process that lifts him out of nature, out of the poem, and out of the successor's way. After the classical period, we might term elegy any lyric meditation proceeding from the thought of death which signals the readiness of the initiate for transcendence to new poetic modes, the "fresh woods and pastures new" of Milton's *Lycidas*. The writing of an elegy, even in the absence of a corpse, is a literary gesture signifying admittance of the male novice to the sacred company of poets.

The masculine elegy marks a rite of separation that culminates in ascension to stature; it rehearses an act of identity that depends upon rupture. But the same is not so for women poets, who seem unwilling to render up their dead. Antigone's symbolic loyalty to her brother, her psychological proximity to the buried spirits, her willing exchange of marriage for tomb in the name of the dead, mark early connections between female mourners and their family dead. As Anne Sexton more recently told an interviewer: "The dead belong to me" (qtd. in Kevles 8). In "Memory," Charlotte Brontë laments that "When the dead in their cold graves are lying / Asleep, to wake never again / . . . / Still how deep in our bosoms they dwell!" (146–47). Sylvia Plath's version of this mutual indebtedness, in "All the Dead Dears," is more pointed: "How they grip us through thin and thick, / Those barnacle dead" (*Colossus* 29). Women writers, lacking mentors, tend to mourn their personal dead rather than predecessor poets. Grace Paley puts these words into Faith's mouth at the end of "Friends": "I was right to invent for my friends and our children a report on these private deaths and the condition of our lifelong attachments" (89). In fact, the task of the male elegist reflects certain psychic models, which seem, in the revisionist elegies of women poets, to be inappropriate to inscribe female experience. Built upon a different set of internalized relations with predecessors, the female elegy is a poem of connectedness; seemingly, women inheritors achieve poetic identity in relation to ancestresses, in connection to the dead, whereas male initiates need to eliminate the competition to come into their own.

We might explain this difference all too sketchily here by recourse to Nancy Chodorow's contrast of female and male psychosexual development: feminine development is characterized by continuity with the mother and an attenuated separation, whereas the male act of identity coincides with the rupture of significant relationship (see "Feminism"; *Reproduction*). Translated into generic terms, this contrast might read as follows: Vergil's Mopsus thus only too willingly enstars Daphnis, canonizing him as *custos* of the land as he conveniently lifts him hors de combat, so that he might take his place in the professional ranks of singing *carmina*. Note the very different model by which a young woman takes on the task of singing, in Judy Grahn's "Funeral Plainsong." A round song, choral and collective, replaces an initiation pattern based upon competition and succession. Inaeed, plainsong here invites contrapuntal development of its theme, imitates linguistically the intertwining of the lives it thematizes. The poem, eschewing the beginnings and ends that punctuation conventionally marks, starts without capitalization:[4]

> i will be your mouth now, to do your singing
> breath belongs to those who do the breathing.
> warm life, as it passes through your fingers
> flares up in the very hands you will be leaving
> wherever you go to, I will arrive
> whatever I have been, you will come back to
> wherever you leave off, I will inherit
> whatever I resurrect, you shall have it
> . . . .
>
> for the bond between women is returning
> we are endlessly within it
> and endlessly apart within it.
> it is not finished
> it will not be finished (80–82)

Similarly, Milton's swain traces King's resuscitation from the waves and his subsequent transcendence to the kingdom of heaven with the confidence of one who is now ready to do his work on earth, whereas, by contrast, the Russian poet Marina Tsvetayeva refuses to let go of the one she mourns in ''Epitaph.'' Transcendence would mean separation, an unthinkable option to her:

> And I won't exchange you for sand
> and steam. You took me for kin,
> and I won't give you up for a corpse
> and a ghost: a here and a there.
> . . . .
>
> You are one thing, corpse and spirit.
> We won't give you up for the smoke of
> censers
> or flowers
> or graves
>
> If you *are* anywhere, it's here in
> us: and we honour best of all those who
> have gone by despising division.
> (77–78)

Michèle Murray and May Sarton observe this different literary genetics in their respective elegies for dead mother figures. In ''Poem to My Grandmother in Her Death,'' Murray refuses with Grahn and Tsvetayeva the absolute separation of death, because in connectedness rather than the psychic agon of the Freudian tribal contest, she stands to gain stature and self-knowledge:

> Finding myself in the end is finding you
> & if you are lost in the folds of your silence
> then I find only to lose with you those years
>
> I stupidly flung off me like ragged clothes
> when I was ashamed to be the child of your child
> I scrabble for them now
>
> In dark closets because I am afraid.
> I have forgotten so much. If I could meet you
> again perhaps I could rejoin my own flesh
>
> And not lose whatever you called love.
> I could understand your silences & speak them
> & you would be as present to me as your worn ring
> (Moffat 261)

May Sarton's version of continuity with the dead also refuses transcendence—figured in her poem by the birds in flight—and the consolation that concludes the masculine elegy since Vergil's fifth eclogue:

> Now the dead move through all of us still glowing,
> Mother and child, lover and lover mated,
> Are wound and bound together and enflowing.
> What has been plaited cannot be unplaited—
> Only the strands grow richer with each loss
> And memory makes kings and queens of us.
>
> Dark into light, light into darkness, spin.
> When all the birds have flown to some real haven,
> We who find shelter in the warmth within,
> Listen, and feel new-cherished, new-forgiven,
> As the lost human voices speak through us and blend
>
> Our complex love, our mourning without end.
> (Moffat 272)

Mona Van Duyn's "Creation," an unconventional elegy by any stretch, accomplishes the very opposite of what we expect of a poem memorializing a death. Instead of lifting the deceased friend out of the poem by means of elegiac apotheosis, her poem literally re-creates, breathes life back into, the dead loved one. In the closing lines of that poem, the elegist goes right to the usurping heart of the masculine elegiac: "Sneak, Poet, Mon- / ster trying to rob you with words" (102). Even as Van Duyn turns over the new leaf that elegy requires, she determines not to displace her dead. Whereas in the masculine elegy death is one's great occasion, one's opportunity to take the stage, Van Duyn's poem refuses to capitalize on the friend's death by refraining decorously from substituting her own face for her friend's at the end of the poem: "Your death was your own," she concludes.

In the last of my brief examples, Adrienne Rich, in "A Woman Dead in Her Forties," wonders "how [I can] go on this mission without you / you who might have told me / everything you feel is true,'' and she calls for an end to the silence that separated the friends in life: ''from here on / I want more crazy mourning, more howl, more keening'' (*Fact* 250).

The female elegist inverts or suspends the masculine elegiac in two ways: she both *deconstructs* the genre's valorization of separation by means of apotheosis (by refusing resolution and the absolute rupture that is death) and *reconstructs* by imagining new or alternative elegiac scenarios that arise from a distinctly feminine experience of attachment and loss. Anne Sexton, for example, hardly associated with codified, international, ''high'' poetic forms like the ceremonial elegy, is, surprisingly enough, author of an entire series of revisionary poems which register both her despair at the finality of death and her dissatisfaction with traditional patterns of inscribing grief. In ''The Truth the Dead Know,'' the speaker ''refus[es] the stiff procession to the grave, / letting the dead ride alone in the hearse'' (49). In ''A Curse against Elegies,'' she says that even ''the dead are bored with the whole thing'' (60). But her deft deconstruction of the genre is most manifest in the two extraordinary elegies for her mother, ''The Double Image'' and ''The Division of Parts''—the pair of poems that conclude her first collection, *To Bedlam and Part Way Back*. In the first poem, Sexton undoes the linear pattern of the conventional elegy from mourning to acceptance, in favor of a constantly deferred reconciliation which better accommodates discoveries and irresolution. In the second poem, she plays out her elegy *against* Christ's Lenten Passion, a pattern of suffering and resurrection which lends its symbolism to the pastoral elegy. The drowned Lycidas of Milton's poem, ''sunk low, but mounted high,'' is, like the dismembered Orpheus with whom he is poetically associated, a kind of Christ. But Sexton's mother's suffering at the hands of a relentless cancer and her own ambivalence toward this mother demand a poetic treatment that must ironize the masculine model of redemption: ''Easter will take its ragged son.'' Refusing to mourn and separate, she strikes, at the end of the poem, an entirely new poetic chord: ''While Christ stays / fastened to his crucifix,'' at the level of the symbolic, the mother descends pentecostally to comfort her daughter, providing a kind of tentative resolution through attachment rather than rupture. Not in the mode of the masculine elegiac, but rather ''without praise or paradise''—those two conventions of the traditional elegy—the mother, ''my Lady of my first words,'' comes *near* to make the poet-daughter into an ''inheritor'' (46).

Amy Clampitt, in a recent elegy for her mother, ''A Procession at Candlemas,'' undertakes a similar reverse elegiac journey back toward the maternal point of origin rather than away from the father-forebear (22–28). The poem substitutes a horizontal transcontinental expedition for the verticality of traditional elegy (the ''enstarring'' of Daphnis), a journey which amounts to a retracing of umbilical indebtedness. In a commentary which accompanied the poem upon its publication in *Vanity Fair*, Helen Vendler unravels the arcane symbolism attendant upon the ''occluded ancient mother'' which all daughters seek to ''rediscover'': ''the rest-in-peace of the placental coracle'' (89, 91). Behind Clampitt's personal, daughter's journey are two historical rituals: the ancient yearly procession to the whitewashed statue of Athena at the Parthenon, and the Jewish law's ritual purification of Mary after childbirth. Seemingly Clampitt wishes to reverse the "mosaic insult" these religious rituals imply, or else purify/ uncover the mother otherwise than has been culturally prescribed. The poem, indeed, cradles the invalid mother, restores her to stature after centuries of cultural devaluation during which she has been "kept / out of sight like the incontinent whimperer / in the backstairs bedroom" (26). Peter Sacks finds it typical of all elegy to repress the maternal and thus places Clampitt in an American tradition stretching from Whitman to Stevens and beyond, but his reading of her as an American poet muffles crucial intertextual resonances between Clampitt's poem and a distinct female tradition of funeral poetry (320–25). At the literal level, Clampitt does ally herself with the settlers whose westward journey she follows or the Indians with whose forced migrations she empathizes, taking the other cars for herds of bison. She asks to be taken herself for an American daughter undertaking an American journey homeward.

But the real ritual passage, the Candlemas procession of the title, is the daughter's psychic return to her mother at the hour of death. Like Sexton's "The Division of Parts," "A Procession at Candlemas" begins with the daughter's inability to grieve, her sense of debts needing settling. An attenuated, circular, difficult structure mirrors a mother–daughter relationship describable in just those terms. The poet's final recovery of the "ancestral fly-way," the "long-unentered nave of childhood," her return through the figurative birth canal to the unnamed place sought in the poem's repeated "Where is it?," her cathartic discovery of a dead bird in the childhood orchard, bring about the peace of Sexton's close, a separation based on attachment and recovery, rather than a severing of ties:

> late on a midwinter afternoon, alone
> among the snow-hung hollows of the windbreak
> on the far side of the orchard, encounters
>
> sheltering among the evergreens, a small
> stilled bird, its cap of clear yellow
> slit by a thread of scarlet—the untouched
>
> nucleus of fire, the lost connection
> hallowing the wizened effigy, the mother
> curtained in Intensive Care: a Candlemas
> of moving lights along Route 89, at nightfall,
> in falling snow, the stillness and the sorrow
> of things moving back to where they came from.
> (28)

Not the least of Clampitt's achievements in this poem is the anger she mobilizes—anger at culture's obscuring of the "wizened effigy" of the mother, anger at the genre's repeated and historical blindness to the "lost connection" of mother and daughter. Beneath her reconstruction of the elegiac scenario is thus a deconstruction of the masculinized form: a difficult but productive continuity between mother and daughter is substituted for the father–son agon it lays bare; transcendence, resting upon disjunction, is roundly denied, even in the spatial configurations of the poem; consolation by means of compensation, the genre's standard mode of accommodating loss, is rendered unnecessary by the act of recuperation itself.

The revision of genre which comes to fruition in these latter-day elegies by Sexton and Clampitt remains consistent with a female tradition of mourning *differently*. But the critique of transcendence that marks women poets' responses to the elegiac form appeared in women's poetry in centuries well before the twentieth. Aphra Behn's seventeenth-century funeral poem for the Earl of Rochester, for example, draws throughout upon pastoral elegiac conventions—nymphs, mourners, flowers, and even pastoral *adynata*, that reversal of nature's courses in the wake of important loss—but it refuses the most important: the "turn" from mourning to consolation upon which Spenser's "November" elegy for Dido and even Wordsworth's displaced elegy the "Immortality" ode rest. Instead of repeating the refrain incrementally, a traditional means of marking linear progression toward elegiac apotheosis, Behn repeats with minimal variation her "Mourn, Mourn, ye Muses, all your loss deplore, / The Young, the Noble *Strephon* is no more" (368–70), as if to suggest that a continuous mourning, a refusal to be compensated for his death, is a more appropriate means of encomium. Eulogy and transcendence are the most salient features of the masculine elegy, and they arise directly from masculine patterns of competition, separation, and individuation. Women poets, by means of resistant counterimagery, pointedly refuse, revise, and reconstruct the elegy.

One elegy stands out among these challenges to a patriarchally determined genre, because it illustrates both deconstructive and reconstructive practice in the female funeral aesthetic, because it is a vocational poem rather than a personal lament, and because it is singularly empowering, a kind of ars poetica in elegiac guise. Sexton's "Somewhere in Africa" (106), a funeral fantasy of the poet-father's passing into the very female, earthly, sexual arms of death, simultaneously accomplishes for the poet what the masculine elegiac achieves for the male poet-initiate, and it also dramatically recasts the elegiac genre, from the displaced perspective of the female mourner and in the distinctive voice of the female elegist:

> Must you leave, John Holmes, with the prayers and psalms
> you never said, said over you? Death with no rage
> to weigh you down? Praised by the mild God, his arm
> over the pulpit, leaving you timid, with no real age,
>
> whitewashed by belief, as dull as the windy preacher!
> Dead of a dark thing, John Holmes, you've been lost
> in the college chapel, mourned as father and teacher,
> mourned with great piety and grace under the University Cross.
>
> Your last book unsung, your last hard words unknown,
> abandoned by science, cancer blossomed in your throat,
> rooted like bougainvillea into your gray backbone,
> ruptured your pores until you wore it like a coat.

> The thick petals, the exotic reds, the purples and whites
> covered up your nakedness and bore you up with all
> their blind power. I think of your last June nights
> in Boston, your body swollen but light, your eyes small
>
> as you let the nurses carry you into a strange land.
> . . . If this is death and God is necessary let him be hidden
> from the missionary, the well-wisher and the glad hand.
> Let God be some tribal female who is known but forbidden.
>
> Let there be this God who is a woman who will place you
> upon her shallow boat, who is a woman naked to the waist,
> moist with palm oil and sweat, a woman of some virtue
> and wild breasts, her limbs excellent, unbruised and chaste.
>
> Let her take you. She will put twelve strong men at the oars
> for you are stronger than mahogany and your bones fill
> the boat high as with fruit and bark from the interior.
> She will have you now, you whom the funeral cannot kill.
>
> John Holmes, cut from a single tree, lie heavy in her hold
> and go down that river with the ivory, the copra and the gold.

"Somewhere in Africa" is a poem so confident in tone, so fully conceived in resolution and strength, that it is as unique in Sexton's corpus as it is among women's elegies. As compellingly as Milton, Sexton wrestles here with what she deems traditional: John Holmes, Boston teacher and poet, stands staunchly for a modernist clarity, impersonality, correctness, which Sexton knows can never serve her. In this elegy she makes her determined choice to serve a poetic deity who is "wild" as opposed to upright (not to mention phallic—"cut from a single tree"), who is forbidden rather than sanctioned, who is, finally and convincingly, female rather than male. If the female subjects of Sexton's poems were, as feminist critics are too quick to point out, often crazy, self-destructive, victimized, the "tribal female" who receives her master in this elegy is healthy, sensual, imposingly alive, "a woman of some virtue / and wild breasts, her limbs excellent, unbruised and chaste."[5] Even godhead becomes feminized as power passes from the masculine authority of John Holmes—here lovingly but firmly allied with the uninspiring "mild God," the "windy preacher" who eulogizes him in the "college chapel"—to this "tribal female who is known but forbidden."[6] In a powerful revision of the elegiac scene, Sexton's "woman naked to the waist" prepares a ceremonial reception for her exacting mentor which amounts to an enfolding of him in a metaphorical womb. Instead of effecting the vertical transcendence more characteristic of the masculine elegy (Milton, for example, describes a skyward arc as he lifts the drooping head of Lycidas), Sexton's mourner asks that John Holmes "lie heavy in her hold," ceremonially flanked by the gifts she returns to him in kind. There might be more than a note of triumph in this recuperation: in the exultant "She will have you now," in the infantilizing of Holmes, horizontally laid and then rocked in her boat. But the effort is not to rehearse the male way of mourning by singing the mentor out of the way; rather, Sexton accompanies her difficult teacher "to his final resting place," in Diane Middlebrook's words, "in her hold, on her terms" (503).

A word needs to be said here, prompted by female revision of the elegiac genre, distinguishing the feminist project from the deconstructionist. Both are oppositional discourses—they have, in fact, the same enemy: phallo-logo-ethno-centrism—and certain deconstructive practices may be welcomed by feminist critics dedicated to dislodging the hierarchies of our Western inheritance. Women elegists, for example, do deploy writing as a strategy for prolonging attachment, a means of deferring resolution or radical separation. Deconstruction, however, takes as its project the undoing of structures of absolute knowledge and value in ways that prevent, deliberately and programmatically, reconstruction, whereas the agenda of feminism—as Catharine Stimpson (274) and Myra Jehlen have noted—calls for deconstruction in the service of reconstruction. It thus makes sense to borrow a methodology from that other oppositional discourse, but not an (even only implied) ideology. A Derridean reading might try to unhinge the texts I have offered as a countertradition to the masculine elegiac by applying the deconstructionist chisel at a predictable point: such a reading would aim at demonstrating that these poems self-deconstruct at the nodal point of a nostalgia for maternal rather than paternal origins. Additionally, a deconstructionist might argue that the notion of a countertradition is in itself a hopelessly idealist construct. But the unsettling coherence of the female elegiac practice across centuries suggests that women poets have clearly enjoyed an elegiac mode of their own, an intertextually verifiable tradition of mourning their dead in a poetic form that calls the genre, as patriarchally codified, into question.

Even though the methodology of deconstruction helps account for female revision of a masculinized genre—the deliberate undoing of generic conventions in women's elegies, the despoiling of generic purity by recourse to attenuated, incomplete, even parodic renderings of elegiac form—I decline to deconstruct women's elegies themselves for the following reasons. First, female subjects still require constitution, a precarious operation that demands working on two fronts at once, *both* occupying a kind of center, assuming a subjectivity, *and* maintaining the vigilant, disruptive stance which speaking from the postmodern margin provides. Second, the recuperation of female poetic voice—women poets speaking their different experience of grief and mourning—would be circumvented, if not elided, by a reduction of the feminine to a revolutionary effect of language. Genre may ultimately be a question of language only, but gender decidedly is not.[7] Finally, as woman's historical situation has differed so greatly from man's, her overt, self-conscious search for origins, for connectedness, may be less suspect and ultimately not deconstructible along the lines of male nostalgia for originary bearings. As Amy Clampitt puts it in the Candlemas elegy: "supposing God might have, might actually need a mother: people have at times found this a way of being happy" (23). The deliberate indeterminacy of the female elegy, perhaps reflective of the more fluid boundaries women enjoy in their attachments to others, I would like to argue here, may thus be of a different order from the self-deconstructing tendency of masculine examples of the genre.

The masculine elegy—as a reading of women's revisionary elegies exposes—thus rests precariously upon timeless patterns of succession and transcendence which amount, inscribed in poetry, to what Harold Bloom has called "refusals of mortality" (*Map* 19). The act of singing for a forebear gains a man temporary reprieve from what the Romantics knew as the dejection of mortality in the eternizing registers of poetic language. As Coleridge defined the genre in "Table Talk," elegy "presents everything as lost and gone or absent and future" (qtd. in Dibattista 188). But anthropologist Jane Harrison would describe such emphasis on human immortality as "really the denial of life, for life is change" (468).

In her subversion of the elegiac, then, the female elegist not only deconstructs these ahistorical, apolitical, and essentially mythic structures; she replaces them with connective tissue, fleshly bonds; she protests final separation by insisting upon not only the difficulty of severing substantial relations but the potential for achieving identity by preserving those very relations in a kind of continuous present. Emily Brontë, in a number of elegiac poems in *Gondal*, for example, refuses the "cosmic epithalamium" which had become, by her time, the defining consoling convention of the elegy: her poems counter the notion of a timeless, ahistorical, transcendental pattern inscribing our reality with "changeful life," the tension of a process that is never consummated in place of fixity (Auerbach, "Changeful Life" 64).[8] In number 182, Rosina even asks to die when Julius does, knowing that in time she will forget to mourn him: as that "divinest anguish" of grief now defines her relation to him, it is as if she fears that ceasing to mourn would most threaten her sense of self (222–23). Virginia Woolf may be up to the same thing in her (often cited as evidence of mental fragility) lifelong "quarrel with grieving" (Spilka 1), her struggle to write successful elegy in her various novels. But Woolf's long refusal to get over her mother's death may, in fact, be deconstructive of masculine norms which do not "meet the case" of female experience. Even Sappho, three centuries before the male way of mourning found its literary form, chided her beloved daughter for weeping at her deathbed: "It's not right to mourn in a house consecrated to the muses," she apparently told Cleis. "That would not be fitting for us" (Loeb 258; my trans.). In fact, refusal of consolation, Sarton's mourning without end, is perhaps the female elegist's most characteristic subversion of the masculine elegiac.[9] A recuperable line of poems stretching from Sappho to Marilyn Hacker's knife-edge "Elegy" for Janis Joplin—a tradition which includes, representatively, Barrett Browning's "Bereavement" (Stanford 109), Charlotte Mew's "Beside the Bed" (Stanford 170), Elinor Wylie's "Little Elegy" (Moffat 14), Amy Lowell's "From One Who Stays" (Moffat 16), Edna St. Vincent Millay's "Dirge without Music" (Moffat 17), and Sharon Olds's "Birthday Poem for My Grandmother" (20)—refuses the closure that elegy conventionally provides, preferring the unfinished chord to the perfect third, the "violent sensations," again in Bernard's words, "all separate," to the false and destructive finality of "conclusion" (157).[10]

NOTES

[1] I cover this ground in the opening chapters of my book *Mourning and Panegyric: The Poetics of Pastoral Ceremony*. For background on the funeral elegy and description of its conventions, see Norlin; Hanford; T. P. Harrison; Lambert; Pigman; Sacks.

[2] Gayatri Spivak addresses the delicacies and dangers of such an alliance in ''Displacement and the Discourse of Woman.'' See also Duyfhuizen, ''Review Essay''; Kamuf, ''Writing Like a Woman''; N. K. Miller, *The Heroine's Text*; the papers in the *Cherchez la femme* issue of *Diacritics*; Bartkowski; Culler, ''Reading as a Woman,'' in *On Deconstruction*; Ryan.

[3] ''Where the hedge is lowest they will soonest leap over,'' Sir Philip Sidney tells us in his *Apology for Poetry*. Since Vergil inaugurated his exemplary poetic career with an imitative collection of bucolics, the pastoral has served as a literary proving ground.

[4] A similar indeterminacy, produced by reduction of punctuation to bare minimum, may be discerned in Nelly Sachs's elegy for her mother, anthologized in Olsen, *Mother to Daughter* 228.

[5] Middlebrook points out the contrast of male and female deities and reads the poem as a record of Sexton's achievement of poetic independence from Holmes. See also McCabe 216–43.

[6] Friends have suggested that Sexton's ''tribal female'' recalls the imposing female figure at the close of Conrad's *Heart of Darkness* and the nameless black woman in Flannery O'Connor's ''The Artificial Nigger.''

[7] This is a paraphrase of opening remarks made by Sima Godfrey at the 1985 SAMLA session Feminism and Deconstruction, at which I presented an early version of this paper.

[8] Auerbach's essay is a reading of Brontë's revision of the closure, the linearity, and the transcendence characteristic of the epic genre which parallels my own work on the elegy. Her foregrounding of Brontë's deliberate valorization of change and mutability has been very helpful to me.

[9] For alternate feminist definitions of elegy, see the application of the term to narrative in Maria Dibattista's essay on *To the Lighthouse*; Jane Marcus's use of the term to classify *A Room of One's Own*; and Gillian Beer's definition of ''elegiac triumph'' as the sustaining of entity.

[10] An early version of this essay first appeared in *Tulsa Studies in Women's Literature* 5.1 (1986): 13–28.

AFTERWORD

From a vantage point of, now, some eight years—six since publication, seven since it first went the lecture circuit, eight since it came to me as I was reviewing the last chapter of my first book on mainly male elegists, eleven since it came to me as a subject and asked to be written—this essay still appears to me to be sound in its appraisal of the dynamic of some women poets' elegies. Now, of course, I would be careful to say ''some'' women poets, to mark the important distinctions among elegies by different women poets, to include discussion of women poets' elegies for one another (barely visible to me at the early moment), and to allow for the possibility that some women poets, for whatever reason, wrote elegies in the masculine form.

But a short recantation (a ''second singing'' in the Socratic sense), afforded me by the format of this celebratory volume, is both timely and welcome. The essay appears to me, for example, from my present vantage point, essentially inside out—that is, my whole demonstration of the recurrent formal strategies of women's elegies is framed not by one but two masculinist boxes. If I were writing the essay today, it would be enough for me to lay out the variety of women's elegies without *either* positioning them binarily against those of men *or* couching the entire discussion in terms of feminism and deconstruction. The latter approach was the direct result of my being asked to write a position paper on feminism and deconstruction, an uneasy marriage against which I spoke by summoning up a rather-too-monolithically conceived female elegy: not deconstructible because already self-deconstructed. But the result—that I could then see women's elegies only in revision of or reaction to men's—was a choice nonetheless. The added fact that the essay first appeared under a title suggesting that figure was ground now pains, not to mention prods, me not a little. But the tasks of feminist criticism still include the responsibility for rethinking foreground and background not only in the texts we work on but in our own palimpsestic writings as well. What the Florence Howe prize once rewarded me for was my own sudden, flashing, independent vision of how elegy could be read, seen through different eyes. What thinking about the prize now reminds me of is the importance of having one's eyesight checked periodically, and the particularly feminist exhilaration of putting on new glasses, yet again, over the same old texts.

~ 1987 ~

Combating an Alien Tyranny: Elizabeth Barrett Browning's Evolution as a Feminist Poet

DEBORAH BYRD

The drama of woman lies in this conflict between the fundamental aspirations of every subject (ego)—who always regards the self as the essential—and the compulsions of a situation in which she is the inessential.

Simone de Beauvoir, 1952

The name [of poet]
Is royal, and to sign it like a queen
Is what I dare not,—though some royal blood
Would seem to tingle in me now and then,
With sense of power and ache.

Aurora Leigh

'Tis Antidote to turn—
To Tomes of solid Witchcraft—

Emily Dickinson

SPEED AND ENERGY, forthrightness and complete self-confidence—these are the qualities that hold us enthralled'' as we read Elizabeth Barrett Browning's *Aurora Leigh*, wrote Virginia Woolf in 1932. As Woolf points out, these qualities emanate not so much from Aurora as from her creator, whose strong and lively presence so pervades the poem that ''[a]gain and again . . . Aurora the fictitious seems to be throwing light upon Elizabeth the actual . . . [making it] impossible for the most austere of critics not sometimes to touch the flesh when his [sic] eyes should be fixed upon the page'' (1: 212). And as Woolf observes, the ''flesh'' the critic touches is that of a woman who knows that the royal blood of poets flows through her veins. ''Elizabeth the actual'' is a subject, speaking boldly of the world as she perceives and experiences it.

Wit and verve, directness and energy, an authorial voice radiating a firm sense of self and a firm sense of purpose—these are the salient characteristics not only of *Aurora Leigh* but of most of the poems that Barrett Browning wrote after 1845. In such works the poet "use[s] the woman's figures naturally" and often is "plain at speech, direct in purpose" when critiquing patriarchy (*Aurora Leigh* 8.1127–31); in some instances, she even transforms poetic forms that her contemporaries considered the exclusive province of men into vehicles for the expression of female and feminist concerns. Since Barrett Browning's reputation as a major Victorian poet rests primarily on these late, woman-centered poems, it is important to identify the experiences that furthered her development of a feminist consciousness and aesthetic. Foremost among these experiences were the poet's encounters with literary texts.[1] Aware of Barrett Browning's erudition, numerous scholars have drawn attention to specific ways in which the poet draws upon or swerves from male writers, especially the acknowledged "masters" of European verse.[2] But with the exception of a few studies of Barrett Browning's debts to Sand, de Staël, Gaskell, and Charlotte Brontë, surprisingly little has been written about the poet's artistic interaction with women authors, particularly women poets.[3]

It is quite true that Barrett Browning's favorite poets were men. She believed that England had produced no "poetess before Joanna Baillie [1762–1851]—poetess in the true sense," and she regarded no nineteenth-century woman poet as highly as she did Wordsworth, Byron, Browning, and Tennyson (Kenyon 1: 30). Barrett Browning's dissatisfaction with English women poets does not mean, however, that she did not participate in a female poetic tradition.[4] As numerous scholars have shown, the nineteenth-century woman writer generally searched for and was empowered by her discovery of literary foremothers and sisters. Even when she chose to modify or depart from the practices of her female predecessors and contemporaries, she often defined herself in relation to other literary women—attempting to avoid making their mistakes, trying to accomplish where they had failed.[5]

Barrett Browning was no exception. She was an avid reader of poems, essays, and fiction by women and took a keen interest in the lives of other professional women writers.[6] Moreover, as a poet she frequently imitated or responded critically to literary texts by other women, regarding such "Tomes of solid Witchcraft" as sources of sustenance as well as instruction. The women poets of her own century and country played a particularly crucial role in Barrett Browning's development, for when she began emulating these poets in the late 1830s, she took the first step toward transforming herself into a woman-identified poet.[7]

Throughout her career Barrett Browning engaged in conversations with writers of both sexes, particularly other poets. Identifying the texts she read and chose to respond to is important, for it can help account for the marked changes in style and vision that characterize each distinctive stage of her career. I cannot in short compass describe all the ways in which this self-proclaimed "book-ferret" was influenced by other writers (Raymond and Sullivan 1: 117). But I will provide an overview of Barrett Browning's poetic evolution, drawing attention to the ways in which her aesthetic principles and practices change as her reading habits and literary tastes alter.

Initially imitating women novelists, then treading closely in the footsteps of her poetic forefathers, in the late 1830s Barrett Browning turned her attention once again to women writers, this time to women poets. In this transitional stage of her career, she sometimes modeled her poetic efforts on those of other women; at other times she attempted, not always successfully, to synthesize aspects of the two distinct (though of course related) poetic traditions to which she was heir. At the height of her powers, Barrett Browning came to view her task as that of writing as ''a woman & man in one,'' a feat she believed her friend Mary Russell Mitford and her idol George Sand had accomplished. She brings into harmony the potentially discordant elements of her dual literary heritage, writing authentically of her own and other women's experiences with the ''forthrightness and self-confidence'' she considered to be more characteristic of male than of female writers.[8]

Surprising as it may seem, the first stage of this precocious poet's literary career spans the brief period from 1814 to 1817, ending when the eleven-year-old became the pupil of Daniel McSwiney. In 1814, at the age of eight, Barrett Browning was designated by her father ''Poet-Laureat [sic] of Hope End'' (Kelley and Hudson, *Correspondence* 1: 10), a position she took seriously for years, considering it her duty to compose poems on birthdays and other important family occasions. Yet it was not until the age of eleven that the Poet Laureate exhibited a decided preference for composing in verse. The longest and most ambitious works of her childhood are written in prose; this is not surprising, for once she had outgrown her taste for fairy tales, reading and ''studying'' novels became Elizabeth's ''most delightful'' pastime (Kelley and Hudson 1: 349–50). Significantly, the novels that she knew and liked best (novels generally selected by her mother) were by women authors such as Maria Edgeworth, Charlotte Smith, and Amelia Opie. Barrett Browning particularly admired the fiction of Edgeworth, in which the woman who gives free rein to her passions and ''forgets womanly duties in the personality of a man'' is criticized, and the young woman who exhibits ''too much sense'' to be considered a ''heroine'' is presented as a character worthy of emulation (Kelley and Hudson 1: 33–34).[9]

As long as she sought to emulate women novelists, and as long as she wrote for as well as about women (most of these early works were directed to Elizabeth's mother or other female relatives), Barrett Browning could write with both authenticity and confidence. Without anxiety she could imagine the kind of woman she would like to become, could attempt to write her own story, to chart the course her future would take. But in 1817 she suddenly began to regard novels as a form of light entertainment and decided to seek her fame as a writer of poems and essays (Kelley and Hudson 1: 33, 350).

Had she begun to read and imitate poems and nonfiction prose by women, Barrett Browning might have continued to assert her subjectivity and might not have suffered—or suffered as intensely—from that female malady that Sandra Gilbert and Susan Gubar term ''the anxiety of authorship'' (*Madwoman* 48–49). But internalizing the patriarchal standards of literary excellence espoused by McSwiney, she began to study and imitate her poetic forefathers—only to feel ''the whole extent of my own immense & mortifying inferiority'' (Kelley and

Hudson 1: 351). Essentially, Barrett Browning began to undergo the process that Judith Fetterley calls ''immasculation,'' began to experience

> not simply the powerlessness which derives from not seeing one's experience articulated, clarified, and legitimized in art, but more significantly, the powerlessness which results from the endless division of self against self, the consequence of the invocation to identify as male while being reminded that to be male—to be universal—. . . is to be *not female*. (xiii)[10]

Thus during the second stage of her literary career, which roughly spans the years 1818 to 1838, Barrett Browning writes as a divided self. The fragmentary ''Essay on Woman'' (c. 1822) shows that she was quite capable of identifying and criticizing writers who espoused partriarchal values. Writing as a disciple of Mary Wollstonecraft, she openly reproaches poets who depict women as timid and subservient creatures, poets who ''Paint . . . The trembling, melting voice of tenderness, / And all that Mother, Sister, Wife impart / to nurture, solace and subdue the heart'' of man.[11] Proclaiming that her goal is ''To bend to nobler thoughts the British fair'' by ''Found[ing] the proud path, where . . . [Woman] stands the equal of her Master Man,'' Barrett Browning leads us to expect that henceforth she will present women as resourceful and self-reliant beings.

Yet it was not until the late 1830s that Barrett Browning began to compose poems in which female characters act assertively and independently. Indeed, most of the poems she wrote before 1838 center on the experiences of men. When the poet does write about real or imaginary women, she generally depicts them as relative creatures, as associates of men of courage and nobility of character. For example, she praises Riego's widow for behaving in a way that enhances our appreciation of her patriot-husband's integrity and valor, urges a young girl to heed the advice her father gives her as she sits meekly at his feet, and tells Bettine, ''The Child-Friend of Goethe,'' that having her existence acknowledged by a man of genius should adequately compensate her for any suffering she has experienced or any sacrifices she has made as the poet's worshiper.[12] Moreover, in the few poems in which men are criticized for treating women like chattel or for being fickle or self-serving, women tend to die of grief or passively bemoan their fate; the poet regards such characters sympathetically, but she presents them as helpless victims rather than as active combatants of patriarchy.[13]

Most of these poems about women are sentimental, lacking the emotional power that comes from writing authentically out of one's own experience of the world. Barrett Browning had written elsewhere that she spurned ''that subserviency of opinion which is generally considered necessary to feminine softness'' and regarded as the most ''odious'' of creatures ''a damsel famed in story for a superabundance of sensibility'' (Kelley and Hudson, *Correspondence* 1: 354–55). Moreover, she did not sit humbly at the feet of her own father, nor was she content to achieve fame as the adoring child-friend of the classical scholars Boyd and Price.[14]

To understand why it took Barrett Browning over three decades to write poems that reflect the reality of her own and other women's lives, one must turn once more to "Essay on Woman." Despite its overtly feminist themes, the poem suggests that henceforth Barrett Browning often will write as a male-identified poet. Indeed, she does so to a certain extent in this poem, for although she refutes Pope's belief in woman's inferiority, she feels compelled to demonstrate that she has mastered "Pope's" verse form, the heroic couplet. In other words, Barrett Browning seems to assume that to be a great poet she must compete with male predecessors on their terms, must excel in the poetic modes that men have considered most valuable. Accepting the patriarchal notion that some verse forms are inherently more noble than others, she apparently does not realize that the idea of a hierarchy of literary forms historically has been used to disparage and to exclude from the literary canon much of the verse written by women.

Or perhaps Barrett Browning did realize that women poets do not fare well when judged by patriarchal standards of literary excellence. Perhaps she failed to finish "Essay on Woman" because, as a teenager, she was incapable of positing critical standards that would allow her to argue persuasively that the accomplishments of her poetic foremothers were as significant as those of her forefathers. After all, of the four women authors cited in the poem, only Anne Dacier and Hannah More wrote in verse, and evidence suggests that Barrett Browning considered both to be second-rate authors.[15] Moreover, if the poet truly believed More and Dacier to be women of genius (as the final stanza of the poem implies), why does she describe her own task as that of *founding*—rather than treading in or enlarging—the poetic path in which woman stands the equal of man? And why did she not complete the poem, giving her predecessors the opportunity to reply to the charge that women, including women poets, are doomed to sigh in obscurity?

I believe that Barrett Browning failed to finish "Essay on Woman" because in the process of writing the poem, she came to the dismal and frightening conclusion that none of her literary foremothers had been a poet of major stature and that therefore the burden of proving that women could excel in poetic composition rested squarely on her own shoulders. Convinced that poets could learn much from imitating their precursors but not wanting to follow in the footsteps of poets whose works she regarded as second-rate, until the late 1830s Barrett Browning equated poetic excellence with and measured her own progress as a poet in terms of her ability to equal or best the literary efforts of the male poets whose artistic achievements she most admired. Not surprisingly, she found it almost impossible to depict women as fully autonomous beings and to express authoritatively her own vision of the world while drawing upon and responding almost exclusively to poetic texts by men, texts that generally convey the authors' assumption that the perspective, concerns, and experiences of men are central and quintessentially human.

At the height of her powers Barrett Browning was to rewrite in original and daring ways and from a woman's point of view some of the "masterpieces" of the Western European poetic tradition. But as works such as *The Battle of Marathon, An Essay on Mind*, and *The Seraphim* reveal, the poet's earliest attempts to write long poems led her to ignore, marginalize, or trivialize the experiences of women.[16] The fact that Barrett Browning wrote such poems at all, however, testifies to her audacity and rebelliousness. For in composing epics, verse dramas, and long philosophical-didactic poems, the poet was deliberately violating the existing norms governing the relationship between gender and genre. Refusing to restrict herself to the portrayal of domestic life and the expression of the affections, she insisted on being read and judged as a poet rather than as a ''poetess''—insisted on writing about subjects that interested her, even if these subjects were ones about which a middle-class Victorian woman was supposed to be uninformed.[17]

In the third stage of her literary career, represented primarily by the two-volume collection of 1844, Barrett Browning continues to allude and respond to her poetic forefathers. But having discovered and begun to participate in a female poetic tradition, she no longer is so overwhelmed by the influence of male precursors that she adopts a male perspective on reality. On the contrary, she generally writes as a woman-identified woman, proclaiming that her central subject—the consciousness of woman—is a subject ''more expressible by a woman than a man.''[18]

''An Island,'' one of the best poems in *The Seraphim*, helps to account for Barrett Browning's transition from an immasculated to a woman-identified poet. In this poem a woman dreams of escaping from the violent and hierarchically ordered world of patriarchy; she longs to settle with a few select others on an island which has neither weapons nor rulers. This peaceful and egalitarian island is clearly a motherland: it is a realm reserved for ''Those who would [ex]change man's voice and use / For [a female] Nature's way and tone,'' a land of undulating, breastlike hills where maternal cows gaze approvingly upon ''The warm mouths milking them for love'' (111–12, 72). If she lived in this nurturing environment, the speaker proclaims, she could compose poems freely and easily, almost ''Unconsciously'' (143). She predicts that in the sweetness of their music, her songs would rival those of Pindar, Aeschylus, and Homer; indeed, she avers that her poetry would be superior to that of her forefathers because she would depict a world of harmony rather than one of strife and discord. In the concluding stanzas, however, the woman not only sadly acknowledges that her ''island-place'' does not exist, but she also expresses her fear that her fantasy of a world in which women's creativity is valued and nurtured is the product of a sinful mind, the dream of a woman who should be content to accept the world and the role that God has chosen for her.

Despite its ambiguous conclusion, ''An Island'' reveals that by 1836 Barrett Browning longed to ally herself with ''two or three'' who shared both her utopian dreams and the dissatisfaction with patriarchy that had prompted them. Fortunately, at about the time she composed ''An Island,'' the poet found such an ally in Mary Russell Mitford, a writer who played an essential role in Barrett Browning's evolution as a feminist poet. For although she was to remark in 1850 that she could ''never *count* upon her [Mitford] in poetry, of which, in my mind, she does not apprehend the essential qualities,'' it certainly was Mitford who urged Barrett Browning to study and consider emulating such popular and prolific poets as Letitia Landon, Felicia Hemans, Anna Barbauld, Mary Howitt,

Joanna Baillie, Eliza Cook, Fanny Kemble Butler, Sara Clarke Lippincott, Anna Seward, Caroline Norton, Georgiana Bennet, and Maria Jane Jewsbury—poets from whose failures as well as successes Barrett Browning was to learn a great deal (Heydon and Kelley 20).[19] Moreover, it was in the pages of *Findens' Tableaux*, which Mitford edited in the late 1830s and early 1840s, that Barrett Browning first seems to have experimented self-consciously with the literary modes and devices that characterize some of the best and most representative poems by late eighteenth- and early nineteenth-century women writers.[20]

It is important to note, however, that Barrett Browning's debts to these poets are quite different in kind from her debt to her poetic forefathers. For rather than borrowing details from a particular poem or entering into a dialogic relationship with a specific female precursor, Barrett Browning writes about the subjects which interested her literary sisters and does so by using the tropes, imagery, and rhetorical strategies that distinguish much of the poetry written by women of the period 1780–1850 from that composed by men of the age. When drawing upon English women poets, Barrett Browning generally responds not to particular texts but to an entire body of poetry, working within the confines of and expanding the possibilities of recognizable and distinctively female *types* of poems.

The female poetic tradition in which Barrett Browning began to participate is one in which authors take as their central subject matter and draw their metaphors from the lives of women. It is a tradition in which authors attempt to define the rights and duties of the Christian woman, portray the struggles and accomplishments of women artists, evaluate heterosexual relationships, depict the benefits of sisterhood, examine the process of female socialization, and ponder the degree to which women do and should participate in the economic and political life of the country. In addition, it is a tradition in which authors sometimes demonstrate their awareness that the fabric of Western society is woven of the intertwined threads of sexism, racism, and imperialism. Most English women poets of the period 1780–1850 write not only of the subjection of women but also—and sometimes simultaneously—of the plight of blacks, Native Americans, Irish Catholics, the poor, and politically oppressed nations of the past and present.

To be sure, none of the poets mentioned above was a consistently vocal critic of patriarchy; in fact, each wrote a number of poems in which woman is presented as fragile and pure, as the obedient helpmate or helpless victim of man. Yet each also wrote a number of "protest poems" in which patriarchal values and institutions are criticized, though usually in indirect and covert rather than explicit ways. For example, these poets generally attribute heroic stature not to their English contemporaries but to individuals of distant times or places who attempt to subvert existing power structures. In other poems, particularly those with contemporary settings, they encode rebellious sentiments in seemingly conventional texts; in such works, statements that seem to endorse patriarchal ideology are voiced ironically or ambiguously or are called into question by the poem's imagery or structure.

As is revealed by such explicitly topical protest poems as "The Cry of the Children" and "Lady Geraldine's Courtship," both of which appeared in the

1844 *Poems*, Barrett Browning soon was to become dissatisfied with such a palimpsestic method of recording her own and other women's concerns. Concluding that "puckerings in the silk," even when stitched by clever literary seamstresses, were more imprisoning than liberating, by late 1844 she was declaring to friends that in the future she was going to meet "face to face & without mask the Humanity [or Inhumanity?] of the age" (Kintner 1: 31).[21] But in many of the poems published in the 1844 collection, she uses the strategies of indirection as well as the tropes that characterize much of the verse of her poetic sisters and foremothers.

For example, these poets write frequently of a young girl's joyous appreciation of, or an older woman's nostalgia for, time spent alone—and usually creatively—in a bower, garden, or other spot in nature.[22] In such poems, the youthful female is not, like Tennyson's Lady of Shalott, "half sick of shadows" (71); on the contrary, she finds her privacy and her escape from social and domestic duties delightful. And the older woman does not, like the persona of Wordsworth's "Intimations" ode, celebrate and yearn for a time of "obstinate questionings / Of sense and outward things" (142–43). She *is* nostalgic, but what she laments is the loss of her belief that as an adult she could engage in meaningful, personally chosen activities. Moreover, unlike the male personae of many of Wordsworth's poems, this middle-aged woman does not believe that she has received "Abundant recompense" for her loss ("Tintern Abbey" 88), nor does she characterize her experience as an inevitable and universal (that is, genderless) one. In "The Lost Bower" (1844), "The Romance of the Swan's Nest" (1844), and "Hector in the Garden" (1846), Barrett Browning carries on this female tradition of articulating in a metaphorical and somewhat veiled way the sadness a woman experiences when she realizes that for women, the transition from childhood to adulthood generally entails a loss of hope, self-esteem, and imaginative freedom.

Similarly, in poems like "The Romaunt of the Page" and "The Rhyme of the Duchess May," Barrett Browning follows her poetic sisters into the Middle Ages, often envisioned by female poets as a time in which at least some women had control over their property and destiny and the courage to venture into the "male" arenas of politics and war.[23] In such poems, Barrett Browning, like other women poets, uses a historical setting, the romance form, and, in the case of "The Romaunt of the Page," ambiguous wording to hide from the unsympathetic reader the fact that she is protesting against middle-class Victorian definitions of the good wife and good daughter. In these poems the poet urges her female readers, as Carlyle had urged male readers of *Sartor Resartus* and *Past and Present*, to cast off their ill-fitting clothes and to benefit from both the wisdom and the mistakes of their forebears, in this case foremothers.

Countless other poems in the 1844 collection—"A Soul's Expression," "The Seraph and the Poet," "Work and Contemplation," "The Lay of the Early Rose," "Wine of Cyprus," and the two sonnets to George Sand, for example—reveal that as Barrett Browning began to view herself as carrying on a female as well as male poetic tradition, her conception of God and of the poet began to change, to become more woman-centered. Perhaps the poem that best reveals the poet's growing determination to assert her independence from her poetic forefathers is *A Drama of Exile*.

A poetic drama that depicts the frame of mind of Adam and Eve immediately after they have been expelled from the Garden of Eden, *A Drama of Exile* is far from being a consummate artistic whole. Yet it is an unsuccessfull poem precisely because the poet is determined to wrestle with the massive figure of Milton, with whom she closely identifies as a Christian but whose view of woman's subordinate status she wishes to refute. The product of this struggle is a poem that contains conflicting views of woman's rights and duties, a drama in which characters lack internal consistency, and a work in which passages vary greatly in poetic power, fluidity, and grace. But though *A Drama of Exile* is riddled with the kind of ambiguity that detracts from rather than contributes to a poem's artistic success, it is a key text in Barrett Browning's poetic evolution and a poem that gives us great insight into the anxieties suffered by the woman poet working in a patriarchal society and within a male-dominated literary tradition. The same can be said of "The Lay of the Brown Rosary," a poem in which Barrett Browning unsuccessfully tries to fuse aspects of the female Gothic tradition with technical and thematic elements of poems by Keats, Wordsworth, and Coleridge.

If *Poems* of 1844 is the volume of a woman who is still suffering from anxieties of influence and who finds it somewhat "easier to gaze . . . On mournful masks and sad effigies / Than on real, live, weak creatures crushed by strong" (*Casa Guidi Windows* 1.46–48), *Poems* of 1850 is the volume of a poet who is drawing in a sophisticated way upon her dual poetic heritage, the work of a feminist who can be witty and playful as well as express righteous indignation. In "The Runaway Slave at Pilgrim's Point" Barrett Browning not only vehemently protests against slavery but also clearly spells out the connections between racism and sexism; in the companion poems "A Woman's Shortcomings" and "A Man's Requirements," she humorously but with equal directness and artistic skill exposes inequities in relationships between Victorian women and men. Moreover, having married a man who shared her desire to identify and combat the evils of patriarchy, she has the courage to make public *Sonnets from the Portuguese*, a poem in which she honestly recounts the vacillation between feelings of fear and joy, self-abasement and self-worth, that she experienced when she began to fall in love with Browning.

Reaffirming in another 1850 poem that the reed rather than the trumpet is her emblem, Barrett Browning announces that henceforth she will be the voice of women, children, and the common man rather than blast forth the "hollow" sounds of "priest or king" ("A Reed" 3–4). Pan, whom the poet associates with freedom, eroticism, and egalitarianism, is not so dead as the last poem of the 1844 collection seems (but only seems) to declare him to be. Moreover, by readopting as her symbol the reed of Pan, the playmate of nymphs who was bested by the more aloof and refined Apollo, Barrett Browning prepares us for her attempt to "blow all class-walls level as Jericho's" (*Aurora Leigh* 9.932) and for the literal and metaphoric union of female and male, pagan and Christian, that is at the heart of her subsequent and greatest poems.

One of these poems is *Casa Guidi Windows*. Writing with confidence about contemporary European politics, Barrett Browning unabashedly stakes her claim to a land into which most of her poetic foremothers had feared even to tread. In so doing, the poet weaves an ornate tapestry out of the three thematic strands that so frequently appear in her earlier poetry: the duties of the artist, the responsibilities of the Christian, and the rights of the oppressed. Having learned to value the wisdom and strength of mothers and to discriminate between good and bad fathers, in this poem Barrett Browning frankly and gratefully acknowledges her literary debts to "dead masters" yet proclaims: "We do not serve the dead" (1.217). Similarly, Barrett Browning the Christian invokes the aid of Christ and the Virgin Mary but castigates a pope who has betrayed his charges, and Barrett Browning the citizen defends the dedicated freedom fighters of her adopted motherland while exposing the cowardice of a "paternal Duke" and the hypocrisy and crass materialism of her powerful fatherland. Finally, Barrett Browning the feminist praises the Italian women and men who are working together to combat their oppressors, but bitterly notes that in "liberal nations" there is "No help for women sobbing out of sight / Because men made the laws" (2.638–39). Almost succumbing to despair at the poem's conclusion, she recovers faith in the possibility of constructive change only when she remembers that some children, among them her own son, are being reared by parents committed to the establishment of a more egalitarian and just society.

In *Aurora Leigh*, an even more ambitious work, the formal and thematic characteristics of both male and female predecessors are welded into a unique, magnificent structure. A "verse novel" that owes much to the author's extensive reading of poems, fiction, and nonfiction prose by women; a first-person account of the growth and development of a woman poet's mind; "a Don Juan, without the mockery & impurity" of Byron, "admitting of much philosophical dreaming & digression" but "having unity, as a work of art" (Raymond and Sullivan 3: 49); and a distinctively female envisioning of the kind of personal and societal paradise that has been lost and the means by which it may be regained, *Aurora Leigh* is certainly one of the most important long poems of the Victorian period. It also is one of the major works of the female literary tradition in English, for in *Aurora Leigh* the poet demonstrates that the epic mode can accommodate the experiences, language, and viewpoint of women.

Having proclaimed in *Aurora Leigh* that it is the task of great poets to represent both the glory and the corruption of "this live, throbbing age" (5.203), Barrett Browning continues in *Poems before Congress* to write openly about the controversial social and political events of her time. But rather than sharing with her readers the observations and meditations of a woman safely ensconced in a Florentine apartment, the poet ventures into the more public arenas of "Italy and the World" and explicitly directs her comments to those who have the power to shape world affairs. Praising rulers who are helping to "deliver" Italy from the womb of a nation that has failed to nurture her, paying tribute to one Italian woman who nurses with equal tenderness dying freedom fighters of varying nationalities, and praising another who not only makes French soldiers regard Italian women with respect but who also creates an atmosphere in which French and Italian soldiers are moved to kiss one another "mouth to mouth," in *Poems before Congress* Barrett Browning boldly advances a notion that had been covertly suggested in the political poems of many of her poetic foremothers and sisters: that the "mother-want about the world" (*Aurora Leigh* 1.40) can be eliminated only if individuals and nations become more womanly.[24] No longer asking—as she had in *Casa Guidi Windows*—to be absolved of an ardent idealism and emotionalism that she explicitly had labeled female, she firmly declares her belief that "A curse from the depths of womanhood / Is . . . good," essential to the apocalyptic transformation of society ("Prologue" to "A Curse for a Nation" 47–48).

Cursing of the power-hungry, apathetic, and cowardly is less evident, however, in the verses on Italy that appear in the posthumously published *Last Poems* (1862). The change in tone is due in part to the poet's belief that the Italian struggle for independence was succeeding, but even more to her growing awareness of the tragedy of war, even one fought for noble ends. Not surprisingly, the horrors of war are most powerfully depicted in poems that focus on the experiences of Italian women, the poet suggesting in both "Parting Lovers" and "Mother and Poet" that "daughters give up more than sons" when nations experience their "birth-pangs" ("Parting Lovers" 52; "Mother and Poet" 93).

But it is not just sympathy for the women of Italy that produces the best poems of Barrett Browning's last years; it is compassion for all women living in patriarchy. For example, in "Where's Agnes?" and "Lord Walter's Wife," the poet criticizes men who cannot or will not regard women as autonomous human beings and who therefore view women either as angelic creatures who "scarcely tread the earth" or as harlots, "mere dirt" ("Agnes" 86–87). And in poems such as "Void in Law," "Bianca among the Nightingales," and "Amy's Cruelty," she openly characterizes men as selfish, untrustworthy, and exploitative, warning women that unless they use great caution when selecting a mate, they may "forefeit all things" by loving ("Amy's Cruelty" 34). Thus Barrett Browning concludes her poetic career by firmly rejecting the notion that she had challenged only tentatively in *A Drama of Exile*: the notion that women, including women poets, must passively endure the "pressures of an alien tyranny / With its dynastic reasons of larger bones / And stronger sinews" (1865–67).

NOTES

[1] Throughout her life Barrett Browning believed that emulating authors one admired benefited rather than harmed a writer. "There is no vanity, but rather wisdom, in following humbly [in] the footsteps of perfection," the poet announces in the preface to *The Battle of Marathon* (1: 9). She expresses the same sentiment thirty years later in *Casa Guidi Windows*, claiming that she could not "sing this song, / If my dead masters had not taken heed / To help the heavens and earth to make me strong" (1.432–34).

[2] See, for example, C. Kaplan; Gilbert and Gubar, *Madwoman*, especially 70, 189, 391, 547; Cooper, "Theory"; Zimmerman; Rosenblum; Mermin; Hayter.

[3] Barrett Browning's debts to women prose writers are explored in C. Kaplan; Donaldson; Hickok, " 'New Yet Orthodox' "; Holloway; Thomson, *George Sand*; Moser. Cooper comments on Barrett Browning's artistic interaction with other nineteenth-century women poets in chapter 2 of her dissertation and discusses ways Barrett Browning's poetry differs from that of her literary sisters in "Working into Light."

[4] As Showalter remarks, a woman writer "confronts both paternal and maternal precursors and must deal with the problems and advantages of both lines of inheritance. . . . The female tradition can be a positive source of strength and solidarity as well as a negative source of powerlessness; it can generate its own experiences and symbols which are not simply the obverse of the male tradition" ("Feminist Criticism" 265).

[5] See, for example, Ruth Miller's discussion of Emily Dickinson's revisions of the poems of her female contemporaries, especially chapter 9.

[6] For the most part, Barrett Browning shared her interest in the lives and writings of women authors with other women—initially with her mother, later with friends such as Anna Jameson, Mary Russell Mitford, Harriet Martineau, and Eliza Ogilvy. The influence that female relatives and friends exerted on Barrett Browning's development is a subject that needs to be explored further, particularly since Kelley and Hudson have demonstrated that it was Mary Moulton-Barrett rather than the poet's father who was "the prime motivator in EBB's early poetic development" (*Correspondence* 1: xxxiv).

[7] To date, the only book-length study of early nineteenth-century English women's poetry (much of which is out of print) is Hickok's *Representations of Women*. My own study of the poetry women published in England during the period 1780–1850 was made possible by a grant from the Committee on Advanced Study and Research of Lafayette College, to whom I express my appreciation.

[8] The phrase "a woman & man in one" appears in an 1844 letter to Mitford in which Barrett Browning notes that it is "a hard & difficult process for a woman to get forgiven for her strength by her grace. . . . [E]very woman of letters knows it is hard" (Raymond and Sullivan 3: 38). In this paragraph I am not arguing that to be a great poet a woman *must* draw upon the works of predecessors of both sexes, but I believe that Barrett Browning held this view and that in many of her finest poems she works out of both a female and a male poetic tradition.

[9] Although the phrase "forgets womanly duties in the personality of a man" is applied by Barrett Browning to Scott's Diana Vernon, it also describes the behavior of many of the female characters Edgeworth criticizes in her novels. For a thoughtful analysis of the way Edgeworth responds as a writer to her father's literary productions and views of women, see Hawthorne.

[10] For other discussions of "immasculation" see Gilbert and Gubar, *Madwoman*; Cooper, "Theory"; Homans; Diehl; and Flynn and Schweickart, especially the essays by Schweickart, Schibanoff, and Fetterley (31–62, 83–106, 147–64).

[11] A transcription of the manuscript poem "Fragment of an 'Essay on Woman' " appears in *Studies in Browning and His Circle* 12 (1984), along with Moser's discussion of the ways Barrett Browning drew on *A Vindication of the Rights of Woman* when writing this poem.

[12] The poems referred to are "On a Picture of Riego's Widow," "The Little Friend," and "To Bettine." The first was published with *An Essay on Mind* in 1826; the others appeared in the *Seraphim* volume. See also "To a Poet's Child" and "Isobel's Child," published in the collections of 1833 and 1838, respectively.

[13] Among the poems in this category are "The Poet's Vow," "The Romaunt of Margaret," and "A Romance of the Ganges."

[14] Barrett Browning's ambivalent feelings about her father are conveyed particularly well in a poem addressed to him on his thirty-third birthday (in which she subtly compares him to Pitt, "who made blest freedoms weep / His name") and in an untitled essay of 1827, written after her father had called her latest production "most wretched" (Kelley and Hudson 1: 59–60, 361). The poet had no need to abase herself before Uvedale Price, who treated her with respect, but she had to actively combat the temptation to become the docile handmaiden of Hugh Stuart Boyd, who often behaved selfishly and maliciously. Barrett Browning's hostility toward Boyd is recorded frequently in her diary of 1831–32 (see, e.g., Kelley and Hudson, *Diary* 39, 148).

[15] In "The Book of the Poets" (1842), More is one of the writers Barrett Browning cites when arguing that during the second half of the eighteenth century England produced no great poets (Porter and Clarke 6: 298). Similarly, in a letter of December 1842, Barrett Browning asserts that Dacier was "a learned writer" but not "a woman of genius" (Raymond and Sullivan 2: 136).

[16] In *The Battle of Marathon* (1820), Barrett Browning praises the Athenian warriors who defended their city-state against the Persians; the fact that the rights and privileges of Athenian democracy did not extend to women does not seem to disturb her. Moreover, the Greek commander, whom the poet repeatedly and without irony terms "sage," responds scornfully to the rousing speech of a patriotic Greek matron and steels his warriors for battle by proclaiming that the Persians "not as heroes, but as women fight; / Grovelling as proud, and cowardly as vain" (756–60, 977–78). Women are totally excluded from *An Essay on Mind* (1826), a work in which Barrett Browning pays tribute to countless males who have furthered the intellectual development of Western "man," and issues of gender are avoided in *The Seraphim* (1838), the poet viewing the Crucifixion through "seraphic" rather than human eyes.

[17] In book 2 of *Aurora Leigh*, Barrett Browning vehemently protests against those who urge women poets to limit themselves to expressing emotions with grace and delicacy and who then argue that poetry by women is inherently inferior to that by men.

[18] In the preface to the 1844 *Poems*, Barrett Browning claims that Eve's state of mind after the fall is "more expressible by a woman than a man"; however, the phrase applies equally well to the other poems about women that appear in this collection.

[19] As the poem "Felicia Hemans" reveals, before meeting Mitford, Barrett Browning was familiar with the verse of Hemans and Letitia Landon, the two most highly regarded English women poets of the 1820s and 1830s. But she does not seem to have read extensively or attentively poetry by other nineteenth-century women writers, most likely because she had internalized her male contemporaries' disparaging view of the productions of poetesses. Women poets are a frequent topic of discussion in Barrett Browning's letters to Mitford, however.

[20] Barrett Browning published the following poems in *Findens' Tableaux:* "A Romance of the Ganges," "The Romaunt of the Page," "The Dream" (later entitled "A Child Asleep"), and "Legend (later "The Lay") of the Brown Rosary."

[21] Although the second quotation comes from a February 1845 letter to Robert Browning, Barrett Browning expresses the same desire to approach "the conventions of vulgar life . . . & touch this real everyday life of our age" in a December 1844 letter to Mitford (Raymond and Sullivan 3: 49). The phrase "puckerings in the silk" is one spoken by Aurora Leigh, who frequently uses sewing as a metaphor for composing poetry. Aurora tells Romney: "I'm plain at speech, direct in purpose; when / I speak, you'll take the meaning as it is, / And not allow for puckerings in the silk / By clever stiches" (8.1127–30).

[22] Following is a partial list of this kind of "nature poem": Eliza Cook's "The Waters," "The Old Water-Mill," "The Old Mill Stream," "The Forest Brake," "When I Wore Red Shoes," and "Stanzas by the Sea-Side"; Maria Jane Jewsbury's "I am Come Back from My Bower," "A Remembered Scene," and "A Summer Eve's Vision"; Felicia Hemans's "To the Mountain Winds"; Letitia Landon's "Erinna," "A History of the Lyre," and "The Enchanted Island"; and Anna Barbauld's "Verses Written in an Alcove." The bower motif appears frequently in women's fiction as well as in women's poetry, as is demonstrated by Annis Pratt and her coauthors.

[23] The idea that women poets often wrote of the Middle Ages and were particularly fond of presenting female characters who disguised themselves as male pages was so common a notion that Frances Trollope could mock the phenomenon in her satirical *The Mother's Manual: Or, Illustrations of Matrimonial Economy. An Essay in Verse* (64). Examples of this kind of poem include Landon's "The Vow of the Peacock," "Inez," and "The Castilian Nuptials," and Sara Clarke Lippincott's [alias Grace Greenwood] "Dreams." For other depictions of women of the Middle Ages, see Hemans's "The Abencerrage," "The Widow of Crescentius," "Woman on the Field of Battle," "The Effigies," and "The Lady of Provence."

[24] References are to these poems: "Napoleon III. in Italy," "A Court Lady," and "The Dance."

AFTERWORD

The preceding essay was first presented at the conference Meeting the Brownings, held in Winfield, Kansas, in April 1986. At the time, I had just completed research for a book on Elizabeth Barrett Browning; the essay was my first attempt to outline the scope and precise nature of this project. That I intended to provide a broad overview of a work in progress rather than substantiate a more narrowly defined thesis was well known to my original audience, from whom I solicited comments on the cogency of my arguments and general approach. Since I make no reference to this context in the published version of the essay, I wanted to draw attention to it here.

I'm still working on the Barrett Browning book, but my methodology, theoretical stance, and conclusions have changed somewhat since the time I wrote "Combating an Alien Tyranny." I continue to be interested in Barrett Browning's artistic interaction with poets of both sexes, and I remain convinced that most of her poems can be viewed as commentaries on literary tropes and genres and/or as readings of particular texts. But I have abandoned a conceptual framework grounded in notions of "evolution," "career," and "literary influence"; I believe that an emphasis on Barrett Browning's habits, tastes, and strategies as a reader is more appropriate for a study that focuses on the poet's complex and shifting responses to others' texts.

My book now opens with a consideration of Barrett Browning's metaphors for the creative process, metaphors that reveal that the poet regarded reading and writing as analogous and integrally related activities, both of which entail the use of the critical *and* imaginative faculties. Often Barrett Browning describes reading as an act of appropriation or deliberate misreading; she suggests that one way a woman working within an androcentric poetic tradition can construct a heritage that empowers her is to read selectively and subjectively, acknowledging and embracing only those authors, texts, or passages that seem good *to* and *for her*. It is only after she has fashioned for herself a tradition in which writers consistently speak out against oppression, Barrett Browning implies, that the woman poet can begin to write with authority and self-confidence; having discovered/invented nurturing foremothers and forefathers, she can openly confront and critique (as well as attempt to move beyond) the masculinist tropes, structures, and texts whose existence she had once tried (and needed) to ignore.

That such theories about reading help us understand and chart Barrett Browning's shifting responses to other poets is now the central argument of my book. Instead of organizing my study in terms of "stages" in the poet's career, in each chapter I examine Barrett Browning's reading(s) of a single poet or group of poets (for example, Milton, the first- and second-generation male Romantics, the male writers of classical Greece) or, in the case of women writers, Barrett Browning's reading(s) of a particular trope or genre (the trope of "woman in drag," the poem of female maturation, verse narratives about women artists). As this organization suggests, I still contend that Barrett Browning generally responds to *types* of poems rather than to a particular text or author when reading women's verse, although I argue that the same dynamics (the movement from embracing to combating) characterizes her interaction with poets of both sexes.

~ 1988 ~

Special Delivery: Twenty-First-Century Epistolarity in *The Handmaid's Tale*

LINDA KAUFFMAN

A woman's life is all like the act of giving birth: a solitary, painful, furtive act.

The Three Marias:
New Portuguese Letters

SET IN CAMBRIDGE before the year 2000, Margaret Atwood's *The Handmaid's Tale* (1986) depicts the aftermath of a paramilitary coup by right-wing fundamentalists who establish a theocracy in the United States, renamed the Republic of Gilead. Born about 1965, the heroine is old enough to remember her feminist mother's activism but young enough to be recruited into surrogate motherhood in the new regime. Toxic wastes, nuclear accidents, and epidemics like AIDS have so decimated the population that reproduction is compulsory: the surrogates, called handmaids, dressed in red habits and veils, are assigned to aging childless couples among the regime's elite. The narrator is stripped of her previous identity and given the name "Offred," a patronymic composed of the possessive preposition and the first name (in her case, Fred) of the Commander whom she services.

The novel seems at first to have little in common with epistolary literature, since letter writing will presumably become extinct in the age of telecommunications and technological wizardry. But Atwood transports the dominant motifs of epistolarity into the twenty-first century, transforming the heroine's "letter" into a tape recording from the 1990s, purposely recorded randomly from memory. The medium changes, but the mode remains the same. The novel's re-presentation of speech is a reconstruction several times removed, for Offred's discourse is muted, mediated, and modified by the interventions of time and technology and by masculine writing appended to her own speech. Her tapes are unearthed and reconstructed in 2195 by a male archivist, whose written transcript is the narrative we read. The representational status of writing and the voice of authority are thus decentered by Atwood's juxtaposition of two entirely different texts, one masculine and one feminine. Atwood apocalyptically foresees the failure of humanism, liberalism, individualism, feminism, and capitalism; disintegration and calamity follow. Postmodernism is therefore stamped on the text as indelibly as the postmark of epistolarity is. My aim in this essay is first to examine the novel's formal relations to epistolary traditions, particularly in terms of masculine writing versus feminine speech. I then explain how the novel functions as an anatomy of ideology, in order to show that apocalyptic politics are as vital as poetics in the special delivery of the postmodern epistolary mode.

Masculine Writing/Feminine Speech: Atwood's Epistolary Predecessors

The Handmaid's Tale has been compared thematically with *The Scarlet Letter* and to "fearsome future" novels like *1984* (McCarthy), but its origins can be traced to the locus classicus of epistolarity, the *Heroides*, for, like Ovid's heroines, Offred narrates from exile, a ceaseless reiteration of her desire and her despair. She is multiply exiled: in obliterating the world she used to know, the Gileadean regime transforms her into "a refugee from the past" (227). When she flees Gilead, she is literally exiled; she makes her tapes while being hidden by the underground resistance movement. Thus, as with Ovid's Briseis, Dido, Penelope, and Medea, both Offred's psyche and the nation are in a state of siege among warring factions; in narrating, Offred situates herself in a landscape that is simultaneously psychic, physical, and political (see Kauffman, ch. 1; Altman 118–20). Whereas in earlier epochs the heroine addressed a reader (real or imagined), Offred addresses an imaginary listener. But like all earlier epistolary heroines, she reveals her pain and compulsively repeats it, as when she confesses:

> It hurts me to tell it over, over again. Once was enough: wasn't once enough for me at the time? But I keep on going with this sad and hungry and sordid, this limping and mutilated story, because after all I want you to hear it. . . . By telling you anything at all I'm at least believing in you, I believe you're there, I believe you into being. Because I'm telling you this story I will your existence. I tell, therefore you are. (268)

What Offred wills is nothing less than a future for the human race, since, at the moment when she actually speaks, its destruction seems imminent. By positing a listener, she affirms her faith in its survival. Far from being a solitary testament of individual feeling, a purely interior discourse of the heart, Offred's obsessions of necessity center on history, politics, and apocalypse. Apocalypse generally connotes catastrophe: terrorism, mass torture, nuclear accidents, deadly new strains of contamination. But apocalypse also signifies revelation of what was, is, and will be; in this sense, Offred is a "handmaid" metaphorically as well as literally; she is the handmaid of history, who prophetically reveals the monstrous shape of things to come for a listener she can only imagine but whom she wills into being by telling.

The epistolary gesture always entails the invention of a confidant who is absent at the moment of narrating, and it is therefore an act of dissimulation as well as of confidence. Offred's narrative embodies both impulses: she dissimulates by disguising all the names and by scrambling the order of her tapes, and she confides by repaying tenacious listeners with her remarkable revelations. As Janet Altman points out, "The epistolary confidant is most fundamentally an archivist"; Offred's listener is literally an archivist (53).[1] Just as the heroine's narrative provides a glimpse into a past that the archivist barely comprehends, his own historical notes provide a glimpse into a future that neither the heroine nor the reader could have foreseen, for by 2195 the entire map of the world has been transformed in terms of territory, language, culture, religion, and politics.

The text thus articulates the problems of transmission and reception, an articulation for which epistolarity is justly renowned and in which the female voice is particularly problematic. As Bernard Duyfhuizen explains, "If a novel in letters is to exist, the act of transmission must include its inverse: the act of retaining or collecting. . . . One part of the narrative of transmission . . . is the story of the collection—how the letters become available to an 'Editor' " ("Epistolary Narratives" 10). That is precisely the story that the historical notes tell. Only after the reader finishes Offred's discourse and turns to those notes do the novel's epistolary origins become apparent: the fiction of found tapes is the next century's equivalent to the fiction of found letters. Professor Pieixoto, Cambridge University's director of twentieth- and twenty-first-century archives, recounts his discovery of Offred's tapes to the Twelfth Symposium on Gileadean Studies, in 2195. More than thirty tapes are found in what used to be Bangor, Maine; they were purposely recorded at random intervals on different musical cassettes to camouflage their chronology, coherence, and significance. Pieixoto determines that the tapes are authentic rather than forged and draws deductions about the handmaid's culture. The very sequence of the sentences we read results from Pieixoto's guesswork; he arranges Offred's "blocks of speech" in a plausible order. He is aided by voice-print experts and technicians who reconstruct a machine long obsolete: the tape recorder. The narrative we read is thus a reconstruction, an approximation, subject to numerous interventions, all of which undermine the voice(s) of authority and the validity of interpretation.

Perhaps the most celebrated predecessor in the tradition of the fiction of found letters is *Lettres portugaises*, published in France in 1669 by Claude Barbin, who added an *avis au lecteur* asserting that the letters were written by a Portuguese nun, Mariane, after her seduction and abandonment by a French chevalier. Barbin recounts his difficulties in "translating" the letters and "verifies" their authenticity, but he may have perpetrated one of the greatest literary hoaxes of all time, for many now believe that Racine's friend Gabriel-Joseph de Lavergne de Guilleragues authored the letters (see Deloffre and Rougeot).[2] Both editor and author, well aware of the public's distaste for fiction, accurately predicted the scandalous appeal the "history" of the nun's passion would have for the public. Like Barbin, Atwood's archivist insists on the authenticity of his discovery and repudiates those forgeries "for which publishers have paid large sums, wishing to trade no doubt on the sensationalism of such stories." One of his moralistic editorial intrusions follows: "It appears that certain periods of history quickly become, both for other societies and for those that follow them, the stuff of not especially edifying legend and the occasion for a good deal of hypocritical self-congratulation" (302). But the archivist commits the very crimes he condemns, for he has little sensitivity to Offred's predicament or her pain. His tone is jocular; Offred's narrative comes to be entitled "The Handmaid's Tale" as a bawdy joke among his colleagues: "the word *tail* . . . being, to some extent, the bone, as it were, of contention, in that phase of Gileadean society" (301). In this pun, the issues of genre (tale) and gender (tail) are joined. Professor Pieixoto does not know how to describe the document as a genre; in terms of gender, he is condescending, ascribing the aleatory construction of the discourse, its lack of style, to the poor education of North American females in the 1980s and apologizing for the quality of Offred's mind. He wishes her record contained more data about the Gileadean regime and yearns for some of the Commander's computer printouts. He ignores the fact that it is precisely because she is female that she is denied access to the kind of information he desires. Pieixoto and his cohorts are merely the most recent of a long series of epistolary editors who appropriate the female voice for their own purposes—fame, fortune, power, self-aggrandizement, and self-congratulation.

His obsession with literal facts is particularly chilling since Gilead, like Puritan America, is founded on a literal interpretation of the Bible, specifically Genesis 30.1–3, where Rachel tells Jacob, "Behold my maid Bilhah, go in unto her; and she shall bear upon my knees, that I may also have children by her." These words result in a monthly "flesh triangle": Offred lies on her back between the knees of Serena Joy, the Commander's wife, while the Commander attempts to inseminate Offred. If and when she delivers a healthy baby, its appropriation and the handmaid's dismissal will follow—an ugly perversion of the spirit of the biblical dictum. How does one respond to such perversions? "One detaches oneself. One describes," says Offred (95).

As so often in epistolary narration, Offred gives us the sense not just of narrating to the moment but of narrating under compulsion: "I don't want to be telling this story," she confesses (273). Just as traditional epistolary heroines draw attention to the blots on the paper, the tearstains on the page, and the self-reflexivity of their acts of writing, Offred repeatedly reminds us that

> this is a reconstruction. All of it is a reconstruction. It's a reconstruction now, in my head. . . . When I get out of here, if I'm ever able to set this down, in any form, even in the form of one voice to another, it will be a reconstruction then too, at yet another remove. It's impossible to say a thing exactly the way it was, because what you say can never be exact, you always have to leave something out, there are too many parts, sides, crosscurrents, nuances; too many gestures, which could mean this or that, too many shapes which can never be fully described, too many flavors, in the air or on the tongue, half-colors, too many. (134)

She emphasizes synaesthesia, the poetic mixture of sensory impressions, because it is the texture of life that language cannot capture; that texture is too ineffably rich and temporally fleeting. She is, moreover, suspicious of all attempts to label, to sum up, to encapsulate, to define: Gilead has shown her too well the repression that results from literally enforcing one way, one truth, one interpretation. The compulsion to describe what cannot be put into words is one of the hallmarks of epistolarity; as the Portuguese nun reflects, "It seems to me that I am doing the greatest possible wrong to the feelings of my heart in trying to make them clear in writing to you" (Deloffre and Rougeot 43; my translation). Offred is similarly overwhelmed by the incapacity of language to encompass experience or feeling; it is always approximate, as she says in describing her affair with Nick: "I'm not sure how it happened; not exactly. All I can hope for is a reconstruction: the way love feels is always only approximate" (263). What is lacking in the archivist's commentary about Offred's discourse is precisely any sensitivity to taste, texture, touch, sound, sight—to the particularity of material existence in a specific historical moment.

That particularity is one of the hallmarks of epistolary writing-to-the-moment, but it has frequently led epistolary theorists to identify the epistle exclusively with individual feeling, as if such feelings could be isolated from social issues or politics. That is one of the myths Atwood dismantles. Epistolarity is in fact intrinsically political, whether one thinks of Ovid's exile, or Clarissa's rebellion against patriarchal bourgeois ideology, or the three Marias' prosecution for obscenity. Exiled, imprisoned, cloistered, or "shut up," epistolary heroines are deeply subversive because for them writing itself is an act of revolt. As the three Marias proclaim, "When woman rebels against man, nothing remains unchanged" (Barreño, Horta, and Velho da Costa 158).[3] Transgression lies in the telling. *The Handmaid's Tale*, then, differs in degree rather than kind from its epistolary predecessors: what remains implicit in a text like *Lettres portugaises*, for example, is merely more explicit in Atwood's novel: sex and politics are indistinguishable as transfer points of power and oppression in a society under siege. The Portuguese nun's seduction is metonymic: she is enthralled by (and in thrall to) a Frenchman stationed in Portugal to expand the empire of the Sun King; once the conquest of woman and colony is accomplished, the chevalier sails home. In Gilead, similarly, woman's body becomes the territory to master; female sexuality is harnessed for the "higher good" of the body politic, and viable ovaries become a "national resource" (65).

The appropriation of the female body and voice is therefore closely allied with other political acts of appropriation and conquest. One begins the process of mastery by stealing the language, a theft that is a recurrent theme in Atwood's poetry as well as her fiction. In the "Circe/Mud Poems" in *You Are Happy* (1974), for example, Circe is initially mistress of the island and namer of all things on it, but Odysseus vanquishes her by possessing her body and stealing her words: she spends her days "with my head pressed to the earth, to stones, / to shrubs, collecting the few muted syllables left over." She resists speaking in the "received language," as if aware that mythology always reproduces the same stories—of seduction, betrayal, conquest, power. She tries to subvert the glorious epic of omnipotent patriarchs by referring to Odysseus's "stupid boat, / your killer's hands." Yet she is helplessly doomed to silence, for she recognizes that he is the narrator of his odyssey, and she knows that "It's the story that counts." Despite her magical powers and prophetic capacities, she beseeches him to answer her questions: "When you leave will you give me back the words? Don't evade, don't pretend you won't leave after all: you leave in the story and the story is ruthless" (2298). She knows that since he is master of the myth, his story will depict her as evil and that she cannot change its contours or course. Atwood thus draws on Ovid's *Metamorphoses* as well as the *Heroides*; like Circe, Offred is powerless, aware that she has no control over the outcome of what she narrates: "I would like to believe this is a story I'm telling. . . . If it's a story . . . then I have control over the ending. Then there will be an ending, to the story, and real life will come after it" (39). The catastrophic events she witnesses are so unreal that Offred tries to believe they are fictional, but she cannot sustain that delusion for long. Her circumstances are too desperate and the regime is too ruthless.

The archivist fails to appreciate the profound implications of Offred's act, for he does not comprehend the effort of will and the leap of faith it requires for her to imagine a listener. Nor does he fully understand her objectives, for the particularity of her predicament is closely allied to the collective fate of women in her society, and one of her aims is to record their individual voices as well as her own. Traditionally, the epistle brings the absent beloved before the writing heroine; the motif of *je crois te parler* enables her to "hold him in her hands," to believe that she is speaking to him. That is a complex process for Offred, because she must first re-create herself, since the regime has turned her into a "missing person . . . disembodied . . . deserted . . . like a room where things once happened and now nothing does" (103–04). She first has to reclaim herself, retrieve her voice; once she does so, she turns to reinscribe the voices of other women. Poignantly, in this context, *je crois te parler* amounts to raising the dead, for Offred tries to bring into being a nonexistent archive of women so as to memorialize, for history, the women she will never see again: her daughter, her mother, her friends, her coconspirators. She re-presents the speech of Moira, for example, the gutsy college roommate who ends up as a prostitute in the Commander's private club. Offred consciously tries to mime Moira's iconoclastic, witty speech: "I've tried to make it sound as much like her as I can. It's a way of keeping her alive" (243–44). As a result, the entire narrative is a polyphony of distinctive female voices, but the archivist is deaf to these nuances. His scholarly, detached approach to the tapes reflects the assumptions of scientific research, technology, and objectivity; it assumes the status of truth. But his "truth" is not the same as women's. In Gilead, as in all previous periods of history, women's history is repressed; Gilead is merely the most recent regime to suppress their voices by prohibiting them from reading, writing, or speaking. The conditions of existence under which Offred labors do not permit the luxury of the archivist's so-called objectivity. As Pierre Macherey observes:

> The act of knowing is not like listening to a discourse already constituted, a mere fiction which we have simply to translate. It is rather the elaboration of a new discourse, the articulation of a silence. . . . What can be said *of* the work can never be confused with what the work itself is saying, because two distinct kinds of discourse which differ in both form and content are being superimposed. (6)

Atwood juxtaposes the handmaid's discourse with "what can be said" by the archivist, who errs in presuming that knowledge is an act of mere translation, once he assembles the proper technological equipment. The traditional definitions of "feminine" speech versus "masculine" writing are thus reaccentuated in Atwood's novel: the feminine is subjective, disordered, associative, illogical; the masculine is objective, orderly, controlled, logical. Such dichotomies have been reiterated by theorists of epistolarity through the ages and have been used to decide whether the letter writer's sex can be determined solely by internal stylistic evidence; with such texts as *Lettres portugaises*, for example, the question continues to be intensely controversial (see Kamuf, "Writing Like a Woman"; N. K. Miller, "Text's Heroine"; Kauffman, ch. 3). Since on a tape recording it is easier to hear whether the speaker is male or female, the question will be less ambiguous in epistolary productions of the twenty-first century.

Ovid's heroines and the Portuguese nun are clearly Offred's ancestors, but her relationship with her missing husband, Luke, most closely resembles Héloïse's with Abelard. Years after Abelard's castration and her conventual incarceration, Héloïse still refuses to face the fact that their separation is permanent; instead she sustains her illusions and her passion in her letters. Offred is equally defiant and illogical; she cannot reconcile herself to the fact that she and Luke will never be free, never make love again, that he may not even be alive. She imagines three alternative fates for him: that he was killed when they were captured; that he is a political prisoner; that he escaped and is working in the resistance movement. She confesses, "The things I believe can't all be true, though one of them must be. But I believe in all of them, all three versions of Luke, at one and the same time. This contradictory way of believing seems to me, right now, the only way I can believe anything" (106). In contrast to Pieixoto's literalness, Offred strives to sustain a spiritual belief. "In reduced circumstances you have to believe all kinds of things. I believe in thought transference now. . . . I never used to" (105). Thus, irrationality, which in former times would be seen as merely personal—and feminine—is here transformed into an explicitly political act, for Offred's survival is at stake in sustaining herself in order to witness to posterity about the fate of other political prisoners. Given the horror of her predicament, her danger, and its apocalyptic proportions, irrational faith is her only defense, for to be able to imagine one listener, she has to imagine the survival of thousands capable of vanquishing Gilead; these are the conditions of her survival and hence her narration. She explicitly relates her discourse to letters when she says:

> A story is like a letter. Dear *You*, I'll say. Just *you*, without a name. Attaching a name attaches *you* to the world of fact, which is riskier, more hazardous; who knows what the chances are out there of survival, yours? . . . *You* can mean more

> than one. *You* can mean thousands. . . . I'm not in any immediate danger, I'll say to you. I'll pretend you can hear me. (40)

Letters have long functioned to defamiliarize the distance between fiction and reality by drawing attention to the fictiveness of the narrative act, as Offred does here. But here, *je crois te parler* is linked not solely to sustaining sexual passion but to the survival of the human race.

The same transformation of the personal to the political through the act of forbidden discourse applies to forbidden reading, which has long been a feminine transgression in fiction, as with the forbidden letters Clarissa receives from Lovelace. But in Gilead, it is not just personal letters that are forbidden; all reading is forbidden to women. The Commander indulges Offred's craving by offering her a secret supply of banned books and magazines: Charles Dickens, Raymond Chandler, *MS.* magazine, *Mademoiselle, Vogue, Esquire, Reader's Digest*. She reads voraciously, trying to absorb as much material as quickly as possible in stolen moments. These materials help her remember a time before Gilead redefined even the language, developing such terms as "unwomen," "unbaby," and "gender traitors" to reshape reality. That is why Offred's surreptitious Scrabble games with the Commander are so subversive: it is her method of stealing the language back again, a proleptic hint of the tape recordings she will eventually make. Language is what she steals and, through language, knowledge and power.

The epistolary novel is the site of numerous transgressions, the formal codes of which are all familiar: adultery in *Les liaisons dangereuses*; prostitution in *Clarissa*; suicide in *The Sorrows of Young Werther*; forbidden reading in all of these. Atwood transforms these familiar codes while leaving their traces legible: since the previous handmaid killed herself when her trysts with the Commander were discovered, suicide is never far from Offred's mind. She is, moreover, defined by the regime as an adulteress, since she married a divorced man. Furthermore, she deceives Serena with the Commander and later deceives the Commander with Nick. Finally, when the Commander takes her to Jezebel's, the private men's club and brothel, she plays the prostitute. But the formal codes are here transformed into political crimes, for reading is not merely "an imaginary or metaphorical transgression."[4] Instead it is a literal crime, punishable by the amputation of a hand. The Gileadean regime punishes those who commit the "crime" of "unchastity" by amputating an arm and the crime of adultery by execution (275). In Gilead, these codes reflect an ideology devoted to the repression of human desire in general and female sexuality in particular.

What caused such sudden and severe societal repression? Offred learns from the Commander that the revolution came about because men felt irrelevant. "There was nothing for them to do with women . . . the sex was too easy. Anyone could just buy it. There was nothing to work for, nothing to fight for. . . . You know what they were complaining about the most? Inability to feel. Men were turning off on sex, even" (210). This revealing statement implies that male potency derives from and depends on the oppression of others. Only by wrapping women in veils and habits, by persecuting "deviants," by suspending civil liberties, do such men derive a sense of meaningful existence. As the three Marias observe, "The basic repression, the one which . . . lies at the very core of the history of the human species, creating the model and giving rise to the myths underlying other repressions, is that of the woman by the man" (Barreño, Horta, and Velho da Costa 219). At one point, Offred prophetically envisions a male listener to her tape and addresses him directly. After declaring that it is impossible to describe anything accurately, in all its fullness, she makes a crucial distinction between masculine and feminine responses to her discourse:

> If you happen to be a man, sometime in the future, and you've made it this far, please remember: you will never be subject to the temptation or feeling you must forgive, a man, as a woman. It's difficult to resist, believe me. But remember that forgiveness too is a power. To beg for it is a power, and to withhold or bestow it is a power, perhaps the greatest. (134–35)

This puzzling statement is perhaps made clearer by relating it to Offred's attitude toward the Commander. She weighs individual responsibility, emotional involvement, and the power of forgiveness as she tries to find the words to describe his monthly violation of her:

> He is fucking . . . the lower part of my body. I do not say making love, because this is not what he's doing. Copulating too would be inaccurate, because it would imply two people and only one is involved. Nor does rape cover it: nothing is going on here that I haven't signed up for. (94)

Offred's comment about forgiveness thus arises in the context of whether it is possible to forgive the Commander, who puts her life in peril by breaking the rules of their intercourse. On the one hand, he becomes an individual person rather than a thing to her, and she to him, which slightly eases her otherwise unbearable existence. On the other hand, she is completely in his power, and he can turn on her, or turn her in, at any moment, as happened to the previous handmaid. It may seem as if Offred is advocating forgiveness, but she goes on to record her childhood memory of a television documentary about the mistress of a Nazi SS officer who was responsible for sending Jews to the ovens. Offred reflects that the mistress "did not believe he was a monster. He was not a monster, to her. Probably he had some endearing trait: he whistled . . . he called his dog Liebchen. . . . How easy it is to invent a humanity, for anyone at all. What an available temptation" (145–46). The temptation of a woman to forgive a man is precisely what Offred abjures; forgiving would result in forgetting, and that is exactly what she records her narrative to prevent: her listeners must remember history and must not eradicate the memory of what has been done to the spirits and bodies of the regime's dissenters and its victims.

Docile Bodies: An Anatomy of Ideology

Offred neither forgives nor forgets; she rebels by keeping the past alive. What the regime would eradicate, she reinscribes. Her first words evoke the "after-image'' of a world long ago and far away: she remembers the basketball games and high school dances held through the decades in the gymnasium where she is imprisoned, which has been turned into a reeducation center to indoctrinate handmaids in their new roles. ''There was old sex in the room and loneliness, and expectation, of something without a shape or name. I remember that yearning, for something that was always about to happen . . . we yearned for the future'' (3). The intensity with which teenagers yearned for the future is grimly ironic in retrospect, since that future has now arrived, emptied of hope, choice, possibility. The ''something without a shape or name'' is desire, and Offred remembers her own ''insatiability,'' a craving all the more poignant now, since desire is precisely what is banned in Gilead.

Her individual memories illuminate not just her intimate relations but political and historical moments, ranging from her mother's feminist activism for abortion rights and against pornography, to her own combined roles as working woman, wife, lover, friend, mother, citizen. But Gilead strips women of their individuality, categorizing them hierarchically according to class status and reproductive capacity. They are, in fact, metonymically color-coded according to their function and their labor: the Commanders' wives wear blue (a remnant perhaps of aristocracy's blue bloods); the handmaids wear red, the color of blood; and ''econowives,'' distributed to lesser functionaries in the regime, wear multicolored dresses, to indicate that they have to perform multiple sexual and housewifely functions. The very term ''econowives'' makes explicit the hierarchical commodification of the female. Men without any status are not ''issued a woman, not even one'' (18). The traffic in women eliminates the individual female personality; she merely becomes an interchangeable unit in the body politic.

The novel thus gives a new and ominous meaning to the phrase ''the body politic'' by laying bare the devices by which subjects of the state are ideologically constructed. Atwood implicitly inquires, ''What is woman?'' The answer: a person of the female sex. Only in certain relations of power and exchange does she become a servant, a womb, or a sexual partner, as Simone de Beauvoir observes in *The Second Sex*, which may have provided Atwood's donnée, for in trying to distinguish production in the Marxist sense from biological reproduction, de Beauvoir observes:

> It is impossible simply to equate gestation with a service, such as military service . . . no state has ever ventured to establish obligatory copulation. . . . All that can be done is to put woman in a situation where maternity is for her the sole outcome—the law or the mores enjoin marriage, birth control and abortion are prohibited, divorce is forbidden. (65–66; 1974 ed.)

That is precisely the situation Atwood imagines: mass marriages are arranged; divorce is prohibited; free will and individual choice cease to exist. Like Héloïse, Mariane, and the many nuns in *The Three Marias*, Offred takes the veil not from internal religious conviction but because external pressures coerce her to harness her sexuality. The only difference between her existence and a nun's is that the latter is forced to be chaste, whereas for Offred and all handmaids copulation is obligatory; birth control and abortion are prohibited; woman is compelled to bring forth or face death.

Apocalypse depicts what has been, what is, and what will be. Atwood depicts what "woman" has been in the Judeo-Christian tradition, from biblical times through the 1980s to the end of the next century. From Medusa to the Virgin Mary, from the biblical handmaid Bilhah to Hester Prynne, from Mary Webster[5] to Maryann Crescent Moon in 2195, the novel assembles the constructions of "woman": monster, madonna, witch, womb, whore, revolutionary, heretic, prostitute, servant, mother. Atwood's purpose is to show that revolutions come and go, but women's fates remain wholly unchanged. The three Marias share the same insight in *New Portuguese Letters*, as they similarly shift forward and backward through time, asking in a woman's diary entry from 1800:

> What woman is not a nun, sacrificed, self-sacrificing, without a life of her own, sequestered from the world? What change has there been in the life of women through the centuries? . . . We are living in an age of civilization and enlightenment, men write scientific treatises, and encyclopedias, nations continually change and transform their political structure, the oppressed raise their voices, a king of France has been sent to the guillotine and his courtiers along with him, the United States of America has gained its independence. . . . What has changed in the life of women? (Barreño, Horta, and Velho da Costa 154)[6]

Rather than being progressive, history, for women, is both regressive and repressive. Atwood is unflinching in depicting the oppression of women before the coup as well as after: before the coup, women were not safe on the streets; portable "Pornomarts" were on every corner; "snuff" films celebrated the murder and dissection of female bodies. The new regime promises an end to rape, pornography, and violence. As Atwood observes, "A new regime would never say, 'we're socialist; we're fascist.' They would say that they were serving God. . . . You can develop any set of beliefs by using the Bible. . . . Repressive regimes always have to offer up something in return" (Interview).[7] Women believed the regime's promises and participated in book burnings, inadvertently colluding in their own enslavement; it is precisely the cooperation of feminists with right-wingers that helps bring about the fundamentalist coup: pornography is banned, but so are all civil liberties. Martial law is imposed, and all undesirables—prostitutes, lesbians, and feminists like the narrator's mother—are forced to clean toxic wastes until they die from contamination. All are labeled "unwomen." Language thus defines reality, which is one reason that Offred spends so much time meditating about words, comparing their meanings before the coup and after, their arbitrariness and construction. Of the word *chair*, for example, she reflects: "It can mean the leader of a meeting. It can also mean a mode of execution. It is the first syllable in charity. It is the French word for flesh. None of these facts has any connection with the others" (110). But in fact there is an associative connection, for the leaders of the revolution enforce their power by torturing the flesh of dissenters. Resisters receive no charity, no mercy; instead, they are executed.

The Handmaid's Tale functions as an anatomy of ideology, exposing the process by which one constructs, psychologically and politically, subjects of the state and then enlists their cooperation in their own subjection. One begins at the level of the flesh. In the reeducation centers, the handmaid is taught to have an entirely different relation to her own body, her "self." As Offred confesses:

> Each month I watch for blood, fearfully, for when it comes it means failure. I have failed once again to fulfill the expectations of others, which have become my own. I used to think of my body as an instrument of pleasure, or a means of transportation, or an implement for the accomplishment of my will. I could use it to run, push buttons of one sort or another, make things happen. There were limits, but my body was nevertheless lithe, single, solid, one with me.
>
> Now the flesh arranges itself differently. I'm a cloud, congealed, around a central object, the shape of a pear, which is hard and more real than I am and glows red within its translucent wrapping. Inside it is a space . . . huge. . . . I see despair coming towards me like famine. To feel that empty, again, again. (73–74)

Atwood's purpose, like Ovid's in the *Metamorphoses*, "is to tell of bodies which have been transformed into shapes of a different kind"; here Offred's body is reduced to the womb, a reproductive factory.

The novel demonstrates the paradox that the ideology of the biological family really comes into its own when the complexity of a class society forces the kinship system to recede (Mitchell 378). Since children are distributed like commodities, the biological kinship system has ceased to exist. But at the same time the patriarchs justify their reign of terror by trumpeting the ideology of the family to the heavens, basing it on an extremist's interpretation of the Bible. The closest corollary to the Gileadean system is slavery in the American South, when black women were similarly prized and priced as breeders. As in slavery, despite the woman's labor, the white slaveholders, like the men in Gilead, retain legal property rights over the product of the woman's body; religiously and legally, it is the man who "produces" the child, just as it has always been.

Bodies are turned into machines in the army, the school, and the hospital; in Atwood's novel, the Red Centers combine all three functions. They are run by the "Aunts," menopausal women whose job is to create a sisterhood and a woman's culture, a grim parody of one of the quaint feminist impulses of the 1970s and 1980s. The Aunts are licensed to torture recruits who resist reeducation. (This emphasis on the collusion of women with their oppressors is significant; one of the regime's strokes of genius is its discovery that the least expensive way to enforce its policies is by using women against each other.) The Red Centers are also hospitals, for here the handmaids practice Lamaze exercises and undergo drug and shock treatments. Their identities as women, wives, mothers, lovers are all erased through discipline, punishment, and torture. As Michel Foucault asks, "Is it surprising that prisons resemble factories, schools, barracks, hospitals, which all resemble prisons?" (*Discipline* 228). Offred is simultaneously a prisoner, a pupil to be reeducated, a patient who is forcibly subjected to monthly gynecological exams to optimize the chances of pregnancy. The novel thus condenses two of Foucault's major subjects: the birth of the prison and the birth of the clinic, the gaze of the panopticon and the gaze of the medical amphitheater (see *Discipline*; *Birth*). In Gilead, all flesh is brought down to the level of the organism.

In revealing the inextricable connections between power and sexuality, Atwood demonstrates the validity of the observation that "sexuality is not the most intractable element in power relations, but rather one of those endowed with the greatest instrumentality" (*Discipline* 103). Offred's reckless trysts with Nick seem to refute Foucault's thesis, but when she is discovered, she says:

> I'll sacrifice. I'll repent. I'll abdicate. I'll renounce. . . . Everything they taught at the Red Center, everything I've resisted comes flooding in. I don't want pain. . . . I want to keep on living, in any form. I resign my body freely, to the uses of others. They can do what they like with me. I am abject. I feel, for the first time, their true power. (286)

Her predecessor's suicide under similar circumstances attests to the powerful mechanisms in force to control sexuality. In Gilead, all citizens are classified in binary categories that control and contain everyone: licit versus illicit sex; reproductive versus nonreproductive ovaries; white versus black; religious believer versus heretic. Homosexuals are executed as "gender traitors"; abortionists are hanged for crimes against the species; Jews must emigrate or convert; blacks are "resettled"; feminists and other deviants—Quakers, Baptists, Catholics, atheists, liberals, leftists—are "disappeared."

To make visible the invisible work of ideology and subjection, Atwood's archaeological investigations uncovered two theocracies as models: Puritan Boston of *The Scarlet Letter* and modern Iran under the Ayatollah Khomeini. Like Hester Prynne, the handmaid is defined by her sexuality, literally marked as a scarlet woman. Like Hester, she lives in a utopia gone awry, where the prison and the cemetery are omnipresent. Hawthorne's "Custom House" seems to have inspired Atwood's preoccupation with the ways in which we subject ourselves to the prison houses of custom: repression is first horrific but soon comes to seem necessary, then customary, and finally "natural." At one point, Offred offhandedly remarks that at present "only" two bodies hang on the wall in what used to be Harvard Yard. The present reality in all its horror is already coming to seem normal—even to her—and the next generation will have no memory, no means by which to measure the relative normality or abnormality of the regime. Indeed, time is carefully manipulated so that all remnants of the past, pre-Gilead reality are obliterated: there are no dates after the 1980s; all historical documents are destroyed, and the Gileadean regime periodically wipes out even its own computer records after various purges.

In a society under siege, when the brutal force of a coup prescribes the law of the land, subjects are defined solely by obedience: the subject who is constituted as subject is he who obeys. As Foucault observes:

> The historical moment of the disciplines was the moment when an art of the human body was born, which was directed not only at . . . the intensification of its subjection, but at the formation of a relation that in the mechanism itself makes it more obedient as it becomes more useful, and conversely. What was then being

> formed was a policy of coercions that act upon the body, a calculated manipulation of its elements, its gestures, its behaviour. The human body was entering a machinery of power that explores it, breaks it down and rearranges it. A "political anatomy," which was also a "mechanics of power," was being born. (*Discipline* 138)

Disciplined like soldiers, the handmaids learn to control their bodies, to respond mechanically, to act as a collective unit. As with a soldier or a nun, each handmaid's body and gestures must reflect her status; she is commanded by signals, not by comprehension. Perhaps the closest model for the behavior desired of her is *dressage*—the leading of horses through their paces—which metaphorically signifies blind obedience (*Discipline* 166).

Obedience is also ensured through the careful regulation of time. As Offred notes, "the bell that measures time is ringing. Time here is measured by bells, as once in nunneries. As in a nunnery too, there are few mirrors" (8). Offred's bodily movements are minutely monitored: so many minutes in the bathroom; so many chances (three) to conceive. Her entire existence as handmaid consists of waiting: waiting for the monthly "ceremony" during which the Commander tries to impregnate her; waiting for the results; and, if they are positive, waiting to deliver the baby. Another way to ensure obedience is to enforce silence; since spies are everywhere, the entire society ceases to speak freely, and the handmaids are allowed to speak only in prescribed pious clichés.

Atwood portrays a regime in the process of establishing the mechanisms of repression that will eventually be invisible. At the moment, they can still be seen: executions still abound; checkpoints stop citizens from fleeing the city; police vans suddenly materialize on the streets and whisk unsuspecting citizens away. However, once Gilead works out the kinks in its repressive mechanisms, all citizens will, like the handmaids in their red habits, exist in a state of conscious and permanent "compulsory visibility" that will ensure the automatic functioning of power. The agents are called the Eyes, and eventually, as in Bentham's panopticon, surveillance will become permanent in its effects, even if discontinuous in its action, for the institutional gaze will be invisible but omniscient (*Discipline* 195–228).

Atwood's novel is thus an exemplary response to the challenge Michèle Barrett recently addressed to feminist literary critics:

> I can find no sustained argument as to *why* feminists should be so interested in literature or what theoretical or political ends such analyses of literature serve. . . . Related to this is the inadequacy of feminist attempts to explore the ways in which material conditions have historically structured the mental aspects of oppression. (65)

Atwood's aim, however, is precisely to demonstrate how material conditions structure mental oppression, for despite all Offred's efforts to remember her prior existence, she has begun to take on the perception the regime wants her to have of herself. When she sees a pregnant woman, for example, she feels the emptiness of her own womb and experiences a sense of failure, futility, and worthlessness. Her breasts become swollen and ache. This is exactly how the material and mental aspects of oppression work in concert, for the Red Center trains her to reflect in her material body the mental impression it strives never to let her forget: that she is nothing but a passive receptacle.

Although Offred internalizes the oppression to which she is subjected, she also resists it. She repossesses her body by making love with Nick, an act for which she could be executed; she is compelled toward him, "expecting at any moment to feel the bullets rip through me" (268). By telling him her real name, she unburies the body, the voice, the self that the regime sought to annihilate, and she demonstrates how uneradicable desire is. As de Beauvoir observes, "It is impossible to bring the sexual instinct under a code of regulations. . . . What is certain is that it does not permit of integration with the social, because there is in eroticism a revolt of the instant against time, of the individual against the universal" (65; 1974 ed.). In this way Offred defies the regime's definitions of her, for she and Nick "make love each time as if we know beyond the shadow of a doubt that there will never be any more, for either of us, with anyone, ever" (269).

Paradoxically, she also resists the regime by taking responsibility for her actions. Offred recognizes that she is guilty of numerous sins, albeit sins different from those defined by the regime. She castigates herself for not paying enough attention to the alarming signs of intolerance—religious, racial, and sexual—in her society before the takeover, and for colluding with the regime in order to survive. Her confession of these sins recalls one of the most remarkable characteristics of the female voice throughout epistolary literature, for from Héloïse to Mariane to Clarissa, heroines have used their letters to engage in merciless self-condemnation. Like Clarissa and the three Marias, Offred puts herself on trial (see Kauffman 44–45, 77–78, 133–36, 187–94). She reveals her participation in the rite of "salvaging," for instance, which means that when a woman is hanged, Offred touches the rope in unison with the other handmaids, then places her hand on her heart "to show my unity with the Salvagers and my consent, and my complicity in the death of this woman" (276). She also confesses to sharing the sensations the regime wants her to have when a political prisoner is brought before the handmaids on trumped-up charges of raping and murdering a pregnant handmaid. In a ritual called "particicution," the handmaids rape and dismember him; only by an extraordinary effort of will does Offred restrain herself, but she nevertheless experiences the "bloodlust; I want to tear, gouge, rend" (279). And she memorializes both her complicity and that corpse in her text:

> I wish this story were different. I wish it were more civilized. I wish it showed me in a better light, if not happier, then at least more active, less hesitant, less distracted by trivia. I wish it had more shape. . . . I'm sorry there is so much pain in this story. I'm sorry it's in fragments, like a body caught in crossfire or pulled apart by force. (267)

While apologizing for the pain in her story, Offred emphasizes that the fact that she is unhappy is less relevant than the fact that she should have been more engaged in collective action to save her society from fanatics. She compares the present with the ominous signs of growing repression in the past before the coup:

> We lived as usual. Everyone does, most of the time. Whatever is going on is as usual. Even this is as usual, now. We lived, as usual, by ignoring. Ignoring isn't the same as ignorance, you have to work at it. Nothing changes instantaneously: in a gradually heating bathtub you'd be boiled to death before you knew it. (56)

She was an apathetic, self-absorbed member of the "post-feminist generation" (see Bolotin). The passage is thus an example of the ways in which one can locate in the same situation the forces of oppression and the seeds of resistance, for while Offred in some respects internalizes the oppression the regime enforces, she simultaneously resists it by confessing her individual responsibility and by making the tape recordings. From *Clarissa* to *The Three Marias*, the heroine's discourse simultaneously reveals her oppression and resistance, collusion and rebellion. That duality, indeed, is yet another hallmark of the female voice in epistolary literature.

Quakers and Catholics also resist the regime; even Southern Baptists start a civil war, which to Atwood proves that there is considerable resistance, even among groups one would have thought would support a fundamentalist takeover (Interview). Her view of the Southern Baptists, however, seems overly optimistic in reality, for the 14.6-million-member denomination in 1987 elected a leader who endorses a literal interpretation of the Bible, insisting that "the narratives of Scripture are historically and factually accurate." A moderate minister who dissented from the majority vote noted that the election "seems to reflect the agenda of the fundamentalist takeover" (*Raleigh News and Observer*).

Thus another reason for feminist literary analysis is that novels like Atwood's are less about the "fearsome future" than about the "fearsome present," for she dismantles received ideas and unquestioned assumptions about religion, sex, politics, women's cultures—and feminism itself. Atwood audaciously creates a heroine who is in a very real sense responsible for the Gileadean coup: she is apathetic politically, complacent about women's struggle for equal rights, absorbed solely in her individual existence. All around her she sees racial hatred, religious intolerance, and sexual repression intensifying daily. If *The Handmaid's Tale* were solely a tragic tale of one woman's suffering, it would merely reinforce the emphasis bourgeois ideology places on the individual, but by focusing equally on the decimation of a culture and several races, Atwood expands the parameters of the epistolary mode. Perhaps the most chilling statement in the novel is that of Professor Pieixoto, who observes: "There was little that was truly original with or indigenous to Gilead: its genius was synthesis" (307). The repressions Gilead devises are a synthesis of all previous cultures: it borrows from the Spanish inquisitors, the Puritans, Khomeini's Iranian followers, the KGB, the CIA. Gilead borrows Hitler's tactics of encircling urban centers, persecuting the Jews, eliminating undesirables, and using female bodies as laboratories for genetic reproduction. Pieixoto comments: "The sociobiological theory of natural polygamy was used as a scientific justification for some of the odder practices of the regime, just as Darwinism was used by earlier ideologies" (306).

Since such ghastly practices come to seem normal while Offred is witnessing them, one inevitably wonders what hope there is of sustaining any sense of outrage nearly two centuries later. Because readers in the 1980s are closer to the period Offred describes, our horror at what may become our imminent destiny is proportionally greater; Pieixoto and his colleagues, however, look coolly back on a distant past. Whereas Offred sees nothing but pain in her narrative, two hundred years later it is merely a source of quaint curiosity to the historians, archaeologists, and anthropologists who hear it. The immediacy of her danger and her descriptions of the evils she witnesses seem so remote in 2195 that her audience cannot even rouse itself to murmur against "the banality of evil"; nothing is condemned by Pieixoto, who warns: "We must be cautious about passing moral judgment upon the Gileadeans. Surely we have learned by now that such judgments are of necessity culture-specific. . . . Our job is not to censure but to understand" (302).

This statement is a direct contrast to Offred's own defiant outrage, for like survivors of other holocausts, she insists that we pay attention to the material conditions of the suffering of specific individuals in a particular historical moment:

> Maybe none of this is about control. Maybe it isn't really about who can own whom, who can do what to whom and get away with it, even as far as death. Maybe it isn't about who can sit and who has to kneel or stand or lie down, legs spread open. Maybe it's about who can do what to whom and be forgiven for it. Never tell me it amounts to the same thing. (134–35)

You can only forgive atrocities that you forget, and Offred reminds us never to forget, never to bury the horrors of history amid vague clichés in which there are no agents and no evils. Judgment is necessary, she insists, to prevent the past from repeating itself.

The archivist's myopia is ironically underscored by the last words of the text: "Are there any questions?" The novel leaves us haunted by myriad questions: What was Offred's eventual fate? What happened during the intervening century and a half to the United States and North America? The human race has survived, and the planet seems to have replenished itself—there are fish, oceans, forests—but what kind of society exists in 2195? Is it less sexist, racist, homophobic, fanatical? Is it more just? Or is it a telling comment that the archivist refuses to condemn Gilead as evil? Perhaps his society has merely perfected Gilead's "genius for synthesis," making the mechanisms of power and repression completely invisible—and thus all-pervasive. What, if anything, have we learned from history?

The novel resists closure, leaving us with disturbing questions rather than soothing answers. Atwood records the failure of humanism, liberalism, individualism, and feminism, but she offers no substitutes, no solutions, no comforting fictions of personal or political redemption—including feminist fictions. As Elaine Hansen observes, "This kind of fiction and feminism alike insists that we uncover and examine the contradictions, the disequilibrium and insufficiency masked by the sense of an ending" (19). Thus in form and content, Atwood purposely dismantles received ideas about the present, as well as about the past and future, a strategy that evokes Fredric Jameson's reflection on future fiction: "The reader will there find an empty chair reserved for some as yet unrealized, collective, and decentered cultural production of the future, beyond realism and modernism alike" (*Political Unconscious* 11). Atwood invents just such a decentered cultural production, for the narrative we read is a collective endeavor, made possible by the resistance movement that presumably rescues Offred, by her courage and defiance in taping her discourse, and by archaeologists and technicians who reassemble her speech. The concentric construction of Atwood's apocalyptic novel encompasses past, present, and future. She makes us into detectives, trying to reconstruct the political history from which Offred's daily chronicle emerges. We discover the struggles and tensions that resulted in the establishment of Gilead's theocracy, and with the appended historical notes, we see history portrayed in its vastest sense, projected into the next century.[8] Through this triple framework, Atwood decenters both history and narrative. By dialogically superimposing the archivist's writing over the heroine's speech, she decenters the representational status of writing while reaccentuating the epistolary postmark.[9]

Atwood's unique contribution to the long tradition of female voices in epistolary literature is to combine epistolary poetics with apocalyptic politics. Despite Gilead's attempts to ban desire, Offred's remains unvanquished. Despite the self-aggrandizement of masculine editors, the interventions of time, and the ideologues who sought to eradicate her, the distinctive female voice of Atwood's heroine remains. Her discourse is a defiant testimony of her innocence and culpability, her defiance and desire, her submission and rebellion to the history being rewritten before her eyes. Like Rennie, Atwood's heroine in *Bodily Harm*, her experiences of a brutal regime so radicalize her that she becomes "a subversive: She was not once but now she is. A reporter. She will pick her time; then she will report" (265). The novel is finally a testament to the urgency of the analytical project that lies at the interstices of feminism and literary theory, for the future Atwood describes is not distant. Instead, like 1984, it has already arrived. Atwood merely defamiliarizes the world around us in the 1980s: whether one thinks of the trials of surrogate motherhood, or the Vatican's recent doctrinal edict against anything but married "normal sexuality," or of the AIDS epidemic and its attendant repressions, or the resurgence of racial and religious intolerance—the seeds of hatred, violence, and repression are already prepared. Whatever "issue" is slouching toward Bethlehem may not yet be more than an embryo, but the seeds of disciplinary power and punishment of the body politic have already been sown. Like Foucault, Atwood is writing a history of the present.[10]

NOTES

[1] Altman examines the oppositions of confidence and dissimulation in epistolary fiction (ch. 2). The dissimulation and duplicity of epistolary heroines (Ovid's, Héloïse, Mariane, Clarissa, and the three Marias) are discussed in Kauffman (17, 23–27, 31, 32, 40–44, 56, 61, 70, 74, 110, 138, 142, 145, 148, 154–56, 179, 187, 201, 207, 288, 301–02, 305).

[2] While in the editors' view the identification of Guilleragues as author is definitive, others argue that although no Portuguese original has ever been found, the work was at least inspired by authentic letters of a Portuguese woman. The controversy is far from being settled; Peter Dronke maintains that the entire issue "remains . . . wide open"; Yves Florenne argues for a female voice (7); Jean-Pierre LaSalle and Thérèse LaSalle offer new evidence and additional letters by the same hand.

[3] The three Marias were prosecuted by the Caetano-Salazar dictatorship from 1972 to 1974. See Kauffman, chapter 8; on epistolary patterns of transgression, see Kauffman 18, 27, 38–40, 49–50, 60, 64–68, 75, 78, 81–84, 89, 119, 132, 155, 229, 280–81, 289, 290–300, 310.

[4] In "Flaubert's Presuppositions," Michael Riffaterre traces a causal connection leading from forbidden reading to adultery, and from adultery to prostitution or suicide:

> The first fatal step leads inevitably to the last fatal leap. These inseparable and complementary poles thus set the limits of the fictional space extending from an imaginary or metaphorical transgression (wicked thoughts nurtured by immoral and forbidden readings) to the most definitive of all actual or literal transgressions—the one that drags the heroine out of existence, and out of the text, simultaneously putting an end to what can be lived or to what can be told in words. The adulteress either commits suicide or sinks into prostitution. (6)

[5] Atwood dedicated the book to Perry Miller, her professor of American literature at Harvard, and to Mary Webster, her Puritan forebear who was hanged as a witch but survived. "She had a tough neck," Atwood wryly observes.

[6] Even after a junior officer's coup overthrew the Caetano-Salazar dictatorship in 1974, the women were still forced to stand trial, an injustice that further demonstrates the validity of their argument that revolutions do little to change women's oppression (Kauffman, ch. 8).

[7] Regarding the current debate about pornography versus censorship, Atwood observes: "Women are in the position of being asked to choose between two things, neither of which is good for them. Why can't they have a third thing that is good for them . . . some kind of reasonable social milieu in which pornography would not be much of an issue because it would not be desired by men?" (Interview).

[8] The novel embodies Jameson's concept of "symbolization," for its structure consists of

> three concentric frameworks [that] function to mark a widening out of the sense of the social ground of a text through . . . first, . . . political history, in the narrow sense of . . . a chroniclelike sequence of happenings in time; then of society, in the . . . sense of a constitutive tension and struggle between social classes; and ultimately, of history now conceived in its vastest sense of . . . various social formations, from prehistoric life to whatever far future history has in store for us. (*Political Unconscious* 75)

[9] Cf. Jameson, *Political Unconscious*, 285, 296. On Bakhtinian dialogism and epistolary reaccentuation, see Kauffman, 18, 23, 25, 33, 79, 82, 120, 282, 298.

[10] Foucault, *Discipline* 31. Mary McCarthy disagrees. She sees nothing "in our present mores that I ought to watch out for unless I want the United States . . . to become a slave state something like the Republic of Gilead." Has McCarthy perhaps lived in Paris too long?

AFTERWORD

This essay is part of a book entitled *Special Delivery: Epistolary Modes in Modern Fiction*, forthcoming from the University of Chicago Press (1991). Part 1, "Producing Women," examines the reinscription of femininity by three leading male theorists: Victor Shklovsky, in *Zoo: Or, Letters Not about Love*; Roland Barthes, in *A Lover's Discourse*; and Jacques Derrida, in *The Post Card*. Part 2, "Women's Productions," focuses on Doris Lessing's *The Golden Notebook*, Alice Walker's

The Color Purple, and Atwood's *Handmaid's Tale*. My thesis is that while the male theorists focus on Woman as a metaphor, the women writers have shifted their frame of reference beyond even feminism, to focus on global politics and apocalypse. The study addresses the vexed question of the politics of subjectivity, arguing for a poststructuralist feminism that takes into consideration the concrete effects of power and the material conditions of women's lives.

Ironically, when *The Handmaid's Tale* first appeared, in 1986, the novel's lack of realism was harshly criticized; some reviewers felt that such events could never happen. Yet since its publication, global events have made it look less like a dystopia than like prophecy. For example, as I write, revelations about the control of women's reproduction in Romania are just beginning to be exposed: under the regime of Nicolae Ceausescu, a state policy was brutally enforced that required every woman to bear five children, despite food shortages and cramped living quarters. The aim was to increase the nation's power as a world force. Women were subjected to forced gynecological examinations every three months to ensure that they hadn't had illegal abortions. Thousands of women suffered permanent injury, sterilization, or death in attempting illegal or self-administered abortions. Atwood actually alludes to these horrors in the novel (305). Since the novel's publication, the United States Supreme Court, in *Webster v. Reproductive Services*, severely undermined abortion rights.

The same bleak picture applies to the environment: the news last night reported that the same trucks used to haul toxic wastes one day are used to haul produce and meat to market the next. We hear daily about many of the environmental disasters Atwood forecasted: dying forests, depleted oceans, contaminated water supplies, massive oil spills in Alaska and Morocco, overflowing landfills containing wastes that will remain for fifty thousand years.

Meanwhile, 14.6 million Southern Baptists continue to be controlled by the most conservative wing, which insists on the literal interpretation of the Bible. Schoolteachers must balance the scientific view of evolution with the creationist's viewpoint.

Surveillance continues to proliferate, its necessity justified on such grounds as threats to national security, or control of the AIDS virus, or establishment of "drug-free workplaces," or other rationalizations. In short, one has only to open the daily newspaper to recognize that Atwood's prophecies have already come true. When historians in 2195 look back on feminism's function in the late twentieth century, will they define it as a passing fashion, a bourgeois movement predominantly for white women, or a bloodless revolution of global political significance? One cannot but wonder what each of us will have contributed to that eventual legacy.

Washington, DC
January 1990

~ 1989 ~

Speaking about the Unspeakable: The Representation of Disability as Stigma in Toni Morrison's Novels

ROSEMARIE GARLAND THOMSON

Whatever is unnamed, undepicted in images, . . . whatever is misnamed as something else, made difficult-to-come-by, whatever is buried in the memory by the collapse of meaning under an inadequate or lying language—this will become, not merely unspoken, but unspeakable.

Adrienne Rich

THE REPRESENTATION OF physical disability is seldom considered in literary criticism from a socially or politically conscious perspective. Because traditional literary-critical discourse tends to treat the representation of disability under the rubric of "the grotesque," a term which makes no distinction between the rendering of monsters, mermaids, or gargoyles and that of actual human beings who are physically different or disabled, it invites interpreting physical disability as monstrosity and alien otherness, dehumanizing us, erasing our histories, and appropriating our experiences for aesthetic purposes (see Holman 245; Muller 7). Therefore, in this examination of the representation of women with physical disabilities or anomalous markings in Toni Morrison's five novels, I hope to initiate instead a sociopolitically conscious discourse of disability which is informed by sociology, anthropology, feminism, Afro-American literary criticism, and narrative analysis, as well as my own personal perspective as a physically disabled, white woman reader and critic.[1]

By turning primarily to sociology, I am foregrounding both social relations and social institutions in my analysis, a move that I take as fundamental in considering both the representation of disabled people and Morrison's project as a black woman writer. All five of her novels are, in a sense, about the social process of stigmatization, the complex distortion of relationships between individuals, among people in families and communities, among larger groups such as races and classes, and finally the distortion that takes place within the self as a result both of stigmatizing and being stigmatized. In a culture that claims to value egalitarianism and institutionalizes democracy, stigmatization is a paradox, a social and political problem needing attention and redress. The literary value of Morrison's novels lies to a great extent in their political potential as explications of stigmatization, its implications, and its effects.

Stigmatization is most accurately seen as a social-control process, a form of social comparison, by which certain people are denied full social status or acceptance because they either acquire or are born with particular traits or attributes which the dominant group defines for one reason or another as discrediting. In other words, stigmatization is the production of cultural otherness. In his groundbreaking work on stigma, Erving Goffman identifies three general categories of traits from which stigmas are usually constructed within a given social unit: first are physical disability, deformity, and anomaly; next are attributes of individual character, such as unpredictable behavior, addiction, dishonesty, or certain sexual habits; finally are race, religion, ethnicity, or gender (4). The umbrella of stigmatization, then, brings together persons in this society who are nonwhite, female, disabled, homosexual, ugly, old, poor, obese, non-Christian, illegitimate, unemployed, illiterate, addicted to substances, and ill, as well as prostitutes and criminals. Although these traits represent quite a diverse range of people, behaviors, and experiences, the process of stigmatization is essentially the same for them all. What stigma theory allows us to do is to focus on the nature of the social relationship, rather than on the particular attributes which have been devalued. For it is important to understand that the problem our society must confront is *not* race, class, homosexuality, or disability: rather, the problem is the oppression and inequality that results from stigmatization.

Even though any human difference is potentially stigmatizable, the dominant group—the one in power in a society—determines which differences are considered undesirable. Stigmas, then, not only reflect the value judgments of the dominant group but also reinforce the value of that group's own idealized characteristics by denigrating traits that are either different or defined as opposite from the dominant group's idealized self-description. Furthermore, the dominant group defines itself as normative, legitimate, and—perhaps most important—identifiable, based on its relative opposition to the groups it stigmatizes. Thus stigmatization involves social relationships, and stigmas themselves are most accurately seen not as essential properties of the stigmatized individuals but, rather, as perceptions of the stigmatizers.[2]

A final aspect of the stigmatizing process is particularly central to my examination of Morrison's black, disabled women. Although stigmatized differences seem to be constructed to unify and define the dominant group, these differences actually represent a continuum rather than an absolute opposition along which most people move at different times. Goffman points out that almost all people in this society diverge in some way from the ideological norm, which he rather wittily describes as the "only one complete unblushing male in America: a young, married, white, urban, northern, heterosexual, Protestant father of college education, fully employed, of good complexion, weight and height, and a recent record in sports" (128). Obviously, those persons who fully meet these criteria are a very small minority (for a definition of *minority*, see Glass). And yet this figure is clearly imprinted upon our collective consciousness. Because we are socialized along with all members of this culture, we who are stigmatized—whether mildly, multiply, or profoundly—absorb the collective cultural prejudices and learn to support the social norms. Therefore, our constant internal struggle—depending on the degree of our stigmatization—involves identity ambivalence. There is a contradiction between what Goffman calls our "felt identity," which is our subjective sense of feeling that we are normal, and our recognition of being in some way marked or devalued (105). We feel at the center of our own universes, and yet we know all too well that we are assigned to the margins of the social universe. This is the internal, personal—therefore less readily apparent—struggle at the heart of cultural otherness which nearly always combines detrimentally with the more obvious institutionalized manifestations of stigmatization such as prejudice, oppression, and discrimination. It is in this struggle that Morrison's physically disabled or anomalous black women triumph. What I hope to show here is the way in which these novels repudiate stigmatization itself.

Although Morrison's novels are most certainly a celebration of black culture, they also remind us that the very shape and spirit of black culture in the United States have been informed by stigmatization—its institutions, its injustices, and its resonating, devastating consequences. I am not suggesting, however, that these novels are full of victimized and demoralized characters leading diminished lives. Indeed, the power of Morrison's texts is summed up for me by the image from *Beloved*, the most recent novel, in which Sethe, a young woman who has just escaped from slavery, is able to look with full horror at the young black men from her community who are hanging dead in the sycamore trees, while at the same time she still recognizes and remembers for her lifetime the beauty of those trees. This affirmation of the human capacity to survive pain, loss, and the denial of one's self and culture without an abridgment of one's experience of passion, beauty, attachment, and joy is thc valuable and empowering achievement of Morrison's novels.

Morrison's five novels are replete with disabled figures, almost all of whom are women.[3] I find eight female characters who are stigmatized by a distinguishing disability or anomalous marking of the body, originating at birth or acquired from life, that causes each of them to be considered flawed, abnormal, other, or accorded a devalued status as a result of that condition. Yet this cluster of women who possess both disabilities or anomalous markings, as well as the reduced social status of being black, poor, female, and—in some cases—old in a culture that views white, middle-class, heterosexual, able-bodied males as normative, is nevertheless curiously empowered and empowering within the narrative context in spite of the women's stigmatization and devalued position in the dominant social order.[4] While some of these women are central and others peripheral, all of them to one degree or another are represented as maternal goddess figures who have a mythical, supernatural aura about them. Moreover, their physical anomalies reflect and correspond to the material effects which are manifestations of stigmatization, the psychological and social process that is always acted out upon the devalued body of the cultural other in the forms of rejection, isolation, lowered expectations, impoverishment—and, most egregiously—murder, rape, and enslavement.

The most fully developed of these characters and the prototype for all eight of them is Eva Peace, the matriarchal grandmother who pervades *Sula* from beginning to end. Eva's leg has been mysteriously amputated, perhaps at her own initiative in an act of tough desperation demanded by poverty to collect insurance money in order to feed her children. Nevertheless, her disability is not rendered by the narrative voice as a diminishment. Rather, her disability augments her dignity and power by inspiring awe, functioning not as a mark of inferiority, victimization, or moral corruption—as is the tradition so often in literature—but as a mark of superiority.

Eva is represented as a goddess/queen/creatrix figure even though she is by dominant standards an old, black, one-legged woman who runs a boarding house. Figured simultaneously as realistic and mythical, she is a revisioned and rewritten black Eve and a female version of the Afro-American trickster whose asymmetrical legs suggest his presence in both the material and the supernatural worlds. However, as Henry Louis Gates, Jr. has noted, rather than suggesting a flaw, the trickster's disability indicates empowerment; mediating between two realms, the trickster is ambivalence personified, violating behavioral norms and reversing the cultural categories that make sense of the social order with his outrageous tricks and actions. His power lies in the ability to transgress and fragment the existing social order, thereby challenging it and creating the possibility for a different order (287; see also Stewart 61–63).

Instead of the biblical myth of heaven's plentitude and Eve's maternal legacy of original sin, Eva's is an alternative mythic narrative of the maternal which is grounded in the necessities of the flesh—of eating, defecating, dying, and the material, realistic demands of earthly survival. Her generative power encompasses both the giving and the sustaining of life through birth and nurturance, but also its other, threatening and paradoxical aspect, taking life back, as she does by burning her "beloved baby boy," Plum, when he becomes a heroin addict and cannot meet the life she gave him (*Sula* 34). Eve's apples are rewritten as a meager three red beets that Eva is left with to feed her sick and hungry children after her womanizing husband abandons her to poverty. Eva is a goddess, not of the Judeo-Christian spiritual order but of the flesh. Her strong, dignified, marked, and enduring body is her ultimate resource.

In contrast to Eve's condemnation of her progeny to physical mortality, Eva's legacy to her world is sustenance. She is the powerful, but not always benevolent and never sentimentalized, provider of food and shelter, the material antidotes to mortality. As the "creator and sovereign" of a "woolly house" that is a huge, rambling, incoherent arrangement of rooms and additions, filled with such varied preoccupations as singing, addiction, and casual lovemaking, and replete with pear trees in the yard—suggesting womb imagery—and "a pot of something always cooking on the stove," Eva directs the activities of her children as well as a continuous stream of friends, boarders, and adopted strays (29–30). She reigns in this unorthodox community household primarily from her incongruous throne, a wagon in her third-floor bedroom where she reads dreams and distributes "goobers from deep inside her pockets" to gaggles of children (29).

Another potent capacity that Eva is invested with is the power of naming and thus defining, a privilege denied Eve in the dominant discourse's myth. Eva names her children and renames others with a kind of mystical and determining vision. For example, in what seems incoherence, she dubs three very different abandoned boys whom she adopts all "Dewey King"; however, the bond of a shared name enables them to emerge from their rejection and isolation and to survive (39).

Having delineated Eva, I now want to examine the seven other empowered and empowering women characters with physical disabilities or anomalous markings in Morrison's novels. In *Tar Baby*, the character Marie Thérèse Foucault is similar to Eva but is more subtly presented. Formerly a wet nurse for white babies in Dominique, where she is known for her "magic breasts," Thérèse is now almost totally blind and works as a washerwoman for the wealthy whites who dominate a nearby island (92). Like Eva, she has mysterious powers as well as being a caretaker, trickster, and an Eve figure, who is referred to as "a lying crone with a craving for apples" (93). It is Thérèse who senses the stalking presence of Son, the novel's protagonist and "tar baby," weeks before any of the sighted characters become aware that he is lurking about. In a kind of continuation of her wet-nurse role, she leaves food for Son and enables him to pilfer the white people's food; she also guides him at the end of the novel through the dark to his ambiguous destiny. Beside her role as a nourisher and mystical guide, Thérèse tricks both Son and her nephew into reconnecting with their black culture, what she terms their "ancient properties," after they have been lured away by white culture (263). Moreover, Thérèse is identified with the mythical, supernatural element in *Tar Baby*, for she is accused of being "one of the blind race" who escaped slavery and now freely roam the island on horseback, seeing with "the eye of the mind" (130–31).

In spite of the quasi-magical powers that Thérèse possesses in one sense, she is powerless, inconsequential, and even invisible within the dominant social and economic sphere. She is poor, old, uneducated, haughty, given to superstition, speaks English badly, and refuses to be grateful to her employers. Each time she is fired, she is rehired by the whites, who don't even recognize her. However, Thérèse's dignity and her empowerment in the novel arise from her refusal to speak to the deferential black servants or "even to acknowledge the presence of the white Americans in her world" or to include them in her imaginative stories: she simply won't look at them. Her blindness suggests, then, her unwillingness to recognize or validate a system of power, values, and language that places her at the bottom (94).

Appearing in *Beloved* are two other empowered, nurturant figures with physical disabilities: Baby Suggs and Nan, both of whom are or have been slaves.[5] After being bought out of slavery by her son, "Baby Suggs, holy"—as she is called in the novel—established a kind of maternal ministry and community welfare center in her intergenerational, female home similar to Eva's, "where two pots simmered on the stove'' and ''the lamp burned all night'' and where she ''loved, cautioned, fed, chastised and soothed'' every black man, woman, and child who passed through (87). Until she was worn out by life, Baby Suggs, holy, led the community in religious rituals in an outdoor clearing. During these paganlike ceremonies, rich with dancing, crying, and singing, she delivered potent, moving sermons imploring the people to deeply love their own flesh, their strong and worthy bodies that were broken, tormented, and despised by others; and afterward she ''danced with her twisted hip the rest of what her heart had to say'' (89). Baby Suggs's knowledge of the flesh and its significance is profound: not only has her flesh been owned by someone else and not only have the eight children she bore with her body been taken from her, but her disabled hip, which makes her limp and suggests the trickster figure, has quite literally reduced her value in the perverse economy of slavery.

Less a goddess figure than Baby Suggs, Nan—who appears briefly but significantly—has the power of surviving, nurturing, and remembering. Reminiscent of Thérèse, Nan is a wet nurse and caretaker whose arm is missing. She provides the young girl Sethe, *Beloved*'s protagonist, with an enabling identity by telling her, in their vanishing African language, the story of Sethe's own birth, revealing that she was the sole child whom her dead, enslaved mother valued, the only one not born of a rape and thrown overboard. Although Sethe never acknowledges it explicitly, one of the shreds of inheritance that she receives from her mother is the certainly ambiguous moral capacity to commit infanticide, a paradoxical power they, of course, share with Eva Peace.

In addition to these four women, who have clearly identifiable physical disabilities, there is another group of women who are anomalously marked, whose physical stigma is presented less as a functional limitation and more as an aberration of form than the cluster I described previously.[6] The first is Pilate Dead, who, born without a navel, is the maverick aunt of Milkman Dead, *Song of Solomon*'s protagonist. As with all these women, her difference sets her apart but also renders her mysterious and powerful within the context of the novel. Like Eva and Baby Suggs, Pilate is the matriarch of an unorthodox household, ''a collection of lunatics,'' where mysterious arts of the flesh such as winemaking, potion making, and lovemaking are practiced and where three generations of women reign like the three Graces or the black goddesses, the Eumenides, who sought vengeance for crimes against family members (20). Ceremoniously wearing her own biblical name ensconced in a tiny brass box hung through her earlobe, Pilate—like Eva—is associated with the power of naming. Recalling Thérèse's trickery, Pilate and her housewomen lure Milkman to her house with their siren song, but instead of destruction, he ultimately finds empowerment there as well as reconnection with his history and ancestors.

Next, Eva Peace's granddaughter, Sula, is also set apart physically by a dark facial birthmark which gives ''her otherwise plain face a broken excitement and blue-blade threat'' and seems to be—like all these women's anomalous markings—the physical manifestation of her social otherness (52). Indicative of her ambiguity within the community, Sula's birthmark is a text interpreted by others, variously as a snake, a tadpole, her mother's ashes, or a rose, depending on each person's relation to her. As a rose, the birthmark suggests the blossoms on the skin that early Christians interpreted as stigmatic marks of grace and alludes, as well, to the African goddess of love, Erzulie, whose sign is a rose (see Goffman 1; Gates 300). The serpent, of course, associates Sula with Eve and her grandmother, the revised black Eve. Sula is also an enabler of others, one who "help[s] others define themselves," even though she is a pariah and disrupts traditional relationships within the social order as well as rejecting the maternal role (95). Her friend Nell's dramatic recognition cry, "girl, girl, girlgirlgirl," attests to the depth of their connection and Nell's debt to it (174).

Finally, both Sethe and her unnamed, enslaved, rebellious, and hanged mother are physically marked. The mother is literally branded as a slave in the manner of the Greeks by a burn on her flesh, and her mouth is permanently fixed in a mocking smile because she has had the master's bit thrust into it so many times. Sethe's mother, in the only direct encounter between them, brandishes her stigma with the dignified and tough pride of a survivor before her daughter as a means of identification. Innocently, the child asks, "Mark the mark on me too," as a bond of identity with her mother, and is answered with a slap (*Beloved* 61). Ironically, Sethe later is inscribed with her own mark, a deep intricate scar on her back, the vestige of a brutal beating received as she escaped from her white masters, that is read by others as a chokecherry tree and as a wrought-iron maze, but that is out of view and, like her own history, too charged with terrible memory for her to easily interpret it herself. Like Sula's birthmark, Sethe's scar is ambiguous; it embodies simultaneously the awful price she paid for her freedom and identity and the courage and will to survive that she showed. This horrible badge so similar to her mother's represents, as well, Sethe's bond with her dead mother and her own redemption from her mother's fate. Later, like Eva, Pilate, Nan, and Thérèse, Sethe joins the household of her mother-in-law, Baby Suggs, where she reigns as a caregiver and food provider.

To highlight these eight women characters and clarify my analysis of their representation in Morrison's novels, I want to contrast them now with the final female figure who has a disability, one who is presented quite differently from the rest of the women I have discussed here. I have characterized the other marked and disabled women as mysteriously empowered within the context of the novels even though they are devalued and excluded from the dominant social order by virtue of their race, gender, class, disability, or marking, as well as their generally unorthodox behavior and attitudes. However, Pauline Breedlove, mother and wife of the hideously victimized Breedlove family in *The Bluest Eye*, has the same multiply stigmatized status as the other female characters I have described, but she is completely disempowered in the novel. Pauline is a washerwoman and caretaker of white children like Thérèse; she has a disabled foot and a limp like Baby Suggs; she has a tormenting and irresponsible husband like Eva; and she has known poverty, abuse, deprivation, and animosity, as have all the women I am discussing here. But Pauline is different from them: she is never represented as a mythical goddess figure, never partakes of supernatural power, never enables other members of her community.

This difference in representation, this narrative disempowerment, results from

Pauline's deference to the dominant order and the concomitant desecration of herself which it demands. Essentially, Pauline betrays her own flesh, and consequently that of her children, husband, and racial community, by internalizing the definition of inferiority and cultural otherness that the dominant—white—society assigns her and by embracing her prescribed role in it as "ugly" and as "the ideal servant" (34, 100). It is not simply the stigmas of being black in a white culture, being a woman in a man's world, limping through a world that idealizes ablebodiedness, or even being poor in a rich society that disempower Pauline and destroy her daughter Pecola. Rather, it is the convergence of circumstances, character, and choice that make Pauline accept these stigmas without question or defiance, that rob her of the dignity, grace, beauty, love of which the other women partake—and, along with that, the potential to transcend stigmatization itself.

Pauline seems to be Morrison's sympathetic study in the unfilled and perverted potential which is often the consequence of stigmatization and its oppressive institutions. Because Pauline is isolated from the sustaining perspective of a community of other black women, because she never hears sermons by women like Baby Suggs, or eats in kitchens like Eva's, or even recognizes the validating solidarity of the whores who live upstairs, she is tragically seduced by the dominant discourse into an inevitable self-loathing. She squanders her potential, finding praise and satisfaction keeping a rich white family's house tidy and loving the blue-eyed, blond-haired white girl who, instead of her own daughter, is valued and defined as beautiful by the dominant culture. Thus Pauline accedes to several destructive dominant ideologies: namely, female martyrdom, bourgeois respectability, Christian denial of the flesh, romantic love, the equation of idealized white physical beauty with virtue, the belief that disability is imperfection, and the role of the ideal praise-lulled black servant in a luxurious white household. Her faith in these ideological sins against blackness, femaleness, and personal integrity functions in the novel as an apostasy whose residual nullification is transferred onto Pauline's daughter Pecola. For this violation, the narrative denies Pauline one of Morrison's chief symbols of empowerment: the inclusive, woman-centered, black home with the communal pot on the stove, in which she might have reigned as yet another enabling goddess figure.

I want to emphasize here that the power and stature the narrative accords thematically to Eva, Thérèse, Baby Suggs, Nan, Pilate, Sula, Sethe, and her mother are founded in their steadfast refusal to support, or sometimes even acknowledge, these ideologies to which Pauline falls prey. By doing so, they avoid the destructive identity ambivalence that I described earlier and deny the norm of the dominant culture—that young, white, middle-class, heterosexual, nondisabled, Christian, etc. fellow whom Goffman delineates. Instead they create their own perspective, a kind of alternative psychological and physical order of self-authorized empowerment and dignity. In other words, the way these particular eight women are represented in Morrison's novels reflects a revised social order, one in which the hierarchies of value, the rules that define norms, and the processes of stigmatization have been rewritten. In effect, then, Morrison's disabled women both produce and are products of an alternative domain with a different perspective, one which is given credence within the context of the novel by the narrative voice.

This rewriting of the social order is accomplished by the rhetorical strategy of juxtaposing the fictional modes of realism and myth so as to reconstitute dominant values. Realism depends on the rules of everyday experience and a shared interpretive perspective for its effect; besides physical laws, it relies on the recognition and, to a certain extent, the agreement with the dominant social norms, expectations, and behaviors. For example, the scene that begins *Song of Solomon*, in which Mr. Robert Smith attempts to fly, is presented realistically. It refers to and is interpreted by our shared cultural experience of disturbed suicidal people perched on ledges above absorbed crowds. Our everyday life experience, the status quo, is confirmed by this presentation and by Mr. Smith's splat on the pavement. However, this grounding—so to speak—of the scene in the everyday world is undercut by Pilate's bursting into song as she watches from below, for singing violates the social rules of the situation. The novel presents Pilate ambiguously in this scene by portraying her, on the one hand, as a bag-lady figure whose crazy action elicits the "realistic" response of sniggering from some people in the crowd and, on the other hand, by simultaneously emphasizing her "powerful contralto" and setting the words of her song off from the rest of the text and italicizing them (5).

Although realism dominates this scene, a domain with other rules has achieved at least a foothold in the novel's opening. This alternative domain is a mythical one peopled by the oddballs and throwaways of the dominant social order, who have names like Pilate and Guitar rather than everyday names like Robert Smith. Myth is a fictional strategy that is one step removed from realism in its referential relationship to everyday experience; however, it retains enough of the trappings of realistic representation to sustain our identification with and willing belief in the fictional realm in a way that irony and metafiction, for example, do not (Stewart 19–21). However, myth rewrites the rules of everyday experience and with them the rules of the social order. Pilate, the character who is most stigmatized within the prevailing social order which realism must refer to, is cast as an empowered goddess figure in the mythical order of *Song of Solomon*, where she inhabits another domain, one which is governed differently, but—more important—one which is validated by the narrative voice. Indeed, it is this mythical order that the novel and its protagonist, Milkman, are progressing toward, culminating in the final, totally mythical scene in which Milkman, empowered by his black heritage, defies the social as well as the physical order by learning to fly. I would read Milkman's gesture not as a suicide, which is what realism requires, but as a revision of Mr. Smith's splat and a release from the social rules which governed that opening scene.

What myth accomplishes in Morrison's novels, then, is that it distances us just enough from the prevailing social order so that we can recognize its constructed nature and question it based on our understanding that it is only one system for interpreting, defining, and ordering experience. In other words, myth allows the novels the potential to clear away the oppressive ubiquity of the dominant perspective and to establish a space, like Eva's, Pilate's, or Baby Suggs's house, where things are run differently. Of course, not only Pilate but Eva, Thérèse, Baby Suggs, Nan, Sula, Sethe, and her mother inhabit the mythical domain that Morrison's novels privilege and are accorded status and power there. In fact, I would argue that Pauline—as well as Ondine and Jadine Childs in *Tar Baby*, Helene Wright in *Sula*, and Ruth Dead in *Song of Solomon*, the other ideal-servant and respectable-lady characters—is disempowered in the narrative context by being excluded from mythic representation. Instead, they are presented through the lens of the dominant social order as diminished by and within the domain from which they accept their values and definitions.

The most salient rhetorical aspect of this privileged mythical domain is its inversion of the dominant social order's rules and practices. Inversions operate to render into nonsense the commonsense, everyday world (Stewart 62). For example, this is the effect gained by several inversions of names in the novels: in *Sula*, the hills where the black people live above the white-inhabited valley are called "the Bottom"; in *Beloved*, the white farm where they are slaves is called "Sweet Home," even though it is neither sweet nor home; in *Song of Solomon*, "Not Doctor Street" and "No Mercy Hospital" are nonsensical names that subvert white authority to name (*Sula* 1, *Beloved* 13, *Song of Solomon* 4).

What we take to be the everyday world of common sense is inextricably laced with the perspective of the social order, with values, hierarchies, and norms that exclude many people who possess certain attributes that the dominant group defines as stigmatizing. Narrative inversions tend to render that dominant social perspective nonsensical and incoherent. That this mythical domain is ruled largely by the poor, black, disabled women I am examining in this essay and that they are figured as powerful goddesses is, of course, the most fundamental inversion of the dominant order and its discourse. Even Eva's throne, an old rocking-chair top fastened onto a child's wagon so that adults actually must look down on her, inverts the dominant hierarchical practice of kings reigning from elegant thrones on high. Nevertheless, her narrative empowerment magically reverses that perspective, giving all people "the impression that they were looking up at her, up into the open distances of her eyes, up into the soft black of her nostrils and up at the crest of her chin" (*Sula* 31).

Furthermore, the values in this mythical domain invert the dominant ones. First, every aspect of the flesh is privileged, as if to undo white, Western culture's denial of the body along with its conception of a separable, abstract soul that supersedes the body. Baby Suggs's sermon on loving your own flesh is the sacred discourse; caretakers of the body are powerful; and even the ghost in *Beloved* is embodied. Sexuality is unrestricted and naturalized, and nourishment is accorded sanctity. Moreover, slavery, poverty, and rape are represented above all as violations of the body which are never mitigated by ideologies of martyrdom, asceticism, or self-denial. The structure of relationships is revised by inversion, as well. Personal power, which is often seen in the dominant society as ownership or control over others, as in the master-slave relation, is used for the most part by the mythic women not to dominate others but to enable, feed, shelter, nurture, and minister to the members of their group. Cooperation, community, and connection are valued, inverting the dominant order's emphasis on the achieving, competing, and possessing individual. Finally, households or other primary relationships tend to be defined in a context of kinship, horizontally across generations—usually of mothers, daughters, and granddaughters, as in Eva's, Pilate's, and Baby Suggs's households—rather than in any vertical, hierarchical order that reflects social or economic stratification, such as the traditional nuclear family or the employer-employee dyad.

However, this domain, along with its reigning figures, is not a discrete alternative realm which transcends history. Rather, these women, even while they are empowered psychologically and mythically, are simultaneously embedded in a social order that defines and determines their existences and relationships. Although there are only a few actual characters in the novels who represent the dominant social order, its perspective and its pervasive, contrapuntal presence are represented as a ubiquitous force which constantly threatens to destroy or undermine the mythical order and that nearly always disrupts it. Thus the slave owner—ironically called Schoolteacher—appears only briefly in *Beloved*, and yet the potential of his power and its dreadful consequences reverberate throughout the novel, rupturing and distorting relationships everywhere within the black community. Even the arguably benevolent representatives of the dominant order like Valerian in *Tar Baby*, Mr. Garner in *Beloved*, and Pauline's appreciative employer in *The Bluest Eye* inflict dissolution and ruin unwittingly, despite good but inept intentions; for their perspective, norms, and values are inevitably incompatible with the well-being of black people. The consequences of stigmatization are vividly and virulently represented in the novels: there is no escape or avoidance; at best there is unembittered survival, dignified endurance, and a liberated perspective which often enables profound joy and love.

The relation of the mythic women to the dominant order, then, is paradoxical, ambiguous: it has power over them at the same time that they have power over it. This brutal paradox is imaged in *Sula* when Eva putatively cuts off her leg to save Plum from starving and later burns him to save him from a slower destruction by heroin, and in *Beloved* when Sethe turns back the slave master by slashing her baby's throat.

However, the question that this essay ultimately asks is: What is accomplished by the text's figuring of these women as having physical disabilities or anomalous markings? First, the women's disabilities serve the rhetorical purpose of intensifying their difference from the dominant norm and with that their stigmatization. The novels want us to understand, furthermore, that any form of stigmatization is not just an abstract social process involving attitudes or opinions, but that its logical consequences have a direct, inexorable, and ineluctable effect on the actual bodies of cultural others. In the revised, mythical order of these novels in which every aspect of the flesh is privileged, the anomalous marks and disabilities do not serve as metaphors for twisted souls, as is so often the case in literature. Rather, these are the valued marks and manifestations of bodily uniqueness and personal history. These disabilities and aberrations are either bodily wounds—the material traces inflicted by the stigmatization process—or they are the congenital differences that stigmatization seizes upon with its institutionalized forms such as oppression, poverty, slavery, and, ultimately, often murder. In other words, these marks are a discourse inscribed by history on the flesh of human beings. This insistence upon the primacy of the flesh in representing oppression is a very important reminder to a society like ours that tends to characterize freedom as an abstract matter involving unrestricted personal choice, beliefs, and opportunity.

Furthermore, by intensifying these black women's differences from the dominant order by endowing them with disabilities and aberrations, the novels make a strong political statement about assimilation as a solution to racial stigmatization. These markings exacerbate rather than ameliorate their physical and psychological difference from the norm, implying that ending oppression requires questioning the norm itself rather than aspiring to conform to it.

My second point is that the condition of having a physical disability or aberration seems to me capable of expressing this ambiguous situation precisely. The anthropologist Robert Murphy argues convincingly that our culture treats disability as a type of liminality, the anthropological concept referring to the ambivalent or ambiguous state of existence between structural social categories (Murphy 131; see also Harpham 3–22). Liminal figures are "transitional beings" within a culture, who are often considered invisible—as is Thérèse by her employers—or structurally dead—which is Pilate's last name (Turner 95). Because they violate social classification, liminal people are also regarded as socially polluted or contaminating, as are Pilate and Sula, for example, in Morrison's novels (Mary Douglas, qtd. in Turner 97).

However, in spite of this negation of status, liminal persons exist simultaneously, according to Victor Turner, in "a realm of pure possibility whence novel configurations of ideas and relations may arise" (97). Seeing disabled people as liminal implies that they become cultural others not so much because they possess a certain attribute—for the experience of having a disability varies tremendously—but that they resist categorization. Like the trickster, they cannot be placed coherently in the realm either of the sick or the well, the normal or the abnormal, the human or the inhuman. In short, disability tends to be more anomalous than essential. The anomalous refuses clear categorization and flies in the face of symmetry: Eva, with one "magnificent" leg and one vanished leg, is in a fundamental way simultaneously normal and abnormal, abled and disabled (*Sula* 31); Thérèse is not categorically, but only mostly, blind; Nan is perfectly able to cradle Sethe in her good arm but cannot do so with her stump. In this dynamic, inchoate state of liminal potential, they are free as well from the restrictions of social roles. This sort of rolelessness or refusal to identify with the position the social order assigns renders the mythical women transitional, free from unambiguous status and in a position to make themselves up apart from the prevailing social rules. Moreover, having a physical disability or aberration existentially alters the other commonly accepted human identities or classifications such as gender, race, or class. Those of us with disabilities are ambiguous; we possess a negatively charged wild card that confounds the categories of the dominant social order. In other words, we embody paradox: our different bodies define us within the society, but at the same time we defy definition.

This ambiguous status arising from an aspect of the physical body is just the appropriate analogy to convey the relation with the dominant order that I believe Morrison's novels advocate black people should have. I take the novels' political position to be that black women must not betray the reality of their enslaved, denigrated flesh, must not deny the historical material conditions which have shaped Afro-American and female culture; but at the same time they must not accede to the reenslavement which that heritage can confer. Thérèse, the washerwoman; Sethe, the cook; Eva, the shelter giver and caretaker; and Baby Suggs, the churchless preacher negotiate this paradox successfully within the narrative context. Pauline, the ideal servant, does not.

Another way of stating this might simply be that these mythic women bear and claim the painful wounds of their inheritance and the marks of their difference with dignity and a profound sense of their own wholeness and that, furthermore, they seize for themselves with pride the right to interpret those wounds and marks. I am reminded here of Leonard Kriegel's moving analysis of a literary character whom he terms the "Survivor Cripple." Like the mythic women regarding their legacy of enslavement and difference, the Survivor Cripple never permits himself to forget what his life might have been like had he not been disabled. The gnosis of the Survivor Cripple is the recognition that "self-creation is limited by the very accidents that give it shape" and that his empowerment lies in "the will to manipulate that which has manipulated him" (22). Their empowerment lies in the terms of their survival, and their survival lies in the terms of their empowerment.

Finally, I want to suggest that, although Toni Morrison has said that she writes for black women, she writes for women with physical disabilities as well, perhaps without intention (Russell 46). Harlan Hahn has pointed out that although many nondisabled people continue to interpret disability as an indication of biological inferiority, many of us with disabilities are entering what can be called the "black-is-beautiful" phase in a developing minority culture in which we redefine our disabilities as a positive source of identity (198). Thus, ironically, these women with disabilities provide me and other women like me with what feminism calls enabling models and, along with that, the seeds for a valid discourse regarding disabled women. Seldom are people with disabilities represented at all in literature, and even less often are we portrayed complexly or with subjectivity. We are too frequently the medium for some other, usually negative, message. I believe that literature has the potential for what Adrienne Rich has called "revision" and that that is precisely what these representations begin to accomplish ("When We Dead" 35; 1979 ed.). Morrison's novels give us an empowering mirror of our selves where a blank or a lie too often exist. For if our experiences and identities as women with disabilities are unspeakable, then our histories will remain unwritten, our feelings and our bodies will remain misrepresented, and our lives will be defined for us by others.

NOTES

[1] I have particular reasons for choosing the adjective "disabled" or the phrase "with disabilities" to name our group in this essay, even though I am not entirely satisfied with these terms. Self-naming, along with issues of identity, history, and community, is only beginning to be articulated in the recently recognized and named field of disability studies, which is rooted in the social sciences, primarily in sociology. The problem is that the word "disability" tends to locate the definition of our condition in our functional impairment instead of recognizing that our limitations are actually more the result of negative attitudes and discrimination on the part of the nondisabled majority. The terms "anomalously marked" (which I have used in this essay), "atypical," or even perhaps the awkward and euphemistic label "physically challenged" seem to me more precise than "disabled" because they do not focus on lack or individual dysfunction or convey a sense of personal misfortune, but rather indicate one's relation to a relative norm. Nevertheless, I want to use "disabled" in order to invoke the social consciousness of the disability rights movement and disability studies along with its grounding in the political and material situations of people with disabilities. Thus I hope that my use of the word "disabled" and my situating of the critical perspective in an "I" that is clearly within a position of cultural otherness will jolt my readers' critical consciousness into a political and material framework. For a further discussion of naming, see Zola.

[2] It appears to sociologists that the social tendency to stigmatize is universal but that the attributes which are deemed stigmas vary across cultures and history. Besides being culturally and historically specific, the defining of certain characteristics as stigmatic is collective; agreement about which traits are considered stigmas and about which people are devalued is endemic to the dominant ideology of each given social unit. Although there is uncertainty as to exactly how the stigmatizing process is acquired, it may grow out of "stranger anxiety," an apparently universal phenomenon which occurs in infants. Its prototype is probably the human tendency to form the categories "like me" and "not like me" and to prefer the former. See Ainlay, Becker, and Coleman 78, 212, 191.

[3] It is interesting to note that Milkman Dead in *Song of Solomon* is the only physically disabled male character in Morrison's novels. Milkman focuses on his mild limp in an effort, which is for the most part unsuccessful, to differentiate himself from his father. I would argue that this marginal disability represents his ambivalent alliance throughout the novel with Pilate.

[4] Disability, particularly mobility impairment, has been traditionally read as impotence or a castration sign, which is, of course, gendered, and which Morrison revises in her novels. See, for example, Peter L. Hays 4, 8. Even Marianne Hirsch's subtle and complex feminist analysis of *Sula* reads Eva Peace's amputated leg as "her castration" and as "lack" in accordance with Lacanian psychoanalytic theory. Hirsch makes the important point that Eva's empowerment is qualified by its necessary embeddedness in the dominant order (181–82).

[5] Denver, Baby Suggs's granddaughter and Beloved's sister, also is physically disabled, having become deaf for two years as a psychological refusal to hear the truth about her sister's death. However, even though she conforms fairly well to the pattern, I have chosen not to include her in this analysis because her disability is temporary. Sethe, Denver's mother, whom I do include in this analysis because of the scar on her back, also has a temporary disability similar to her daughter's that should be noted: she stutters from the time that her mother is hanged until she first sees Halle, her husband-to-be.

[6] By encompassing formal aspects such as birthmarks and functional conditions such as mobility impairments in the single category of "disability," I do not mean to deny the various individual experiences and meanings of these conditions. Nor am I suggesting an equivalence among all forms of stigmatization. Rather, I intend here to show the interrelated sociopolitical nature of these experiences. In particular, I hope to demonstrate that Morrison's narratives frame femaleness, non-whiteness, and atypical form or disability not as biological conditions which are inherently limiting but as conditions profoundly informed by an unaccommodating social environment as well as its physical and institutional manifestations.

~ WORKS CITED ~

Abrams, M. H. "The Deconstructive Angel." *Critical Inquiry* 3 (1977): 425–38.

Ainlay, Stephen, Gaylene Becker, and Lerita Coleman, eds. *The Dilemma of Difference: A Multidisciplinary View of Stigma*. New York: Plenum, 1986.

Allen, Robert J. "Pope and the Sister Arts." *Pope and His Contemporaries: Essays Presented to George Sherburn*. Ed. James L. Clifford and Louis Landa. New York: Oxford UP, 1949. 78–88.

Allestree, Richard. *The Ladies Calling*. London, 1673.

Altieri, Charles. "The Hermeneutics of Literary Indeterminacy: A Dissent from the New Orthodoxy." *New Literary History* 10.1 (1978): 71–79.

Altman, Janet. *Epistolarity: Approaches to a Form*. Columbus: Ohio State UP, 1982.

Ambelain, Robert. *Adam dieu rouge*. Paris: Niclaus, 1941.

Atwood, Margaret. *Bodily Harm*. New York: Simon, 1982.

———. "Circe/Mud Poems." *You Are Happy*. Toronto: Oxford UP, 1974. Rpt. in *Norton Anthology of Literature by Women*. Ed. Sandra Gilbert and Susan Gubar. New York: Norton, 1985. 2296–98.

———. *The Handmaid's Tale*. Boston: Houghton, 1986.

———. Interview. With Cathy N. Davidson. *MS*. Feb. 1986: 24–26.

Auerbach, Nina. *Communities of Women: An Idea in Fiction*. Cambridge: Harvard UP, 1978.

———. "This Changeful Life: Emily Brontë's Anti-romance." Gilbert and Gubar, *Shakespeare's Sisters* 48–64.

———. *Woman and the Demon: The Life of a Victorian Myth*. Cambridge: Harvard UP, 1982.

Ault, Norman. *New Light on Alexander Pope*. London: Methuen, 1949.

Axtell, James T., ed. *The Educational Writing of John Locke*. Cambridge: Cambridge UP, 1968.

Bagg, Robert. "The Rise of Lady Lazarus." *Mosaic* 2 (1969): 9–36.

Barreño, Maria Isabel, Maria Teresa Horta, and Maria Velho da Costa. *The Three Marias: New Portuguese Letters*. Trans. Helen R. Lane. New York: Bantam, 1976.

Barrett, Michèle. "Ideology and the Cultural Production of Gender." *Criticism and Social Change: Sex, Class and Race in Literature and Culture*. Ed. Judith Newton and Deborah Rosenfelt. New York: Methuen, 1985. 65–85.

Bartkowski, Frances. "Feminism and Deconstruction: A Union Forever Deferred." *Enclitic* 7.1 (1982): 70–77.

Baym, Nina. "Melodramas of Beset Manhood: How Theories of American Fiction Exclude Women Authors." *American Quarterly* 33 (1981): 129–39.

———. *Woman's Fiction: A Guide to Novels by and about Women in America, 1820–1870*. Ithaca: Cornell UP, 1978.

———. "The Women of Cooper's *Leatherstocking Tales*." Cornillon 135–54.

Beer, Gillian. "Hume, Stephen, and Elegy in *To the Lighthouse*." *Essays in Criticism* 34 (1984): 33–55.

Behn, Aphra. "On the Death of the Late Earl of Rochester, by Mrs. A. B." *The Works of Aphra Behn*. Vol. 6. New York: Blom, 1915. 368–70.

Benson, Jackson J. *Hemingway . . . : The Writer's Art of Self-Defense*. Minneapolis: U of Minnesota P, 1969.

Berger, John. *Ways of Seeing*. New York: Penguin, 1972.

Bernikow, Louise, ed. *The World Split Open: Four Centuries of Women Poets in England and America, 1552–1950*. New York: Vintage, 1974.

Blackmur, R. P. "A Burden for Critics." *Hudson Review* 1 (1948): 170–86.

Bleich, David. *Subjective Criticism*. Baltimore: Johns Hopkins UP, 1978.

Bloom, Harold. *Kabbalah and Criticism*. New York: Seabury, 1975.

———. *A Map of Misreading*. New York: Oxford UP, 1975.

Bolotin, Susan. "Voices from the Post-feminist Generation." *New York Times Magazine* 17 Oct. 1982: 28–31+.

Booth, Wayne. "Arts and Scandals 1982." *PMLA* 98 (1983): 312–22.

———. "Freedom of Interpretation: Bakhtin and the Challenge of Feminist Criticism." *Critical Inquiry* 9 (1982): 45–76.

———. "The Rhetoric of Fiction and the Poetics of Fiction." *Now Don't Try to Reason with Me*. Chicago: U of Chicago P, 1970. 151–69.

Boswell, James. *Boswell's Life of Johnson*. Ed. George Birkbeck Hill and L. F. Powell. 6 vols. Oxford: Clarendon, 1934–64.

Boyce, Benjamin. *The Character Sketches in Pope's Poems*. Durham: Duke UP, 1962.

———. *The Theophrastan Character in England to 1642*. Cambridge: Harvard UP, 1947.

Boyers, Paul. "A Case against Feminist Criticism." *Partisan Review* 43.4 (1976).

Bradstreet, Anne. *The Works of Anne Bradstreet*. Ed. Jeannine Hensley. Cambridge: Belknap-Harvard UP, 1967.

Brontë, Charlotte. *The Complete Poems of Charlotte Brontë*. Ed. C. W. Hatfield. St. Clair Shores: Scholarly, 1971.

Brontë, Emily. *The Poems of Emily Jane Brontë*. Ed. C. W. Hatfield. New York: Columbia UP, 1941.

Brower, Reuben A. *Alexander Pope: The Poetry of Allusion*. Oxford: Clarendon, 1959.

Browne, Ray B. "Two Views of Commitments: 'The Paradise of Bachelors and the Tartarus of Maids.' " *American Transcendental Quarterly* 7 (1970): 43–47.

Brownell, Morris. *Alexander Pope and the Arts of Georgian England*. Oxford: Clarendon, 1978.

Browning, Elizabeth Barrett. *The Complete Works of Elizabeth Barrett Browning*. Ed. Charlotte Porter and Helen A. Clarke. 6 vols. New York: Crowell, 1900.

Burney, Fanny. Ms. 658 of the Early Journal of Fanny Burney. Henry and Albert A. Berg Collection. New York Public Library, Astor, Lenox, and Tilden Foundations.

———. *Evelina: Or, The History of a Young Lady's Entrance into the World*. Oxford: Oxford UP, 1968.

Butler, Marilyn. *Maria Edgeworth: A Literary Biography*. Oxford: Oxford UP, 1972.

Campbell, Joseph. *The Hero with a Thousand Faces*. 2nd. ed. Princeton: Princeton UP, 1968.

———. *The Masks of God: Creative Mythology*. New York: Viking, 1968.

———. *The Masks of God: Occidental Mythology*. New York: Viking, 1964.

Carpenter, Frederic. "Puritans Preferred Blonds: The Heroines of Melville and Hawthorne." *New England Quarterly* 9 (1936): 253–72.

Cherchez la femme. Spec. issue of *Diacritics* 12 (1982).

Chodorow, Nancy. "Feminism and Difference: Gender, Relation, and Difference in Psychoanalytic Perspective." *Socialist Review* 46 (1979): 51–69.

———. *The Reproduction of Mothering: Psychoanalysis and the Sociology of Gender*. Berkeley: U of California P, 1978.

Christ, Carol. *Diving Deep and Surfacing: Women Writers on a Spiritual Quest*. Boston: Beacon, 1980.

———. "Margaret Atwood: The Surfacing of Women's Spiritual Quest and Vision." *Signs* 2 (1976): 316–30.

———. "Some Comments on Jung, Jungians, and the Study of Women." *Anima* 3 (1976): 66–69.

Cirillo, Albert R. "Salvation in *Daniel Deronda*: The Fortunate Overthrow of Gwendolen Harleth." *Literary Monographs*. Vol. 1. Ed. Eric Rothstein and Thomas K. Dunseath. Madison: U of Wisconsin P, 1967. 203–43.

Cixous, Hélène. "The Laugh of the Medusa." Trans. Keith Cohen and Paula Cohen. *Signs* 1.4 (1976): 875–93.

Clampitt, Amy. *The Kingfisher*. New York: Knopf, 1985.

Clark, Alice. *Working Life of Women in the Seventeenth Century*. London: Routledge, 1919. New York: Kelley, 1968.

Cody, Richard. *The Landscape of the Mind*. Oxford: Clarendon, 1969.

Cohen, Ted. "Metaphor and the Cultivation of Intimacy." *Critical Inquiry* 5 (1978): 3–12.

Colby, Robert A. *Fiction with a Purpose: Major and Minor Nineteenth-Century Novels*. Bloomington: Indiana UP, 1967. 256–302.

Coleman, Patrick. "The Idea of Character in the *Encyclopédie*." *Eighteenth-Century Studies* 13.1 (1979): 21–47.

Cooper, Helen Margaret. "Elizabeth Barrett Browning: A Theory of Women's Poetry." Diss. Rutgers U, 1982.

———. "Working into Light: Elizabeth Barrett Browning." Gilbert and Gubar, *Shakespeare's Sisters* 65–81.

Cornillon, Susan Koppelman, ed. *Images of Women in Fiction: Feminist Perspectives*. Bowling Green: Bowling Green U Popular P, 1972.

Crowley, William. "Melville's Chimney." *Emerson Society Quarterly* 14 (1959): 2–6.

Culler, Jonathan. *On Deconstruction*. Ithaca: Cornell UP, 1982.

———. "Reading as a Woman." *On Deconstruction*. Ithaca: Cornell UP, 1982.

Daly, Mary. *Beyond God the Father: Toward a Philosophy of Women's Liberation*. Boston: Beacon, 1973.

———. *Gyn/Ecology: The Metaethics of Radical Feminism*. Boston: Beacon, 1978.

———. Paper delivered at the conference The Prism of Sex. Madison, WI, Sept. 1977.

d'Arblay, Madam. *Memoirs of Dr. Burney*. 2 vols. London: Moxon, 1832.

Davis, Cynthia A. "Heroes, Earth Mothers, and Muses: Gender Identity in Barth's Fiction." *Centennial Review* 24 (1980): 309–21.

Davis, Merrell R. "The Flower Symbolism in *Mardi.*" *Modern Language Quarterly* 2 (1941): 625–38.

Davis, Natalie Zemon. " 'Women's History' in Transition: The European Case." *Feminist Studies* 3.3–4 (1976): 83–103.

de Beauvoir, Simone. *The Second Sex*. Ed. and trans. H. M. Parshley. New York: Random House, 1952; Vintage, 1974.

Deloffre, Frédéric, and J. Rougeot. "L'énigme des *Lettres portugaises.*" Deloffre and Rougeot v–xxiii.

———, eds. Lettres portugaises, Valentins, *et autres oeuvres de Guilleragues*. Paris: Garnier, 1962.

de Rougemont, Denis. *Love in the Western World*. Trans. Montgomery Belgion. Garden City: Doubleday, 1940. New York: Pantheon, 1956.

de Vere, Edward. "Woman's Changeableness." *Shakespeare Identified in Edward de Vere . . . and the Poems of Edward de Vere*. By J. Thomas Looney. 3rd ed. Vol. 1. Port Washington: Kennekat, 1975. 595.

Dewey, John. *Art as Experience*. New York: Capricorn Books, 1958.

Dibattista, Maria. "*To the Lighthouse*: Virginia Woolf's Winter's Tale." *Virginia Woolf: Revaluation and Continuity*. Ed. Ralph Freedman. Berkeley: U of California P, 1980. 161–88.

Dickinson, Emily. *The Complete Poems of Emily Dickinson*. Ed. Thomas H. Johnson. Boston: Little, 1960.

Diehl, Joanne Feit. " 'Come Slowly—Eden': An Exploration of Women Poets and Their Muse." *Signs* 3 (1978): 572–87.

Dillingham, William B. *Melville's Short Fiction, 1853–1856*. Athens: U of Georgia P, 1977.

Dinnerstein, Dorothy. *The Mermaid and the Minotaur: Sexual Arrangements and Human Malaise*. New York: Harper, 1976.

Donaldson, Sandra M. "Elizabeth Barrett's Two Sonnets to George Sand." *Studies in Browning and His Circle* 5 (1977). 19–22.

Douglas, Ann. *The Feminization of American Culture*. New York: Knopf, 1977.

Douglas, Mary. *Purity and Danger*. London: Routledge, 1966.

Dronke, Peter. Article. *Times Literary Supplement* 5 Nov. 1976: 1397.

Duyfhuizen, Bernard. "Epistolary Narratives of Transmission and Transgression." *Comparative Literature* 38 (1985): 1–26.

———. "Review Essay: Deconstruction and Feminist Literary History." *Tulsa Studies in Women's Literature* 3 (1984): 159–67.

Eby, E. H. "Herman Melville's 'Tartarus of Maids.' " *Modern Language Quarterly* 1 (1940): 95–100.

Edwards, Lee R. "The Labors of Psyche: Toward a Theory of Female Heroism." *Critical Inquiry* 6 (1979): 33–49.

———. "Women, Energy, and *Middlemarch.*" *Massachusetts Review* 13 (1972): 222–38.

Edwards, Thomas R. *This Dark Estate: A Reading of Pope*. Berkeley: U of California P, 1963.

Ehrenpreis, Irvin. "The Cistern and the Fountain: Art and Reality in Pope and Gray." *Studies in Criticism and Aesthetics, 1600–1880*. Minneapolis: U of Minnesota P, 1967. 156–75.

Eisenstein, Hester, and Alice Jardine, eds. *The Future of Difference*. Boston: Hall, 1980.

Eliot, George. *Daniel Deronda*. New York: Harper, 1966.

———. *The George Eliot Letters*. Ed. Gordon S. Haight. 7 Vols. New Haven: Yale UP, 1954–55.

———. "Margaret Fuller and Mary Wollstonecraft." *Leader* 13 Oct. 1855: 988–89. Rpt. in *Essays of George Eliot*. Ed. Thomas Pinney. London: Routledge, 1963. 199–206.

———. *Middlemarch*. Ed. Gordon S. Haight. Boston: Houghton, 1956.

———. Prelude. *Middlemarch*. New York: Washington Square, 1963. 1–2.

Ellis, Anne Raine, ed. *The Early Diary of Fanny Burney*. London: Bell, 1907.

Ellmann, Mary. *Thinking about Women*. New York: Harcourt, 1968.

Elshtain, Jean B. *Public Man, Private Woman*. Princeton: Princeton UP, 1981.

Empson, William. "Ignorance of Death." *Collected Poems*. New York: Harcourt, 1935. 58–59.

Fabricant, Carole. "Pope's Portraits of Women: The Tyranny of the Pictorial Eye." *Women and Men: The Consequences of Power*. Ed. Dana V. Hiller and Robin Ann Sheets. Cincinnati: Univ. of Cincinnati Office of Women's Studies, 1977. 74–91.

Farwell, Marilyn R. "Virginia Woolf and Androgyny." *Contemporary Literature* 16 (1975): 436–42.

Fetterley, Judith. *The Resisting Reader: A Feminist Approach to American Fiction*. Bloomington: Indiana UP, 1978.

Feuerbach, Ludwig. *The Essence of Christianity*. Trans. Marian Evans. London, 1854.

Fiedler, Leslie. "Come Back to the Raft Ag'in, Huck Honey!" *An End to Innocence: Essays on Culture and Politics*. Boston: Beacon, 1955. 142–51.

———. *Love and Death in the American Novel*. New York: Criterion, 1960.

Finch, Anne. *Selected Poems of Anne Finch*. Ed. Katharine Rodgers. New York: Ungar, 1979.

Findlay, J. N. *Hegel: A Reexamination*. New York: Collier, 1962.

Firestone, Shulamith. *The Dialectic of Sex: The Case for Feminist Revolution*. Rev. ed. New York: Bantam, 1971.

Fish, Stanley E. *Is There a Text in This Class? The Authority of Interpretive Communities*. Cambridge: Harvard UP, 1980.

———. "Normal Circumstances, Literal Language, Direct Speech Acts, the Ordinary, the Everyday, the Obvious, What Goes without Saying, and Other Special Cases." *Critical Inquiry* 4 (1978): 625–44.

Fisher, Marvin. *Going Under: Melville's Short Fiction and the American 1850s*. Baton Rouge: Louisiana State UP, 1977.

Flaubert, Gustave. *Madame Bovary*. Trans. Francis Steegmuller. New York: Modern Library, 1957.

Flax, Jane. "Mother-Daughter Relationships: Psychodynamics, Politics, and Philosophy." Eisenstein and Jardine 20–40.

Fliegelman, Jay. *Prodigals and Pilgrims: The American Revolution against Patriarchal Authority*. Cambridge: Cambridge UP, 1982.

Florenne, Yves. Introduction. *Lettres de la religieuse portugaise*. Paris: Librairie générale française, 1979.

Flynn, Elizabeth A., and Patrocinio P. Schweickart, eds. *Gender and Reading: Essays on Readers, Texts, and Contexts*. Baltimore: Johns Hopkins UP, 1986.

Foucault, Michel. *The Birth of the Clinic: An Archaeology of Medical Perception*. Trans. A. M. Sheridan Smith. New York: Vintage, 1975.

———. *Discipline and Punish: The Birth of Prison*. Trans. Alan Sheridan. New York: Vintage, 1975.

———. *Power/Knowledge: Selected Interviews and Other Writings*. Ed. Colin Gordon. New York: Pantheon, 1980.

Freud, Sigmund. *Civilization and Its Discontents*. Trans. James Strachey. 1930. New York: Norton, 1961.

———. "Femininity." *New Introductory Lectures on Psychoanalysis*. Trans. James Strachey. 1933. New York: Norton, 1965. 112–35.

———. *The Future of an Illusion*. Trans. W. D. Robson-Scott. 1927. New York: Anchor-Doubleday, 1964.

———. *General Introduction to Psychoanalysis*. Trans. Joan Riviere. 1916–17. New York: Permabooks, 1956.

———. *An Outline of Psychoanalysis*. Trans. James Strachey. 1940. New York: Norton, 1949.

———. "The Relation of the Poet to Daydreaming." *Delusion and Dream and Other Essays*. Ed. Philip Rieff. Boston: Beacon, 1956. 122–33.

Friedman, Susan Stanford. "Creating a Women's Mythology: H. D.'s *Helen in Egypt*." *Women's Studies* 5.2 (1977): 167–93.

———. "Mythology, Psychoanalysis and the Occult in the Late Poetry of H. D." Diss. U of Wisconsin, Madison, 1973.

Frye, Northrop. *Fearful Symmetry: A Study of William Blake*. Boston: Beacon, 1962.

Furman, Nelly. "The Study of Women and Language: Comment on Vol. 3, No. 3." *Signs* 4 (1978): 182–85.

Furness, Clifton Joseph, ed. *The Genteel Female*. New York: Knopf, 1931.

Gallant, Christine. "The Archetypal Feminine in Emily Brontë's Poetry." *Women's Studies* 7 (1980): 72–94.

Gallop, Jane. *The Daughter's Seduction: Feminism and Psychoanalysis*. Ithaca: Cornell UP, 1982.

———. "Psychoanalysis and Feminism." Eisenstein and Jardine 106, 114–21.

Gates, Henry Louis, Jr. "The Blackness of Blackness: A Critique of the Sign and the Signifying Monkey." *Black Literature and Literary Theory*. Ed. Gates. New York: Methuen, 1984. 285–321.

Geertz, Clifford. "Ideology as a Cultural System." *The Interpretation of Cultures: Selected Essays*. New York: Basic, 1973.

———. "Thick Description: Toward an Interpretive Theory of Culture." *The Interpretation of Cultures: Selected Essays*. New York: Basic, 1973.

Gilbert, Sandra M., and Susan Gubar. *The Madwoman in the Attic: The Woman Writer and the Nineteenth-Century Literary Imagination*. New Haven: Yale UP, 1979.

———, eds. *Shakespeare's Sisters: Feminist Essays on Women Poets*. Bloomington: Indiana UP, 1979.

Gilligan, Carol. *In a Different Voice: Psychological Theory and Women's Development*. Cambridge: Harvard UP, 1982.

Glass, Ruth. "Insiders—Outsiders: The Position of Minorities." *New Left Review* 17 (1962): 34–45.

Goffman, Erving. *Stigma: Notes on the Management of Spoiled Identity*. Englewood Cliffs: Prentice, 1963.

Goldenberg, Naomi. "A Feminist Critique of Jung." *Signs* 2 (1976): 443–49.

Gornick, Vivian. "Woman as Outsider." *Woman in Sexist Society: Studies in Power and Powerlessness*. Ed. Gornick and Barbara K. Moran. New York: Basic, 1971. 126–44.

Grahn, Judy. "Funeral Plainsong from a Younger Woman to an Older Woman." *Lesbian Poetry: An Anthology*. Ed. Elly Bulkin and Joan Larkin. Watertown: Persephone, 1981. 80–82.

Greenburg, Caren. "Reading Reading: Echo's Abduction of Language." McConnell-Ginet, Borker, and Furman 300–09.

Gregory, John. *A Father's Legacy to His Daughters*. London: Strahan and Cadell, 1774.

Griffin, Dustin H. *Alexander Pope: The Poet in the Poems*. Princeton: Princeton UP, 1978.

Gross, Theodore L. *The Heroic Ideal in American Literature*. New York: Free, 1971.

Gubar, Susan. " 'The Blank Page' and the Issues of Female Creativity." *Critical Inquiry* 8.2 (1981): 243–62.

———. "The Echoing Spell of H. D.'s *Trilogy*." *Contemporary Literature* 19 (1978): 196–218.

———. "The Female Monster in Augustan Satire." *Signs* 3.2 (1977): 380–94.

———. "Mother, Maiden, and the Marriage of Death: Women Writers and an Ancient Myth." *Women's Studies* 6 (1979): 301–15.

Habakkuk, H. J. "Marriage Settlements in the Eighteenth Century." *Transactions of the Royal Historical Society* 4th Ser. 32 (1950): 15–30.

Habermas, Jurgen. "Wahrheitstheorien." *Wirklichkeit und Reflexion: Walter Schulz zum 60. Geburstag*. Pfullingen: Neske, 1973. 211–65.

Haberstroh, Charles. *Melville and Male Identity*. Cranbury: Fairleigh Dickinson UP, 1980.

———. "Melville, Marriage, and *Mardi*." *Studies in the Novel* 9 (1977): 247–60.

Hacker, Marilyn. *Presentation Pieces*. New York: Viking, 1974.

Hagstrum, Jean H. *The Sister Arts: The Tradition of Literary Pictorialism and English Poetry from Dryden to Gray*. Chicago: U of Chicago P, 1958.

Hahn, Harlan. "Civil Rights for Disabled Americans: The Foundation of a Political Agenda." *Images of the Disabled, Disabling Images*. Ed. Alan Gartner and Tom Joe. New York: Praeger, 1987. 181–203.

Haight, Gordon S. *George Eliot: A Biography*. New York: Oxford UP, 1968.

Hanford, James Holly. "The Pastoral Elegy and Milton's *Lycidas*." *PMLA* 25 (1910): 403–47.

Hansen, Elaine Tuttle. "Fiction and (Post)Feminism in Atwood's *Bodily Harm*." *Novel* 19 (1985): 5–21.

Harding, M. Esther. *Woman's Mysteries: Ancient and Modern*. New York: Harper, 1971.

Harpham, Geoffrey Galt. *On the Grotesque: Strategies of Contradiction in Art and Literature*. Princeton: Princeton UP, 1982.

Harrison, Jane. *Themis: A Study of the Social Origins of Greek Religion*. 1912. London: Merlin, 1963.

Harrison, T. P. *The Pastoral Elegy: An Anthology*. Austin: U of Texas P, 1939.

Harte, Bret. *Condensed Novels*. 1871. Upper Saddle River: Literature House, 1969.

Harvey, W. J. "The Intellectual Background of the Novel: Casaubon and Lydgate." Middlemarch: *Critical Approaches to the Novel*. Ed. Barbara Hardy. London: U of London Athlone P, 1967. 25–37.

Hawthorne, Mark D. *Doubt and Dogma in Maria Edgeworth*. U of Florida Monographs, the Humanities. Gainseville: U of Florida P, 1967.

Hays, H. R. *The Dangerous Sex: The Myth of Feminine Evil*. New York: Pocket, 1964.

Hays, Peter L. *The Limping Hero: Grotesques in Literature*. New York: New York UP, 1971.

Hayter, Alethea. " 'These Men Over-Nice': Elizabeth Barrett Browning's 'Lord Walter's Wife.' " *Browning Society Notes* 8 (1978): 5–7.

H. D. *The Gift*. New York: New Directions, 1982.

———. *Helen in Egypt*. 1961. New York: New Directions, 1974.

———. *Hermetic Definition*. New York: New Directions, 1972.

———. Letters to Viola Jordan. Beinecke Library, Yale Univ.

———. *Tribute to Freud*. 1956. Boston: Godine, 1974.

———. *Trilogy*. 1944, 1945, 1946. New York: New Directions, 1973.

———. *Vale Ave*. Ms. Beinecke Library, Yale Univ.

Hegel, George W. F. *The Phenomenology of the Spirit*. Trans. James Baillie (1910). Trans. rev. Carl J. Friedrich. *The Philosophy of Hegel*. Ed. and introd. Friedrich. New York: Random, 1953. 399–519.

———. Preface. *The Phenomenology of the Spirit*. Rpt. in *Hegel: Texts and Commentary*. Trans. and ed. Walter Kaufmann. Garden City: Doubleday, 1966.

Hemlow, Joyce. *The History of Fanny Burney*. Oxford: Oxford UP, 1958.

Henderson, Joseph L. "Ancient Myths and Modern Man." *Man and His Symbols*. Ed. Carl G. Jung. New York: Dell, 1964. 95–156.

Heydon, Peter N., and Philip Kelley, eds. *Elizabeth Barrett Browning's Letters to Mrs. David Ogilvy, 1849–1861*. New York: Quadrangle and the Browning Inst., 1973.

Hickok, Kathleen K. " 'New Yet Orthodox': The Female Characters in *Aurora Leigh*." *International Journal of Women's Studies* 3 (1980): 479–89.

———. *Representations of Women: Nineteenth-Century British Women's Poetry*. Westport: Greenwood, 1984.

Hirsch, Marianne. *The Mother/Daughter Plot: Narrative, Psychoanalysis, Feminism*. Bloomington: Indiana UP, 1989.

Holloway, Julia Bolton. "*Aurora Leigh* and *Jane Eyre*." *Brontë Society Transactions* 17 (1977): 126–32.

Holman, Hugh C. *A Handbook to Literature*. New York: Odyssey, 1972.

Homans, Margaret. *Woman Writers and Poetic Identity: Dorothy Wordsworth, Emily Brontë, and Emily Dickinson*. Princeton: Princeton UP, 1980.

Hopkins, M. A. *Hannah More and Her Circle*. New York: Longmans, 1947.

Howard, Leon. *Herman Melville*. Berkeley: U of California P, 1951.

Howe, Florence. "Feminism and Literature." Cornillon 253–77.

———. "Literacy and Literature." *Myths of Coeducating: Selected Essays, 1964–1983*. Bloomington: Indiana UP, 1984. 111–24.

Howe, Florence, and Ellen Bass, eds. *No More Masks! An Anthology of Poems by Women*. Garden City: Anchor-Doubleday, 1973.

Hoy, David Couzens. "Hermeneutic Circularity, Indeterminacy, and Incommensurability." *New Literary History* 10 (1978): 161–73.

Hughes, Ted. "The Chronological Order of Sylvia Plath's Poems." *The Art of Sylvia Plath*. Ed. Charles Newman. Chicago: Swallow, 1970.

Hyppolite, Jean. *Genesis and Structure of Hegel's* Phenomenology of the Spirit. Trans. Samuel Cherniak and John Heckman. Evanston: Northwestern UP, 1974.

Iser, Wolfgang. "The Reading Process: A Phenomenological Approach." Tompkins 50–69.

Jacobus, Mary. "Is There a Woman in This Text?" *New Literary History* 14 (1982): 117–41.

James, Henry. *The Portrait of a Lady*. Riverside Edition. Ed. Leon Edel. Boston: Houghton, 1963.

Jameson, Fredric. *The Political Unconscious: Narrative as a Sexually Symbolic Act*. Ithaca: Cornell UP, 1981.

———. *The Prison-House of Language: A Critical Account of Structuralism and Russian Formalism*. Princeton: Princeton UP, 1974.

Jeffrey, Julie Roy. Introduction. *Frontier Women: The Trans-Mississippi West, 1840–1880*. American Century Series. New York: Hill, 1979.

Jehlen, Myra. "Against Human Wholeness." Columbia University Seminar on Women and Society. New York, Spring 1985.

Jones, Betty H., and Alberta Arthurs. "The American Eve: A New Look at American Heroines and Their Critics." *International Journal of Women's Studies* 1 (1978): 1–12.

Jones, M. G. *Hannah More*. Cambridge: Cambridge UP, 1952.

Joyce, James. *A Portrait of the Artist as a Young Man*. London: Cape, 1916.

Jung, C. G. *The Collected Works*. Trans. R. F. C. Hall. 20 vols. Princeton: Princeton UP, 1968.

Jung, Emma. *Animus and Anima*. Trans. Cary F. Baynes and Hildegard Nagel. New York: Spring, 1957.

Kamuf, Peggy. *Fictions of Feminine Desire: Disclosures of Héloïse*. Lincoln: U of Nebraska P, 1982.

———. "Rousseau's Politics of Visibility." *Diacritics* 5.4 (1975): 51–56.

———. "Writing like a Woman." McConnell-Ginet, Borker, and Furman 284–99.

Kaplan, Cora. Introduction. *Elizabeth Barrett Browning: Her Novel in Verse* Aurora Leigh *with Other Poems*. London: Women's, 1978.

Kaplan, Sydney Janet. *Feminine Consciousness in the Modern British Novel*. Urbana: U of Illinois P, 1975.

Kauffman, Linda. *Discourses of Desire: Gender, Genre, and Epistolary Fictions*. Ithaca: Cornell UP, 1986.

Keener, Frederick M. *An Essay on Pope*. New York: Columbia UP, 1974.

Kelley, Philip, and Ronald Hudson, eds. *The Brownings' Correspondence*. 4 vols. to date. Winfield: Wedgestone, 1984– .

———, eds. *The Unpublished Diary of Elizabeth Barrett Browning, 1831–1832*. Athens: Ohio UP, 1969.

Kellner, Robert. "Sex, Toads, and Scorpions: A Study of the Psychological Themes of Melville's *Pierre*." *Arizona Quarterly* 31 (1975): 5–20.

Kennard, Jean E. "Convention Coverage: Or, How to Read Your Own Life." *New Literary History* 13 (1981): 69–88.

———. *Victims of Convention*. Hamden: Archon, 1978.

Kenyon, Frederic G., ed. *The Letters of Elizabeth Barrett Browning*. 2 vols. New York: Macmillan, 1899.

Keogh, J. G. "Pope's 'Epistle to a Lady,' 1–4." *Explicator* 31.5 (1973): item 37.

Kevles, Barbara. "The Art of Poetry: Anne Sexton." McClatchy 3–29.

Kintner, Elvan, ed. *The Letters of Robert Browning and Elizabeth Barrett Barrett, 1845–1846*. 2 vols. Cambridge: Harvard UP, 1969.

Kolodny, Annette. "The Feminist as Literary Critic." Critical response. *Critical Inquiry* 2.4 (1976): 821–31.

———. "Literary Criticism." *Signs* 2 (1976): 404–21.

———. "A Map for Rereading: Or, Gender and the Interpretation of Literary Texts." *New Literary History* 11 (1980): 451–67.

Koppelman, Susan. "Florence Howe Award Position Papers." *Concerns* 6.2 (1976): 14–22.

Korshin, Paul J. *Typologies in England, 1650–1820*. Princeton: Princeton UP, 1982.

Kramer, Cheris, Barrie Thorne, and Nancy Henley. "Perspectives on Language and Communication." *Signs* 3 (1978): 638–51.

Kramer, Heinrich, and Jacob Sprenger. *Malleus Maleficarum*. 1486.

Kriegel, Leonard. "The Wolf in the Pit in the Zoo." *Social Policy* (Fall 1982): 16–23.

Krieger, Murray. *The Theory of Criticism: A Tradition and Its System*. Baltimore: Johns Hopkins UP, 1976.

Lambert, Ellen. *Placing Sorrow: A Study of the Pastoral Elegy Convention from Theocritus to Milton*. Chapel Hill: U of North Carolina P, 1976.

LaSalle, Jean-Pierre, and Thérèse LaSalle. *Un manuscrit des lettres d'une religieuse portugaise: Leçons, interrogations, hypothèses*. Papers on Seventeenth-Century French Literature 6. Paris: Biblio 17, 1982.

Leranbaum, Miriam. *Alexander Pope's 'Opus Magnum,' 1729–1744*. Oxford: Clarendon, 1977.

Lerner, Gerda. *The Majority Finds Its Past: Placing Women in History*. Oxford: Oxford UP, 1979.

Levenson, Shirley Frank. "The Use of Music in *Daniel Deronda*." *Nineteenth-Century Fiction* 24 (1969): 317–34.

Lévi-Strauss, Claude. *The Savage Mind*. Chicago: U. of Chicago P, 1967.

———. "The Structural Study of Myth." *Journal of American Folklore* 68 (1955): 428–44. Rpt. in *The Structuralists: From Marx to Levi-Strauss*. Ed. Richard T. DeGeorge and Fernande M. DeGeorge. New York: Anchor-Doubleday, 1972. 169–94.

Lewes, George Henry. *The History of Philosophy from Thales to Comte*. 4th ed. London: Longmans, 1871.

Leyda, Jay. *The Melville Log*. New York: Gordian, 1969.

Locke, John. *Two Treatises of Government*. Ed. Peter Laslett. Cambridge: Cambridge UP, 1967.

Lukács, Georg. *Writer and Critic*. New York: Grosset, 1970.

Macherey, Pierre. *A Theory of Literary Production*. Trans. Geoffrey Wall. London: Routledge, 1978.

MacKinnon, Catherine M. "Feminism, Marxism, Method, and the State: Toward Feminist Jurisprudence." *Signs* 8 (1983): 635–58.

Macpherson, Crawford B. "The Social Bearing of Locke's Political Theory." *Western Political Quarterly* 7 (1954): 1–22.

Malcolm X. *The Autobiography of Malcolm X*. Written with Alex Haley. New York: Grove, 1964.

Marcus, Jane. "Liberty, Sorority, Misogyny." *The Representation of Women in Fiction*. Ed. Carolyn Heilbrun and Margaret Higgonet. Baltimore: Johns Hopkins UP, 1983.

Markley, Robert. "Beyond Consensus: *The Rape of the Lock* and the Fate of Reading Eighteenth-Century Literature." *New Orleans Review* 15.4 (1988): 68–77.

Martin, Wendy. "Anne Bradstreet's Poetry: A Study of Subversive Piety." Gilbert and Gubar, *Shakespeare's Sisters* 19–31.

McCabe, Jane. " 'A Woman Who Writes': A Feminist Approach to the Early Poetry of Anne Sexton." McClatchy 216–43.

McCarthy, Mary. Rev. of *The Handmaid's Tale*, by Margaret Atwood. *New York Times Book Review* 9 Feb. 1986: 1+.

McClatchy, J. D., ed. *Anne Sexton: The Artist and Her Critics*. Bloomington: Indiana UP, 1978.

McConnell-Ginet, Sally, Ruth Borker, and Nelly Furman, eds. *Women and Language in Literature and Society*. New York: Praeger, 1980.

Meeks, Wayne A. "The Image of the Androgyne: Some Uses of a Symbol in Earliest Christianity." *History of Religions* 13 (1973): 165–208.

Melville, Herman. "After the Pleasure Party." *Poems of Herman Melville*. Ed. Douglas Robillard. New Haven: College and University P, 1976.

———. *Collected Poems of Herman Melville*. Ed. Howard Vincent. Chicago: Hendricks, 1947.

———. "Fragment from a Writing Desk." Rpt. in *Melville's Early Life and* Redburn. By William H. Gilman. New York: New York UP, 1951. 265–71.

———. *Mardi*. Evanston: Northwestern UP and the Newberry Library, 1970.

———. "The Paradise of Bachelors and the Tartarus of Maids." *Great Short Works of Herman Melville*. Ed. Werner Berthoff. New York: Harper, 1969.

———. *Pierre: Or, The Ambiguities*. Evanston: Northwestern UP and the Newberry Library, 1971.

———. *Redburn*. Evanston: Northwestern UP and the Newberry Library, 1969.

———. *Typee*. Evanston: Northwestern UP and the Newberry Library, 1968.

Merezhkovsky, D. S. "Tolstoy's Physical Descriptions." *Anna Karenina*. By Leo Tolstoy. Trans. Louis Maude and Aylmer Maude. Ed. George Gibian. New York: Norton, 1970. 802–10.

Mermin, Dorothy. "The Female Poet and the Embarrassed Reader: Elizabeth Barrett Browning's *Sonnets from the Portuguese*." *ELH* 48 (1981): 351–67.

Middlebrook, Diane. "Housewife into Poet: The Apprenticeship of Anne Sexton." *New England Quarterly* 56 (Dec. 1983): 483–503.

Miller, Edwin Haviland. *Melville*. New York: Braziller, 1975.

Miller, Jean Baker. *Toward a New Psychology of Women*. Boston: Beacon, 1976.

Miller, Nancy K. *The Heroine's Text: Readings in the French and English Novel, 1722–1782*. New York: Columbia UP, 1980.

———. "The Text's Heroine: A Feminist Critic and Her Fictions." *Diacritics* 12 (1982): 48–53.

Miller, Ruth. *The Poetry of Emily Dickinson*. Middletown: Wesleyan UP, 1968.
Millett, Kate. *Sexual Politics*. Garden City: Doubleday, 1970.
Mitchell, Juliet. *Psychoanalysis and Feminism: Freud, Reich, Laing, and Women*. Harmondsworth: Penguin, 1975.
Moers, Ellen. *Literary Women: The Great Writers*. Garden City: Anchor-Doubleday, 1976.
Moffat, Mary Jane, ed. *In the Midst of Winter: Selections from the Literature of Mourning*. New York: Random, 1982.
Moody, William Vaughn. *The Poems and Plays of William Vaughn Moody*. Vol. 1. Boston: Houghton, 1912.
More, Hannah. *Complete Works*. 19 vols. London: Cadell, 1801–19.
———. *The Works of Hannah More*. 2 vols. Boston: Goodrich, 1827.
Morrison, Toni. *Beloved*. New York: NAL, 1987.
———. *The Bluest Eye*. New York: Washington Square, 1970.
———. *Song of Solomon*. New York: NAL, 1977.
———. *Sula*. New York: NAL, 1973.
———. *Tar Baby*. New York: NAL, 1981.
Moser, Kay. "Elizabeth Barrett's Youthful Feminism: Fragment of 'An Essay on Woman.' " *Studies in Browning and His Circle* 12 (1984): 13–26.
Muirhead, John H. *The Platonic Tradition in Anglo-Saxon Philosophy: Studies in the History of Idealism in England and America*. London: Allen, 1931.
Muller, Gilbert H. *Nightmares and Visions: Flannery O'Connor and the Catholic Grotesque*. Athens: U of Georgia P, 1972.
Munz, Peter. *When the Golden Bough Breaks: Structuralism or Typology?* London: Routledge, 1973.
Murphy, Robert. *The Body Silent*. New York: Holt, 1987.
Murray, Henry. Introduction. *Pierre*. By Herman Melville. New York: Hendricks, 1949.
Neely, Carol Thomas. "Feminist Modes of Shakespeare Criticism: Compensatory, Justificatory, Transformational." *Women's Studies* 9 (1981): 3–15.
Neumann, Erich. *The Great Mother: An Analysis of the Archetype*. Trans. Ralph Manheim. Princeton: Princeton UP, 1963.
Norlin, George. "The Conventions of the Pastoral Elegy." *American Journal of Philology* 32 (1911): 294–312.
Nussbaum, Felicity. *The Brink of All We Hate: English Satires on Women, 1660–1750*. Lexington: UP of Kentucky, 1984.
———. "Pope's 'To a Lady' and the Eighteenth-Century Woman." *Philological Quarterly* 54 (1975): 444–56.
Ohmann, Carol. "Emily Brontë at the Hands of Male Critics." *College English* 32 (1971): 906–13.
Okin, Susan. *Women in Western Political Thought*. Princeton: Princeton UP, 1979.
Olds, Sharon. *The Dead and the Living*. New York: Knopf, 1984.
Olsen, Tillie, ed. *Mother to Daughter, Daughter to Mother*. Old Westbury: Feminist, 1984.
———. *Silences*. New York: Delacorte-Seymour Lawrence, 1978.
Ortner, Sherry. "Is Female to Male as Nature Is to Culture?" *Woman, Culture, and Society*. Ed. Michelle Zimbalist Rosaldo and Louise Lamphere. Stanford: Stanford UP, 1974. 67–87.

Paley, Grace. *Later the Same Day*. New York: Farrar, 1985.

Parkin, Rebecca. "The Role of Time in Alexander Pope's 'Epistle to a Lady.' " *ELH* 32 (1965): 490–501.

Pennington, Montagu. *Memoirs of the Life of Mrs. Elizabeth Carter*. 2 vols. London: Rivington, 1816.

Pigman, G. W. *Grief and English Renaissance Elegy*. Cambridge: Cambridge UP, 1985.

Plath, Sylvia. *Ariel*. New York: Harper, 1965.

———. *The Bell Jar*. New York: Bantam, 1971.

———. *The Colossus*. New York: Vintage, 1968.

———. *Crossing the Water*. New York: Harper, 1971.

———. *Winter Trees*. New York: Harper, 1972.

Plumb, J. H. "The First Flourishing of Children's Books." *Early Children's Books and Their Illustration*. Ed. G. Gottlieb. Boston: Godine, 1975. xvii–xxx.

Pollak, Ellen. Comment on "The Female Monster in Augustan Satire," by Susan Gubar. *Signs* 3.3 (1978): 728–32.

———. "Rereading *The Rape of the Lock*: Pope and the Paradox of Female Power." *Studies in Eighteenth-Century Culture* 10 (1980): 429–44.

Poovey, Mary. "Fathers and Daughters: The Trauma of Growing Up Female." *Women in Literature: Men by Women*. Ed. Janet Todd. New York: Holmes, 1981. 10: 550–61.

Pope, Alexander. *The Works of Alexander Pope*. Ed. Whitwell Elwin and William J. Courthope. 10 vols. 1886. Ed. John W. Croker, et al. New York: Gordian, 1967.

———. *The Twickenham Edition of the Poems of Alexander Pope*. Gen. ed. John Butt. 11 vols. New Haven: Yale UP; London: Methuen, 1939–61.

Pops, Martin. *The Melville Archetype*. Kent: Kent State UP, 1970.

Poulet, Georges. "Criticism and the Experience of Interiority." Trans. Catherine Macksey and Richard Macksey. Tompkins 41–49.

Pratt, Annis. "Archetypal Approaches to the New Feminist Criticism." *Bucknell Review* 21.1 (1973): 3–14.

Pratt, Annis, et al. *Archetypal Patterns in Women's Fiction*. Bloomington: Indiana UP, 1981.

Price, Martin. *To the Palace of Wisdom*. Garden City: Doubleday, 1964.

Quinn, Vincent. "H. D.'s 'Hermetic Definition': The Poet as Archetypal Mother." *Contemporary Literature* 18 (1977): 51–61.

Raleigh News and Observer [NC] 17 June 1987: 1+.

Raymond, Meredith B., and Mary Rose Sullivan, eds. *The Letters of Elizabeth Barrett Browning to Mary Russell Mitford, 1836–1854*. 3 vols. Winfield: Armstrong Browning Library, 1983.

Rich, Adrienne. *The Fact of a Doorframe: Poems Selected and New, 1950–1984*. New York: Norton, 1984.

———. "It Is the Lesbian in Us . . ." *On Lies* 199–202.

———. *Of Woman Born*. New York: Norton, 1976.

———. *On Lies, Secrets, and Silence: Selected Prose, 1966–1978*. New York: Norton, 1979.

———. "Transcendental Etude." *The Dream of a Common Language: Poems, 1974–1977*. New York: Norton, 1978.

———. ''Vesuvius at Home: The Power of Emily Dickinson.'' *On Lies* 157–183.

———. ''When We Dead Awaken: Writing as Re-Vision.'' *Adrienne Rich's Poetry*. Ed. Barbara Charlesworth Gelpi and Albert Gelpi. New York: Norton, 1975. 90–98. Rpt. in *On Lies* 33–49.

Richardson, Betty. ''Florence Howe Award.'' *Concerns* 4.2 (1974): 3–5.

Riddel, Joseph N. ''H. D. and the Poetics of 'Spiritual Realism.' '' *Contemporary Literature* 10 (1969): 447–73.

Riffaterre, Michael. ''Flaubert's Presuppositions.'' *Diacritics* 11 (1981): 2–11.

Roberts, William, ed. *Memoirs of the Life and Correspondence of Mrs. Hannah More*. 2 vols. New York: Harper, 1834.

Robinson, Lillian S. ''Criticism—and Self-Criticism.'' 1974. Robinson, *Sex* 53–68.

———. ''Criticism: Who Needs It?'' 1976. Robinson, *Sex* 69–94.

———. ''Cultural Criticism and the *Horror Vacui*.'' 1972. Robinson, *Sex* 47–52.

———. ''Dwelling in Decencies: Radical Criticism and the Feminist Perspective.'' *College English* 32 (1971): 879–89. Rpt. in Robinson, *Sex* 3–21.

———. *Sex, Class, and Culture*. Bloomington: Indiana UP, 1977.

Rogers, Katharine M. *The Troublesome Helpmate: A History of Misogyny in Literature*. Seattle: U of Washington P, 1966.

Rosenblum, Dolores. ''Face to Face: Elizabeth Barrett Browning's *Aurora Leigh* and Nineteenth-Century Poetry.'' *Victorian Studies* (1983): 321–38.

Rosenfelt, Deborah. ''A Tribute to Florence Howe.'' *NWSAction* 2.4 (1989): 8–9.

Rowland, Beryl. ''Melville's Bachelors and Maids: Interpretation through Symbol and Metaphor.'' *American Literature* 41 (1969): 389–405.

Ruether, Rosemary. ''Misogynism and Virginal Feminism in the Fathers of the Church.'' *Religion and Sexism*. New York: Simon, 1974.

Russell, Sandy. ''It's OK to Say OK.'' *Critical Essays on Toni Morrison*. Ed. Nellie Y. McKay. Boston: Hall, 1988. 43–46.

Ryan, Michael. *Marxism and Deconstruction: A Critical Articulation*. Baltimore: Johns Hopkins UP, 1982.

Sacks, Peter. *Elegy*. Baltimore: Johns Hopkins UP, 1985.

Sappho. *Lyra Graeca*. Vol. 1. Trans. J. M. Edmonds. Loeb Classical Library. London: Heinemann, 1963.

Sarton, George. *History of Science*. Cambridge: Harvard UP, 1952.

Savile, George. *The Lady's New Years Gift: Or, Advice to a Daughter*. London, 1688. *The Complete Works of George Savile, First Marquess of Halifax*. Ed. Walter Raleigh. Oxford: Clarendon, 1912. New York: Kelley, 1970.

Schenck, Celeste. *Mourning and Panegyric: The Poetics of Pastoral Ceremony*. University Park: Penn State P, 1988.

Schochet, Gordon. *Patriarchalism in Political Thought*. Oxford: Oxford UP, 1975.

Scholem, Gershom G. *On the Kabbalah and Its Symbolism*. Trans. Ralph Manheim. New York: Schocken, 1969.

Scholes, Robert. *Structuralism in Literature: An Introduction*. New Haven: Yale UP, 1974.

Segre, Cesare. ''Narrative Structures and Literary History.'' *Critical Inquiry* 3 (1976): 271–79.

Sexton, Anne. *The Complete Poems*. Boston: Houghton, 1981.

Showalter, Elaine. "The Double Critical Standard." *A Literature of Their Own* 73–99.

———. "Feminist Criticism in the Wilderness." *Critical Inquiry* 8 (1981): 179–205. Rpt. in *The New Feminist Criticism: Essays on Women, Literature, and Theory*. Ed. Showalter. New York: Pantheon, 1985. 243–70.

———. *A Literature of Their Own: British Women Novelists from Brontë to Lessing*. Princeton: Princeton UP, 1977.

———. "Women and the Literary Curriculum." *College English* 32 (1971): 855–62.

Shurr, William H. *The Mystery of Iniquity*. Lexington: UP of Kentucky, 1972.

Smith, Catherine. "The Invention of Sex in Myth and Literature." *The Binding of Proteus*. Ed. Marjorie W. McCune, et al. Lewisburg: Bucknell UP, 1980. 252–61.

Spacks, Patricia Meyer. *An Argument of Images: The Poetry of Alexander Pope*. Cambridge: Harvard UP, 1971.

———. *The Female Imagination*. New York: Avon, 1975.

———. *Imagining a Self: Autobiography and Novel in Eighteenth-Century England*. Cambridge: Harvard UP, 1976.

Spengemann, William C. *The Adventurous Muse: The Poetics of American Fiction, 1789–1900*. New Haven: Yale UP, 1977.

Spilka, Mark. *Virginia Woolf's Quarrel with Grieving*. Lincoln: U of Nebraska P, 1980.

Spivak, Gayatri. "Displacement and the Discourse of Woman." *Displacement: Derrida and After*. Ed. Mark Krupnick. Bloomington: Indiana UP, 1983.

Sprinchorn, E. M. Introduction. *Miss Julie*. By August Strindberg. San Francisco: Chandler, 1961. i–xxx.

Stanford, Ann, ed. *The Women Poets in English: An Anthology*. San Francisco: McGraw, 1972.

Stanley, Julia Penelope, and Susan W. Robbins. "Toward a Feminist Aesthetic." *Chrysalis* 6 (1977): 55–71.

Stein, Allen. "Hawthorne's Zenobia and Melville's Urania." *American Transcendental Quarterly* 26 (1975): 11–18.

Stein, William Bysshe. *The Poetry of Melville's Late Years*. Albany: State U of New York P, 1970.

Stewart, Susan. *Nonsense: Aspects of Intertextuality in Folklore and Literature*. Baltimore: Johns Hopkins UP, 1978.

Stimpson, Catharine. "Feminism and Feminist Criticism." *Massachusetts Review* 24 (1983): 272–88.

Stirling, J. H. [James Hutchinson]. *The Secret of Hegel*. London, 1865.

Stone, Lawrence. *The Family, Sex, and Marriage in England, 1500–1800*. New York: Harper, 1977.

Strauss, David Friedrich. *The Life of Jesus*. Trans. Marian Evans. London, 1846.

Strindberg, August. Preface. *Miss Julie*. Trans. E. M. Sprinchorn. San Francisco: Chandler, 1961.

Swann, Brian. "Eyes in the Mirror: Imagery and Symbolism in *Daniel Deronda*." *Nineteenth-Century Fiction* 23 (1968–69): 434–45.

Taine, Hippolyte. Introduction. *History of English Literature*. Trans. H. Van Laun. New York: Holt, 1886. 1–21.

Tatham, Campbell. "The Gilesian Monomyth: Some Remarks on the Structure of *Giles Goat-Boy*." *Genre* 3 (1970): 364–75.

Taylor, Anne Robinson. *Male Novelists and Their Female Voices: Literary Masquerades*. Troy: Whitston, 1980.

Taylor, William R. *Cavalier and Yankee: The Old South and American National Character*. New York: Harper, 1961.

Thompson, Henry. *The Life of Hannah More*. London: Cadell, 1838.

Thomson, Patricia. *George Sand and the Victorians: Her Influence and Reputation in Nineteenth-Century England*. New York: Columbia UP, 1977.

———. *The Victorian Heroine: A Changing Ideal, 1837–1873*. London: Oxford UP, 1956.

Tilton, John W. "*Giles Goat-Boy*: An Interpretation." *Bucknell Review* (1970): 92–119.

Tolstoy, Leo. *Anna Karenina*. Trans. Constance Garnett. Ed. Leonard J. Kent and Nina Berberova. New York: Modern Library, 1965.

Tompkins, Jane, ed. *Reader-Response Criticism: From Formalism to Structuralism*. Baltimore: Johns Hopkins UP, 1980.

Travis, Mildred. "*Mardi*: Melville's Allegory of Love." *Emerson Society Quarterly* 43 (1966): 88–94.

Trollope, Frances. *The Mother's Manual: Or, Illustrations of Matrimonial Economy, An Essay in Verse*. London: Treuttel, 1833.

Tsvetayeva, Marina. *Selected Poems*. Trans. Elaine Feinstein. London: Penguin, 1974.

Turner, Victor. *The Forest of Symbols*. Ithaca: Cornell UP, 1967.

Van Duyn, Mona. *Merciful Disguises: Published and Unpublished Poems*. New York: Atheneum, 1973.

Van Ghent, Dorothy. *The English Novel: Form and Function*. New York: Reinhart, 1953.

Vendler, Helen. "Notes on a Poem." *Vanity Fair* Apr. 1983: 89+.

Vickers, Nancy J. "Diana Described: Scattered Woman and Scattered Rhyme." *Critical Inquiry* 8.2 (1981): 265–79.

Wasserstrom, William. *Heiress of All the Ages: Sex and Sentiment in the Genteel Tradition*. Minneapolis: U of Minnesota P, 1959.

Watts, Emily Stipes. *The Poetry of American Women from 1632 to 1945*. Austin: U of Texas P, 1977.

Weinbrot, Harold D. *Alexander Pope and the Traditions of Formal Verse Satire*. Princeton: Princeton UP, 1982.

Wheelwright, Philip. *The Burning Fountain: A Study in the Language of Symbolism*. Rev. ed. Bloomington: Indiana UP, 1968.

Woolf, Virginia. "*Aurora Leigh*." *Collected Essays of Virginia Woolf*. Vol. 1. Ed. Leonard Woolf. New York: Harcourt, 1953.

———. *A Room of One's Own*. New York: Harcourt, 1929.

———. *Three Guineas*. New York: Harcourt, 1938.

———. *The Waves*. New York: Harcourt, 1931.

———. "Women and Fiction." *Granite and Rainbow: Essays*. London: Hogarth, 1958. Rpt. in *Collected Essays*. Vol. 2. London: Hogarth, 1966. 141–48.

Zimmerman, Susan. "*Sonnets from the Portuguese*: A Negative and a Positive Context." *Mary Wollstonecraft Newsletter* 2 (1973): 1–11.

Zola, Irving Kenneth. "Self, Identity, and the Naming Question: Reflections on the Language of Disability." Unpublished essay.

~ INDEX ~